Yankee Dutchmen under Fire

CIVIL WAR IN THE NORTH

Yankee Dutchmen under Fire

Civil War Letters from the 82nd Illinois Infantry

TRANSLATED AND EDITED BY

Joseph R. Reinhart

THE KENT STATE UNIVERSITY PRESS
Kent, Ohio

Library of Congress Catalog Card Number 2012048729

ISBN 978-1-60635-176-5

Manufactured in the United States of America

LIBRARY OF CONGRESS CATALOGING-IN-PUBLICATION DATA

Yankee Dutchmen under fire : Civil War letters from the 82nd Illinois Infantry / translated and edited by Joseph R. Reinhart.

p.   cm. — (Civil War in the North)

Includes bibliographical references and index.

ISBN 978-1-60635-176-5 (hardcover : alk. paper) ∞

1. United States. Army. Illinois Infantry Regiment, 82nd (1862–1865) 2. United States—History—Civil War, 1861–1865—Personal narratives. 3. Illinois—History—Civil War, 1861–1865—Regimental histories. 4. United States—History—Civil War, 1861–1865—Regimental histories. 5. United States—History—Civil War, 1861–1865—Participation, German American. 6. United States—History—Civil War, 1861–1865—Participation, German. 7. United States—History—Civil War, 1861–1865—Participation, Jewish.

I. Reinhart, Joseph R., editor of compilation.

E505.582nd.Y36

973.7'473092—dc23

2012048729

17 16 15 14 13   5 4 3 2 1

To my brothers Greg and Paul and my sister Judy.
Greg served in the United States Army in Vietnam and
Paul served in the Kentucky Air National Guard.
Thanks for your service to our country.

Contents

Maps and Illustrations

Maps

Illustrations

Acknowledgments

Many persons and institutions have been involved in the preparation of this book and deserve recognition and thanks.

I owe special thanks to the Newberry Library, Chicago, Ill., for preserving on microfilm copies of the *Illinois Staats-Zeitung* for the Civil War years and making them available to researchers. Many of the letters in this work were discovered in copies of such microfilm. The library also furnished a typed English translation of Pvt. Max Schlund's diary. Special thanks is also due to the Thomas Jefferson Library at the University of Missouri–St. Louis, where I obtained copies of the letters of Rudolph Müller and other information located in the Friedrich Hecker Papers archived there. The Abraham Lincoln Presidential Library in Springfield, Illinois, granted me access to both microfilm copies of several German American newspapers, the diary of Friedrich August Braeutigam, and other documents. The United States Army Military History Institute provided copies of the letters of Friedrich P. Kappelmann. Benjamin Stephen, Giles Hoyt, and Liesel Knudson provided invaluable, prompt, and critical assistance in translating certain problematic parts of the letters and are due my sincere appreciation.

I am grateful to Dick Skidmore, who has edited a journal and a collection of letters in his own right, for his careful reading of a near final copy of the manuscript and providing important criticism and recommendations. Eric Benjaminson also read and criticized a near-final draft of the manuscript and deserves thanks for his suggestions. My thanks to Scott Hartwig, Chief Historian at the Gettysburg National Military National Military Park, for critiquing the Gettysburg chapter and making several critical suggestions for changes. Mark A. Moore, author and mapmaker, also deserves thanks for his close review of the Final Battles chapter and for furnishing a detailed map of the Battle of Bentonville. Nonetheless, any errors in this work are solely my responsibility.

My thanks to those who provided photos: Frances L. Luebke, Chicago History Museum, Missouri History Museum (St. Louis); and Jerome Hunt.

I also want to thank the librarians, archivists, and others at the Bellarmine University Library (Louisville, Ky.), Belleville (Ill.) Public Library, Chicago Public Library, Chicago History Museum, Danville (Ill.) Public Library, Filson Historical Society (Louisville), Hennepin County Library-Minneapolis, Illinois State Archives, Louisville Free Public Library, Manatee County (Fla.) Public Library System, Missouri History Museum, Library and Research Center (St. Louis), Morrison-Talbott Library (Waterloo, Ill.), National Archives, New College Library (Sarasota, Florida), Sarasota County (Fla.) Public Library, University of Kentucky, W. T. Young Library, University of Louisville, Ekstrom Library, University of Miami Library, University of South Florida Library, and the United States Army Military History Institute (Carlisle Barracks, Pa.).

I also extend thanks to Christian B. Keller, who loaned me his microfilm copies of the *Illinois Staats-Zeitung,* Marilyn Lotz, Tom Lowry, Richard M. McMurry, Mike and Vicki Peake, Dennis Suttles, Kari Stacy, Lee White, John S. Gray, Andrea Mehrländer, Hank Meves, and Melissa Petersen.

Finally, I want to thank my wife Virginia for her love, and her patience and understanding while I spent untold hours immersed in translating and editing the letters in this work.

A Note about Translation and Editing

The editor translated the following letters, except where noted, from German into English. The goal of the translation was to convey the meaning the letter writer intended and therefore is not an exact word-for-word translation.

For clarity and the convenience of the reader, some original German sentences were divided into separate sentences in English, and some punctuation marks were added or deleted. Also some paragraphs were combined or divided. When the meaning of a word or phrase was unclear, letters and/or words were added using square brackets, and misspelled names or misidentified persons were corrected using square brackets. Illegible words in the correspondence are identified by a question mark or text in square brackets. German words or phrases italicized in the original printed text are italicized. Italics are also used to indicate instances where the letter writer used an English word or provided an explanation of an English word or the German equivalent. Newspaper names have also been italicized. The original spellings of places and names have been retained.

The letters are generally presented in the chronological order of the events described rather than the date published or written. There were some misspelled German words in a few of the letters discovered in German-language newspapers, but the translator attributes this primarily to typesetting errors or the typesetter misreading the original handwritten word.

Some scattered handwritten sentences or phrases that were illegible or defied sensible translation have been omitted from the letters. Mention of some names and/or immaterial information about the persons named has also been omitted. Finally, portions of the three letters authored by Pvt. Friedrich P. Kappelmann have been omitted due to restrictions placed by their owner on the percentage of text in his letters that may be published.

Introduction

*H*istorians and other scholars of the American Civil War largely overlooked its ethnic component for many decades after the war, despite the fact that 25 percent of the Union's more than two million fighting men were born outside of the United States.[1] Fortunately, the number of books about immigrants, especially Germans, in the Civil War has increased greatly in the last two decades.

The majority of the Union's foreign-born soldiers were Germans or Irish but many other ethnic groups were represented in much lesser numbers. The Union's 200,000 German-born soldiers comprised almost ten percent of the North's fighting force and 40 percent of its immigrant component. Moreover, as historians Walter D. Kamphoefner and Wolfgang Helbich point out, "Germans . . . made up as large a contingent as African-Americans, whom most historians see as essential to the war effort." Perhaps 150,000 Irish immigrants fought in the Union army.[2]

The large majority of German-born soldiers fought in mixed regiments that were predominantly Anglo-American (defined here as persons born in the United States and descended mainly from colonial-era English and Scots-Irish colonists). Often, when their numbers were sufficient to form a company (83 to 101 officers and men), Germans served in all or mostly German companies within the mixed regiments. This allowed German-speakers who understood little English to serve in the military.[3] Approximately 40,000, or one in five, native Germans fought in ethnic German regiments. These regiments were organized mostly in large cities and areas where there were large concentrations of Germans. Historians have identified more than thirty German regiments. The Confederacy's German-born population of less than 80,000 persons was barely more than 6 percent of the Union's German-born population of 1.2 million persons, and it fielded no German regiments.[4]

German and other ethnic regiments were a unique element of the American Civil War and certainly increased the visibility of their particular ethnic group's participation beyond the level that would have existed if its members had been scattered in Anglo-American regiments. This visibility was a double-edged sword, however, in that while an ethnic group could point with pride to the contributions and accomplishments of its regiments, they also proved convenient scapegoats when things went wrong. For example, the German soldiers of the Eleventh Corps were blamed for the disastrous defeat of the Union's Army of the Potomac at the Battle of Chancellorsville in Virginia (discussed later in this introduction).[5]

Immigrants fighting in the 82nd Illinois Volunteer Infantry Regiment wrote the fifty-nine soldiers' letters that appear in the following chapters. The 82nd Illinois was one of three German regiments formed in the Prairie State and one of only two regiments in the entire Union army containing a company of Jews. It was also the second German regiment organized by Col. Friedrich Franz Carl Hecker, a popular leader of the unsuccessful German Revolution of 1848, who had settled on a farm in Summerville, Illinois, in 1849.[6]

The accompanying letters are valuable for much more than their rarity.[7] First, they reveal how the 82nd Illinois differed from Anglo-American regiments and provide valuable information about life in a German regiment, as well as how some German Americans viewed the war, themselves, their fellow Germans, Anglo-Americans, other ethnics, and the enemy. Second, the letters shed light on the broader ethnic dimensions of the war, especially ethnic identity, ethnic pride, ethnic prejudice, ethnic solidarity, and how the German American press linked the home front to the battlefront, ultimately raising ethnic consciousness.[8] Third, vivid first-hand accounts of camps, marches, and such hard-fought battles as Chancellorsville, Gettysburg, Resaca, New Hope Church, Kolb's Farm, and Bentonville, as well as of personal experiences during Maj. Gen. William T. Sherman's Atlanta campaign, the March to the Sea, and the Carolinas campaign, provide new primary source material to military historians and frontline accounts to persons interested in Civil War battles and campaigns. Finally, some of the correspondence reflects the political climate during the American Civil War.

Historians affirm that contemporary letters such as those in this study are superior to memoirs and reminiscences written years or even decades after the events occurred because memory is frequently clouded by time and perceptions sometimes change. Of course, public letters, unlike private ones, omit intimate expressions to loved ones and friends, and their authors consciously or unconsciously tend to describe their own actions and those of their unit in a favorable light.[9]

II

Thirty of the soldiers' letters that follow originally appeared in wartime issues of German American newspapers. These "public" letters begin in July 1862, when the regiment was being organized, and end in July 1864, while the battle-tested regiment was entrenched by the Chattahoochee River near Atlanta. Their authors vary in rank, age, city or village of birth, education, prewar occupations, and religious beliefs. Fourteen of the public missives are unsigned or signed only with initials or a pseudonym. This was not unusual for published letters at that time. Biographical information about the identified letter writers is generally located in a paragraph preceding or immediately following the individual's first letter, in the epilogue, or in the endnotes.

The preponderance of the public letters appeared in the *Illinois Staats-Zeitung* (Illinois State Newspaper)—Chicago's and Illinois's leading German American newspaper. The *Staats-Zeitung* was Republican, anti-slavery, and strongly pro-Union. It promoted the organization of German regiments and published numerous letters from soldiers fighting in Illinois's German regiments.[10]

German Americans relied on their ethnic press as an important source of information about the war because many lacked skills in English, and Anglo-American newspapers carried little or no information about Germans and were often viewed as despicable nativist (anti-Catholic and anti-foreigner) organs. Of special interest to German readers were the exploits and treatment of their native landsmen. Besides letters from soldiers detailing army life, battles, complaints, boasts, and opinions, major organs like the *Illinois Staats-Zeitung* further helped connect the German American community to the battlefront by providing news about German American military leaders, military units and their battles, casualty lists, needs, and editorials. German American newspapers that did not publish soldiers' letters or whose editors opposed the war would sometimes publish casualty lists and news about German American military leaders. Even newspapers that strongly opposed the war, and there were more than a few, would still condemn nativist attacks on Germans in the army and encourage political and other actions to defend against such abuse and to promote common interests.[11]

Newspapers received by soldiers in the field informed them of important events back home, other German Americans in the military, and the progress of the war in other theaters. Historian Stephen D. Engle argues that German American newspapers were important in raising the ethnic consciousness of Germans in the Union and credits Franz Sigel, a hero of the German Revolution of 1848 and a Union general, with successfully utilizing the link between community and battlefield to help unify the Union's Germans despite their political differences.[12]

About one-half of all German American newspapers, including the *Illinois Sta-ats-Zeitung,* were owned and/or edited by Forty-eighters—a term for participants in the failed German Revolution of 1848 and uprisings of 1849. Forty-eighters had battled to establish a more democratic government in their homelands, to unify Germany's various states into one nation, and to bring about economic and social reforms. During the Civil War Forty-eighters in Union states promoted and helped organize German regiments and often served as their colonels; eleven became Union generals.[13]

Forty-eighter editors and other Forty-eighter leaders played an influential role in raising the ethnic consciousness of America's Germans, defining German American ethnicity, enunciating common concerns, and mobilizing them politi-cally in defense of their common interests. In Chicago and other cities, Forty-eighters also founded secular German American institutions such as *Turnvereine* (gymnastic societies whose members were called Turners), men's singing societ-ies, immigrant aid societies, and central meeting halls.[14]

Most Forty-eighters condemned organized religion, especially Roman Cathol-icism and conservative Lutheranism, and particularly their hierarchy and clergy. Part of the Forty-eighters' opposition to organized religion stemmed from the churches supporting the aristocracy, thereby helping to defeat the revolution; they also believed the Roman Catholic Church was anti-democratic. The ranks of the Forty-eighters included freethinkers, agnostics, atheists, deists, humanists, pan-theists, and some very liberal Protestants. A large number of Forty-eighters were socialists or communists and some Anglo-Americans called them "red Republi-cans." Roman Catholics and Lutherans generally avoided the radicals as much as possible.[15]

Forty-eighters comprised only four to six thousand of the one million Ger-mans who immigrated to the United States in the decade following the failed revolution, but they were highly visible.[16] While most German immigrants bus-ied themselves trying to make a living and avoid nativists, these political, social, and economic radicals saw imperfections in certain American institutions and customs, and vociferously criticized them and agitated for reforms. Their shrill anti-slavery cries, calls for removal of the Bible from public schools, the orga-nization of labor unions, and an end to the spoils system in politics; along with elimination of temperance and Sunday laws, were broadcast by their German American newspapers and speeches. This displeased most old-stock Americans, who tended to associate all Germans with the Forty-eighters, thereby increasing friction and furthering strong anti-German sentiment. The Forty-eighters also caused dissension within the German community itself.[17]

Although the nativistic Know Nothing and American parties, whose support-ers attacked immigrants' religion and culture and strove to reduce immigrants' political power, were virtually dead before the Civil War began, their former members and like-minded persons did not abandon their anti-Catholic and anti-immigrant feelings. Nativists still disdained Roman Catholics because they believed their church was un-American. Among other things, Anglo-American opponents of Catholicism asserted that the church was anti-democratic and anti-enlightenment, and was led by a tyrannical foreign power (the Pope) who wanted his minions to subvert American institutions and change the country's predominate Protestant culture. Many detractors also railed at the Catholic Church's lack of support for the temperance movement and suspected that Catholics' allegiances to Rome were stronger than to the United States. Anti-immigrant sentiments in general resulted from the feeling that immigrants not of Protestant English or Scots-Irish descent consisted of inferior races, had alien customs, took jobs from Anglo-Americans, and would not quickly assimilate.[18]

Mid-nineteenth-century German immigrants were a complex and diverse lot. Further, as historian Christian B. Keller explains, they "were struggling to define themselves within American Society as an ethnic group and sort out internal differences that kept them strongly divided."[19] These newcomers came from political entities that were or had been independent kingdoms, duchies, principalities, and free cities with their own political and tribal histories, and some of these states had warred against each other. Even though they were German-speaking, these Teutonic immigrants were also set apart by differences in idiom and dialect, religion, political views, and class. They mostly identified themselves with the political entity of their birth (such as Baden, Bavaria, Prussia, and so forth) rather than with the central part of Europe then called Germany (Germany did not become a nation-state until 1871). Anglo-Americans, on the other hand, seldom distinguished between Bavarians, Prussians, or Hessians, but referred to them all as Germans or, pejoratively, as "Dutch," "Dutchmen," or "damn Dutch." "Dutch" was a corruption of the German word *Deutsch* (meaning German). Approximately two-thirds of German Americans were Protestants and about one-third were Roman Catholics—and, as in the Old Country, the two groups were not on friendly terms and did not mix. There were also Jews and Freethinkers. In spite of their differences, however, as Keller points out, as the 1850s progressed some feeling of *Deutschtum* or pan-German consciousness began developing, and increased American nativism in the 1850s, along with restrictive social practices and differing cultural standards, caused many Germans to question the value of rapid assimilation.[20]

Prior to the founding of the Republican Party in 1854, the vast majority of Germans clung to the Democratic Party because it was friendly to immigrants and opposed temperance and Sunday laws.[21] Some shifting occurred with the founding of the Republican Party in 1854; Forty-eighters became the most politically active and influential Germans in this new party. At the Republican convention in Chicago in 1860, several Forty-eighters served as delegates. They succeeded in getting the party to adopt two "Dutch planks." One plank demanded equal rights for all citizens, including the foreign-born, and the other promoted a liberal homestead law that gave settlers free land under certain conditions. The desire of many Germans to keep the territories free, so they would not have to compete with slave labor, and the promise of a homestead law helped pull them into future president Abraham Lincoln's party. Although a significant number of Germans abandoned the Democratic Party in 1860, Lincoln failed to receive a majority of the German vote. Many members of the American Party (Know Nothings) had joined the Republican Party after the slavery issue gained dominance, so most Germans still felt the Republican Party was tinged with nativism and was the home of supporters of temperance and Sunday laws. Roman Catholics amounted to about one-third of the free and border states' 1.2 million native Germans and most remained staunch Democrats because of the above-mentioned reasons.[22]

Despite some postwar claims that Germans were united in the desire to abolish slavery, this was not so. Generally, only certain Forty-eighters, Turners, members of the small *Freimännerverein* (Freemen's League), and German Methodists and Baptists in the North fostered immediate abolition. For example, the *Turnerbund* (the national coordinating organization for *Turnvereine*) adopted a resolution

Col. Friedrich Hecker, *Hecker-Regiment; Veteran Verein 24er Illinois Volunteers. Fest-Commers zu ehren Kameraden aller deutschen Regimenter. Dienstag Abend, den 28 August, 1900 in der Turnerhalle der Nordseite, Chicago.*

stating slavery was "contrary to all concepts of freedom," and that Turners are "opposed to slavery," and "particularly . . . against the extension of slavery to the free territories," but did not mention the abolition of slavery. Expansion of slavery into the territories was a more immediate threat to immigrants because of, as historian Bruce Levine argues, "the prospect that the coveted soil of the West would be preempted by a home grown aristocracy that cordially despised free labor. Immigrant farmers and workers who tried to live there would see their living standards and social status driven down to levels prevailing in the Old World." Moreover, some German abolitionists did not favor equal rights for blacks, even if they were free.[23]

Five of the regiment's officers wrote a total of twenty-six of the private letters interspersed throughout various chapters. The 82nd Illinois's fiery colonel, Friedrich Hecker, wrote two of the public letters and two of the private letters presented in this work. The second of his private letters was sent to his close friend and fellow revolutionist Gustav Struve after the Battle of Chancellorsville, fought on May 1–4, 1863, and described his wounding and how he escaped capture. Moreover, Colonel Hecker was the recipient of all but six of the other private letters in this volume.[24] Hecker was a leading Forty-eighter, a Turner, a farmer, and previous commander of the 24th Illinois (First Hecker Regiment). The patriotic but inexperienced colonel resigned as commander of the 24th Illinois on December 21, 1861, because of bitter disputes with certain officers in the regiment, who found fault with his harsh efforts to enforce strict discipline and his explosive nature. Colonel Hecker began organizing the 82nd Illinois (Second Hecker Regiment) in June 1862 and led it until October 19, 1863, when he was promoted to a brigade command. The 82nd Illinois transferred to his new brigade.[25]

First Lt. (later Capt.) Rudolph Müller wrote twenty-one of the private letters in this collection to Colonel Hecker between February 23, 1864, and June 9, 1865. Müller's missives began while the colonel was on sick leave and continued after Hecker resigned from the army in March 1864; they ended shortly before the regiment boarded railroad cars near Washington, D.C., to return to Illinois after the war's end. The correspondence reveals that Hecker and Müller were close friends and confidants. Fourteen of Müller's letters have never before been published in English; seven of his letters or significant parts thereof (translated by the late Hildegard Benedick), appear in Eric Benjaminson's 2001 article, "A Regiment of Immigrants: The 82nd Illinois Volunteer Infantry and the Letters of Captain Rudolph Müller." All of Müller's letters in this volume are the current editor's translations. More information about his letters is included later in this introduction.[26] Eric Benjaminson, who introduced the editor to the 82nd Illinois and a portion of Rudolph Müller's letters through the above-mentioned article, aptly described Müller as, "an intelligent, well-read man who had strong, almost violent opinions. Experienced and cynical, brave and critical, Müller wrote with a sure hand on his regiment, the situation of German immigrant troops in the Union army, the Jewish soldiers in his regiment, wartime politics, and combat."[27]

Eighteen-year-old Adj. Eugene Weigel wrote one of the personal letters to his family on July 9, 1863, shortly after the Battle of Gettysburg. Eugene's father was a close friend of Colonel Hecker and had fought under him during the revolution. Lt. Col. Edward S. Salomon's single letter condemned the Illinois state legislature's actions regarding the Emancipation Proclamation and Capt. John Hillborg's missive objects to Colonel Hecker requesting a German be made an officer in the Scandinavian company. Finally, small excerpts from two diaries of other soldiers of the regiment are included in various chapters.[28]

Articles published in the *Illinois Staats-Zeitung* about the organization of the 82nd's Jewish company and a published report signed by three prominent members of the Jewish community describing their visit to the regiment's camp (Camp Butler) near Springfield, Illinois, are included with the soldiers' letters. These accounts reveal how Chicago's small Jewish community of approximately 1,500 persons contributed to the formation of Hecker's second regiment, what some of the city's Jewish leaders did and said to rally their community to support the war effort, and they provide some details of life and certain events at Camp Butler. A letter written in March 1865 to *Illinois Staats-Zeitung* editor Wilhelm Rapp by a Turner residing in Savannah, Georgia, is also included. This letter describes the writer's encounters with several officers of the 82nd Illinois during the Union army's occupation of Savannah and reports on some events concerning the regiment after it left Savannah for South Carolina. The letter was signed only F. K.[29]

The editor cautions that the letters appearing in this study and their authors are so few in number they are not necessarily representative of the beliefs and attitudes of all Germans in the 82nd Illinois. Nor can they be considered representative of all Germans in the Union army. Because of the regiment's Forty-eighter and Turner leadership element, Roman Catholics and probably Democrats were surely underrepresented in the unit. Approximately 30,000 of the 130,000 Germans in Illinois were Roman Catholics and it was widely known that Colonel Hecker hated Catholics. The letters must therefore stand alone, and provide only anecdotal evidence.[30]

III

Nine of the 82nd Illinois's companies and its headquarters mustered into service on September 26, 1862, at Camp Butler. Its tenth company mustered in on October 29, 1862, bringing the aggregate number of enlistees to approximately 850 officers and men.[31] The last company mustered in—Company I—consisted of Scandinavians. Governor Yates had transferred this company and a mostly-German company (D) from the 3rd Board of Trade Regiment (113th Illinois) to complete Hecker's regiment. German regiments often recruited other ethnics and Anglo-Americans to bring individual companies up to the requisite minimum number of soldiers; sometimes one or more companies of non-Germans were included to complete the regiment. Germans immigrants of course predominated in Colonel Hecker's new regiment. Germans served as the field officers, comprised a large majority of the regiment's soldiers, were in the majority in nine of its ten companies, and initially commanded eight of its companies (later increasing to all ten companies).[32]

Besides the Jews in Company C, a small number of Jews also served in some other companies of the 82nd, including Company K's first captain Joseph B. Greenhut. Lt. Col. Edward S. Salomon, a Jew who had served as a first lieutenant in the 24th Illinois under Colonel Hecker, initially became second in command of the 82nd and later commanded the combat unit. All but a few of the Jews in the regiment were natives of Germany.[33]

The proud new German regiment departed for Virginia on November 3, 1862, where it joined the Eleventh Corps of the Army of the Potomac. Almost one-half of the Eleventh Corps's soldiers were German Americans.[34] Maj. Gen. Franz Sigel, mentioned earlier in this introduction, led the corps until he resigned on February 12, 1863. West Point–educated Maj. Gen. Oliver O. Howard superseded Sigel. General Howard was a deeply religious teetotaler who was not popular with his German American troops, especially after banning beer in the corps in May 1863.[35]

The 82nd Illinois suffered heavy casualties in the Battle of Chancellorsville on May 2, 1863, and in the Battle of Gettysburg on July 1–3, 1863. The regiment and its corps traveled west in September 1863 to reinforce the Army of the Cumberland then under siege at Chattanooga, Tennessee. The siege was broken by Federal forces on November 25, 1863. On April 4, 1864, the two Eleventh Corps divisions posted near Chattanooga and a Twelfth Corps division combined to form the Twentieth Corps of the Army of the Cumberland.[36]

Colonel Hecker's resignation on March 21, 1864 (while he was home on sick leave), along with Forty-eighter Maj. Gen. Carl Schurz's exclusion from a division command in the new Twentieth Corps, marked the end of the 82nd Illinois serving in a brigade and division commanded by native Germans. The 82nd Illinois would serve its final fourteen months mainly under Anglo-American brigade and division commanders.[37]

In early May 1864 Maj. Gen. William T. Sherman's grand army (consisting of the Army of the Cumberland, the Army of the Tennessee, and the Army of the Ohio) began a grueling campaign that resulted in the capture of Atlanta, Georgia, on September 2, 1864. The Fourteenth Corps and Twentieth Corps of the Army of the Cumberland formed the Left Wing of General Sherman's army, which made the famous March to the Sea (Savannah campaign) in November and December 1864 and then foraged and fought its way through South and North Carolina. The last campaign ended with the surrender of Gen. Joseph E. Johnston's Confederate army on April 26, 1865, at the Bennett Place near Durham Station (now Durham), North Carolina. Johnston's surrender occurred more than two weeks after Gen. Robert E. Lee surrendered his Army of Northern Virginia at Appomattox Courthouse. The 82nd Illinois marched with its corps from Raleigh, North Carolina, to Alexandria, Virginia, arriving on May 20, 1865, and four days later participated in the Grand (Victory) March in Washington, D.C.[38]

After mustering out in Washington on June 9, 1865, approximately three hundred officers and men of the 82nd arrived in Chicago on June 16 to a rousing welcome from their families, friends, and others. This represented approximately 30 percent of the original number of men who had mustered in. During its thirty-one months of service, four officers and ninety-eight enlisted men sacrificed their lives in combat and sixty enlisted men died of disease. Some of the latter group died in Confederate prison camps. Many more men were discharged for disabling wounds or diseases or other causes. Still others were in hospitals, had deserted, or otherwise disappeared.[39]

IV

Historian William L. Burton asserted, in *Melting Pot Soldiers: The Union's Ethnic Regiments,* that "[w]ith any ethnic regiment, . . . it is difficult to grasp just how important ethnicity was to the average soldier. Once the beer and language are discounted, what was left?" Wolfgang Helbich, Christian B. Keller, and other scholars, however, have had no difficulty coming to a different conclusion. Wolfgang Helbich correctly asserts, "German regiments [were] noticeably (and often abrasively) different from their American counterparts, so, too, were German-born soldiers. . . ." Keller agrees and points out that "[f]rom a distance to the uninformed observer, the German American regiments looked exactly the same as all other infantry units in the Federal service. A closer examination, however, would have revealed differences that specifically addressed the regiment's ethnicity." The letters in this study and an examination of the muster and descriptive rolls for the 82nd Illinois Infantry support Helbich and Keller's conclusions.[40]

German immigrants and Anglo-Americans joined in the fight to preserve the Union for a combination of reasons. Principal reasons applicable to both groups included patriotism; the desire to preserve the Republic, liberty, and democracy; community and peer pressure; adventure; eliminating slavery; and simply a paycheck. Some German Americans, however, had the additional reasons of paying back the country that provided them with economic opportunities and constitutional guarantees; proving they were loyal and worthy citizens; and hoping to eliminate nativist prejudices against Germans.[41]

Recruit George E. Heinzmann of Company B of the 82nd Illinois urged fellow Germans "to unite with me under Hecker's standard and Sigel's in the battle for the Republic and for freedom." Colonel Hecker trumpeted fighting for "freedom," and late in the war Rudolph Müller stated he was fighting for the "flag." Other letters are silent on reasons for enlisting. Without doubt there were men who joined Hecker's regiment for other reasons, such as the need for money or peer pressure, but it is unlikely they would admit it in a public letter.[42]

Wolfgang Helbich argues that among reasons for enlisting, patriotic feelings were significantly lower on the list for German Americans than for Anglo-Americans, who were "born and raised in America, imbued with American traditions and values." He suggests that many more Germans joined the Union army for economic reasons than out of patriotic feelings. Keller believes that "[p]racticality dictated the decision to enlist for most Germans." Unfortunately, there is insufficient evidence available to quantify the relative importance of the various reasons for Germans enlisting in the 82nd Illinois or the Union army.[43]

Motivations for enlisting in a German regiment varied. Engle explains that many Germans wanted to be among men of their own culture who shared common values, experiences, and historical memories. Many did not understand English or "wanted to fight under a commander who understood their Germanness," and some "feared nativist hostility in the ranks" of Anglo-American units; still others responded to an appeal from German leaders and editors to raise the visibility of German participation in the war, while some saw a better opportunity for advancement than in predominately Anglo-America units.[44]

The average age of men in German regiments was usually higher than those in the Union army as a whole. At muster-in the average age of the men in the 82nd Illinois was approximately twenty-nine, and 20 percent of the men were under twenty-two. The same was true for the German component of the regiment. On the other hand, the average age for enlistees in the entire Union army in July 1862 approximated just over twenty-five, with somewhat over 40 percent of these enlistees under twenty-two.[45]

Besides the age difference, the 82nd Illinois differed from the average Union regiment in the prewar occupations of its members. For example, while nearly 50 percent of soldiers in the Union army came from farms, farmers aggregated only 20 percent of the 82nd's members. In the 82nd Illinois, where almost one hundred different walks of life were represented, six categories accounted for a majority of the men's occupations at enlistment: farmers, day laborers, clerks, carpenters, tailors, and shoemakers, in descending order. Laborers amounted to 10 percent. Accordingly, the Second Hecker Regiment was more urban and contained fewer farmers and more craftsmen and artisans, than the army as a whole.[46]

German and Anglo-American regiments usually contained men from the same Union state and also predominantly from the same region of the state. German regiments, including the 82nd, contained men from all or most of the different German kingdoms, duchies, principalities, and independent cities in Central Europe.[47]

Ethnic traits such as language, culture, and customs distinguished German American fighting men and regiments from Anglo-American ones. Language was the most significant difference. In some German regiments, such as the 9th Ohio and 32nd Indiana, German was the language of both command and conversation. Whether the 82nd Illinois used German for regimental commands is uncertain; however, it may have been used at the company level in the German-dominated companies. Certainly, the Germans and German-speaking Swiss and Austrians used German as the language of conversation and often of song. Interestingly, at his court martial hearing for desertion, Company G's Pvt. Robert Stoddart, a native of Scotland, testified that the members of the 82nd Illinois, "with few exceptions, could not speak the English language. . . . My ignorance of the German language rendered my position amongst so many Germans, where I heard hardly any other language spoken, very disagreeable and very lonesome, and I tore myself away." This may not have been the real reason for his desertion, but certainly some other non-German members of the regiment felt this way.[48]

Germans did not surrender their love of lager once they joined the Union army, and early in the war some German regiments even received a beer ration. To many Germans it was a necessity, like bread. Colonel Hecker's men consumed many barrels of lager while in Illinois, but it became harder to obtain after they moved to Virginia and beyond. First Sgt. William Loeb of Company C pleaded in a letter dated September 2, 1862, "Send beer in special trains, much beer and your name shall be emblazoned in golden letters in the memories of our soldiers."

Unfortunately for the thirsty Teutons, Maj. Gen. Oliver O. Howard's ban on their favorite beverage made camp life less bearable.[49] A taste for traditional German foods also distinguished German soldiers. Food such as sausages (including liverwurst), sauerkraut, and pungent cheese were sought after in camps of German regiments and sold by German sutlers assigned to these organizations.[50]

Music and song were important parts of German culture, and for Turners the German song not only served as a social function but also helped build solidarity among fellow members. German units could easily be recognized as such when they sang their favorite German marching songs while tramping up or down the road. Groups sang German and also American songs while encamped. Pvt. Carl Lotz wrote to the *Staats-Zeitung* on December 2, 1862, about singing "the so much celebrated new song 'O you dear Augustin[e].'" And, Rudolph Müller informed Cololel Hecker on Oct. 25, 1864, "[t]he . . . [*Quarter*]*Master* staff, which celebrated the day with [illegible word], answered with the songs *Hecker, Struve,* etc., melody *Schleswig-Holstein.*"[51]

When practical, German regimental camps reflected the culture and taste of their members. Pvt. Frank Schönewald of Company K wrote in a letter to the *Illinois Staats-Zeitung* that, in celebrating Colonel Hecker's birthday, "[w]e saw from morning to night nothing but trees, flowers and such materials belonging to a German folk festival. . . . In front of their tents, which were set up in straight rows, each company had planted a number of trees, and decorated with wreaths, whereby the entire camp was transformed into shady allées. Lights were attached to the trees, which looked very pretty." Turners also constructed gymnastic equipment for their use.[52]

Colonels of German regiments sometimes ignored the law stipulating that a regiment's chaplain must be a "regularly ordained minister of some Christian denomination."[53] Colonel Hecker appointed Edmund Julius Reichhelm as chaplain. A Forty-eighter educated for the judiciary and a veteran of one year's service in the Prussian army, the new chaplain acted as the regiment's postmaster and concentrated on helping the surgeons and the wounded, giving proper honors at burials, and elevating the morale of the soldiers.[54] Pvt. Frederick Braeutigam of Company F commented in his diary on October 5, 1862, on the occasion of the new chaplain's first regimental address, that "[i]t was a very liberal speech without the slightest religious reference. Theme on the basis of true freedom."[55] Other German regiments, such as the 32nd Indiana, 12th Missouri, and 9th Ohio, had Forty-eighter chaplains as well.[56]

Any hopes German Americans entertained that their show of loyalty to the Union and the sacrifices made by their men serving in the military would soften or end anti-German prejudices and Anglo-American nativism were dashed as the war progressed. Nativism took many forms in the Federal army from making fun of Germans and insulting and cursing them, to blaming them for thefts and calling them cowards, to assigning them more than their fair share of the harder duties such as train guard and loading and unloading freight. Some Germans accused Anglo-American commanders of using Germans as cannon fodder. A member of the 82nd Illinois identified only as W. A. reported in a letter published in the (St. Louis) *Westliche Post* on August 27, 1862, that "[j]ust now we nearly had a little battle between a just arrived American [regiment] and Hecker's. It was prevented only by calling several hundred armed guards . . . It would have resulted in bloodshed because of nativism and hatred toward the Germans, but the combatants lacked the weapons." A disrespectful Anglo-American colonel even cursed at Colonel Hecker.[57]

Even worse, immediately after Lt. Gen. Thomas J. "Stonewall" Jackson's divisions routed the Eleventh Corps at Chancellorsville in May 1863, nativist newspapers, soldiers' letters, and word of mouth spread rumors and charges that panic, confusion, and cowardice prevailed in the corps's German element. The Germans, who felt they had fought as well as could be expected under such unfavorable circumstances, were insulted and sensed the onset of anti-German sentiment as strong as in the mid-1850s.[58]

On July 5, 1863, two days after the battle of Gettysburg ended, and still stinging from nativist slurs, an 82nder identified only as R. wrote: "This time even the most vicious nativist will not be able to deny that the 11th Corps fought excellently"—an obvious reference to Chancellorsville. Keller maintains that "Germans never got over what happened in the Virginia woods in May 1863," and that "they suddenly lost their ardor for the war and began to look to one another for support rather than a Union which seemed to despise them and disdain them for their sacrifices." It was long after the war ended before the largest portion of the responsibility for the defeat was placed on Maj. Gen. Oliver O. Howard and Maj. Gen. Joseph Hooker. A much smaller portion of responsibility for the loss does, however, fall on some members of the Eleventh Corps who ran or did not fight well.[59]

Finally, it is likely that German Americans sometimes misinterpreted orders, actions, or statements as a sign of prejudice against them. As Burton observed, "[t]hat prejudice and favoritism existed was beyond doubt. It was equally certain that individuals rationalized their condition by ignoring other factors and laying all blame at the door of prejudice." Importantly, Anglo-Americans and other ethnics serving in German regiments also frequently complained about their treatment, claiming prejudice hindered their promotion, well-being, and so forth.[60] Certainly, Capt. Ivar A. Weid of Company I anticipated problems when he advised Governor Yates on September 13, 1862, "I think it is wrong to order my

Company into Hecker['s regiment]. Germans and [S]candinavians never agree. They are national enemies." The following letters are virtually silent regarding any conflicts between the Germans and Scandinavians.[61]

Strong expressions of ethnic pride and biases are found in correspondence of the soldiers of the 82nd Infantry and its civilian supporters. One example is found in a letter dated August 28, 1862, whose author is unidentified: "We appear . . . to be a thorn in the eye of the American regiments here. It seems nearly as if they could not endure the strapping appearance and the cheerful nature of the 'Dutchmen.' However, we will show them our superiority. We do not want to know anything about the boring and stupid chit-chat in their daily meetings and the chaplains from other regiments, who meanwhile creep through our camp, make sour faces and see that their invitation to the meeting sits poorly with us; mawkishness and meetings are inadmissible commodities with us."[62]

According to Wolfgang Helbich, "the contradictory collective images elevating one's own and disparaging other ethnic groups have less to do with reality than with psychological needs and insecurities heightened by a sense of competition and the constant awareness of cultural difference." In addition, in a more recent work Helbich and Walter D. Kamphoefner agree: "The unpopular Germans insisted on believing they were better soldiers and could thus win the respect of Americans, and many Americans were eagerly waiting for the chance to prove that these incompetent foreigners were inferior to real Yankees . . . both sides were blind to the irony of the situation."[63]

Unlike his comrades who wrote to newspapers, Rudolph Müller knew that Colonel Hecker would not publicize anything in his missives that might embarrass or anger anyone in his regiment or brigade, cause problems for himself, or reflect poorly on the German combat unit. Müller's letters give the reader a close-up view of a radical German American's wartime experiences, his relations with his fellow Germans, opinions regarding certain senior Anglo-American officers and President Lincoln, and much more. Like his comrades' letters, Müller's correspondence mentions beer, sausages, German songs, festive occasions, and pride in the regiment, as well as detailed descriptions of battles, camps, and marches.

When the highly opinionated officer wrote to his close friend and former commander he expressed his opinions in no uncertain terms. He vented his anger and frustrations, as well as telling of fighting, the agony of wounded soldiers after a battle, boredom during sieges, suffering from harsh conditions, his political views, and sometimes pity for others. Müller revealed the bad as well as the good, and provided names. Unlike the above-mentioned public letters, Rudolph Müller's correspondence criticized Germans as well as Anglo-Americans, revealing instances of intra-ethnic conflict and prejudice within his regiment.

Anglo-Americans received praise when he believed they deserved it. Among the praised are division commander Brig. Gen. Alpheus S. Williams and army commander Maj. Gen. William T. Sherman, though he also criticized the latter general in some cases. Brigadiers Hector Tyndale and James S. Robinson, however, did not measure up to his high standards.[64]

Lt. Col. Edward S. Salomon, successor to Hecker as regimental commander, was the principal target for Müller's barbs. The Rhineland native detested Salomon because of his constant striving to gain popularity with both his superiors and certain subordinate officers for the purpose of increasing his rank. Müller disliked anyone who tried to increase his military status through self-promotion and currying favor with superiors. He admitted Salomon was a good officer and stated he would not oppose his promotion; it was Salomon's method that offended him. Adj. William Loeb, another Jew, was also among those Müller disdained, and he was generally disgusted with other officers who closely associated with Salomon. Regardless of his low opinion of certain officers, he had immense pride in his regiment as a whole.

Certain comments Müller makes about Salomon, such as calling him the "Creole from Jerusalem" and stating that he felt like he was living in a synagogue, certainly ring of anti-Semitism. Although Salomon and his fellow Jews were Germans they were different and this apparently bothered Müller. He disliked Salomon so much that he stated he would rather serve on the staff of Colonel McGroarty, an Irishman, than under Salomon.[65]

Müller had become so disturbed by Salomon's self-aggrandizing behavior that in March 1864 he confided to Hecker: "I am in conflict with myself about my next move. I do not want to leave the regiment, don't want to give up and leave the game to the Creole from Jerusalem. Having to serve under him, whom I despise from the depth of my heart, is bitter. Then again it appears my duty is to remain with our flag and to join in with the few brave officers who remain free of the stain."[66] Müller stuck with the flag but continued to criticize Salomon and express discontent with other people and things.

Müller, like other radical Republicans, believed the Lincoln administration had failed to pursue the war with the full resources of the North and he railed at a disturbing lack of support for the war at home. Although he did not specifically mention the emancipation of slaves, most radical Republications also criticized Lincoln for moving too slowly in freeing them.[67] Müller expressed the opinion on October 25, 1864, that "[t]hey are . . . miserable shopkeepers, these citizens of the Republic, who are lacking almost all characteristics of genuine republicans, and after 3 years of bloody war still have not learned that the peace can be achieved only through decisiveness and the rapid development of its entire strength." On May 27, 1865, he even stated that President Lincoln's death could benefit the country in a certain way.[68]

Despite his burning desire to pursue the war more aggressively, Müller believed that some in the army had acted too harshly in South Carolina. On April 2, 1865, he wrote: "Our army has taken on the character of bandits and murdering arsonist bands through the forage system, which everyone [illegible word], and it is sad to have come so far that one must almost blush to say he belongs to Sherman's army and campaigned through S. C."[69]

Now to the wartime letters that kept thousands of German Americans in Chicago and other places informed of the camps, marches, and battles of the Second Hecker Regiment, and the correspondence that provided Colonel Hecker with an insider's view of his former regiment through the ethnic lens of his future son-in-law, Rudolph Müller.[70]

One

Organization of the Regiment

*T*he letters and newspaper articles in this chapter were written during the organization of the 82nd Illinois Volunteer Infantry Regiment. They begin on July 22, 1862, and end on August 19, 1862. The regiment's first recruits signed up in June, and in mid-July groups of recruits began assembling at Camp Butler near Springfield, Illinois, while recruiting continued.[1] Recruiting soldiers was more difficult in the summer of 1862 than in the early days of the war when men enthusiastically rushed to the colors after Fort Sumter in Charleston Harbor was fired upon by South Carolina artillery and the war was expected to be short lived. Reports of the large number of men already killed and wounded in the fighting, along with the return home of many men crippled in the war, dampened the enthusiasm of many military-age males. Many cities and business organizations resorted to offering bounties to induce men to enlist to fill quotas set by the government and conscription of militiamen was to be used for any unfilled quotas.[2] The following letters express enthusiasm and pride and call for more men to join the regiment. The formation of the Jewish company in Chicago and life in the German regiment while training at Camp Butler are also described.

Illinois Staats-Zeitung
July 25, 1862
Springfield, Ill.
July 22, 1862

The 3 companies of the new Hecker Regiment arrived here from Highland on Sunday [the 20th] and our regiment appears to be complete and ready for field duty.[3] We are supplied very well, excellently uniformed and armed, so we are lacking nothing at all. We have moved from Camp Butler and pitched our tents on a charming elevation shaded by trees in the neighborhood of the old camp.

Our soldiers are highly motivated. We are serious and united by love for the cause and possess a youthful spirit necessary for good and valiant soldiers. Between the time the men complete their daily duties and retire to their nice airy tents to rest for the next day's work, they amuse themselves with gymnastics, dancing, etc., and it is truly a pleasure to watch them. How great the joy will be when the paymaster pays each one $40 today. (This $40 consists of $25 bounty, $13 pay, $2 recruiting money, and to this $40 will probably be added a $60 bounty for each man recruited in Cook County.)[4] Even more, however, we are looking forward to the arrival of our colonel. Under his leadership we will prove through our actions that the 71st [82nd] Illinois Regiment is not inferior to the older German regiment where it counts—showing the Rebels what Germans blows are.

I might mention that our officers are trying hard to educate us to be competent soldiers through amicable treatment and at the same time through military rigor. Through their work they have already earned the respect and devotion of everyone in this short time. More soon.

X

Illinois Staats-Zeitung editor's note. Of the three above-mentioned companies, one is from Chicago, another is from St. Louis [Mo.] and the third is from Highland [Ill.]. Additional companies of the regiment from different parts of the state will enter Springfield during the next 8 days.

George E. Heinzmann appealed to his fellow Turners to join the regiment in the following letter, dated August 6, 1862. Turners were members of a distinctly German gymnastic society called a *Turnverein* or *Turngemeinde*. Transplanted from Germany, the Turner movement grew quickly from one *Turnverien* in Cincinnati in 1848 (founded at the suggestion of Friedrich Hecker) to 150 local *Turnvereine* or *Turngemeinden* with 10,000 members across the county by 1860. A national organization (the *Turnerbund*) coordinated programs and activities. The Chicago *Turngemeinde* was founded in 1852. This uniquely German organization espoused order, discipline, and comradeship, and helped its members develop and maintain strong bodies through physical education (gymnastics, fencing, drilling, and sharpshooting), and improve their minds through lectures and libraries. Some Turner societies even contained one or more companies of militia.[5] One of their slogans, *"Bahn Frei!"* translates to "Clear the way" or "Watch out," and signaled their aggressiveness. As historian Bruce Levine writes, like

George Heinzmann, Company B (*Ge-schichte der Chicago Turn-gemeinde aus mündlichen Ueberlieferungen und Vereinsdokumenten zusammengestellt*)

Forty-eighters, "Turners were no random cross section of the immigrant population." Although the majority of Turners were not Forty-eighters, they shared all or much of the *Weltbild* or worldview of these highly idealistic men.[6] A large number of Turners fought in the Union army in both German and mixed regiments. For example, there were two infantry companies of Turners in the 24th Illinois and Turners fought in both the German 43rd Illinois Infantry and 82nd Illinois Infantry regiments.[7]

Heinzmann, born in the Grand Duchy of Baden, was a 25-year-old painter who mustered in on September 26, 1862. Elected first lieutenant of Company B, Heinzmann advanced to captain on March 12, 1863, and mustered out on June 9, 1865. After the war he received a brevet (honorary) promotion to major retroactive to March 13, 1865. Company B was funded by Anton C. Hesing, part owner of the *Illinois Staats-Zeitung,* and was called the Hesing Sharpshooters.[8]

Illinois Staats-Zeitung
August 6, 1862
Chicago
August 6, 1862

Clear the way!

How long do you still want to tarry? You should no longer want to deprive your besieged country of your services, and even if you wanted to, you cannot, because *Conscription,* forced levying, is at the door. Why not volunteer and do now under agreeable terms what you will have to do after August 15?[9] Turners are represented in all armies of the Union. Our beleaguered homeland and our Turner brothers in the field are facing a fearsome enemy and need help, immediate help. Why hesitate any longer? For long enough, Turner brothers, we have practiced swordsmanship with fencing masks on our faces, with the saber and rapier in our hands; we have strengthened and toughened our bodies long enough through gymnastics to bear the stresses and strains of military service.

The time has come to stand the test of arms and strength in the face of the enemies of the Republic, the enemies of freedom. I enlisted yesterday as a "*Private*" in Br[u]ning's company of the new Hecker Regiment, have already taken the oath of allegiance, and now call on my Turner brothers most sincerely and insistently to take the same step and unite with me under Hecker's and Sigel's standards in the battle for the Republic and for freedom.[10]

Alert, free, happy! Clear the Way![11]

George Heinzmann

Twenty-four-year-old Otto Balck, a native of Schwerin in the Duchy of Mecklenburg-Schwerin in northern Germany, expressed pride in the regiment and praise for Colonel Hecker in his public letter from Camp Butler. The light-haired, gray-eyed former clerk from Chicago mustered in as a private, Company A, on September 26, 1862; was appointed sergeant-major on October 23, 1862; mustered in as first lieutenant, Company C, on July 1, 1863; and was appointed the regimental adjutant on August 3, 1863. Balck was wounded at Chancellorsville, Virginia, in May 1863 and again near Ringgold, Georgia, in 1864. He mustered out with the regiment in June 1865 and was brevetted captain effective March 13, 1865.

Illinois Staastzeitung
August 12, 1862
Camp Butler
August 8 [1862]

Several times already, through some circumstances unknown to me, members of our company, the first in the new Hecker regiment, have experienced unpleasant delays in your valued newspaper arriving on schedule.** In the name of my comrades I would like you to find out if you could do something about this matter, to use your influence to speed its delivery. Because our company, as is generally known, was recruited in Chicago, you will understand how we eagerly await your newspaper. On the other hand, we are obliged to read your daily edition on the day published because of the lively interest and the patriotic zeal with which the *Ill. Stsztg.* helped with the formation of the First as well as the Second Hecker Regiment.

Our company was mustered in yesterday at Springfield as the first company of the new Hecker regiment.[12] Major [Edward S.] Salomon came to our camp from Chicago for this purpose. He brought a significant number of new recruits with him and was greeted with three strong German hurrahs. That same afternoon we traveled to Springfield by railroad where the mustering in was conducted by U.S. Mustering Officer Hill in the presence of Major Salomon as well as Hecker's newly elected quartermaster, Panse.[13]

According to what we have heard, our enthusiastic company made a thoroughly favorable impression in Springfield because post commander Fonda called us the best of the troops in camp here. Such a statement on the part of an American toward an exclusively German company certainly is saying something. Each individual is proud of this company and also to belong to this regiment. The spirit is excellent and the camaraderie could not be better. I do not need to explain further that it is a pleasure to serve under such circumstances. The members of our company are thoroughly strong young men, full of courage and lust for life—solely German. We are not exaggerating when we state that it excited us when we saw the joy of our countrymen and the admiration of the Americans in Springfield who enthusiastically observed us. Yesterday, the handsome uniforms and the military deportment of the men pleased everyone.[14]

Most of us belong to the educated working class and many are members of the workers' union (*Arbeiterverein*). I do not know what unit our undecided German countrymen in Chicago should join, but they could do no better than to come to us. The recruiting office of the major [Salomon] offers the best opportunity. Men will find manly cheerfulness, joviality, song, and good comradeship with us, and all that makes the soldier's life comfortable.

The name of Colonel Hecker has brought together excellent material for the second time and all signs are that the second regiment will soon be complete, and Company "A" is certain that it will not cede any superiority to the old regiment. The colonel has already visited us several times and each time was greeted with cheers. His enemies have not been able to rob him of his old popularity.

We lie outside the camp in excellent tents in the shade of green trees. The camp itself has become too small for the newly recruited regiments. Tents shoot up daily like mushrooms on its south side and each day significant numbers of new recruits are moving in from all parts of the state. We are comfortable in stating that if all other states followed the encouraging example of Illinois, the fate and the future of our glorious Union would be secured forever.

The mustering in of further companies of our regiment is proceeding quickly.

> Your servant,
> Otto Balck
> Orderly Sergeant *pro tem*
> Co. A, Hecker Reg. No. 2.

**The *Ill. Stsztg.* as a rule delivers to the post office early, so the blame for such delays could lie with the local post office. We will continue to do all within our power to prevent such mischief. Anyway we call to your attention that we have sent 25 copies post free by express. [*Illinois Staats-Zeitung* editor's note.]

Maj. Edward S. Salomon (mentioned in the letter above) would be promoted to lieutenant colonel of the regiment on September 26, 1862. Salomon was born in Schleswig in the Duchy of Schleswig in 1836. He received a good basic education, then moved to Hamburg at sixteen and engaged in the mercantile business there until he left for America in 1854. In 1855 the ambitious immigrant was living in Chicago and working as a clerk. He next worked as a bookkeeper and then became a lawyer. In 1861 he was elected alderman of the 6th Ward. Salomon married Sophie Greenhut in February 1860. Sophie was the daughter of a well-known Chicago Jewish family and the sister of Capt. Joseph B. Greenhut of Company K of the 82nd Illinois. Salomon mustered in the 24th Illinois Infantry Regiment on July 8, 1861, and served as first lieutenant, Company H, until he resigned in sympathy with Colonel Hecker's resignation in December 1861. He mustered out of the 82nd Illinois on June 9, 1865, and on June 22, 1867, was brevetted as a colonel and a brigadier general effective as of March 13, 1865.[15]

The following news articles described four public meetings called by Jewish leaders in Chicago to promote the formation of a Jewish company for Colonel Hecker's regiment. The speakers included not only leaders of the Jewish community but also the owners and editors of the *Illinois Staats-Zeitung* (Lorenz Brentano, Sheriff Anthony C. Hesing, and Wilhelm Rapp), Caspar Butz, Lieutenant Governor Francis A. Hoffmann, Col. Friedrich Hecker, Maj. Edward S. Salomon, and Jacob Lasalle, captain of the Jewish company.[16]

Illinois Staats-Zeitung
August 14, 1862
German War Assembly
Yesterday evening at 8 o'clock in Concordia Hall on Dearborn Street, a large

and enthusiastic war assembly was held and attended mainly by our Israelite fellow citizens.[17] President M. Gerstley presided; the speech was brief, avid, and inspiring. The resolutions, which had been drafted by . . . the Resolutions Committee, appear proper.[18] However, the main thing is that nearly $6,000 was subscribed and they hope that the sum will increase by several thousand dollars today. A company will be formed under the auspices of this assembly, and according to the resolution it will join the Hecker Regiment. Six of those present immediately signed up as volunteers. Mr. Lasalle the recruiting officer looks for further enrollments and will make the full particulars known. Three cheers for the volunteers and three more cheers for Col. Hecker ended the meeting. And we add on our part three cheers and a [*tigor?*] for our patriotic Israelite fellow citizens.

Illinois Staats-Zeitung
August 15, 1862

The second war meeting of Chicago's Israelites took place yesterday evening in Concordia Hall on Dearborn Street. The forty brave men who had already enlisted in the company of the Hecker Regiment forming under the auspices of the local Israelites marched into the hall with the Great Western Band. Upon loud calls by many of those present, Mr. Henry Greenebaum delivered a splendid address in which he reminded the Israelites that they all owe especial faithfulness and sacrifice to the Union because it has granted them the full political, social, and religious freedoms that they had to do without in many lands in the Old World.[19]

The same loud cheers raised by Mr. Greenebaum's speech were no less enthusiastic for the patriotic remarks of Messrs. Schwarzenberg, Strauss, and Maj. Salomon. The latter announced that Hecker and Sigel extended a most hearty welcome to the Israelite company and the assembly greeted these two celebrated names with enthusiastic applause.[20] Meanwhile, recruiting for the company makes great progress. Among those who have joined are many veterans and it is firmly believed that the company will be filled today.

The Israelite ladies of Chicago, who are no less patriotic than the Israelite men, subscribed yesterday in the amount of $152 and will purchase a flag for the Israelite company of the Hecker Regiment. Briefly—our fellow Israelite citizens are totally imbued with the noble human and freedom loving spirit.

Illinois Staats-Zeitung
August 16, 1862

The third war meeting of Chicago's Israelites took place last evening in Concordia Hall and was as enthusiastic as the previous one. The president announced that the muster rolls of the company already contained 94 men who had been sworn in by Capt. Christopher, a United States Mustering Officer.[21]

Lieutenant Governor Francis A. Hoffmann was the keynote speaker of the evening and was often interrupted by stormy applause. He eloquently imparted to our Israelite fellow citizens the great benefits they are receiving from this Republic and explained and impressed upon them that duties to the hard-pressed Republic arise from these benefits.

Mr. Hoffmann advocated with urgent and sincere words that the more stalwart part of the audience should join the German Hecker Regiment and closed with the inspiring and enthusing wishes and desires: not only should the territorial existence of the Republic be maintained, but when this war has ended the last chain must fall, the last shackle must be broken open, and the residents of the Republic must look favorably upon universal freedom regardless of the person or their color. After Mr. Hoffmann's speech the subscription began anew.

Around eleven o'clock the Concordia Guard[s]—this is the name of the Israelite company of the Hecker Regiment—paraded in front of the seats of the *Illinois Staats-Zeitung* with fife and drum under the command of Major Salomon.

After the Great Western Band played several patriotic airs, Mr. Wilhelm Rapp delivered a stormy address to the assembly in which he gave sincere and warm praise to the numerically small number of Israelites of Chicago for the patriotic and unmatched energy with which they brought into existence in forty-eight hours such a fine and, through patriotic subscriptions, such a well-equipped company.

During his speech the speaker reminded those present that Friedrich Hecker had already worked in Baden's [Lower] Chamber for the "emancipation of Jews," with magnanimousness and ardent zeal, after he declared openly and honestly in front of all German people in the year 1846 that his initial opposition to this great and just measure was a serious mistake. He deserves the full trust and affection of our Israelite citizens. After that, the company marched off to its headquarters amid thundering hurrahs for Hecker, for Sigel, and for the editorial staff of the *Illinois Staats-Zeitung.*

Illinois Staats-Zeitung
August 19, 1862
The Large War and Hecker Meeting on Yesterday Evening

There was a glorious demonstration yesterday evening! Long before eight o'clock the entire, large Bryan Hall—with the patriotic male and female Israelite citizens in the forefront—was filled so densely by German citizens that thousands could not find a seat. The Germans came in crowds to show their respect and love for the noble, storm-tested hero of the people Friedrich Hecker.[22]

Mr. M. A. Mayer opened the assembly and nominated Mr. M. Gerstly for president, as well as a number of vice presidents and secretaries. Accepted by acclamation.[23]

Mr. Gerstley introduced Colonel Hecker with a short speech, then after a powerful and succinct address by Mr. Greenebaum, Madam Leopold presented the magnificent Federal flag for the regiment in the name of the Israelite ladies. Mr. Otto Steitz made the flag, which will be returned tomorrow. The actual flag will be finished in a few days and delivered in a suitable manner.[24]

Col. Hecker gave the flag to Capt. Lasalle of the Israelite company of the Hecker Regiment and then delivered an address about the war. His speech was full of extreme patriotic fire and splendid youthful energy. The pauses between the speeches that followed were filled with patriotic melodies by the great Western Band and the singer Lombard. The next speakers were Mr. Th. B. Bryan, first in English, then German; Mr. W. Rapp; and Mr. Caspar Butz.[25]

After short addresses by Mr. Greenebaum and Sheriff Hesing, and after a brief request of Colonel Hecker, the assembly ended. A list was started at once for the subscription of contributions and immediately notable contributions were subscribed. Later still, Mr. Brentano made a short speech. To say the least the assembly ended with thundering hurrahs for Friedrich Hecker that did not want to end.

A total of $11,000 was raised in only one week for use as bounties ($100 to each enlistee) and to outfit the Jewish company. The Jewish community that raised the money and equipped the soldiers of the Concordia Guards consisted mainly of German speakers from Bavaria, Prussia, and Poland, and many in this community identified with the city's general German population. They read German language newspapers and literature, favored German music, and attended the German theater. Although Jews organized their own social life and maintained their own societies, associations, and lodges (including the Concordia Club), prominent Jews and some less distinguished ones also belonged to non-Jewish German organizations. Jews were also elected to some public offices. Tobias Brinkman, professor of history and Jewish studies, tells us: "Between 1850 and 1880 the German community [in Chicago] was open and inclusive, German leaders did not discriminate against Jews." Nevertheless, Brinkmann states, "While there is plenty of evidence for the involvement of prominent Jews in the German community, there are, especially for the early period, almost no documents that indicate widespread involvement in it."[26]

Two

Camp Butler

*A*n unidentified member of the Concordia Guards described his company's trip to Camp Butler and the first days there in the following letter. Military necessity probably required the hungry Jews to consume the pork products mentioned.

Illinois Staats-Zeitung
August 28, 1862
Camp Butler near Springfield
August 25, 1862

To the editor of the *Illinois Staats-Zeitung*

Today I finally have time to send you a short description of our trip to Springfield and Camp Butler, and our local camp life. We left Chicago on the 19th of this month. On the way to Springfield we were held up for 6 hours because a freight train ran partway off the track. Therefore we only arrived here about noon on the 20th. We paused 20 minutes for breakfast at the Burlington Station, where everyone could have the pleasure of quickly eating a meal of bread, coffee, and ham for the inexpensive sum of 50 cents cash. In Springfield we ate in a Russian (Irish) boardinghouse at noon (boiled cabbage, bacon, and cold water). After the noon meal we drove to the camp.[1]

We spent the first night under the greatest of all tents, the blue of the sky. Thanks to the energy of our colonel, covers were delivered to us toward midnight. The first things our brave Colonel Hecker took care of were provisions and barracks; the second day after our arrival we already slept under cover. Our food is good, sufficient, and is also well prepared because our company hired a cook from the Tremont House. Even if we do not have as many goodies as in the Tremont, our nourishment is substantial and healthy. Our Colonel Hecker is very demanding, but he is still friendly. No leaves will be given and privates will be treated the same as officers. Our colonel eats at the same table and the same food as his soldiers. He can be found in the camp all the time and actually appears to be made of iron and steel. At the parade he sees the slightest mistakes by officers as well as soldiers, and all who say he is no soldier do not know him. The men of our company are all healthy and cheerful. The single problem is that we have to go 2 miles to get water. The weather is pretty and warm. There are 7 infantry regiments, a battery, and a company of cavalry in camp. [2]

Our Captain Lasalle is very popular with his men as is our 1st Lieutenant [Mayer] Frank. Much satisfaction prevails in our company.[3]

Your esteemed newspaper is much missed here and should you be so friendly as to send one or more examples for our company, we all would send you a vote of thanks.

> Sincerely,
> F. S. [This could possibly be 1st Sgt. William Loeb, whose let-
> ter dated September 2, 1862, appears later in this chapter.]
> Concordia Guards
> Hecker Reg.

The editor believes that Pvt. John Lebhertz of Company B, a forty-three-year-old native of Prussia, authored the following letter. Lebhertz was just five-foot, six-inches tall, married, and had worked as a butcher in Chicago in civilian life. He was detached from the regiment at its muster out in June 1865.

> *Illinois Staats-Zeitung*
> August 29, 1862
> Camp Butler, near Springfield, Ill.
> August 26, 1862

To the editor of the *Illinois Staats-Zeitung*

It has been a week since we left Chicago and tore ourselves out of the arms of sweet lager dreams, so this sender is free to tell you something of our camp life. The departure of our company from Chicago was, so to say, not very [illegible word], because many already saw themselves in higher dreams as a general sitting on horseback in a splendid uniform, which idea dissipated as they flew out

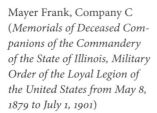

Mayer Frank, Company C (*Memorials of Deceased Companions of the Commandery of the State of Illinois, Military Order of the Loyal Legion of the United States from May 8, 1879 to July 1, 1901*)

of the cars Tuesday morning, and the [three illegible words] this lustrous dream, was very bad to have.

We rode in wagons from Springfield to Camp Butler, where we were met with much joy, until the joy grew so great that one man could not find his way except to the lager barrel, where he consoled himself too much. In order to warn him against this sort of failure in the future he had to spend 48 hours in the guardhouse, where he actually spent six days because of an error.

I do not believe that our company is musically adept, because no harmony can be found in it; the presence of our colonel, however, should significantly improve this because he reads the meaning of the notes quite accurately, and the sounds often fade away in the guardhouse.

Colonel Hecker arrived here last Wednesday and since then has been busy with the organization of companies and making the camp as comfortable a residence as possible for us. Our time is sufficiently filled, as you can see from the following Regimental Order No. 1:

5:00 in the morning, reveille and roll call.

6:00 ditto, drills of the officers and noncommissioned officers.

6:30 ditto, breakfast.

7:30 ditto, company drills.

7:30 ditto, guard mounting.

10:00 to 11:30 ditto, battalion drills.

12:00 noon, dinner.

2:00 to 3:00 in the afternoon, instruction and roll call.

3:00 to 5:00 ditto, battalion drills and dress parade.

6:00, evening supper.

7:00 to 9:00, instruction of the officers.

9:30 ditto, roll call.

Our regiment is rather far advanced because of the exactingness of our colonel and yesterday we held a parade; it went so well that many regiments already in the field for a year probably could not have performed better. The discipline of our colonel goes to the extreme, and I think we will thank him for it, because his intention is good and well calculated and I therefore share with you a little address he delivered last week:

"Soldiers! I have a great responsibility resting on me. You are mostly married [a review of the soldiers' records proves that most were single] men. Your wives and children have made me responsible for you. I want to make soldiers out of you, competent soldiers who do not meet misfortune due to disorder and carelessness, as was the case at Bulls [Bull] Run and Pittsburg Landing, and so forth.[4] I want Gen. Sigel, as I have said to him through his adjutant, to lead soldiers and not *molasses* [mawkish] boys. That is the reason for my strictness. You all will thank me, not only as your colonel but also as your friend." Three thundering hurrahs resounded and everyone was pleased with having such a competent and gallant colonel.

Incidentally, with few exceptions we are healthy and cheerful. We only seldom see a glass of good Chicago lager; the water here is very bad and also very scarce. I want to close by telling you a story about water, which occurred here last week. Every now and then the boys go to a farm located about a mile from here to get water. It soon came to light that the owner was an avid and, even more, a good for nothing *Secesh,* and he had forbidden the *boys* to come onto his property to fetch water again or he would shoot them. When last week several men went there to draw water again the *Secesh* came out the door and ordered the *boys* to leave his yard or he would shoot them. Our *boys* paid no attention to him but only laughed at him. Enraged, the old man shouted to his wife to bring his rifle to him and as soon as the old man came out of the door with it in his hand, our boys snatched it out of his hand without further ado. That brought the story to an end; however, in my opinion this *Secesh* had a quite proper opinion of himself, because he thought that he was not worthy to give water to Union *boys.*

Nothing further for today,
>   Respectfully,
>   J. L. [John Lebhertz?]
>   Co. B, (Capt. Br[u]ning.)

The next two letters bring to light the tensions between the Germans of Hecker's regiment and Anglo-Americans troops at Camp Butler. The author of the first letter is unidentified. Colonel Hecker wrote the second letter.

> *Westliche Post*
> August 31, 1862
> Camp Butler, near Springfield, Ill.
> August 27, 1862

Just now we nearly had a little battle between a just-arrived American [regiment] and Hecker's. It was only prevented by calling several hundred armed guards. I will send the details to you as soon as I know they are reliable. It would have resulted in bloodshed because of nativism and hatred toward the Germans, but the combatants lacked weapons. The Hecker Regiment had extra sentinels encircle its camp, and a colonel of the just-arrived Americans, not wearing a uniform, wanted to pass through this line, but was somewhat harshly refused. Several "*d__d sons of b__*," came from the American side and in no time there was a crowd of 700 to 800 gathered against the Hecker Regiment, which now was placed under arrest. The young Americans and the sentinels treated Colonel Hecker shamefully. It is really sad to me that these people are always very dissatisfied; if no beer were sold, something else would not suit them. Tomorrow the details.[5]
>   W. A.

On September 4, 1862, the *Louisville Anzeiger* published an excerpt from a letter written by Colonel Hecker that originally appeared in the St. Louis *Neue Zeit* in regard to the above-mentioned incident.[6]

> *Louisville Anzeiger*
> September 4, 1862

On the morning of the 27th, about ten o'clock, I was busy with regimental matters in Springfield. After completion of these matters I immediately returned to camp. As soon as I arrived in my tent and was busy giving orders, I heard a great commotion and learned from a report of an orderly that a riot between some men of the camp and men of my regiment caused the noises. I girded saber and sash, took the tambour with me and learned the following: I had surrounded my camp with guards to keep better order and so that the men could practice the crucially important field guard duty. When men from the regiment of a certain Col. Day, which was lying next to us, tried to force the guards, heeding to proper protocol, the officer of the day in charge was called, who, in full uniform with sash and saber, tried to calm the disorder in accordance with *Army Regulations* and instructions.[7]

Upon arriving at that place he reported to me that a man with a straw hat, white topcoat, and in civilian clothes, without any insignia that could identify him as an officer, sided with the party who caused the ruckus and stated that he was the colonel of the regiment. To the reply of the officer on guard duty, that he neither knew him in person nor could deem from his clothes that he really was the person he claimed to be, he answered to the officer on duty, who was dressed with the in-signia of his appointment as officer of the day, that he was a "*good d—d saucy dutch son of a b—*." Upon having said this, the officer of the day, the son of a soldier, and a man who had fought in Schleswig-Holstein and here, had him brought to the guardhouse. I immediately had the drums roll to get them off the square and all companies of the regiment reported in good order in front of their tents.[8]

This order was followed without question. At the same time I went to the guardhouse. I took the colonel located there with me to my tent, and had Col. Schnell from a different regiment accompany me as a witness, to listen to what Col. Day had to say about the incident.[9] While I was listening to his story and learned from him that he supposedly was deliberately mistreated three times in the scuffle, I received the message that the camp commander, Col. Fonda, had ordered our camp to be surrounded by guards and declared the regiment under arrest. He did this even though my men had meanwhile been ordered to their tents and had immediately followed the command, so that my camp was in a state of complete calmness. I immediately went to him and explained that a regi-ment could only be put under arrest if its commander is not able to handle the men and that my regiment had absolutely followed my orders and that if all regi-ments had such discipline, something like this could not happen. I demanded that he lift the arrest and bring a court martial against Col. Day and my officer of the day, so the whole truth could be revealed. The arrest order was immediately lifted. I turned to the governor, lieutenant governor, and adjutant general for suf-ficient satisfaction, which has been promised to me and will be meted out to us, to the colonel, and the regiment, even though we are Germans. Of that I am sure. This is the true course of events.[10]

> Friedrich Hecker, Col.
> Commanding 82nd Ills. Volunteers.

Following Colonel Hecker's first letter in this compilation, it is appropriate to reveal more about this German American leader's life up to this point. Friedrich Hecker was the first and among the most popular of the German political refugees who came to America. Born in Eichtersheim in the Grand Duchy of Baden on September 28, 1811, and educated in law at Heidelberg University, Hecker practiced law in the city of Mannheim and later served in the Baden State Assembly. He evolved into one of Baden's elite intellectuals and a highly active and vocal leader in the growing republican movement in his native southwestern German duchy. The future Union army brigadier fled from Germany after he and Gustav Struve (another revolutionary republican) proclaimed a German republic at Constance on April 12, 1848, and their small rebel army was defeated at Kandern in southwestern Baden eight days later.[11]

Hecker was greeted by thousands of cheering German Americans upon his arrival in New York on October 5, 1848. In 1849 he purchased a farm near the settlement of Summerfield in St. Clair County, Illinois, located approximately thirty miles east of St. Louis, Missouri. In 1856 Hecker became active in the new Republican Party because of its opposition to the expansion of slavery into the territories and "stumped" for presidential candidates John C. Frémont in 1856 and Abraham Lincoln in 1860.[12]

Upon the outbreak of the Civil War in April 1861, Hecker and his oldest son Arthur crossed the Mississippi River and enlisted in Col. Franz Sigel's 3rd Missouri Regiment as privates. Sigel, a former officer in Baden's army, was also a hero of the revolution and later rose to major general in the Union army. The fifty-year-old Hecker left Sigel's regiment in late May 1861 to take command of a German regiment being organized in Chicago. Initially called the Hecker Rifles, the unit was officially designated as the 24th Illinois Volunteer Infantry Regiment. Besides Germans, the regiment contained three companies of Hungarians. As previously stated the patriotic but inexperienced colonel submitted his resignation on December 21, 1861, because of bitter disputes with certain officers in the regiment.[13] Hecker's military career was resurrected in June 1862 by Illinois governor Richard Yates's pressing need to organize more regiments and strong support from the *Illinois Staats-Zeitung* and Caspar Butz. The latter was a writer for the *Staats-Zeitung,* a leader in Chicago's German community, a Forty-eighter, and a close friend of Hecker's. Friedrich Hecker soon received a commission and threw himself into organizing the 82nd Illinois Volunteer Infantry Regiment.[14]

Regimental and ethnic pride, along with some prejudices, are revealed in a letter written by an unidentified member of Company A.

<hr>

Illinois Staats-Zeitung
September 1, 1862
Camp Butler
August 28, 1862

Although the new Hecker Regiment still cannot report any skirmishes and engagements since the dispatch of my last correspondence, many a thing has happened that might be interesting to you.

As expected with certainty, so it happens; in a short time our regiment will be nearly full; 9 companies are already organized and a tenth is in the process of formation—all companies are assembled here in the camp and our camp ground has been significantly expanded.

On the 20th of August, Colonel Friedrich Hecker took over command of his new regiment and since that time has placed his headquarters in the camp. From that moment, with his well-known energy, he began the formation of the companies, the organization of the regiment, and the setting up of the new camp, so that in a few days a military appearance prevailed in the heretofore rather unorganized mass there, and orderliness was soon established. That day was one of importance for the regiment in another respect. The 82nd Regiment had on this day the honor of receiving its new flag. Company A, commanded by the brave Captain Anton Bruhn, the first and largest of the regiment, had been designated to receive the flag at the railroad station in Springfield, to escort the flag, and at the same time to welcome the company of Captain Lasalle from Chicago.[15]

We marched to Springfield in the early morning hour in full uniforms and around 10 o'clock positioned ourselves at the railroad station. Loud cheers greeted the arriving train. After the newly arrived company stood opposite ours and the grand flag was uncovered, Captain Bruhn led three thunderous cheers for the Concordia Club in Chicago that resounded through the streets of our capital and I might add that our whole regiment sends our deep heartfelt thanks to the Israelite ladies from Chicago, the noble and kind donors of the beautiful flag. We carried our flag through the streets in a triumphal procession and later into our camp. That same evening Colonel Hecker assumed command in person.

The day before yesterday, to our joyful surprise, Mr. Caspar Butz from Chicago, Hecker's longtime friend, who deserves so much credit in the organization of our new regiment, came to see the state of our development. He arrived in the company of Lieutenant Colonel Salomon and two of the supervisors from Cook County and, with cordial words, the colonel presented him to Company A, which bears his name (Butz's Rifles). Our company is especially obliged to give him particular thanks, because he and Edw. S. Saloman are the men who used their influence for the bounty of $60 for us, the payment of which the two supervisors have brought along. Mr. Butz then gave a fiery speech to the company in which he appealed to our hearts regarding our duty as citizens and soldiers, asked us to show thanks to this land, to which all of us are obligated in such manifold ways, and finally asked us to place unconditional confidence in his old friend, our leader, Friedrich Hecker.

The company answered with three cheers for the patriot Caspar Butz. Then Mr. Butz delivered three hurrahs for the colonel, who then pointed out to him that our company was the best and best disciplined of the regiment, and not to overlook the credit due to Captain Anton Bruhn, who brought us here. He praised our captain three times as a competent soldier and excellent drillmaster and all voiced approval from their hearts. He briefly thanked them. Unfortunately, Mr. Butz must have had very little time, for he immediately took his leave of us.

We will probably leave the camp soon and go to Virginia and will be incorporated into Franz Sigel's command. Anyone who still has the desire to join us, come soon. I do not want to conceal that we appear to be a thorn in the eyes of the American regiments here. It seems almost as if they could not endure the strapping appearance and the cheerful nature of the "Dutchmen." However, we will show them our superiority. We do not want to know anything about the boring and stupid chit-chat in their daily meetings and the chaplains from other regiments, who meanwhile creep through our camp, make sour faces, and see that their invitation to the meeting sits poorly with us; mawkishness and meetings are inadmissible commodities with us.—Therefore we drink our lager on Sundays, of course, when we can obtain it, even if there is some difficulty connected with it; otherwise, thank goodness, we have not yet experienced any deficiency of this noble substance, although the Springfield beer cannot measure up entirely to the product from Chicago. Chicago has many things that make it unforgettable to us even if we are far away, but the brewers should in no way attribute this fact to themselves alone.

Soon I hope to be able to provide interesting messages to you from General Sigel's army in Virginia.

      Beta

      [Company A]

First Sgt. William Loeb of Company C, who would later have an adversarial relationship with Rudolph Müller, appealed to German men to fill up the regiment and praised Colonel Hecker as "fatherly," possibly to allay any fears that enlistees might have as a result of unfavorable publicity the colonel received while heading the First Hecker Regiment. Nineteen-year-old 1st Sergeant Loeb was born in Bechtheim in Rhenish Bavaria and was a prewar merchant. Loeb was promoted to second lieutenant on July 7, 1863, and to first lieutenant on May 3, 1864. He mustered out in June 1865 and later was brevetted captain retroactive to March 13, 1865.

———

Illinois Staats-Zeitung
September 5, 1862
Camp Butler
September 2, 1862

In spite of several correspondences from members of our company found in your valued newspaper, and through which families whose relatives in the Concordia Guards have received news about their condition, I would still like to add a few lines that would be of interest to your readers and friends of our "old man [Hecker]."

Our regiment is complete and only needs a few patriots to bring it to the maximum strength allowed. From old soldiers—and those are not a few in the regiment, it is admitted and declared that our Col. Fried. Hecker is fatherly to his soldiers—whom he treats with love—and provides far better for his soldiers than is done in many a regiment. But moreover "our old man" is a soldier from head to toe, and has earned respect among all American officers residing in the local camp. It is really a joy to see our regiment march, which was born only 2 months ago, in comparison to the dawdling one-year-old American regiments.[16]

Do not hesitate long! Forward German patriots! Fill up our ranks, so that in the near future we are able to show in the face of the enemy that no more grass grows where the Hecker boys strike with "their old one."

Our Captain Lasalle has already schooled us in such a way that we need not fear conducting competitive drills with three-month soldiers. First Lieutenant Frank is proficient in every respect, just like Lieutenant Bechstein.[17]

While reading through these lines I find that I nearly forgot the main point. To you my dears, Best, Busch, Brand, and all other manufacturers of the exalted liquid, now come words from my heart, the emotions and feelings of our regiment. Have pity on 800 drooling throats. Send beer in special trains, much beer, and your name shall be emblazoned in golden letters in the memories of our soldiers, and a

William Loeb, Company C
(courtesy of Frances L. Luebke)

Te Deum [hymn of praise] would ascend to the heavens after receipt of the barley juice, and our dear lord God, tears of joy will flow from the eyes of his brave lads.
Wilhelm Löb [Loeb]
Concordia Guard[s]

The two news articles following describe a regimental flag the Jewish women of Chicago provided to the regiment and the addition of the final two companies to the regiment.

Illinois Staats-Zeitung
September 6, 1862

The new flag of the Hecker Regiment was finished today and will be sent to Springfield on Monday. It is a further gift of the Israelite ladies who were not satisfied that the Concordia Guards had already been gifted with a splendid flag, so they have decided not to allow the regiment to face the enemy without a regimental flag. The flag, made by the famous artist Mr. Steiss [Steitz], is 6 feet by 6½ feet as is prescribed by regulations and made out of a single piece of heavy blue silk material.

On the front it has the inscription, above:

HECKER REGIMENT

And "82nd Regiment of Ill Vols." below.

Between these two inscriptions is the Coat of Arms of the United States.

Above on the backside is: Presented by the Jewish Ladies, and below: Chicago, August 18th 1862 (Date of the great assembly in Bryan Hall and flag presentation).

In the middle is the portrait of Friedrich Hecker, which was designed by a well-known artist, Mr. Wilhelm Voegtlin, who relocated here from Wisconsin, and its completion is expected today.[18]

Illinois Staats-Zeitung
September 16, 1862

Departure of the Company of Capt. Marx and the Norwegian Company of Capt. Weird [Weid]

On Saturday Mr. Henry Greenebaum, who was specifically named as recruiting officer for this purpose, delivered the order from Adjutant General Fuller to Lieutenant Colonel Salomon, to lead the companies of Capt. Marx and Capt. Weird [Weid], belonging to the 3rd Board of Trade Regiment, into Camp Butler at Springfield, because they have been assigned to the Hecker Regiment.

Yesterday afternoon around 5 o'clock Marx's company struck its tents and left its camp. Captain Weird's [Weid's] company was not ready to march because several of its soldiers had not received their bounty. The Great Western Band escorted Captain Marx's company (First Lieutenant Warner and [Second] Lieutenant Kirchner) and the company of Captain Yates (Governor's Guards), as well as the companies of Clark and Southland; all marched to the St. Louis and Alton Railroad Station, where later Captain Weird's [Weid's] company appeared. Yesterday evening, both companies, which now make the Hecker Regiment complete, departed for Springfield under command of Lieutenant Colonel Salomon.[19]

The following report describes a visit of a committee sent to Camp Butler by the Jewish women of Chicago to check on the conditions at Camp Butler and the Concordia Guards. During the war a committee also maintained contact with the men of the Guards and their families. The report contains the same expressions of pride and prejudice as many of the soldiers' letters.[20]

Illinois Staats-Zeitung
September 16, 1862
Report of the Committee sent by the Israelite Women

To the editor of the *Illinois Staats-Zeitung*

We arrived in Springfield last Thursday morning at 6 o'clock with the flag previously described to you in order to hand it over to the Hecker Regiment in the name of Chicago's Israelite women. After we had a good breakfast with Mr. Burkhardt, a really proficient German innkeeper who operates the Jefferson House, to our joy we saw Colonel Hecker, to whom we immediately made known the purpose of our trip. He was certainly happy about it but he could not accompany us into the camp because he had to take care of business with the government for his regiment.[21]

Camp Butler is northeast of Springfield, and the Hecker Regiment's camp is located across from the actual Camp Butler. We found everything at Hecker's camp lively and cheerful. Some companies exercised, one other stood on guard, and another rested after guard duty. What strikes a visitor immediately is that order and cleanliness rule in the Hecker Regiment's camp, in contrast to the surrounding American regiments. The strength, order, and caring hand of the colonel is noticeable everywhere. The Hecker Regiment is the only one in camp with complete uniforms. Further, it possesses a full quantity of shelters, while other regiments still have to do without. The tents are not new but serve their purpose. The board is good and the men receive more than enough.

Colonel Hecker looks after his soldiers early and late, procures everything that is lacking, seeks to train a model regiment, and he succeeds more and more. Even the Americans recognize that his regiment is the best disciplined and drilled in the camp. He achieves good results through rigor and through untiring efforts in drilling.

Because of the miserable gossiping and lies that were circulated by some malicious persons in Chicago over his relationship with his officers and soldiers, we particularly investigated the sentiments of the men. And what did we find? General satisfaction, general devotion to Hecker, general praise for his true care for the regiment, and for his military training. With regard to the Concordia Guard[s] especially, its members laughed after we announced to them the horrifying rumors circulating in Chicago that they are supposed have transferred from Hecker's regiment. In no company is the devotion to Hecker greater and more intimate than in the Israelites' company; they, just like the others, have fully gotten used to Hecker's bawdy, candid, and always honest and straightforward behavior. "The old one is admittedly coarse," a soldier told us, "but he is a rough gemstone, whom we have discovered and therefore respect and we love him."

To be sure a little dissatisfaction is not lacking for a few. There are officer candidates and position seekers who have not attained their selfish goals and now and again try to muckrake and agitate; however, their influence does not go far, because the men are very loyal to their company officers. We have had numerous opportunities to communicate with the officer corps; it is generally indisputable that they are the most educated and most dignified men you can encounter in any regiment. They are strict while on duty but otherwise are comradely toward subordinates. The officers and men ardently wish to be led into the field and to Sigel as soon as possible.

Quartermaster Panse has given up his position as staff officer with General Schofield in St. Louis in order to serve under Hecker and to prove that a person can be an honest quartermaster. Colonel Hecker told us that Quartermaster Panse would leave his office poorer than when he entered it.[22] Adjutant General Fuller, with whom we have communicated, assured us that Mr. Panse is the most trustworthy quartermaster he knows in the entire Illinois army. Panse served under Sigel in Missouri, fought bravely at Carthage and Wilson's Creek, and fell into the hands of the Rebels severely wounded. After several days as a prisoner he gained his freedom again. His left arm is still paralyzed from this event.[23]

During our stay in the camp Lieutenant Colonel Salomon was absent in Chicago on regimental business. However, as we learned from members of the regiment, he is generally popular and highly respected as a man and as an officer. Major Rolshausen is "every inch a soldier"; he previously served in the Hesse-Darmstadt artillery. Adjutant Weigel, the son of the well-known fighter for progress, Dr. Weigel in St. Louis, is a young man of amiable manners and we hear his military competency is generally praised. During our visit we saw American officers come to him and ask him about arranging guard detail, etc., and asking advice, and they promised such visits to him frequently.[24]

In the evening we strolled through the camp and observed a picture of soldiers' camp life. We saw the soldiers of the Hecker Regiment assembled in several groups. The Turners formed grand pyramids; some delighted themselves through sociable games or through recitations and humorous presentations, some with singing. These activities form a highly pleasant contrast with life in the camps of the other regiments, where it is rather stiff and monotonous.

Later we went into the colonel's tent, where we met different officers and were surprised with an excellent serenade by the regiment's singing society, composed mostly of members of Companies A and C, earlier kinsmen of the Chicago Workers Union and Singing Alliance. After their performance the singers addressed us individually and we were compelled to make speeches.[25]

First, Joseph Frank made a few remarks in which he heartily thanked the singers on behalf of the committee.[26] Then Henry Greenebaum spoke. He directed his words to the "members of the singing society of the new Hecker Regiment" and expressed his joy over the organization of a singing society in the regiment, because he sees it both as a significant means for advancement of education and as a noble endeavor. He remarked that one could perhaps also find a singing club in an American regiment, but at most it will sing Methodist songs, while the German singing club offers a truly artistic treat; sings of truth, freedom, and right; and combines pretty and cheerful artistry with the military and patriotic. Finally, A. Hart spoke.[27] He emphasized particularly how pleasantly he was surprised by the splendid and satisfied conditions in the regiment and how much he likes the respect paid to Colonel Hecker everywhere in the camp.

We returned to the colonel's tent after the serenade. He was away on business in Springfield again. Meanwhile, he had ordered the quartermaster to treat us hospitably and that happened in large measure.

Friday morning Colonel Hecker came galloping into the camp. Battalion drills now took place under his command. The other regiments and their colonels observed the wheeling [several illegible words] and the various [several illegible words] already to be the best drilled. Hecker was on his impressive stallion, full of fire and life. His commands were loud and sonorous and bear witness to his complete confidence in his military skills. His sharp eye noticed every deficiency and mistake, and he pointed out each error with humorous gruffness. His own fire electrifies his soldiers. After the exercises concluded the officers were called to in front of his headquarters by bugle and the necessary measures taken for presentation of the flag. Hecker displayed a drawing he had sketched about the disposition of the different companies and of the color guard for this purpose.

About 2 o'clock the regiment was in position; among other things, the committee came forward with the flag and presented it with military honor. Henry Greenebaum stated in the name of the committee, the following:

It is impossible to express the feeling that has taken possession of him. He has the honor to present the regimental flag to the regiment through its brave colonel in the name of the Israelite ladies of Chicago. With pleasure the committee has witnessed the splendid material of which the Hecker Regiment consists. They bring honor to America's Germanhood and will provide firm support for our adoptive homeland in the current crisis.

We have seen with our own eyes that all of the regiments in the camp are seeking to learn from the Hecker Regiment. It is a model of discipline, military deportment, competence, and development. In order to be just to the donors of this flag, I must use this opportunity to say a word about the leader of the regiment. We recognize him as one of the leading representatives of the German proclivity for proficiency, German faithfulness, justice, and love of freedom in America. The regiment can join this man with pride and satisfaction and follow him to victory or death.

He, the speaker, only now understands the consequence of the words, which he so often and happily sang as a boy in the old homeland:

"Hecker, grand German man,
Who can die for freedom"[28]

The Germans are granted a lofty mission in America; they are disbursed among the American population as bearers of higher and nobler ideas. Their duty is contained in the words: freedom, equality, forward for truth! He does not doubt that every soldier from the right wing to the left wing is infused with the same feeling about Colonel Hecker that he, the speaker, has. The new Hecker Regiment has proven what can be achieved through discipline and military organization in a very short time. He does not want to state that nothing more needs to be learned; some more time will probably be required until the unit consists of complete soldiers, until your colonel is satisfied in every way and no more opportunities are found to criticize anything.

At the conclusion the speaker pointed out that the regiment was certainly surprised that the ladies of Chicago had Hecker's likeness painted on the flag as the most appropriate slogan they could give him. The flag will probably not be as splendid when it returns from the battlefield. It probably will be shot through by enemy bullets, and torn, blackened by powder, but at the same time will come victoriously from the battlefield. Hecker's soldiers will be received as victorious heroes by their fellow citizens.

Colonel Hecker took the flag and turned it over to the color guard with the following words: "Comrades! Your captains recommended you to me today as the best corporals in the regiment. Take the flag. Before it falls into enemy hands, you should sacrifice your life, and every officer should have shed his lifeblood. Soldiers rally around it and persevere, so just ten of you come back like the 4th Polish Regiment."[29]

Addressing the committee the colonel thanked the noble donors in his and the regiment's name, and promised that the regiment would faithfully protect the magnificent gift. Three flags have been given to the regiment.[30] Three virtues confer dignity to man and soldiers: boldness, bravery, and discipline, the everlasting boldness of unshakeable bravery and iron discipline. "Pledge," Hecker called to his soldiers, "that you intend these attributes for your flags. Only a few of you will return; however, if other regiments dissolve in frantic flight, we, as German men, will stay and fight. Where we are buried it should be said: here German men fell."

He then described the important benefits for which we adoptive citizens are indebted to this country. He also described the intense efforts through which most adoptive citizens have gradually established an existence here. Abroad many worked with the pen but had to swing the axe here, and the craftsman had to earn his livelihood here through twice the sweat. Through these efforts, however, our new country has become even more beloved, and has to be most dear to the European freedom fighters and refugees who found asylum under the star-spangled banner.

Certainly the door of the homeland has now opened again for most of the banished. They are free to return home and have received urgent invitations from relatives and friends abroad to return to the old homeland or at least to visit it, but in their eyes, one who would turn his back while this large and unfortunate republic is in its gloomiest hour of trial, while it bleeds out of thousands of wounds, is nothing other than a villain.[31]

The German American freedom fighter should not think about a fire in the homeland until this rebellion is overcome, slavery is destroyed, and the republic is restored on the basis of freedom and equality; and then he might only return to the old homeland for the purpose of procuring victory there, for the principles for which he fought here, in order to wrest away the tyranny and aristocracy there forever.

Hecker closed his splendid address, delivered with youthful fire and noble ardor, amid thundering hurrahs from his soldiers. The above is only a small summary. After the ovation ended, Hecker stated, "So much fire ought to be quenched with beer," and he allowed the quartermaster to dispense ample beer to the soldiers returning to their tents by company.

Meanwhile, the hour of departure had come for us. Based on our desire the colonel assembled the officers again, so that we could bid farewell to them. Quite opposite to the colonel's usual practice, a large part of the officers received leaves in order to accompany us to Springfield. Soldiers, to whom we had related sordid rumors and the gossip in Chicago, urged us to reveal Hecker's slanderers, in case they return to Chicago healthy and well, and want to hold them accountable and to get rough with them. One told us: "You tell these liars simply, I will knock the teeth down the throat of the first one I nab." Soldiers expressed their bitterness toward their colonel's slanderers in similarly rough and overly rough ways.

After the closest and most diligent observations we may say: all is well in the Hecker regiment. Order, provisions, and drills are exemplary, and above all one has to attribute this to the administrative and military talent of Colonel Friedrich Hecker, who is loved and respected by his soldiers, who looks after the welfare and the military training of his soldiers with true zeal.

> Henry Greenebaum,
> Joseph Frank,
> A. Hart

On September 22, 1862, President Abraham Lincoln issued the preliminary Emancipation Proclamation, declaring that on January 1, 1863, the slaves in the states or parts of the states still in rebellion would be free. This action pleased Colonel Hecker and other anti-slavery German Americans, and Hecker expressed his support of the proclamation in a letter to his friend the Honorable Isaac N. Arnold, an anti-slavery Republican member of the U.S. House of Representatives (1861–1865).[32]

> *Illinois Staats-Zeitung*
> October 1, 1862

Colonel Friedrich Hecker was asked to speak by the committee at the great assembly in Bryan Hall on the previous Saturday, and, because he could not appear because of his military duty, had directed the following letter to the Honorable Isaac N. Arnold:

> Camp Butler, near Springfield, Ill.
> September 26, 1862

To the Honorable. I. N. Arnold
Chicago, Ill.
Dear Sir:

Your letter from the 24th of this month arrived and I am infinitely sorry that because of the mustering in of my regiment and the acquisition of good weapons for it, the interest of the service demanded my absence.

The proclamation of the president will create a new epoch in the history not only of America, but of all civilized nations.

This proclamation plunges like a thunderbolt among the open and secret traitors and at the same time breaks up the network of transatlantic diplomacy. The president has destroyed all that was spun on Downing Street and Rue Rivoli. It is generally admitted that I have loved freedom from my youth and that I have fought in Europe for the freedom of a people who grieved under the heartless despots. It is therefore unnecessary to furnish my view again about the president's proclamation. But I will say I agree with it and that I will support it in my heart. I have read and reread it and as often as I have, my heart was full of joy and said to me that posterity will give him the well-deserved name:

"Abraham Lincoln,
the Emancipator"
Respectfully,
Friedrich Hecker

Colonel Hecker was successful in obtaining good weapons for his regiment. The soldiers received British Enfield rifles that fired .577 caliber conical bullets called Minié or minnie balls.

Pvt. Frank Schönewald of Company K described how the regiment celebrated Colonel Hecker's birthday. Private Schönewald, who stood only five-foot, five inches tall, was twenty-five years old, married, and a bookkeeper. He was born in the vicinity of Cologne in the Kingdom of Prussia. The Chicago resident was appointed first sergeant of his company on September 19, 1863 and later was commissioned as a second lieutenant but not mustered at that rank. He mustered out with the regiment in 1865.

Illinois Staats-Zeitung
October 4, 1862
Camp Butler
October 1, 1862

You will excuse that I have not written to you for so long. I was sick but am now healthy again.

The day before yesterday we celebrated Colonel Hecker's birthday. The eve of the happy day was announced through a special display of lights, likewise through splendid concert and dance music by our band, led by Alexander Henschel. After music director Henschel tired, Lieutenant Colonel Ed. S. Salomon delighted us with his pretty musical pieces. In addition, the various companies entertained themselves through singing, dancing, gymnastics, etc.[33]

On Monday, the actual day of celebration, we saw from morning to night nothing but trees, flowers, and such materials belonging to a German folk festival, which were brought into our camp by the hands of our brave Hecker boys. Everyone was busied preparing a pleasant surprise for our dear colonel. However, in the evening—what a view! In front of their tents, which were set up in straight rows, each company had planted a number of trees, and decorated with wreaths, whereby the entire camp was transformed into shady allées. Lights were affixed to the trees, which looked very pretty. The Concordia Guard[s] illuminated their (Lasalle) street with red, white, and blue lanterns. Likewise, Hesing Street (Capt. Br[u]ning's company) was decorated with a mass of lights and foliage, but the prettiest place was the temple of Company K, Capt. Greenhut. Using trees that were placed so that their crowns came together at the top produced a really pretty temple. A rather large candelabra hung in the middle of it, and the background and sides were embellished with banners of every sort. One stated: "Hail to Hecker on his 52nd birthday," another, "Victory or Death," and etc., but one banner hung up in the entrance, the largest, with the words, "Our Dear Hecker on His 52nd Birthday," drew the most attention. The poem on it was authored by Dreissen [Drissen], Company K, and stated:[34]

> You call us to move into the field with you,
> To the battle for freedom, right, and honor,
> We gather joyfully around your flags,
> Loyal to the example of our ancestors;
> Because when it is called: For freedom and for right,
> There stands the German, if still genuine his heart,
> Lead us well now, you heroic German man,
> And our sword shall show what it can achieve.

Our whole camp looked like a sea of lights. A large friendly fire burned in the distance and illuminated everything around it red. Each company received a barrel of beer from our generous colonel and you can imagine that it went cheerfully here. Everywhere our colonel appeared he was received with thundering hurrahs, which did not want to come to an end.

Music, songs, recitations, and dancing concluded this festive day and it was said to be the general wish that this anniversary could often be celebrated together with our beloved colonel. Overall, each company tried to surpass the other, and yet I never saw such unity in our regiment, than where it counted, to provide joy to our colonel.

Last Sunday we had a large division review, at which our old one led the senior command and our regiment was particularly praised as the best-drilled regiment of the division. You will excuse us therefore if each of us is proud to belong to the Hecker Regiment.

The condition of the health of the regiment is rather good and gets better each day.

For now live well, certain that I am and remain respectfully yours,
Frank Schönewald[35]

The writer of the letter that follows was not a member of the Second Hecker Regiment but gives a first-hand account of what he observed during a visit to its camp.

Illinois Staats-Zeitung
October 9, 1862

From a correspondence in the *Evening Journal* of Springfield, Ill., we extract the following: [36]

"Lieutenant Governor Hoffmann visited the camp of the 82nd or Hecker Regiment yesterday at the invitation of Col. Hecker and afterward reviewed the regiment on the large review field adjoining the camps. I was present by invitation and enjoyed the visit and review more than anything in the military line that I have been present at since the commencement of the war.

I found the regiment's camp in most excellent order. Everything was as neat as a pin. The sentries were set up in accordance with regulations, with arms and accoutrements properly furnished, with clean uniforms put on with a degree of exactness and taste that would do credit to a regiment in the regular army. Colonel Hecker received the lieutenant governor in front of his headquarters, where the ceremony of introduction to all officers took place. Shortly after reviewing the camp and socializing, the lieutenant governor and his aide were called to dinner, in which various officers of the regiment, including the major, chaplain, etc., took part. The table was under an arbor in front of the colonel's headquarters.

It was to all intents and purposes a "camp dinner" for us, but it was prepared in a manner that would do honor to a Soyer. There were several courses, including beef, veal, mutton, and poultry, and apple fritters for dessert. Because the group had an excellent appetite, the food received all praise and was washed down by splendid Rhine and Champagne wines.[37]

The conversational powers of Col. Hecker are really extraordinary. The subjects discussed ranged from German metaphysics all the way down to military matters and the peculiar aptitude of various nationalities for certain pursuits in life. The special cultural and technological endeavors of the French, English, American, German, and other peoples were dwelt upon, and illustrated by Col. Hecker in a very effective manner indeed. The readiness with which he quoted in the original words from Caeser's *Commentaries*, Horace, Virgil, etc., astonished me.[38] However, it must be remembered that Col. Hecker was an advocate in the Superior Court of Baden and engaged by the Swiss confederation to revise their present constitution. And that even now, although but lately pardoned from the death penalty, and holding extreme liberal views, should he return to Baden he would receive a high official position on account of his familiarity with the internal condition of the Dukedom, etc.

The regiment was called out after dinner and marched to the field where it performed various drills with great precision. It was first formed in line in front of the United States flag, saluting the lieutenant governor, who took his place by the national ensign. It was then formed into columns of companies and passed the lieutenant governor in review, in slow and quick time, the officers saluting as they passed. Afterward, different maneuvers were performed. The regiment marched out of the field in a column of fours, with the band playing and colors flying, saluting the lieutenant governor as it passed the gates, and escorting him back to the camp.

A luncheon at the colonel's headquarters was enlivened by an animated conversation on various topics, in which all those present took part, including Col. Anneke, chief of artillery on Gen. McClernand's staff, Rev. Reichhelm, Major Rollshausen [Rolshausen], and other gentlemen. The lieutenant governor and his staff returned to the city around 6:00 in the evening, evidently highly pleased with their visit.[39]

Colonel Hecker's regiment will march from here at the latter end of the present week and will be attached to the division [army corps] of Gen. Sigel. I learned that the Norwegian [Scandinavian] company attached to the regiment is highly pleased with its situation and being with Col. Hecker. Although the colonel is a very rigid disciplinarian, he is evidently well liked by his regiment, and it exhibits a proficiency in discipline and drill that shows that he has expended an immense amount of labor on it.[40]

[Unsigned]

In light of the above correspondence, it is interesting that Pvt. Friedrich A. Braeutigam, Company F, confided in his diary on October 5, 1962 [in English] that during Lieutenant Governor Hoffmann's visit "[o]ur regiment had a review for him in the afternoon, and I participated. Unfortunately we made several blunders today, and as a result the Col. became very angry and blew up at our adjutant and Capt. Bruhn from Comp. A; both were placed under arrest."[41]

Capt. Matthew Marx wrote to the *Staats-Zeitung* to dispel rumors that he and the other officers of Company D were unhappy after their company's forced transfer from the Third Board of Trade Regiment to Colonel Hecker's regiment. A second letter from the captain appears in chapter 6.

Marx had lived in Brooklyn, New York, for seven years before moving to Chicago in 1858 and practicing law. The forty-three-year-old captain was a native of Wiesbaden in the Duchy of Nassau. Marx served as adjutant for the 1st Washington Independent Regiment Illinois State Militia from the winter of 1858–1859 until he enlisted in Captain Thielemann's Independent (Illinois) Cavalry Company in June 1861. He rose from private to second lieutenant to captain. Marx served in Missouri and Kentucky before resigning his commission in March 1862 due to deteriorating health. He later organized what would become Company D of the Second Hecker Regiment. Captain Marx was discharged on October 7, 1863, to join the Invalid Corps (Veterans Reserve Corps) and served as commander of Company I, 4th Regiment, Veteran Reserve Corps; he later became acting assistant quartermaster performing light office duty until he was discharged in April 1865.

Illinois Staats-Zeitung
October 11, 1862

A Declaration of Captain Mathew Marx of the New Hecker Regiment

It has already been repeated to me that I wanted to leave the Hecker Regiment and my treatment is not acceptable. Therefore I find myself induced, because these statements are completely untrue, to state here in my interest and in the name of the remaining officers of my company, that we are not only satisfied with the treatment by Colonel Fr. Hecker toward everyone in my company but also are very satisfied with the whole organization. This is slander in the news.

Respectfully.

Mathew Marx
Captain of the New Hecker Regiment

The 82nd Illinois completed its organization on October 29, 1862 with the mustering in of Capt. Ivar Weid's Company I, and on November 3, 1862, departed for the seat of war in Northern Virginia, where they would join Maj. Gen. Franz Sigel's Eleventh Corps of the Army of the Potomac. The Eleventh Corps was formally designated as such on September 12, 1862, and consisted mainly of the three divisions formerly comprising the First Corps of the former Army of Virginia. Several new German regiments including the 82nd Illinois joined the Eleventh Corps after its organization.

Three

Off to the Seat of War

he Second Hecker Regiment marched from Camp Butler, Illinois, at 4:00 a.m. on November 3, 1862, and boarded a train at Springfield for Chicago. At 9:00 p.m. on November 4, a train crammed with Colonel Hecker's troops chugged out of Chicago and headed east, reaching Cleveland, Ohio, at sunset. The train reached Dunkirk, New York, on the southeastern edge of Lake Erie about 7:00 a.m. on November 6, and that night the men detrained at Elmira, New York, and climbed into open cattle cars for the trip south to Baltimore, Maryland. Pvt. Friedrich A. Braeutigam wrote in his diary, " We suffered terribly at night from the cold and the next day." The thirty-five-year-old native of Saxony noted that while traveling alongside the Susquehanna River, "It vividly reminds me of the Fatherland, the area along the Rhine and the Main, of the vineyards and the old ruins." Surely he was not alone in his thoughts given the many German immigrants on the train.[1]

The travel-weary troops arrived in Baltimore at approximately 3:00 a.m. on November 8 and by 2:00 p.m. were on the march to the nation's capital city some forty miles to the southwest. The regiment finally halted at Camp Seward in Arlington Heights, Virginia, on November 9. Eight days later, Hecker's command headed west to Fairfax Court House, where General Sigel had established his headquarters as part of the defenses of Washington. The German regiment arrived at its new camp on the night of the eighteenth after a march aggregating twenty-six miles.[2]

The following unsigned letter includes a brief mention of the regiment's trip to Baltimore, a deadly incident that occurred at Camp Butler while the regiment trained there, and observations about some earlier battles in Virginia.

Illinois Staats-Zeitung
December 2, 1862
Camp Sigel by Fairfax Court House, Va.
November 27, 1862

In spite of our closeness to Washington, we see everything here but the world, and often do not see any newspapers for 3 to 4 days, much less letters. Hopefully, this will change for the better, because we have received equipment for the transport and receipt of mail.

Others will have already informed you about our trip here: from Elmira to Baltimore [261 miles]. We were all transported like cattle, from colonel to *Private,* and it took 2 days to cover this relatively short distance.

You will receive a short report about the Camp Butler affair, but today only this much: The coroner's jury in Springfield has found the soldiers not guilty. Lieutenant Colonel Salomon just came from the side of Colonel Hecker; neither Lieutenant Colonel Salomon nor Adjutant Weigel nor the others still stand accused in the shooting, because they did not have revolvers in their hands. Lt. Fuchs, who tried to stop the team of mules, had the bullets fly by his ears, so that he was in more danger than anyone. Lieutenant Colonel Salomon called forcefully, after he heard shots: "don't fire, stop, stop."[3]

The man shot dead provoked it by his extremely beastly behavior. He drove the mule team at the officer of the day, drove over him, then directed it at the lieutenant colonel, who had to leap to the side, then at Colonel Hecker, who had to hurry out of the way. He had full control of his team and sought to deliberately run over the men, especially the guard who was supposed to arrest him. When the men saw his brutal conduct, when he tried to run down the officers and soldiers and tried to bring disaster, they were naturally excited. Shots fell like lightening and in the tumult no one could see from where they came.[4]

The driver's crime was even more serious because he stood under the orders of our officers and by striking the officer of the day, who was in full uniform according to the laws and regulations, he deserved to be killed. Through specific general orders the officer present is entrusted in certain cases to shoot the offender (to shoot on the spot). Today I announce to you only that Colonel Hecker has given a complete report about this event to the post commander Colonel Fonda at Camp Butler.[5]

Sigel and Schurz greeted us warmly. Some of us have visited the battlefield of [Second] Bull Run in the company of some of Sigel's excellent officers. They explained the entire course of the August battle to us. The full burden that day lay on Sigel's weak corps. Had Kearny done his part on the first day the enemy would have been flanked and the reinforcement of Jackson by Longstreet would have been thwarted, i.e., the former defeated before the latter arrived. Had McDowell done his part the reinforcement also would not have been possible; and if he had stood fast when he arrived on the battlefield, instead of leaving it, then the total defeat of the Rebels would have been certain. Further, had Pope sent the available reserve troops into the battle, the fate of the enemy would have been sealed; he retreated on the second day of the battle, because Sigel's small corps had so pressed him. Yes—if on the last day of the battle all the troops not led into the fire had quickly been thrown at the enemy, and if they had advanced ruthlessly on this day the Rebels would have suffered the most terrible defeat of the entire war. It must be said of the Rebels that they had selected excellent positions, placed their artillery in controlling positions, and largely showed boldness and audacity in their maneuvers.[6]

It still appears that a large battle took place on the battlefield of [Second] Bull Run. Bullets of every caliber, mounted pieces, remains of horses, sunk-in graves, human skulls, totally ruined caissons, wheels, destroyed rifles, etc., constitute a serious ensemble, and the trees are literally peppered with bullets.

Yesterday, Gen. Schurz's scouts had an encounter with a standing picket of the Rebels. They advanced to within 2½ miles of New Baltimore and hit on the Rebels there, who numbered about 40 men strong. Although only 8 in number, the scouts attacked, shot the officer together with his horse, lost 2 men, and reported the position of the advanced post.[7]

Gustav Struve, who looked excellent, said goodbye to military service in order to work in the press again. He resigned because Prince Salm [-Salm] was named commander of the concerned regiment in Hetterich's [Hedterich's] place [through the influence of his wife? *Illinois Staats-Zeitung* ed., comment]. We should insist that it not be permissible, in accordance with the Constitution, for soldiers to associate closely with European princes, counts, and barons.[8]

In conclusion, it only remains to say that Sigel's army corps is still not as strong as it is supposed to be according to newspaper reports.

[Unsigned]

Another anonymous letter provides a further glimpse of camp life and some words of General Sigel.

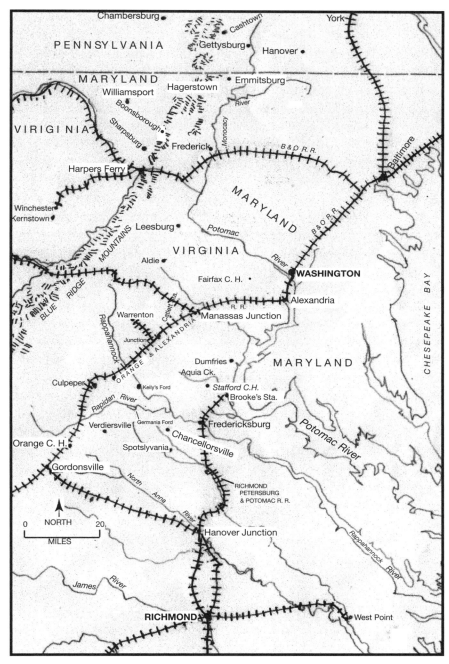

Theater of Operations November 1862 to September 1863

Illinois Staats-Zeitung
December 6, 1862
Fairfax Court House, Va.
November 30, 1862

We lie here only three hundred feet from Fairfax Court House where Sigel has his headquarters and are really under his command now. Last Tuesday, Gen. Sigel reviewed our regiment and the German 107th Ohio Regiment.[9] He [Sigel] climbed down from his horse and examined each man closely. After he was finished he spoke with the officers. Everyone heard what he said, namely: You should not be rude to the soldiers, rather treat them well and leniently; it is your duty to take care of everyone. For him an officer is not any better than a private soldier in the ranks who has to do his part. Every soldier's life is worth millions and anyone who is treated unjustly will receive justice from him. Our regiment conducted several maneuvers and Sigel was very satisfied, then Colonel Hecker expressed that he is strict to be sure, but he understands military service excellently.

We have established ourselves very well here. There is a stove in every tent. We dig a hole in the ground, obtain some old sheet iron and some bricks for a chimney, which we find enough of here, and our tents are warmer than your rooms will ever be. If only everything was not so expensive and the paymaster would come, e.g., a pack of tobacco that costs 5 cents in Chicago brings 20 cents here.

Private Carl Lotz of Company H wrote a lengthy and informative correspondence from Camp Sigel at the beginning of December. Lotz, a twenty-seven-year-old native of Hohensolms in Prussia, and a merchant, was living in St. Louis, Missouri, when he enlisted in Capt. Emil Frey's company. He was later appointed sergeant major and promoted to second lieutenant, Company G, on May 3, 1863, and first lieutenant, Company G, on March 12, 1864. Lieutenant Lotz was also brevetted captain effective March 13, 1865 and mustered out with the regiment.[10]

Illinois Staats-Zeitung
December 11, 1862
Camp Sigel by Fairfax Court House, Va.
December 2, 1862

Surely the expanded readers' circle of the *Illinois Staats-Zeitung* wants to hear a little news about the new Hecker regiment and, therefore, the following lines should be welcome:

In order not to cover old ground regarding our trip from Chicago to Washington, permit me to begin right away with information about Camp Seward and draw a little picture for you of this camp.[11] It is about 5 miles south of Washington on the most sacred ground of Virginia, separated from the capital by the Potomac, which has become so famous in recent history.

Lying atop a small hill, Camp Seward provided a wonderful view of Washington and its picturesque surroundings on the majestically flowing Potomac with its splendid banks and the softly rocking ships on its broad surface, and also of the much discussed Arlington Heights and its many forts. One nearby fort is the most excellent Fort Richardson, which is located about half a mile south of us. This fort controls a large part of the region there, with its 11 heavy guns, 18 cannons, and 3 mortars. Two of its cannons were seized at Camden [Port Royal] during the 7 days battles near Richmond.[12]

Camp Seward's air was completely clean and healthy, the water excellent and abundant, and it was possible to obtain sufficient, good-quality provisions from nearby Washington. Further, we possessed so much more of odds and ends, which are important in the field. The single little mischief of our former camp was that sometimes the firewood was far away; otherwise nothing remained to be desired. With such excellent characteristics of Camp Seward, there stirred within many a man the wish to let it become permanent. You will probably not be surprised that their desire was thwarted, and indeed, through a sudden marching order that called us to Sigel's army corps.

One afternoon general march was sounded, the regiment formed in *Line of Battle,* and with knapsacks on our shoulders, we grasped our rifles, and took leave from the days of Aranjuez, accompanied by the tears of a heaven weeping over our fate.[13] In the beginning we marched toward Alexandria in a rather cheerful mood; however, the march soon changed into a strenuous and uncomfortable one, caused by heavy knapsacks, wet clothes, slippery ground, and the onset of night. We continued forward in the darkness, in which we could not see our hands before our eyes. One man who had taken a hard fall stood up cussing and ranting. Another complained in not very couched verbalisms about his neighbor, whose rifle had poked him in the ribs rather hard. The others marched on in mostly quiet resignation.

Lieutenant B. [Bechstein?],[14] known to many in Chicago circles, and my humble self, who had just now grasped the humor of despair, intoned the celebrated new song, "O, you dear Augustin," when he suddenly disappeared before my eyes.[15] Frightened, I looked around for him without being able to see him initially. Raging, he finally emerged from a hole the depth of which he probably wanted to measure for the enrichment of geological science. Still laughing heartily over this little intermezzo, I made a misstep and made the same journey from which Lieutenant B. had returned. We finally reached Alexandria after much torment and great suffering, paused about 1½ hours, and then marched one mile farther to Camp Banks, where we were greeted very friendlily by soldiers who had been released on parole.[16] Tired as dogs (because we had advanced 10 miles from 4:30 in the afternoon until 10 o'clock at night, the hour we arrived in camp, and the 1½ hours' rest in Alexandria, was in rank and file, with the packed knapsacks on our backs on an open street) we lay down and fell asleep very soon. I can assure you that the unaccustomed load of a heavy, 40-lb. knapsack and a rifle had worn down my body rather severely.

The next morning at 10 o'clock we decamped again to make a march of about 17 miles that was very similar to that of the previous day. Then it rained gently around 7 o'clock in the evening at our destination, Fairfax C[ourt] [House]. We arrived there with sore feet, abused backs, and empty stomachs. We were ordered back ½ mile, where we pitched our camp, and, in spite of the wet earth and growling stomachs, laid ourselves down to rest after the great strain and unpleasantness of the march. I deem it necessary to tell you that none of the above-indicated distances were direct, but included detours, which the regiment was forced to make because of the route ordered to our colonel. Thus, we lay here in a wasteland, a desolate region cut off from the civilized world, without newspapers, tobacco, whiskey, or objects that otherwise would perhaps not become very noted, except that for soldiers lying in a field, they are of much significance and contribute very much to the improvement of their rather dismal lives. Therefore the chess game, which your correspondent attended to earlier and which also banished very boring hours, must be given up because of a lack of suitable space. For example, I am writing these lines on a cracker box lying crossways over a meat box.

Our environment carries traces of the war throughout. Whenever we come across a fence, half of it has disappeared for use as firewood; the few scattered, mostly unoccupied farmhouses are riddled with bullet holes. Some remain only as fragments that have survived a blazing fire. Even Fairfax, a miserable nest, is in the above-mentioned condition. Very few civilians inhabit it, at the most, an enterprising Middle Eastern man, who is tenaciously attached to the almighty dollar, like a predator to his prey, endeavoring to lure the last cent out of the pockets of the poor soldiers for inferior goods at enormous prices. Chickens, eggs, milk, and butter are things that disappeared from this region a long time ago and positively belong to the class of unobtainable luxury items. The water here is *en Canaille* [terrible]. In contrast, the provisions delivered to us are very good considering the conditions; likewise is the present state of health of the regiment.

The climate is rather mild here. Frequently, however, there are very cold days, which can be very bitter in our thin canvas-walled tents. However, need leads to innovation. If you entered our tents you would find nice "Brickstone-Stoves." Fires burn frolicsomely in most of them, because there is no lack of wood.

At best, the biggest part of life isn't goods (merchandise), but the biggest part of evil is a *Sutler,* who most of the time does not have the most necessary items for a soldier. He only wants to sell the little trash he has with a minimum 200–250 percent [markup]. So we live here now in an arcadia of purest [?] water, awaiting things that will come, and by God I want it to come in any manner, preferably in the form of battle.

A different spirit has prevailed ever since we found ourselves under the command of Major General Sigel. The general orders are consistently specific, strict, and entirely appropriate. The great machine called an army corps is made to operate properly. All regimental and company books have been inspected and an inspection of the camp is supposed to take place today. A few days ago, as you already know, Major General Sigel and General Schurz, together with their entourage, made an inspection of our regiment as well as the pure German 107th Ohio Regiment right next to us.

Major [General] Sigel appears to be troubled and his pale face bears traces of the strains endured and the insults suffered. But now and then a look flashes from his eyes, sharp, fierce, and penetrating deep into your heart, which convinces everybody that within this small, ailing body lives a healthy, grand, and energetic spirit.

General Schurz made a very imposing impression on me. His slim figure, excellent military bearing, and intellectual face provide a splendid appearance. The inspection seems to have pleased Major General Sigel and after we performed some evolutions for him again he delivered a brief address to the officers, in which he, among other things, commended the considerate treatment of the subordinates. Then he galloped off from there with his entourage under the enthusiastic hurrahs of our boys, leaving them with various opinions.

I have nearly forgotten to tell you that Sigel presently has his headquarters in Fairfax. I am sorry that I cannot give you any information about the location of the enemy.

Surprisingly, I heard from Mr. Sch.[?], who was returning from Chicago, that in the anti-Hecker circles, which are known to be mainly composed of Democrats who, of course, do not particularly like the radical Republicanism of Colonel Hecker, the old spitefulness is being launched again.[17] Moreover, one shouldn't really be surprised by this, for it is an old story that remains forever new, and when it happens the heart breaks, but not into pieces. We generally believe that Colonel Hecker will soon advance to brigadier general, a position, which he is not only fully able to handle, but in which he will achieve many great things.

The unfortunate Camp Butler affair is supposed to be exploited in a very exaggerated way. Although I now do not want to justify it, there is indeed much to excuse. You will concede to me, that a man, who was ordered to drive the things of a regiment that was ready to march to the railroad, instead of following the instructions received, sought to withdraw, and drove around in the camp like crazy searching for a passage, ran over one here, knocked another to the ground with a blow from his whip, and endangered the security of many, made the remainder furious enough to provoke the well-known unfortunate act. But one could have done better by firing at one of his four mules instead of at the teamster.

It has not further surprised me to learn that a coroner's jury of the state of Illinois has arranged to charge several accused persons who had the least to do with it and one who had not the smallest pistol in his hands.

In the hope that you, as well as the esteemed readers' circle of your newspaper, have not become bored by my sketches,

Respectfully yours,

[Pvt.] Carl Lotz

One embarrassing statistic that the readers of the *Illinois Staats-Zeitung* would not find in its pages, and that the newspaper's editor may not have known, is that seventy-one of Colonel Hecker's soldiers deserted between October 2, 1862, and November 7, 1862. All but a few of these desertions were recorded within one week before and one week after the regiment marched off from Camp Butler on November 3. This represented almost two-thirds of the ninety-seven desertions for the regiment's entire period of service. There was a wide disparity in desertions by company. On the low side were Company H with one deserter and Company B with five deserters; on the high side were Company C with sixteen deserters and Company K with twenty-four deserters. The large number of desertions in October and November of 1862 likely indicates that many of the deserters enlisted for the bounty money and a paycheck and slipped away before the regiment left Illinois. Other men likely did not take to soldiering or decided not to risk life and limb on the battlefront. The ninety-seven desertions approximated 10 percent of the total number of men who mustered into the regiment and is a bit higher than the average of 9 percent for deserters in the Union army as a whole.[18]

While Sigel's Eleventh Corps was manning the defenses of Washington, President Lincoln dismissed Maj. Gen. George B. McClellan as commander of the Army of the Potomac and replaced him with Maj. Gen. Ambrose Burnside. Burnside launched a failed attack on Gen. Robert E. Lee's army at Fredericksburg on December 13, 1862, and withdrew from the area on December 15. In the meantime, the 82nd Illinois broke camp on Saturday, December 11, and began marching toward Fredericksburg as part of the Grand Reserve Division, arriving at Stafford Court House on December 16. Private Braeutigam noted in his diary on December 16 that his regiment: "ran out of food and supplies yesterday," and the "men are completely starved and exhausted." The next day he wrote, "Haven't got anything to eat yet. General dissatisfaction and impatient grumbling . . . everything is barren and forsaken." Fortunately, provisions arrived that evening, but he complained two days later, "Very low rations. Grumbling among the troops."

Sometime during the march to Stafford Court House or soon after its arrival there the 82nd Illinois officially became a part of Brig. Gen. Alexander von Schimmelfennig's First Brigade of Maj. Gen. Carl Schurz's Third Division. Schimmelfennig had served in the Prussian army before joining the revolutionaries in 1848. Col. Wladimir Krzyzanowski, a native of Poland who had taken part in the revolution in 1848, led the Second Brigade of Schurz's division.[19]

The regiment moved to near Aquia Creek on December 19, and the men soon began building log cabins for their winter quarters. On December 22, Capt. Emil Frey of Company H took time to write a missive to the editor of his hometown newspaper back in Illinois. To the delight of the relatives and friends of his soldiers from Highland, he mentioned something about each of them. He also bragged a little about the company. Remarkably, Captain Frey returned to Switzerland after the war ended and in 1894 became that country's president.[20]

Der Highland Bote
January 9, 1863
Camp near Stafford [Va.]
December 22, 1862

To the editor of the *Highland Bote:*

Our regiment presently camps near Stafford Court House, 10 miles above Fredericksburg. We are attached to Schurz's division and Schimmelpfennig's [Schimmelfennig's] brigade and since the unfortunate assault at Fredericksburg have awaited things that are supposed to come.—Our company, the second strongest in the regiment, has meanwhile busied itself with the construction of cabins, although we do not exactly know when we will receive orders to march again and all the trouble and work will have been in vain.

Besides Highland and its environs, Chicago, Ottawa, Aurora, Decatur, Trenton, and St. Louis are more or less strongly represented in the company—a somewhat varied assembly, only without noticeable influence on the comradely behavior of the men toward each other. Among the Highlanders, of course, we must note "big Widmer [Wittmer]." He is the flag bearer of the regiment and in spite of all attempts we could find no one in the Army of the Potomac to match him. The brothers Wildhaber are wild indeed, as their name says, only not less devoted in the service; Geisbühler and Bircher are satisfied in front of their self-built cabin warming by the fire; Hans [Johann] Kistling is small indeed and scandalous, but large in the baking of crackers and dangerous when angry; Cpl. Tscharner is universally respected and spry in spite of his 44 summers, cursing and damning the soldier's life only on nightly marches; and Ruedi [Rudolph] Müeller [Muller] has let his beard grow as evidence of his emancipation from civilian life and to the horror of his wife, and which also dismays all good wives. [Names of and comments about approximately twenty other soldiers from Highland, Illinois, omitted from this letter by the editor.][21]

That is the Highland stock of our company; add to this the youthfully strong and mostly physically large men from Chicago, etc., and you have a company, which certain impartial people have maintained might be the finest of the regiment and that is what we want. So much is certain, disagreements and frictions, which were the consequence of the many different elements thrown together through chance, shortcomings in discipline, which followed changed expectations, frustrated ambition, and all too much enjoyment of beer available in abundance and hard liquor—all have stopped since we left Camp Butler.

Everyone must do his duty and when all the men uniformly discharge their duty, obedience will come easily to the individual; it becomes a habit. The men have the firm conviction that they lead a far happier and more comfortable life than under the opposite circumstances—and act accordingly. Our company adds directly to the best of the regiment and it did not surprise us that Colonel Hecker recently assigned us to the post of honor of the regiment. We covered the brigade in a position lying 7 miles in front toward the mass of Stuart's cavalry. We held this post for 3 days, during which time the brigade advanced to Sumfrees [Dumfries, Va.].[22]

That is all for today. More soon.

Polite greetings.

Your servant,

E. F. [Emil Frey]

Four

A New Year Begins

The 82nd Illinois remained encamped near Aquia Creek, Virginia, until January 20, 1863, when it joined in Maj. Gen. Ambrose Burnside's infamous "Mud March," which was cancelled after three days due to impassable roads. The 82nd halted at Hartford Church until February 6, and then moved to Stafford Court House, where it remained with its corps until the start of the Chancellorsville campaign on April 27, 1863.[1]

On January 1, 1863, while the regiment lay at Aquia Creek, President Abraham Lincoln signed the final Emancipation Proclamation declaring that the slaves in the states or the parts of the states still in rebellion should be "thenceforward, and forever free." Adverse reaction to the preliminary Emancipation Proclamation issued the previous September, along with the suspension of writs of habeas corpus, had helped Democrats win governorships in New York and neighboring New Jersey, and legislative majorities in Illinois, Indiana, and New Jersey. On January 5, 1863, the Illinois legislature resolved: "That the emancipation proclamation of the president is as unwarrantable in military as in civil law, a gigantic usurpation, at once converting the war, professedly commenced by the administration for the vindication of the authority of the constitution, into the crusade for the sudden, unconditional, and violent liberation of 3,000,000 of negro slaves; a result which would not only be a total subversion of the Federal Union, but a revolution in the social organization of the Southern States, the immediate and remote, the present and far-reaching consequences of which to both races cannot be contemplated without the most dismal foreboding of horror and dismay. The proclamation invites servile insurrection as an element in this emancipation crusade, a means of warfare, the inhumanity and diabolism of which are without example in civilized warfare, and which we denounce, and which the civilized world will denounce, as an ineffaceable disgrace to the American name." The officers of the 82nd Illinois Infantry were appalled by the legislature's action and issued formal resolutions of their own condemning the legislature's action.[2]

[Original letter in English]

Headquarters 82nd Regt. Ills. Vols.
Camp near Stafford C.[ourt] H.[ouse] Va.
February 14, 1863

To his Excellency
Governor Richard Yates

At a meeting of the Officers of the 82nd Regt. Ills. [Ill.] Vols. held this day Lieut. Col. Edward S. Salomon was chosen chairman and Adjutant Eugene Weigel secretary, and the following resolutions were offered, and unanimously adoptet [adopted]:

In consideration of the critical position of our country and of the intrigues of miserable politicians and partisans, who while the true and loyal citizens of our state, with the sacrifice of blood and life, endeavor to destroy the enemies of our most sacred rights,—aid and abet these enemies, at home, by means of treasonable, and our state degrading resolutions, be it resolved:

1. That we, the German soldiers and the citizens of Illinois, who have declared themselves willing to sacrifice all for the preservation of the Union, have heard with the greatest indignation of the miserable treachery of the men, who dare to call themselves our representatives.

2. That we endorse with pleasure the emancipation proclamation of our President, and are at any moment ready to execute it with arms in hand.

3. That we regard our Governor Richard Yates, as one of the noblest, truest and most high minded patriots of the United States, and that we refute the infamous attacks and slanders, which have been made upon him by secesh-sympathizing members of the legislature of Illinois, as low and mean in the highest degree, and that we regret that we are no longer at Camp Butler, to have an opportunity of liberating the halls of our capitol, from this detestable scum.

4. That we condemn the majority-report of the house committee on federal relations most decidedly, and that we consider the authors and all those, who voted in favor of this report as rebels and traitors, who deserve to be hung by the side of Jeff. Davis and consorts.

5. That we, contrary to this report, consider the minority report of the same committee, as the noble expression of the sentiments of true patriots, and acknowl-

edge and esteem the same as such with all our heart, and that we are convinced that the same will be endorsed by every soldier of the state of Illinois.

6. That we hope and wish, that the rebellion may soon be suppressed, but *only* by force of arms, and that then the traitors in the north as well as the leaders of the rebellion in the south, may not evade their just punishment.

7. That these resolutions be published in the *Ilinois Staats-Zeitung* and the *Chicago Tribune,* and copies thereof be sent to the Governor of Illinois and to our representatives in Congress, as well as to our Colonel Friedric[h] Hecker, who, unfortunately, was prevented by disease, from participating in this demonstration.

> Edw. S. Salomon
> Lieut. Col. comdg. 82nd Regt. Ills. Vols.
> Chairman
> Eugene Weigel, Adjutant,
> Secretary.

The above resolutions were read to the regiment at Dress Parade & unanimously adopted.

> Edw. S. Salomon
> Lt. Col. Comdg.[3]

Capt. Ivar A. Weid of Company I resigned on January 17, 1863, and Governor Yates commissioned 1st Lt. John Hillborg, a thirty-five-year-old native of Sweden, to replace him. Colonel Hecker recommended a German from Company C to fill Hillborg's former position in Company I. Hecker's letter to the governor explains why he chose a German to be second in command of the Scandinavian Company.[4]

[Original letter in English]

> Head[q]uarters 82d Regt. Ills. Vols.
> Camp Schurz, Va., April 1st 1863
> His Excellency Richard Yates
> Governor of Illinois

Sir!

By resignation of Captain M. [I.] Weid and 2d Lieutenant Hansen [Hanson] of Company "I" of this regiment two vacancies occurred. Your Excellency appointed 1st Lieut. John Hillborg as Captain in this company. His commission arrived here, whilst he was on sick leave, and I have not received yet his notification of the acceptance of the promotion. Your Excellency further promoted the Orderly Sergeant Erickson 2d Lieutenant under date of December 10th 1862, in place of 2d Lieut. Hansen [Hanson], resigned, so that there is still a vacancy to wit: the place of a 1st Lieutenant in the above company which, composed of Scandinavians, needs more than any other Company an efficient Officer. Those two, who have resigned, had been elected, but proved in no way to correspond to the expectations. Lieut. Erickson has been promoted only a short time ago and is not yet fit as yet to advance to the place of 1st Lieutenant in preference of more meritorious Officers.[5]

Captain Hillborg being absent sick, and as the time of an active campaign is fast approaching, and it being of the greatest interest for the service to have all vacancies filled, and that as soon as the acceptance of 1st Lieut. Hillborg of the Captaincy, granted in your commission, is shown, I respectfully recommend 2d Lieut. *Frederick Bechstein* of Company "C" to be promoted to 1st Lieutenant of Company "I." 2d Lieut. Bechstein, who has served in Europe and to the satisfaction of his superiors here, is in my humble opinion entitled to the promotion above mentioned.

Should this recommendation find favor and be approved, a vacancy to be filled, is created in Company "C," and I would most respectfully recommend that, as above referred to the acceptance of the Captaincy by said 1st Lieut. Hillborg, *Otto Balck,* Serg't [Sgt.] Major of the regiment, be appointed 2d Lieut. of Company "C." His Excellency Lieut. Governor Francis A. Hoffmann knows him personally, and I can add, that he deserves to be promoted as 2d Lieutenant of Comp'y [Company] C."

> I have the honor to sign
> most respectfully
> your obedient servant
> Fr. Hecker
> Col. comd'g 82d Reg't Ills. [Ill.] Vols.[6]

Newly commissioned Captain John Hillborg objected to a German being made an officer in his company and wrote directly to the governor urging that a Scandinavian be appointed as his company's 1st lieutenant. It is unknown whether Colonel Hecker ever learned of Hillborg's letter, but Hecker prevailed in this matter, much to the disappointment of Hillborg and probably most men in Company I.

(Original letter in English)

Camp near Stafford C. H., Va.
April 11, 1863

Hon. Richard Yates
Governor of the State of Illinois

I hereby most respectfully take the liberty to address the following lines to your Hon.[or] in behalf of my comp.[any], which is the Scandinavian Comp. recruited by Capt. Ivar Alexander Weid in Chicago, Ill., last year intended for the Board of Trade Regt. and which was ordered to join the 82nd Regt., Col. Fred Hecker. By Capt. I. A. Weid's and Lieut. F. Hanson's resignments [resignations] there became 2 vacancies in the comp. I as 1st Lieut. was promoted to captain in Jan. 1863 and 1st Sgt. Chr. Erickson as 2d Lieut. in Debr [Dec]., 1862 leaving the 1st lieutenantcy [lieutenancy] empty. Yesterday on my return from a furlough, I found that this vacancy was intended to be filled by a 2d Lieut. Beckstein [Bechstein] of Co. C ([G]erman). Gov. my comp.[any] consists only of Scandinavians and I should very much regret to see anny [any] other officers to be put into my comp.[any] especially as I feel convinced that I got men able to fill anny [any] vacancy in the same; and notwithstanding this is [it] it [is] necessary for anny [any] officers in this comp. to [k]now the Scandinavian language because two-thirds can't speak English and hardly none German, therefore I take the liberty to apply to your Hon. hoping that the promise your Hon. give [gave] to the late Capt. Weid is not yet forgotten; now I most respectfully ask your Hon.; if possible, to let my comp. have the chance to fill its own vacancies by which your Hon. would greatly oblige not only me but my whole Comp.

Your most obedient
John Hillborg
Capt., Co. I, 82d Regt Ill. Vol.[7]

Colonel Hecker did not have to confront the disgruntled captain because Hillborg submitted a letter of resignation and a surgeon's certificate of disability on May 19, 1863. Hillborg was suffering from neuralgia and a peptic ulcer. Interestingly, he mustered into the 55th Illinois Volunteer Infantry Regiment on January 31, 1864, and served as a private until mustered out on August 14, 1865, in Little Rock, Arkansas.[8]

Not a single letter from a member of the Second Hecker Regiment appeared in the *Illinois Staats-Zeitung* between December 23, 1862, and May 7, 1863, probably due to the lack of major events while the unit was in its winter quarters. Had any letters been published they likely would have mentioned the inclement Virginia weather, including foot-deep snow on February 21, six inches of snow on March 20, and flurries on Easter Sunday, torn up shoes, the regiment's adverse reaction to General Sigel's resignation as Eleventh Corps commander on March 11, and a review of their corps by President Lincoln near Brooke's Station on April 10.[9]

Most disturbing to the Germans of the Eleventh Corps and elsewhere in the North was Sigel's unexpected resignation. As Christian Keller explains, "Suffering from poor health, chafed by the smallness of his corps compared to the others in the Army of the Potomac, annoyed by the lack of promotions of fellow German officers (for which he believed Army Chief of Staff Henry W. Halleck was responsible), and deluded by his own inflated sense of importance, Franz Sigel resigned command of the Eleventh Corps." The Eleventh Corps's three divisions each contained just two brigades. Most other divisions contained at least three brigades. Sigel reconsidered his rash decision at the urging of the German American community and in April unsuccessfully tried to get his command back. President Lincoln and his War Department however stuck with Sigel's replacement, Maj. Gen. Oliver O. Howard.[10]

Although General Howard had a good military record to date, he was a poor fit with the Eleventh Corps. The Germans in the Eleventh Corps were not only upset that their beloved leader Sigel was not replaced by Carl Schurz or another German but that his successor was a temperance advocate and so deeply religious that he would not write orders on a Sunday. Naturally, this Maine Yankee's religious attitude and pronouncements rankled the "freethinkers" among the Germans and some Anglo-Americans, too.[11]

The commander who selected Howard over Schurz for the Eleventh Corps's command was Maj. Gen. Joseph Hooker. President Lincoln had replaced General Burnside with General Hooker back on January 26, 1863. Hooker had previously commanded the Army of the Potomac's Center Grand Division at the Battle of Fredericksburg. Hooker restored the morale of the army, which had plunged dramatically after the defeat at Fredericksburg and the notorious "Mud March," by improving the quantity and quality of rations, replacing torn up shoes and uniforms, improving sanitation, and granting furloughs. The Massachusetts native also ordered the soldiers of each corps to wear a distinctive cloth badge to identify his corps and division. For example, the Third Corps's symbol was a diamond, the Eleventh Corps's was a crescent, and the Twelfth Corps's was a star. The First Division's color was red, the Second Division's was white, the Third Division's was blue, and the Fourth Division's was green. The 82nd Illinois's soldiers therefore wore a blue crescent on their kepi caps or hats.[12]

Five

The Battle of Chancellorsville

O n April 27, 1863, Major General Hooker began to launch a powerful force of more than 70,000 troops on a march that would swing behind Gen. Robert E. Lee's 60,000-man army entrenched at Fredericksburg, while the First Corps and Sixth Corps, 40,000 troops under Maj. Gen. John Sedgwick, fixed Lee's force at Fredericksburg. This maneuver required the Eleventh and Twelfth Corps to cross the Rappahannock River at Kelly's Ford and again at the Rapidan River at the Germania Ford. The Second, Third, and Fifth Corps were to ford the Rapidan to the east of the Eleventh and Twelfth Corps using Ely's Ford and the United States Ford. Because Lee's army was outnumbered by two to one, Hooker was sure that Lee's forces would be crushed or would flee. Unfortunately for Hooker's army, Lee did not wait to be caught in the middle.[1]

On May 1, Maj. Gen. Henry W. Slocum's two Twelfth Corps divisions advancing east on the Orange Plank Road and Maj. Gen. George Sykes's division of Maj. Gen. George G. Meade's Fifth Corps advancing east on the Orange Turnpike met strong resistance from several divisions Lee sent from Fredericksburg to check Hooker. In view of his lack of information about Lee's deployments and the almost impenetrable wilderness on both sides of the roads, General Hooker ordered Slocum's Twelfth Corps and Meade's Fifth Corps to pull back and take up defensive positions around Chancellorsville. Hooker hoped Lee would attack his larger fortified army.[2]

On the morning of May 2, Meade's corps and Maj. Gen. Darius N. Couch's Second Corps faced east and stretched south for two miles from the Rapidan to Chancellorsville, while Slocum's corps, Maj. Gen. Daniel E. Sickles's Third corps, and Howard's corps faced south and extended westward from Chancellorsville for three miles. Howard's three divisions comprised the far right flank of its army.

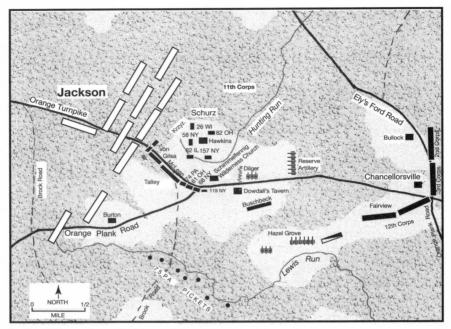

Battle of Chancellorsville, May 2, 1863

Brig. Gen. Charles Devens Jr.'s First Division formed Howard's far right and was hemmed in by the forest, while Maj. Gen. Carl Schurz's Third Division and Brig. Gen. Adolph von Steinwehr's Second Division were able to deploy reserve regiments in clearings north of the turnpike. That same morning Lee split his army and sent Maj. Gen. Thomas J. "Stonewall" Jackson's 27,000-man corps on a wide arc around the Union army's right flank, screened by the dense woods locals called the Wilderness. At approximately 5:30 p.m. the first of Jackson's three battle lines, extending for one mile on each side of the turnpike, came crashing out of the forest, surprising the Eleventh Corps's 10,500 soldiers then manning their army's right flank.[3]

Several German officers had previously warned Howard and Hooker that their corps was poorly positioned in case of a flank attack and that there was activity in the forest but they were ignored, with devastating consequences. Contributing to the Eleventh Corps's defeat was the fact that Brig. Gen. Francis C. Barlow's brigade of von Steinwehr's division had been detached to support Sickles's corps and part of Slocum's, while they pursued what Sickles thought was a large body of retreating Rebels. This isolated Howard's corps and removed its reserve.[4]

First to be hit by Jackson's strong battle line were the two west-facing regiments of Col. Leopold von Gilsa's brigade of Devens's division (the 153rd Pennsylvania and 54th New York). The Pennsylvanians and New Yorkers resisted until almost surrounded and then fled to avoid capture or death; they had no chance against Stonewall Jackson's masses. Von Gilsa's other two regiments were faced south and could not turn in time to face the charging enemy line and therefore could give little resistance. Parts of von Gilsa's brigade ran east through Brig. Gen. Nathaniel C. McLean's brigade (also of Devens's division) with the screaming Rebels on their heels, while destructive grapeshot and canister tore into McLean's right flank. Nevertheless, McLean's regiments resisted as long as feasible considering the unstoppable overwhelming force rushing at them. The Ohioan's regiments variously fired off from three to six rounds each at the enemy before retreating rapidly. Heavy casualties evidenced the cost of their resistance.[5]

Next to be hit was Carl Schurz's division. Schurz's division lay mostly east and north of McLean's brigade. Schimmelfennig's five regiments were deployed in two lines facing south. The first line rested on the turnpike next to McLean's left and contained the 74th Pennsylvania, 61st Ohio, and 68th New York. The 82nd Illinois and the 157th New York formed the second line. North of these two lines and facing west were Colonel Krzyzanowki's 58th New York and 26th Wisconsin regiments and the 82nd Ohio (unattached to a brigade). Krzyzanowki's 75th Pennsylvania stood on picket duty south of the turnpike, and his 119th New York regiment was posted at the juncture of the Orange Plank Road and the Orange Turnpike. Capt. Hubert Dilger's six-gun Ohio battery stood east of the juncture.[6]

Schimmelfennig's regiments posted at the turnpike were unable to form up to resist the enemy because men, guns, caissons, and horses of Devens's division escaping down the road slammed into them, followed by the rapidly advancing enemy. Various fragments of these three regiments hastened east to a rise of ground between the Wilderness Church and the woods to its west. Here they quickly prepared for battle in previously prepared shallow rifle pits. The Wilderness Church (a small Baptist chapel) sat in a small grove that lay 150 yards north of the turnpike. Krzyzanowki's 58th New York was flanked after firing for a few minutes and then fell back to the Wilderness Church line. The 26th Wisconsin fought valiantly for about twenty minutes and only fell back under Schurz's orders when the enemy pressed the regiment from their front and flanked it on both sides.[7]

Soon after the battle began Colonel Hecker moved his command back a short distance to the top of a small hill and faced it toward the advancing Southerners. The regiment stood its ground under a hailstorm of enemy lead and iron and fired at least six rounds before General Schimmelfennig ordered Hecker to retreat. After pulling back only fifteen to twenty yards Hecker ordered a charge, but was immediately wounded, as was Major Rolshausen. Capt. Joseph Greenhut led the bloodied regiment back to the loosely formed Wilderness Church line, halting it several times to return the enemy's fire. Some 5,000 Federals (mostly from Schurz's division) and six guns of Capt. Hubert Dilger's Ohio Battery temporarily held this line against four Confederate brigades.[8]

When Schurz's troops were forced from this line after approximately twenty minutes they retreated to one with shallow entrenchments being defended by four regiments of Col. Adolphus Buschbeck's brigade of von Steinwehr's division and one gun. The Buschbeck line swelled to about 4,000 Eleventh Corps troops and extended north-south for approximately one thousand yards. This line began to fold around 7:00 p.m. when it became flanked on its north end. This stubborn stand at the Buschbeck line lasted approximately twenty-five minutes and forced the Rebels to halt and reorganize before they could resume their attack. The Federal survivors then reformed at the western end of another clearing near Chancellorsville, where they were well covered by friendly artillery and reinforced by Hiram Berry's Third Corps division around 9:00 p.m. After even more troops arrived the exhausted Eleventh Corps soldiers then moved from the Fairview clearing to an open field near the Chancellor mansion, where they rested for about two hours before trudging to the United States Ford and entering entrenchments there. Although Jackson's attack forced the Eleventh Corps back for approximately two miles, as Christian Keller points out, "the delaying action at the Buschbeck line was credited with allowing the artillery reserve and baggage trains of the Eleventh Corps to escape and permitting the rest of Army of the Potomac to react to the Confederate flank attack."[9]

Official reports place the Eleventh Corps losses at 2,412 killed, wounded, and missing. Schurz's division lost 920 soldiers; Schimmelfennig's brigade lost 419 men; and the 82nd Illinois lost 155. In Schurz's division only the casualties of the 26th Wisconsin exceeded those of the 82nd Illinois.[10]

Although the fighting was over for the Eleventh Corps, this was not the case for the rest of Hooker's army. On May 3, the Confederates attacked a salient in Hooker's line and in fierce fighting, supported by massed artillery, broke through the Union line at Chancellorsville. Hooker pulled his troops out of the salient and they entrenched in a U-shaped line anchored on the right and left at the Rappahannock River. On May 3, General Sedgwick marched through Fredericksburg but was defeated in fighting on May 3 and 4 at Salem Church. He retreated back across the Rappahannock at Bank's Ford before dawn on May 5. Hooker retreated across the Rappahannock at the United States Ford on the night of May 5–6, ending his disastrous campaign. Aggregate losses in the Army of the Potomac for the campaign exceeded 17,000 and Confederate losses approximated 13,500. Among the Rebel army's losses was General Stonewall Jackson, who was accidentally shot by his own men on the night of May 2.[11]

The Army of the Potomac returned to its old camps north of the Rappahannock. The battle-worn 82nd Illinois camped with its division in Camp Schurz at Brooke's Station, located just south of Stafford Court House, and waited for what would come.[12]

The following letters and excerpts provide first-hand accounts of the Second Hecker Regiment's participation in the campaign and the Battle of Chancellorsville. In two of the letters the writers incorrectly state that Colonel Hecker was shot while holding a flag. As the colonel wrote in a letter to Gustav Struve (presented later in this chapter) he was shot a short time after handing the flag to the regiment's color bearer.[13]

Despite the criticism heaped on the Germans of the Eleventh Corps by Anglo-American officers and men and nativist newspaper editors, parts of the Eleventh Corps fought well under the circumstances.

Belleviller Zeitung
May 21, 1863
Camp Schurz
May 11 [1863]

We left our camp very early on Monday, April 27. We were so heavily loaded down that we were barley able to carry everything. In addition to our clothing, blankets, tents, overcoats and 60 cartridges, we had rations for eight full days in our knapsacks. If you knew that we had to march 15 to 20 miles a day with a load of over 80 lbs. in such heat that we have now with clear days, you could easily understand how tired and exhausted we felt in the evening when we were granted a few hours of sleep. However, that was the least of it.

We approached the Rappahannock on the evening of Tuesday, May [April] 28. This river was the partition between life and death for us. That night, at about 9:30, we marched quietly over the barely completed pontoon bridge. We thought we would get into a fight here, but the Rebels were not present in force because of General Hooker's stratagem and so we arrived on this side of the river untouched. That same night we advanced three miles farther and camped in a spruce forest. We were greeted by the Rebels' cannon fire with the onset of daylight. They had awaited our arrival and had moved opposite us while we rested in the woods from which they had attacked our pickets with some canister early in the morning; however, they suspected our overwhelming power, because they rushed off just as fast as they had come. Before we could spot them they were gone again and we continued on our way without any hindrances. From here on out we did not get any more rest. We marched by day, and we had to stand picket or reconnoiter at night. We barely had time to cook something warm and, driven by hunger and fatigue, ate the meat mostly raw, like it was just cut off the cattle, without salt or anything else.

Friday evening after a wide detour we finally reached the scene of our imminent battle. We were attacked with shells and small arms fire on this same evening; but because our regiment was in the center we had nothing to fear at this time; although we still had another dangerous post to occupy that night. The road [Orange Turnpike] was being fortified on one side with barriers. We therefore had the assignment to cover the workmen and to expect an attack. However, all went well and it was quiet.[14]

The next morning, Saturday, May 2, the first time the regiment was under fire, we served as skirmishers and searched for the enemy's flank; we were nearly cut off from our army. However, it still turned out okay. Except for being dead tired, we reached our old position on an elevation, covered to the right by shrubs, on the left side by a hill on which the other regiments of our division camped.[15]

We lay there under the torrid heat of the sun until about 4:00 [5:30] p.m. Suddenly the air trembled from heavy musket fire. Stonewall Jackson had attacked us on our weakest side and had already broken through. They came in thick, close columns carrying a black flag as a symbol of death and destruction. Like a severe storm they hit us with lion-like power—an endless mass. We stood in ranks as quick as lightening and formed around our flag. We moved back to the next hill and deployed in line of battle. Barely had this happened than bullets whistled past our ears. We lay down on our stomachs on command and took off our knapsacks to be able to fight without any hindrances. However, as we stood up to fire we saw everyone in wild flight and the enemy advanced freely towards us in a body. We gave them several rapid volleys, one after the other; but then almost everyone fled. We saw our battle line dwindle and disintegrate.

Hecker, however, did not want to give up any ground. As the column began to disintegrate, he commanded, "fix bayonets"—and some of our soldiers wanted to lunge against the enemy with their bayonets, while others had already retreated. Then, Hecker was hit in the leg by a bullet and plunged from his horse with the flag in his hand. The time for standing had now passed; all who could flee did so. Our wounded and dying fell to the ground left and right. The bullets, canister, and shells rained without stop; they flew around our ears with a dreadful hiss, seeking victims.

Who could imagine that he could escape this slaughter? Gasping and groaning, those remaining finally reached the nearest woods, the enemy close on their heels; but here death also spit its deadly poison toward those seeking protection. Everyone now ran into a thicket and looked after his own well-being the best he could. It was 2 to 3 days before many of the missing returned to the regiment again and many had fallen into the hands of the enemy.

After our company came together again it was only 22 men strong—there was handshaking and a reunion; each one thought the other was dead! We had 7 dead and 7 wounded. Captain Grünhut [Greenhut] from Chicago had acted very bravely; he was one of the last to return from the battlefield with our flag in his hand.

Sunday, May 3, the battle began anew. The cannonade roared with the gray of the morning. Heaven and earth seemed to spit fire. The battle lasted four full hours. The enemy lost a mass of men; corpses of the dead lay on one another like hail. The fighting continued at the entrenchments and barricades behind which we lay without the least rest. Tuesday night about 1 o'clock, while we served as sentinels at a barricade, and believed we would be attacked at every moment, an order arrived to retreat. Indescribable astonishment hit us; we believed the enemy was surrounded and that we could call him to account, and we should now withdraw? However, it was thus—soon after that we were in the middle of a storm again. We suffered through a rainy night on the march, with soaking, frozen-stiff limbs. We endured four nights and days without sleep, and had nothing to eat! We carried our entire fortunes on our bodies; knapsacks, blankets, clothes, and everything were gone, in the hands of the Rebels, and what we wore was tattered.

We arrived at the bank of the Rappahannock at daybreak, after we had marched the whole time on the double quick. Here in the gray misty morning raiment, a magnificent panorama unfolded before our eyes. When we arrived on the last hill, we looked down into the deep Rappahannock Valley, and we beheld the entire force of the Army of the Potomac, spread out before us like a painting. The valley was sown thick with soldiers as far as the eye could see. Truly a noble, splendid view, but a faint-hearted feeling crept up on me that this great force was retreating without having accomplished anything. We arrived at our old camp in the deep of night with terrible weather and roads and now rested on the laurels that we have won.

[Unsigned]

Illinois Staats-Zeitung
May 14, 1863

Excerpt from Letter
Camp Schurz
May 7 [1863]

Saturday, May 2, our battalion moved to the skirmish line, but after one hour it was ordered back. We heard gunfire nearby all day. Ever since we arrived at

Chancellorsville we were continually under arms and slept on our rifles. On the aforesaid Saturday evening [May 2], the order arrived that the troops of our division could make themselves comfortable. We could cook, etc. However, just fifteen minutes later we heard heavy rifle fire in front of our right wing. The order "to fall in" came about 5:30 p.m. The regiment was barely under arms when the First Division [Devens's], located 200 paces from us, rushed back in disorder. The enemy came from a side where he was not at all expected. He had taken us by surprise. Our division's (the 3rd Division under Schurz) position was very poor. We moved back somewhat and our regiment was posted in the line of battle on a small hill. We lost several men during this maneuver. We lay down to await the time that we could give the enemy a full volley. During this time the bullets whistled around us so thickly that we felt the air pressure. We remained on the ground for a minute, then we stood up, shot effectively, and moved back down the hill ten steps. The enemy came on, not respecting our cannonry, until his ranks thinned out. Some regiments retreated; the others remained, however, and Colonel Hecker grabbed the flag [rest of paragraph illegible].

We moved back about 100 paces to rifle pits, where we made a final try, but it failed. The order to fall back came and we retreated. Our regiment conducted itself well, better than most others. What we lacked was only a general. The deployment of our corps was terrible according to the judgment of all experts.

Besides Colonel Hecker, Major Rol[s]hausen was wounded. Lt. Babst of Company B was severely wounded and is missing. In Company F, Lt. Hoppe was mortally wounded. Second Lt. Spönnemann is dead. From Company G, 2nd Lt. Schander [Schonder] is dead. In the crush of business I cannot furnish a list. The battle on May 2 was a difficult one for us, but it was not our soldiers' fault.[16]

During the night of the 2nd to the 3rd our brigade occupied an entrenchment to keep the enemy in check. We expected them from the direction of Fredericksburg. We occupied the post until 4:00 a.m. Around this time, on the spot where our regiment stood hours before, cannon and rifle fire began that shook the earth. [illegible sentence.] The enemy, however, was driven back.

We had a splendid position, but were relieved Sunday night at 11 o'clock. Our brigade marched back to its camping place. The 11th and 12th Corps dug and occupied entrenchments. A reserve regiment and a battery stood between each brigade. Our regiment moved into the reserve at 3 o'clock in the morning. Then, around 8 o'clock, we had to occupy the entrenchments again. We were not relieved until Monday evening; however, not to rest, but to serve on advance post duty. Tuesday afternoon we were relieved from advance post duty and moved into the entrenchments again. We withdrew from there at 1 o'clock in the morning, and arrived in our old camp by Falmouth [Stafford Court House] at 10:00 p.m. last night, totally exhausted. Incidentally, we have already received orders to be ready to march again.

[Unsigned]

Illinois Staats-Zeitung
May 13,1863
Camp Schurz
May 8, 1863

Yesterday, we returned to our old camp with a fateful day behind us. I am too exhausted and too busy to be able to report to you sufficiently. Be satisfied with the following for today.

The powerful attack by Jackson's corps in Sunday's battle was shocking and happened quite unexpectedly for us. The regiments of our corps had their rifles stacked in pyramids, and cavalry had been sent out to see whether there were Rebels nearby. The cavalry returned with the report that they could not see any. Then 40,000 [27,000] Rebels broke out of the forest and before we could look around they had already fired twice. Although we were 12,000 [10,500] against 40,000 [27,000], we fought courageously; however, we had to gradually retire. The bloodshed was horrible. The dead lay 4 feet high.

Colonel Hecker was as brave as a Spartan. He posted himself 15 feet ahead of our front, and had a U.S. flag in his hand when he was struck by a bullet in his shoulder [thigh] and fell from his horse. Major Rollshausen [Rolshausen] was wounded in the calf at the outset. After Hecker had been disabled, Captain Grünhut [Greenhut] of Company K took command of the regiment based upon orders from Major Rollshausen [Rolshausen]. He is the subject of praise and admiration. He showed himself as the bravest of the brave, calm, prudent, valiant.

After arrival in our camp, Captain Lasalle of Company C (the senior captain) took command of the regiment. The heroic courage of Lieutenant Frank of Company C also deserves to be emphasized.[17] The conduct of Captain Heinzmann of Company B and of 2nd Lt. Babst of the same company was similarly brave; sadly the latter was so severely wounded that his recovery is doubtful. Because our brave regimental adjutant Lieutenant Weigel lay sick in Washington, Lt. [Rudolph] Müller from Company E functioned in his position and performed excellently. Lieutenant Dammann of Company E was just as brave. In Company F, 1st Lt. Hoppe, who stood in for Capt. Weber, who was absent on leave, led the company with much courage and was severely wounded. Lieutenant Spönemann died a hero's death. Command of his company temporarily rests with Lieutenant

Bechstein. Company G lost its brave Lt. Schander [Schonder], who was seriously wounded. Lt. Fuchs from Ottawa led Company K after Capt. Grünhut [Greenhut] took command of the regiment during the battle, and he conducted himself imperturbably well. Our boys fought well and courageously in spite of the often very unfavorable situation of the battle.[18]

As I hear, Colonel Hecker was taken from Washington to his sister in Philadelphia. Unfortunately, I cannot send a list of our dead and wounded at the present time because none of our doctors was on this bloody campaign and, up until now, no one with us has seen or heard anything about them, although long since the terrible Saturday battle has been known in all corners and ends of the country. Imagine the indignation!

No regards to Dr. Schloetzer![19]

[Unsigned]

Illinois Staats-Zeitung
May 14, 1863

Excerpt from Letter [not same writer as the May 7 letter]

Camp Schurz
May 8 [1863]

We had a very bad position in the Saturday battle. All was calm until 4:00 p.m., when we suddenly heard a strong infantry fire on our right. We immedi-

Joseph B. Greenhut, Company C (courtesy of the Chicago History Museum [ICHi-36624, photographer-unknown])

ately hurried to our rifles and had taken our position, when the regiment posted on our right retreated in disorder after the Rebels attacked them in the line [of battle]. Our regiment retired in good order to a hill, where we received orders to lie down. At this moment the regiments located in front of us and on our right ran back in disarray; the Rebels hurried after them in good order and were hard on their heels. We directed a deadly fire at the enemy for five minutes. Because Hecker had been shot in the shoulder [thigh] and, immediately after that, our major had been shot in the calf, the situation became desperate. The larger part of our regiment fell back in disorder and, no matter where we were, we were in danger of being annihilated or captured. Capt. Greenhüt [Greenhut] ran forward and grabbed the flag that Hecker was previously carrying and shouted to the officers and soldiers that they should hold fast. About 50 men complied with the call. We retreated slowly through the forest and fired constantly [illegible text]. The Rebels, therefore, were very careful in their advance.

We formed to the right of the 157th N.Y., which had taken a position in the rear. Here we allowed the Rebels to come within 50 yards of us, whereupon Captain Greenhut ordered us to fire. Our shots mowed down the enemy. They followed us for a half mile, whereupon they tired of our fire and began to retreat. We moved to the place where our brigade began to reform again.

[Unsigned]

A letter written by nineteen-year-old private Friedrich P. Kappelmann to his parents on May 10, 1863, described the horrible sights he observed during his shocking baptism of fire on May 2, 1863. Kappelmann mustered into Company B at Camp Butler and transferred to the Ambulance Corps in January 1863. He carried a navy Colt revolver instead of an Enfield Rifle Musket. This change in weapons was more convenient because he had to locate and carry wounded soldiers to ambulances instead of trying to kill the enemy. Kappelmann survived the war and mustered out with his regiment.[20]

May 10, 1863
Camp Schurtz [Schurz]

Dear Parents:

Terribly many people have fallen, particularly in our regiment. Our company has lost eighteen men and the 2nd lieutenant. The battlefield was a gruesome sight. The wounded were lying around everywhere and the dead of both sides were lying around like cut glass, one without a head, another one with both legs gone, the entrails were hanging out of another man, still another one without his arms. The bullets were flying like during a hailstorm. The Rebels were fighting like tigers. Our regiment would have stood its ground better, but the attack came unforeseen, and we were caught down. Captain George Heinzmann got away alive. I still want to say that if Sigel had been in command the 11th Corps would not have been so badly defeated.

Greetings from your son.

Friedrich P. Kappelmann

The following excerpt is from a private letter written by Colonel Hecker while he was recovering from his wound received at the Battle of Chancellorsville. The letter was written to Gustav Struve, a friend and fellow Forty-eighter.

Written from his sickbed.
Philadelphia, Pennsylvania[21]

[Gustav Struve]

Because the 82nd Regiment was on higher ground, I could see everything. My men stood like rocks and fired ceaselessly although we stood in a terrible hailstorm of bullets, shells, balls, case shot, and pointed projectiles from rifled cannon. I constantly rode back and forth among the men and, although my jacket was perforated like a sieve, I remained calm. I now wanted to attack with the bayonet to stop the enemy, even with dreadful losses; I took the flag on my horse and called, "*Hurrah! Charge bayonet.*" The men stood firm, I called to them not to let their flag and their old colonel down. The men stood and fired, but did not make a bayonet attack and actually were right not to do this. I estimate the enemy force that attacked us at twenty-five thousand men.

These Rebels are soldiers, they attacked like a swarm of bees without regard for their lives (whiskey and powder were found in their canteens).[22] Their artillery performed splendidly. They barely noticed the resistance that my and the 157th New York Regiment put up; they also set up two batteries opposite us and spewed an extremely effective hail of projectiles at us. After I had handed the flag to the ensign and ridden from the left to the right wing encouraging the troops, I was shot through the left thigh, close to the trunk of my body. The snuffbox I carried in my pants pocket saved my life, so that I only have a hole in my thigh into which I can insert three fingers diagonally. The neck of the femur bone is grazed, the large thigh vein exposed. I will probably limp for the rest of my life. Only on horseback will it not be noticeable. In a few weeks I want to give the rebels a bloody payback for my pain.

After I was shot, of course, I had no foothold, and shortly afterward my rearing horse threw me off. I gave the major my sword and asked him to take over command and leave me to my fate. Five minutes later he was shot from his horse. One hundred and fifty men of the four hundred and fifty men in my regiment littered the battlefield, and now my brave regiment wavered and moved back in good order toward Buschbeck's brigade, which was behind it and covered it. Schurz and Schimmelfennig did their best to rally the troops. Ten steps behind Schurz, Dessauer was shot; his adjutant von Seille was wounded near him.[23] No corps in the world of so much lesser numbers and in such a position could have stopped the enemy. The best proof is that Hooker had to employ his artillery, forty pieces, and had to use his whole available force to finally stop an enemy already exhausted by several hours of violence and running, and then his troops still had to fall back to within three quarters of a mile of Chancellorsville.

What he [Hooker] could not accomplish with this huge force could hardly be expected of a weak corps, overrun due to his and Howard's negligence. I am objective. No one has said to me, nor could say, that I did not stand firm.

Now to my rescue: As I lay on the ground bleeding severely and saw that my regiment wavered, I called to the men not to worry about me, and later when Lieutenant Beckstein [Bechstein] and six men wanted to carry me away and I saw that this would only adversely effect the retreat, I ordered them to leave me to my fate.[24] I now lay between the attacking enemy and our retreating division. The thought of becoming a prisoner was painful to me, so I crawled to the field fortifications of Buschbeck's brigade using my hands and feet. They had already trained their guns on me. When the guys recognized me, I was pulled over the breastworks and lay there until these (breastworks) fell, too; so I crept between the firing of both sides to the edge of the forest, where the last regiment of Buschbeck's brigade protected me, and indeed Lieutenant Colonel Cantador, compassionately called out: "O, Colonel Hecker!" His men carried me a stretch until I saw that the regiment was falling into disorder, and ordered them to leave me to my fate.[25] They did and I dragged myself ten to twelve yards farther. A saddled horse stood there with its bridle shot away, bleeding from three wounds. One eye had been shot out, its knee was grazed, and it had a flesh wound in its back. Some stragglers lifted me onto it and the poor animal on which I did not sit, but hung, toddled off as well as it could.

An adjutant of General Slocum who found me in this rueful situation took me with him and brought me to a field hospital during the night, where I was bandaged. Our brigade wagon train soon arrived with ambulances of the Third Division. I was placed in an ambulance where I spent the entire horrible Sunday [May 3] of the battle.[26]

I was first taken to Falmouth, then Aquia Creek, then Washington; finally, I found myself under the faithful care of my brother-in-law and sister.[27]

The battle was horrible. You can have no concept of the hail of bullets and the roar of the firearms. You could not understand another person ten paces away. Hooker's batteries mowed down the Rebels by the hundreds by Chancellorsville. I estimate the losses of both sides at forty thousand men killed, wounded, and missing. It was obviously the bloodiest battle of the war. I am pleased that I was not crippled and can walk again. For the pain caused by the scoundrels I will send as many of them as possible to hell. You are now fully informed. Because you still have not left, if I cannot see you personally, we can still write each other.

Adieu, my dear old friend.

Cordially yours,

Hecker

The first of 1st Lt. (later Capt) Rudolph Müller's private letters to Colonel Hecker follows. Despite the regiment's losses and the criticism heaped on Germans of the Eleventh Corps by Anglo-American editors and soldiers, Müller was proud of the regiment's performance in its first battle. The lieutenant's claim that someone in the 82nd Illinois shot General Stonewall Jackson is, of course, incorrect.

Capt. Rudolph Müller, Company D, previously 1st Lt., Company E (courtesy of Jerome L. Hunt)

Camp *near* Brooke's Station
May 18th, 1863

Colonel Friedrich Hecker,

I am writing to you with cordial wishes for a speedy recovery. After we pitched our camp about one mile from our previous one, we made it homelike. Salomon and Eugene wrote to you before I did. The latter gave me a brotherly embrace; however, I do not know what I have done to deserve it.[28]

Panse will have informed you of everything worth knowing, so there remains little for me to say. The change of camp has had a good effect on the men. Instead of being in the midst of the dilapidated and empty huts of the old camp, which naturally made us ponder the fates of many of our former comrades, we now live on a pretty, open hill surrounded by woods. The headquarters of Schurz and Schimmelfennig are located nearby.

Regrettably, Fuchs has resigned. Greenhut is on leave. Marx and Schloe[t]zer have returned. Brendel will depart as a result of the return of Schloe[t]zer.[29] As I learned today, the official news is that our whole army will remain quiet a long time and await replenishment of the regiments through conscripts. Whether remaining idle is wise, I dare not judge. It does not make sense to me. As a result of the above-mentioned news, I have requested 15 days leave and would like to go to Philadelphia; however, Eugene told me that I would no longer find you there. Then I would go to St. Louis and would like to visit you at your farm.

Our wounded in the *hospital* are well situated and receive all necessary care. I visit the hospital almost daily. Babst is significantly better today; he still has the bullet in him. Likewise, Balck still has the bullet stuck in his wound; it cannot be removed and is very sensitive for him. Hoppe has a slight leg wound and feels better. From my company 4 of 46 men died; 15 were wounded, of whom 7 were captured and paroled, 2 were captured unwounded. Two of the wounded each had a leg amputated. Unfortunately, my orderly, Zais[s]er, a brave man, is also among the dead. He volunteered for a reconnaissance mission and fell victim to an enemy bullet.[30]

The opinion about us appears to be gradually becoming more favorable. A real pity that our brave regiment, and one can boldly call it that, came under fire for the first time under such unfavorable circumstances. Unfortunately, we could not prevent what happened with the best of wishes, and if a mistake was actually made, (it appears to me) it was that we did not retreat earlier and in an orderly manner. We have proven, however, that we can stand up like all the others. The 26th Wisc., ours, and 157th New York were the only ones that stood against the first attack. Under a terrible crossfire and nearly being encircled, ours was the last that yielded. Jackson was out in front, so that is why it is not improbable that someone in our regiment shot him. In any event we must hold onto the *claim* of the fortunate shot.[31]

With high esteem, I remain,
Yours truly,
Rud[olph] Müller, Lt.

The writer of the letter dated Camp Schurz, May 7, 1863, published in the *Illinois Staats-Zeitung* on May 14, 1863, accurately summed up the situation with respect to the 82nd Illinois Regiment at the Battle of Chancellorsville: "Our regiment conducted itself well, better than most others. What we lacked was only a general. According to the judgment of all experts the deployment of our army corps was terrible."

Unfortunately for Hecker's regiment and the Germans in the Eleventh Corps, the reports that first appeared in the *New York Times, New York Herald,* and many other major English-language newspapers blamed the loss on the "cowardly Dutchmen" of the so-called German Corps, even though only half the corps consisted of Germans and no small corps in its position could have performed much better in the circumstances. A *Times'* correspondent erroneously reported: "But to the disgrace of the Eleventh Corps be it said that the Division of General Schurz, which was the first assailed, almost instantly gave way. Threats, entreaties and orders of commanders were of no avail. Thousands of these cowards threw down their guns and soon streamed down the road towards headquarters." A *Herald* correspondent also blamed Schurz's division for "the disastrous and disgraceful giving way," and stated he was told the men, "fled like so many sheep before a pack of wolves." Smaller newspapers picked up the story from these New York papers and it was spread throughout the North. Private letters from soldiers in other corps often blamed the Germans for the defeat and ridiculed them as cowards, although these commentators had been far from the scene of Stonewall Jackson's overpowering attack. Generals Schurz and Schimmelfennig and other German officers protested to higher authorities about the falseness of the claims and wanted their names and those of their men cleared but to little avail. Hooker, Howard, and the rest of the Army of the Potomac were content to let the Dutchmen take the blame for the defeat.[32]

On May 6 the *Chicago Tribune* printed the allegations made in the *New York Times* and *New York Herald,* but the next day, to its credit, cautioned its readers to wait for more details before rendering a judgment against the Germans because they had fought courageously in earlier battles and some Americans had fled before the enemy in other battles including the Battle of Bull Run (First Manassas).[33]

Christian Keller found, "in the weeks to come the English-language press would attempt to assuage the Germans and erase the falsehoods created by its over-hasty reactions to the defeat at Chancellorville."[34] For example, on May 28, 1863, prompted by a complaint from General Schurz, the New York Times printed a letter from the correspondent who had written that Schurz's division, "almost instantly gave way," stating that he was in error. "Yet," as Keller avers, "the damage had been done, and no amount of apology could erase the first impression created in German and non-German minds. . . . The morale of the Germans, and their ardor for the Union, would never be the same again."[35]

The German American press displayed a rare unity in its outrage over the charges made against German fighting men and their commanders. Keller's recent research into wartime German-language newspapers uncovered "attempts to disprove the allegations, defend the courage of the soldiers, and place the blame for the defeat where it supposedly belonged."[36]

On May 7, 1863, the Illinois Staats-Zeitung tried to refute the allegation in the New York Times by explaining which regiments and commanders were German and which non-German and how the regiments and commanders reacted to the attack. The Staats-Zeitung declared: "Today we want to show through some preliminary data how unjust it is to blame the misfortune on the 11th Corps, which was thrown back by Stonewall Jackson's troops, who were four times greater in number, in particular to lay the blame on the Germans, and to speak of 'cowardly Dutchmen' in the manner of the correspondents of the New York Times." After identifying which units in the Eleventh Corps were German and which were not, and which ones stood and fought and which ones did not, the editor proclaimed: "However, we do not imitate the evil example of the Times correspondent; we make no hateful distinctions between nationalities; we draw the above parallels merely to show how groundless, disreputable and stupid it is to make the Germans specifically responsible for the disaster and supposed ignominy of the Eleventh Army Corps of the Army of the Potomac."

As Christian Keller points out, the ugly and demeaning experience of Chancellorsville forced German Americans in the North "first to defend themselves, and then to look to one another for solace and support. They would continue looking inward after Gettysburg." The Chancellorsville affair, asserts Keller, was a "severe jolt" for German Americans in the North, "on the road to Americanization."[37]

Six

The Battle of Gettysburg

fter his army's great victory at Chancellorsville, Gen. Robert E. Lee devised a plan to carry the war onto Northern soil. Lee's main objective was to draw the Army of the Potomac from the line of the Rappahannock River and disrupt its plans for a summer campaign. Lee intended to engage the Yankee army in battle if a favorable opportunity presented itself, because only a military victory, particularly in a Northern state, offered the military and political gains critical to striking a possibly war-changing blow to Northern morale. Secondarily, as Gettysburg historian Scott Hartwig explains, "Pennsylvania offered a rich landscape untouched by war, where Lee could supply his army and accumulate additional supplies for the fall. This would relieve Virginia from the burden of feeding his army and allow that state a respite from the occupying armies."

Therefore, on June 3, 1863, while the Eleventh Corps and the rest of Maj. Gen. Joseph Hooker's Army of the Potomac remained in defensive positions north of Fredericksburg, General Lee quietly began withdrawing his Army of Northern Virginia from Fredericksburg in order to invade Pennsylvania.[1]

Hooker began shifting his army northward on June 12, at which time it was at least forty miles behind Lee's most advanced divisions. By June 17 Hooker stood halfway between Lee's army and Washington, D.C. Lee's army continued marching northward and by June 27 was on Pennsylvania soil. The Federal army's seven infantry and one cavalry corps were concentrating in central Maryland on June 27, and that same day General Hooker offered his resignation as army commander over a dispute with General Halleck concerning the use of troops guarding Harper's Ferry, West Virginia.[2] To Hooker's surprise, President Lincoln accepted his resignation and on the next day Lincoln selected Fifth Corps commander Maj. Gen. George Gordon Meade to head the Army of the Potomac. This forty-eight-year-old Pennsylvanian resolved to find and engage Lee's army. That night Robert E. Lee learned that the Army of the Potomac had reached Frederick, Maryland, and ordered his army to concentrate east of South Mountain in

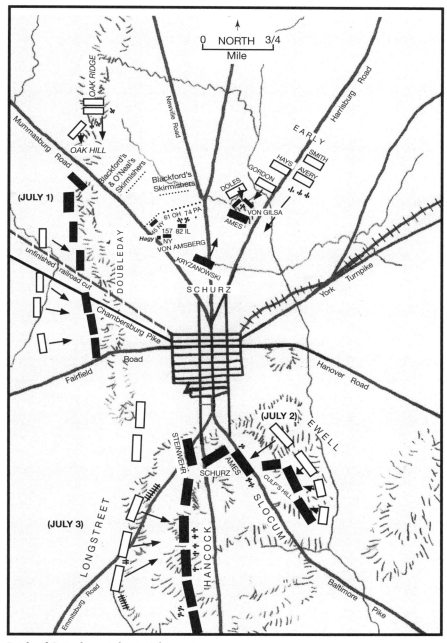

Battle of Gettysburg, July 1 to July 3, 1863

the Cashtown–Gettysburg area to prevent Meade's army from cutting off his line of communication to Virginia and to draw the Unionists north where Lee might have an opportunity to fight them on ground of his choosing. Lt. Gen. James Longstreet's corps and Maj. Gen. A. P. Hill's corps began moving east from the Chambersburg area and Maj. Gen. Richard S. Ewell's corps headed southwest from Carlisle and York.[3]

At approximately 7:30 a.m. on July 1, Brig. Gen. John Buford's pickets began exchanging fire with the van of Maj. Gen. Henry Heth's division of A. P. Hill's corps about three miles west of Gettysburg. By 10:30 a.m. the Confederate infantry had pushed Buford's stubborn troopers back to McPherson's Ridge (located northwest of the town). The Union's First Corps hastened north through Gettysburg and deployed on McPherson's Ridge. The First Corps faced west except for the far end of its right flank, which faced north. By 11:30 a.m. the First Corps had repulsed attacks by two brigades of Heth's division. Unfortunately for the Union side, Maj. Gen. John F. Reynolds (the Right Wing and First Corps commander) was killed early in the fighting. Maj. Gen. Abner Doubleday assumed command of the First Corps, while command of the Right Wing devolved to Maj. Gen. Oliver O. Howard. In turn, command of the Eleventh Corps shifted to Maj. Gen. Carl Schurz; leadership of Schurz's Third Division transferred to Brig. Gen. Alexander Schimmelfennig; and Col. George von Amsburg of the 45th New York took over Schimmelfennig's First Brigade (which included the 82nd Illinois).[4]

Marching from near Emmitsburg, Maryland, early that morning, the van of Schimmelfennig's Third Division reached Gettysburg at approximately 1:00 p.m. and proceeded to take a position on the First Corps's right flank. The trailing First Division, (now commanded by Brig. Gen. Francis C. Barlow) was ordered to connect with the right flank of Schimmelfennig's division. The Second Division (von Steinwehr's) remained in reserve on Cemetery Hill, one-half mile south of the town.[5]

Colonel von Amberg's First Brigade moved up to the right of the First Corps between the Mummasburg Road and the Carlisle Road. The Mummasburg Road veered northwest from the north–south Carlisle Road. The 45th New York advanced onto the open plain and pushed out a skirmish line of four companies, with their left on the Mummasburg Road and facing Oak Hill. Its remaining six companies moved up later.[6]

Schurz had been ordered to seize Oak Hill to extend and protect the right of the First Corps but the Confederates were already there. Page's Battery and a battalion of Alabama sharpshooters halted the aforementioned New Yorkers after an advance of about 400 yards. Brig. Gen. George P. Doles's tough brigade of Georgians backed up both the artillery and the Alabama sharpshooters located in

von Amsburg's front. Capt. Hubert Dilger's Ohio battery followed the New Yorkers onto the plain, intending to silence the enemy battery. The 61st Ohio and 74th
Pennsylvania advanced and extended the First Brigade's skirmish line over to the
Carlisle Road; however, there were too few men to form a normal line of battle.
Colonel von Amsberg initially posted the 157th New York and the 82nd Illinois
in reserve, with the 157th near the Hagy farm. Because the 82nd's official report
of the battle is missing, it is difficult to ascertain precisely the movements of the
regiment. Historians have generally reported that most of the afternoon the 82nd
supported the batteries of Capt. Hubert Dilger and 1st Lt. William Wheeler, whose
13th Independent New York Battery came up after Dilger's. Two of the letters that
follow immediately provide new details about the actions of the 82nd not previously published in English. Unfortunately, they do not tell the full story.[7]

Col. Krzyzanowski's Second Brigade of the Third Division moved up on von
Amsburg's right but not far enough to connect with the latter's skirmish line. After
Capt. W. J. Reese's four 3-inch rifled guns arrived at Oak Hill and opened up on
Schimmelfennig's division, Lt. William Wheeler's battery of rifled guns came forward and dropped trail on Captain Dilger's right. Dilger advanced his six Napo-
leons a few hundred yards and after his guns resumed firing Lieutenant Wheeler
moved his guns forward and again unlimbered them to Dilger's right. The 157th
New York and the Second Hecker Regiment moved up to continue to support
the batteries. Colonel von Amsburg's brigade was subjected to aggressive enemy
artillery fire and musketry in its position, which was devoid of any natural or
man-made protection.[8]

The First Division's commander, Francis C. Barlow, who had replaced Brig.
Gen. Charles Devens Jr. after the Battle of Chancellorville, led his division from
the town up to Blocher's Knoll (now known as Barlow's Knoll), ahead of and too
far to the right to connect with Krzyzanowski's brigade. After Howard refused
to send Schurz reinforcements to fill this gap, Schurz ordered Krzyzanowski's
brigade to advance and cover the gap Barlow had created.[9]

Meanwhile, around 1:30 p.m., after Confederate artillery had bombarded the
First Corps and Eleventh Corps off and on for ninety minutes, Rebel infantry attacks on the First Corps resumed. The First Corps repulsed the attacks, but new
Confederate brigades entered the fight around 2:30 p.m. and pressed the First
Corps's divisions back to Seminary Ridge in bitter fighting. During this period,
Maj. Gen. Jubal Early's division (Ewell's corps) approached Barlow's two brigades
on their right, and after strong initial resistance, Barlow's troops began a disor-
ganized retreat. Colonel Krzyzanowski advanced his brigade in an effort to support Barlow, but in a close-range firefight with Brig. Gen. George Dole's brigade
of Georgians, the Confederates prevailed and Krzyzanowski's line melted away.

Schimmelfennig dispatched the 157th New York to attack Doles's right flank but Doles's brigade changed its front and decimated the outgunned New Yorkers. Its line broken, the Eleventh Corps began to retreat toward Gettysburg.[10] While Schimmelfennig's and Barlow's divisions were retreating, Howard finally sent Col. Charles R. Coster's brigade of von Steinwehr's division into battle. It hastily deployed at the brickyard on the northeastern edge of the crossroads town. Coster's regiments were soon chewed up by the Confederate brigades and the survivors joined the mass of soldiers, wagons, and guns trying to make their way through the crowded and unfamiliar streets of Gettysburg while pursued by the victorious enemy troops. Renewed attacks on the First Corps at Seminary Ridge began about 3:00 p.m.[11] The blue-clad Unionists fought hard until a Confederate regiment penetrated through a gap in the corps's defensive line and unhinged it, forcing a final retreat. By 4:00 p.m. both Union corps were streaming back to and through Gettysburg.[12]

Most of the retreating Federals made it back to Cemetery Hill, but not all. Of approximately 20,000 engaged, slightly more than 9,000 were killed, wounded, or captured. Some of the Federals were killed and a large number were captured in or near the town. Although many commentators have called the retreat a "rout," it did not reach that degree. The First Corps's and Eleventh Corps's retreats ended when the exhausted soldiers reached Cemetery Hill on the southern edge of Gettysburg. The two corps had lost the battle on July 1, but their sacrifices had gained valuable time for the rest of their army to arrive on the high ground, giving the Army of the Potomac the advantage of an excellent defensive position, with good interior lines and good communications. Despite fighting reasonably well under extremely difficult circumstances, the Eleventh Corps was again criticized, especially by some members of the First Corps, who blamed the "Dutch" corps for not holding the right flank. Considering that Schurz had too few men to adequately defend the northern approaches to Gettysburg, no good defensive cover, and that the enemy held all the commanding terrain, the criticism is unjustified.[13]

By mid-morning on July 2 all but the Sixth Corps had arrived and the army lay in a line resembling an inverted fishhook. The shank was anchored at Little Round Top and ran north for approximately a mile and a half along Cemetery Ridge. It then curved around Cemetery Hill and Culp's Hill, ending on the southeastern end of the latter eminence. The Eleventh Corps's divisions on Cemetery Hill generally faced in a northerly direction, forming most of the curve in the fishhook, with Schurz's division on the left. To the Eleventh's immediate left was the Second Corps and on its immediate right was a division of the First Corps.[14]

Meanwhile, in response to enemy sharpshooters firing from houses about one-half mile distant from Cemetery Hill, General Schurz ordered Lieutenant

Colonel Salomon to send one hundred men to capture the houses. As mentioned in Capt. Matthew Marx's letter, presented below, the combat team successfully completed its mission. Capt. Joseph B. Greenhut led the group of volunteers and later recalled that they "stormed those houses driving out those sharp-shooters, and keeping possession of those houses the balance of the day."[15]

At about 3:30 p.m., Southern artillery opened up on the Union's left and when it ceased at 4:00 p.m. Longstreet's corps assaulted Little Round Top and much of Cemetery Ridge. Longstreet's divisions gained ground through fierce and bloody fighting but failed to break the reinforced Federal line. Southern batteries began to bombard Cemetery Ridge and Culp's Hill around 4:00 p.m. but were silenced by counter battery fire. Then, when it was almost dark, three brigades of Maj. Gen. Edward Johnson's Confederate division (Ewell's corps) attacked Culp's Hill from the east. Brig. Gen. George S. Greene's brigade of the Twelfth Corps repulsed the attacks from its high, well-placed entrenchments on the main hill, although Brig. Gen. George H. Stuart's Rebel brigade captured the lower summit. The 82nd Illinois and three other regiments from its brigade plus three regiments from the First Corps reinforced General Greene after he requested help around 7:00 p.m. General Schurz reported that his four regiments entered the woods and "drove the enemy from our rifle-pits."[16]

Soon after fighting on Culp's Hill began, Maj. Gen. Jubal Early dispatched two brigades to attack the eastern slope of Cemetery Hill and held one in reserve. Maj. Gen. Robert R. Rodes's division was supposed to attack its western slope at the same time. Early's troops soon ousted two battle-weakened Eleventh Corps brigades at the foot of the hill. Hand-to-hand fighting raged around two batteries in the darkness atop the hill as their Union artillerists and infantrymen of the Eleventh Corps (who had hastily retreated up the slope and rallied around the batteries) battled the Southerners. Several regiments from von Steinwehr's division and a brigade from the Second Corps hastened to the scene and fell upon the nearly victorious Rebels, who were driven off. General Rodes of Ewell's corps cancelled his division's planned attack against the western slope of Cemetery Ridge, sparing lives on both sides.[17]

Action on the third day of the battle (July 3) began at 4:30 a.m. when twenty-six Twelfth Corps guns on Culp's Hill opened up on the enemy in the captured breastworks as blue-clad infantry prepared to launch an attack down the slope. Edward Johnson's division beat the Federals to the punch, however, and attacked at daylight. This attack failed, as did thrusts at 8:00 a.m. and 10:00 a.m. By 11:00 a.m., Johnson knew that he could not take Culp's Hill and began withdrawing what was left of his command. Confederate infantry did not attack the Eleventh Corps's position and therefore the 82nd Illinois was not engaged in the day's fighting. Colonel

Hecker missed the fighting on July 1 and 2, but returned from medical leave in time to command his regiment on July 3.[18]

Lt. Gen. James Longstreet was supposed to launch a massive attack on the Union left or left center on the morning of July 3, in conjunction with General Johnson's attack on Culp's Hill. Fortunately for Meade's army, it was delayed. When Lee arrived early in the morning Longstreet was not ready and advised Lee against the attack. Lee modified his plan and ordered a major attack on the Union center. This attack was delayed for some time while Johnson's troops fought on Culp's Hill. By 11 a.m., the Rebel soldiers were exhausted and withdrew across Rock Creek. Confederate artillery finally commenced firing about 1:00 p.m. and the infantry attack commenced around 3:00 p.m. Longstreet's force comprised Pickett's newly arrived division of his own corps and eight brigades from A. P. Hill's corps, about 13,000 men in all. General Pickett's famous charge, which really should be called the Pickett–Pettigrew charge, failed to break through the Union center on Cemetery Ridge and Robert E. Lee's army headed back to Virginia the next day having suffered its first major defeat of the war.[19]

Three days of slaughter at Gettysburg cost the Army of the Potomac almost 23,000 killed, wounded, and missing out a force of 88,000 troops and the Confederacy suffered more than 22,000 casualties out of its force of 75,000 soldiers. The Eleventh Corps lost 3,800 men out of approximately 8,200 engaged. Approximately 1,400 of the Eleventh Corps losses were missing or captured. The 82nd Illinois suffered 4 men killed in action, 19 wounded, and 89 missing out of 310 officers and men engaged in the battle. Although the regiment incurred the least number of casualties in its brigade, it had the third highest of the number of missing. Twelve of its missing died in Confederate prison camps.[20]

The following letter refers to actions of Company H of the 82nd Illinois, and its author is identified only as R.

Illinois Staats-Zeitung
July 11, 1863
Camp of the Hecker Regiment by Gettysburg
July 5 [1863]

Before our departure (because the order has already been issued) I tell you in a hurry that we arrived in Gettysburg at 1 o'clock in the afternoon after a forced march on July 1. Our strength was diminished by strain and hunger. After we saw the first house of the city, the command sounded "double quick." We marched on the double quick to the scene of the battle. We stood in the reserve at the beginning; later, two companies of the regiment were released and took part in the fight.

We fought for two hours but due to the enemy's overwhelming power we had to withdraw behind the town where we took a strong position. We had 2 officers wounded and 2 missing during this clash. The horse that Lieutenant Colonel Salomon had received as a gift in Chicago was shot in the lower body; he was injured falling from his horse, but not severely.

The enemy attacked us on July 2, but they were so overwhelmingly blasted to pieces by our side that you can have no idea of the dead that still lie on the battlefield even now. The ground is sown with dead on all sides where the battle raged. I have seen it. A horrible sight! Even the most vicious nativists will not be able to maintain that the 11th Corps fought other than excellently.

We attacked the enemy with hurrahs and subjected them to devastating fire. Lt. Colonel Salomon's horse was shot in the body in this affair. It was the horse on which Colonel Hecker was wounded at Chancellorsville, thus the second one. He, however, was not hurt.

Our losses in dead and wounded are light, but we lost more men as prisoners because many soldiers remained in the houses of the city for too long on the first day. Lt. Charles W. Biese and Capt. [Emil] Frey [both from Company H] were wounded [only captured]. Lt. Schröder and Lt. Hepp are missing and presumed captured. Colonel Hecker returned to us again. We are marching off in haste.[21]

In a hurry.

    Yours,

    R. [unidentified]

In the preceding letter, R. mentions that "two companies of the regiment were released and took part in the fight," but does not identify the specific companies or exactly when they took part in the fight. Capt. Matthew Marx of Company D states in the following letter that after he joined his company and Company K, which were both supporting Dilger's battery, he "suddenly saw that Lieutenant Colonel Salomon led our regiment into the fire composedly and coolly." The captain added, "I saw how the Rebels came out of the bush down the hill in masses and how our boys hastened to meet the enemy with shouts of joy and hurrahs. That is the 11th Corps! I saw the Rebels fall into disarray and when the enemy saw our boys he screamed, 'oh distress,' as a large crowd of them fastened a white handkerchief on a pole, threw away their weapons, and surrendered."[22] The preceding statements lead the editor to believe that Salomon may have advanced at least two companies of the 82nd Illinois to support the left wing of the 45th New York about 1:30 p.m., when the New Yorkers poured heavy fire into a line of Confederates, who unknowingly exposed their left flank, while attacking the extreme right flank of the First Corps. The surprised Confederates who were not killed or wounded retreated or surrendered. Whether Salomon's companies caused any enemy casualties is unknown.[23]

Writing from the 82nd's camp near Boonesboro, Maryland (forty miles southwest of Gettysburg), Capt. Matthew Marx praised Lieutenant Colonel Salomon highly in his detailed letter covering the campaign and Battle of Gettysburg.

Illinois Staats-Zeitung
July 20, 1863
Camp by Boonesboro, Md.
July 8, 1863

At 3 o'clock in the afternoon on June 12 we suddenly received an order to march, and marched immediately through Maryland to Pennsylvania. Our march lasted 19 days and only a few were rest days. We only had these [rest] days because our general had to wait for further orders; he knew our destination just as little as the soldiers. He had only received orders to arrive at a certain place at three o'clock in the afternoon, and camp until further orders.

As is known, Colonel Hecker was absent and Lieutenant Colonel E. S. Salomon commanded the regiment. The officers and the men already had respect for Lieutenant Colonel Salomon, and he also won their affection during this march. He led the regiment with such calmness and care that instead of tiring [us], the march was a true picnic, like in Wright's Grove, lager and ladies excepted.[24] If only the rain had not marred our fun. After the first 3 or 4 days of marching, which were hardly bearable with the terrible heat and the dust, it started raining, with only short interruptions. With very few exceptions, the farther we advanced the worse the road became, until we came upon a sort of German causeway. Very soon, however, we had to march across fields again, where there was no road and our pioneers tore down fences and had to build bridges over brooks and rivers. The part of Maryland that our army marched through is a true paradise, and the residents should enjoy one of the best harvests that the fields have ever generated, except where our army destroyed them with our camping sites. I lamented over the nicest wheat fields that we marched through or camped in and that our animals used for grazing.

On June 30 we reached Emmitsburg, pitched our camp on a clover field at the skirt of a forest, and expected a rest day on the following day, July 1; however, the god of war had decided otherwise. That night, at eleven o'clock, our regiment's adjutant came to my dog hut (which the American generals call a shelter tent). Adjutant Weigel has grown in importance since he has been in the army and has changed from a boy into a man.[25] He had to duck so low to see into my tent that he soon fell headlong over my hut and awakened me out of my wet slumber (we lay, of course, in rainwater 6 inches deep), while he very softly called into my tent: the lieutenant colonel wants to see the officers immediately. We pulled ourselves together. Long Haunes (as my former sergeant was called, whose name has now changed to Lieutenant Berthold [Barthold] Kruckenberg)[26] and I met in front of the first lieutenant's tent, who told us quietly that the order had just been issued that we should hold our men ready because we must depart that night. In spite of that we lay the whole night in the camp on alert; no further marching orders came.

As the rainy morning broke, the hope arose that we would not need to march in the rain, but that was not to be. The potatoes the soldiers had received for the first time in months, and that were half rotten, were barely half cooked when we heard the signal: "So we live, so we live, so we live each day!"—this is our brigade's signal—and immediately after that the signal to decamp and march sounded. The potatoes were cut up and in a hurry the soldiers picked up the few cooked pieces from the clover field and ate them with great *Oier* [?]. At that moment many a soldier did not think about the fact that he might not number among the living that evening or would lie on the battlefield with crushed arms or legs.

We marched to Gettysburg, Pa., on the double quick without resting, where the 1st Corps was already under a punishing fire beyond the city. Recently, and particularly on this march, I had been ill, and near Gettysburg could not go farther. Dr. Brown gave me a certificate, so I could be picked up by an ambulance.[27] Ambulances followed the division, so I had to wait for one to come by. However, I soon met a local farmer, who told me that Gettysburg was only a half-mile distant and that the 1st Corps was engaged in a desperate fight there. I now summoned up all my strength and hurried to my regiment. It was an impressive sight to see how the women and girls of Gettysburg tried to give our troops refreshments while they were marching through the city (but we had no time for that, because the troops marched through on the double quick), and how they also washed off the blood, bandaged up, and attended to the wounded.

I reached the regiment as it was forming up in line of battle on the extreme left wing of our corps. Our lieutenant colonel told me that my company [D] and Company K had been detached to provide support for Dilger's battery, and I should join them. I went there immediately. Once there, I found the troops lying flat on the ground to protect themselves from the Rebels' terrifying bombs, shells, and case shot. The enemy batteries directed crossfire at Dilger's battery, the one they feared the most.

I stood for a while to look over the battlefield and suddenly saw Lieutenant Colonel Salomon leading our regiment into the fire, composedly and coolly. I saw how the Rebels came out of the bush down the hill in masses and how our boys hastened to meet the enemy with shouts of joy and hurrahs. That is the 11th Corps! I saw the Rebels fall into disarray, and when the enemy saw our boys they screamed, "oh distress," as a large crowd of them fastened a white handkerchief onto a pole, threw away their weapons, and surrendered. However, at the same moment, the balls of the enemy batteries whizzed past my ears, so I found it best to lie down. I heard the deadly small-arms fire and the enthusiastic shouts of our troops while lying there. Suddenly, I heard a horrible scream, a second and a third, which followed a frightful wail. I raised my head and saw Ernst Fuhrmeister, my sergeant, without any legs. A ball had torn one completely off and smashed the other one to pieces at the knee. The blood ran in streams and the violent [illegible word] the bone. Emil Giese lay just behind me with a shattered leg and next to Friedrich Kallenbach [Calmback], who likewise had a shattered leg. Finally, John Boher [Bolken] crawled using his hands and feet; blood streamed from his head and back, and all this happened within 10 minutes. Gustav Giese, my sergeant now, rushed immediately to help his brother, ignoring the terrible rain of bullets, in order to take him to the hospital in Gettysburg, where he was later captured by Rebels. He was paroled and, as I hear, is supposed to be in Chicago. Sergeant[s] Fuhrmeister and Kallenbach [Calmback] died that evening from loss of blood. Emil Giese's leg was amputated above the knee and I hear that he is in good spirits and out of danger. Heinrich Meins [Mignell], the bugler, had his already once amputated arm made a bit shorter because a minnie ball smashed it. He lay near Emil Giese, and I was told he is out of danger and cheerful, considering the circumstances. I sent an extra attendant from the company for both men, so they could receive good care.[28]

Soon, however, the scene on the battlefield changed. The Rebels had received reinforcements and attacked with such masses that the corps had to give way, in spite of the 11th Corps, and particularly our boys, refusing to retire. Upon Lieutenant Colonel Salomon's encouragement, the men retired in the best order after the signal was given and marched as if on the parade ground. They were engaged by the pursuing Rebels in the city and fired on by them in the crowded streets. Lieutenant Colonel Salomon suffered internal injuries when his horse was shot dead and fell on him. Captain Heinzmann brought him out of the street and to our ambulance. The fate of the regiment, however, lay close to his heart, because after several hours, feeble and sick as he was, he assumed command again.[29]

General Schimmelfen[n]ig's horse was also shot[?]; he was cut off from the brigade, which was already out of the city. He therefore hid in a woodshed for three days without food and drink, in order to avoid being captured by the Reb-

els. He was protected by his overcoat (a private soldier's overcoat), which prevented the Rebels from seeing his stars. They thought he was a private and did
not bother themselves with him because they had the city and he could not get
out of it.[30] The Rebels now had possession of the city and made prisoners of our
sick and wounded who were still there. This was the end of the first day (July 1).
The troops were now deployed in a new and more advantageous line of battle
on different hills south of Gettysburg. Various corps arrived, took positions, and
slept with their weapons in battle formation.

The next day at 4:00 p.m. the Rebels attacked our center and a terrible cannonade soon raged. Our regiment lay between four batteries. The balls fell around
us like snowflakes, and killed Dr. Schloetzer's horse, Adjutant Weigel's, and one
of Colonel Hecker's, which stood just behind the front of our regiment.[31] You
should have seen how our brave Lieutenant Colonel Salomon stood in front of
the regiment so calmly, like we were having a dress parade, laughing and joking
with the officers and soldiers, and how our boys laughed and joked among one
another that the Rebels aimed so poorly that most of the balls went over us; however, one hit in our regiment and smashed into the head of a soldier of Company
K, who was killed immediately.[32] Toward evening, after the Rebels were driven
away from our left flank by heavy fire and severe losses in dead and wounded,
they flanked our right wing and our regiment came under fire again.

I was not with them because I was the officer of the day in charge of the brigade guard, which had occupied the outer houses of the city, and whose assignment was to maintain effective rifle fire at the Rebels who occupied the adjacent
houses, and to shoot every enemy officer and soldier within range. I had to go
from house to house and bullets whistled past my ears as soon as I showed myself. One bullet ricocheted; it was flattened and hit me in the right shoulder. It
caused only a small bruise.

Our detachment returned the next morning and took up a position in the
line of battle in order to lie anew under the terrible rain of balls; we lay there the
whole day. In the evening the Rebels tried to storm a battery on our right wing
and also Capt. Dilger's battery, in the center. They launched a desperate bayonet charge but were bloodily repulsed. The officers and soldiers of our regiment
have informed me that on that evening (the 2nd) after the Rebels attacked our
right flank one snuck up quite near and grabbed our flag in order to steal it, but
through the alertness of our soldiers he was shot dead.

That night [afternoon] our men lay behind a stone fence and Lieutenant Colonel Salomon stood on it during the heaviest fire to observe the effect of our fire,
continuing to encourage and exhilarate our men, as if they were shooting at a
target. Thus went the third day of battle.

Skirmishers on both sides exchanged several shots on the morning of the fourth; otherwise it was quiet. All at once the news spread that the Rebels had fled during the night, abandoned the city and the battlefield, and only left behind their pickets and several batteries to deceive us, and that they intended to move across the Potomac and Rappahannock as fast as possible. However, we were already on their heels again. We left our campsite, marched all day and night, and now stand firmly opposite them again. Also, the news just arrived that they fled again. Whether we must follow them is still uncertain.

We captured 30,000 [12,200] prisoners and the battlefield is sown with dead Rebels. All the stables and barns in and around Gettysburg are full of wounded Rebels.[33] We also lost many men. I calculate about 18,000 [22,800] were killed, wounded, and missing.[34] I cannot give an exact report of the casualties in our regiment because we still are on the march and no morning reports are available. I took 2 officers and 30 men into the battle with me and brought 16 back. Among the dead are Sgt. Fuhrmeister and soldier Kallenbach [Calmback]. Wounded: Sgt. Greenwald, slightly, in the foot; Corporal Bringel [Briegel], slightly, in the finger; Corporal Bolken, grazed on his head and back. Bugler Memmel [Mignell] in the arm, amputated. Emil Giese, left leg shattered, amputated; Anton Karsten [Carstons], bruised on the chest by a shell.[35] Captain Marx, a rebounding shot hit his right shoulder blade. The rest are missing. The officers and soldiers showed themselves to be soldiers and men; the new lieutenants have all especially given great effort.

To the regret of our entire regiment, an order from Gen. Howard has detached our lieutenant colonel to command the 153rd Pa. Regiment, 1st Division, our corps. Colonel Hecker will command our regiment again.[36]

Respectfully,

M. Marx, Capt.

In a private letter to his family, Adj. Eugene Weigel described his wounding on July 2, 1863, and contrasted Lieutenant Colonel Salomon's leadership with Colonel Hecker's. Weigel was born in 1845 in Kirchheim in Rhenish Bavaria, and came to America in 1848. In September 1861, at sixteen, he enlisted in the 3rd Regiment United States Reserve Corps in St. Louis, and mustered in on October 31, 1861, in Rolla, Missouri. In January 1862, his regiment consolidated with the Gasconade Battalion to form the 4th Missouri Infantry Regiment; Weigel served in Company A. His regiments served in central and southwestern Missouri. Private Weigel was discharged on September 14, 1862, to become adjutant of the 82nd Illinois Infantry. Adjutant Weigel was commissioned as a captain on August 3, 1863, but not mustered in at that rank until May 12, 1864. The competent young officer served on Brig. Gen. Alpheus Williams's staff as an aide-de-camp

Capt. Eugene F. Weigel, Company F (Scherer's Photographic Studio, 1862. Courtesy of Missouri History Museum, St. Louis.)

during the Carolinas campaign. He mustered out on June 9, 1865. On June 25, 1866, he was brevetted with the rank of major.[37]

Headquarters 82d Regt. Ill. Vols.
Boonesborough [Boonsboro], Md.
July 9, 1863

My dears,[38]

I finally have some time to write to you because we have been on the march the entire time. Unfortunately, my [horse] Charly was shot dead in the Battle of Gettysburg, while I was saved only by a miracle. On the 2nd we occupied a position in a graveyard behind the city, and the Rebels tried their hardest to drive us out of there. They showered us with a true hail of bullets and shells, and

there were cracks, howls, and hisses as if all of the devils in hell were let loose. Of
course, our batteries answered just as strongly. In the battle on the 1st my horse
was quite calm and made nothing of the bullets. On the 2nd he was quite crazy,
so that I had to dismount and hold him by the reins. As I stood there, a 6-lb. ball
went through the breast of my horse and hit me in the stomach, so that I was
hurled back 3–4 feet and was carried back [to the rear] only half conscious. It
turned out okay; the next day I was with the regiment again. My stomach is still
blue today as a result. My canteen was full of water and saved me. It was smashed
as flat as a pancake but repelled the ball. The Rebels suffered terribly; their dead
covered the ground by the thousands. It was good that we got away from there
because the stench was unbearable. I am sorry that my horse is gone; however,
I immediately replaced it with a Rebel horse that is not as good, but it trots very
well. It belonged to a Rebel doctor and is a gray horse named Pauline.

Lieutenant Colonel Salomon acquitted himself excellently and is very popular; he stands out favorably compared to the "Old One [Colonel Hecker]" because he acts coolly and composedly, while the latter immediately gets excited
and makes an awful fuss. Since he has been back he has already been afflicted
with his paranoia again. He thinks the whole world wants to have him out of the
way. Fortunately, Dr. Börner [Boerner] arrived here yesterday and I am pleased
to have him as our doctor.[39]

Our men have to endure terrible strains. Without shoes, half starved, battle
fatigued, and soaked daily by rain, they have had to constantly march, and advance 34 miles a day.

Yesterday, the Rebels were driven back in a very lively *Cavalry* battle. Lee is
supposed to have occupied a position ten miles from here. If we defeat him there
soundly, the campaign will hopefully be at an end. I received a letter today from
Lou.[40] Because I have little time to write, you must advise her of this letter.

Our regiment numbers 200 muskets, our brigade 900, and the division 1,700.

Until later, Adieu and kisses to all of you, yours,

Eugene [Weigel]

The 82nd Illinois and its corps joined in the pursuit of Lee's defeated army
back into Virginia, commencing on July 5. The regiment marched south to Emmitsburg and Middletown, Maryland, then northwest to Williamsport, back to
Middletown, then south to Warrenton Junction [now Cavelton], Virginia, located approximately fifty miles southwest of Washington D.C. The 82nd and its
corps arrived at Warrenton Junction on July 25, 1863, then engaged primarily in
guarding the Orange and Alexandria Railroad in the vicinity of Warrenton.[41]

Seven

After Gettysburg to Chattanooga

With some exceptions, the Anglo-American press did not portray the retreat of the Eleventh Corps on July 1, 1862, in the negative manner that they did the Battle of Chancellorsville. Some even praised the corps's soldiers for fighting bravely before being forced to retreat. German American editors praised their native landsmen's contributions to the victory at Gettysburg. As Christian B. Keller states, "from their viewpoint . . . the honor of the Germans had been vindicated by their soldiers' battlefield performance, and the slurs of the nativists had been refuted."[1] Nevertheless, the so-called German Corps and its German American fighting men received some harsh criticism from soldiers in their own army, and this, argues Keller, "biased earlier Gettysburg scholars against the Germans perpetuating the 'cowardly Dutchmen' idea." This negative stereotyping of German Americans and the Eleventh Corps at Gettysburg by some historians continued well into the twentieth century. Within the last three decades several scholars, such A. Wilson Green, D. Scott Hartwig, David G. Martin, and Keller, have studied the Eleventh Corps's performance at Gettysburg and concluded that the German Americans fought as well as they could, given the situation into which they were thrown. The first three historians named focused on the corps as a whole; Keller went further and examined the actions of the primary German American regiments from Pennsylvania, the 27th, 73rd, 74th, and 75th regiments of the Eleventh Corps. He also looked at the performance of the 98th Pennsylvania of the Sixth Corps on July 2. Keller's impression was that these five Keystone State regiments acquitted themselves well in the battle.[2] Other regiments, such as the 26th Wisconsin and 45th New York, also fought well and no one has pointed a finger at the 82nd Illinois as shirking its duty.[3] Of course, not all German Americans or, for that matter, all Anglo-Americans or other nationalities fought as hard or retreated as calmly as other soldiers from the same places of birth.

Even today, the alleged cowardice of the German soldiers at Gettysburg has not faded. Battlefield tours now incorporate Major General Schimmelfennig's hiding place, which is identified by a historical marker. Not letting the facts get in the way of a good story, licensed battlefield guides at Gettysburg still tell the story of General Schimmelfennig hiding in a "pig sty" in Gettysburg for several days to avoid capture. The editor experienced this himself. Although the general hid by a woodshed next to a pig sty, the story has been changed to say that he hid in a "pig sty," and that he had earlier donned a private's coat to hide his rank, indicating cowardice.[4]

Following the Battle of Gettysburg, eight Anglo-American regiments were attached to the existing brigades of the Eleventh Corps, diluting the corps's German element. The aforementioned regiments previously belonged to Brig. Gen. George H. Gordon's Second Division of the Fourth Corps in the Department of Virginia; General Gordon was placed in charge of the First Division, Eleventh Corps. General Schimmelfennig requested a transfer out of the Army of the Potomac and was assigned to command the First Brigade (formerly von Gilsa's), First Division, Eleventh Corps. On August 5, 1863, the First Division was ordered to South Carolina for duty.[5]

The Second and Third divisions of the much-maligned Eleventh Corps left the Army of the Potomac on September 25, 1863, as part of a large relief force sent to Tennessee to help lift a Confederate siege of Maj. Gen. William S. Rosecrans's Army of the Cumberland at Chattanooga. Rosecrans's army had retreated to Chattanooga after its disastrous defeat in the Battle of Chickamauga, fought in northern Georgia on September 19 and 20, 1863.[6] The rest of the relief force consisted of the Twelfth Corps and four divisions from Maj. Gen. Ulysses S. Grant's command in western Tennessee.[7] Maj. Gen. Joseph Hooker commanded the Eleventh and Twelfth corps (16,000 troops), and Maj. Gen. William T. Sherman led the divisions coming from the west (17,000 troops).[8] Major General Grant was appointed to overall command at Chattanooga and he replaced Rosecrans with Maj. Gen. George H. Thomas.[9]

On September 25, 1863, Colonel Hecker's Illinois regiment marched to Manassas Junction, Virginia, with its division, and climbed into railroad cars for the 1,200-mile journey to Bridgeport, Alabama, near Chattanooga. The infantry of the Eleventh Corps detrained at Bridgeport on October 2 and waited for orders to move to Chattanooga.[10]

On October 19, 1863, while the 82nd Illinois was still camped at Bridgeport, Colonel Hecker was elevated to command of the Third Brigade of the Third Division of the Eleventh Corps, and the 82nd Illinois transferred to his brigade. The

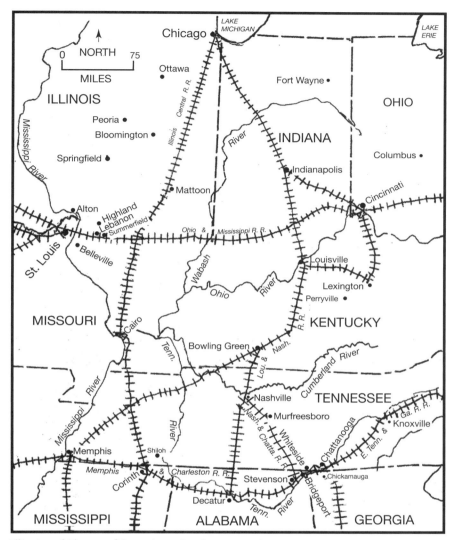

Illinois and Theater of Operations, October 1863 to August 1864

new brigade consisted of the 80th Illinois, 82nd Illinois, 75th Pennsylvania, and the 68th New York. Only the 80th Illinois was not a German regiment.[11]

The Eleventh Corps remained at Bridgeport until the night of October 27, when it, followed by Maj. Gen. John W. Geary's Second Division of the Twelfth Corps, crossed the Tennessee River and marched toward Chattanooga. The Eleventh Corps linked up with Brig. Gen. William B. Hazen's brigade of the Army of the Cumberland on the afternoon of October 28 at Brown's Ferry (located about a mile and a half west of Chattanooga by land but nine miles distant by the Tennessee River). Hazen's command had driven off the Alabama troops guarding the landing at Brown's Ferry on the night of October 26–27. This operation opened up a desperately needed supply line into Chattanooga.[12]

After the Eleventh Corps had encamped by Brown's Ferry, Confederates attacked Geary's Twelfth Corps division about 11:00 p.m. at Wauhatchie, Tennessee (about three to four miles south of Brown's Ferry). Geary's soldiers repulsed the Confederates in nighttime fighting before the Eleventh Corps's brigades sent to their assistance arrived.[13]

The 82nd, its division, and corps settled down in the Lookout Valley until November 22, working on entrenchments and enduring shelling by Confederate batteries located on Lookout Mountain. The following unsigned published letter describes the regiment's operations between November 22 and December 19. On November 23 the 82nd Illinois and its brigade engaged in skirmishes on November 23, when its corps advanced to Citico Creek near Orchard Knob to cover the left flank of the Fourth Corps, which had just seized that eminence and its entrenchments. The 82nd Illinois and its division functioned in a reserve role during the siege-breaking battles of Lookout Mountain and Missionary Ridge, fought on November 24 and 25, 1863, respectively. The Union achieved its stunning victory on the 25th, when four divisions of the Fourth Corps of the Army of the Cumberland stormed up the long east face of Missionary Ridge, driving off the Confederates entrenched on its crest.[14] Almost immediately after the siege was broken, Major General Sherman undertook an expedition to aid Maj. Gen. Ambrose Burnside's two corps at Knoxville. By the time the relief force reached Maryville, Tennessee, on December 5, however, word arrived that Burnside had repulsed Lt. Gen. James Longstreet's Virginia corps on November 29, 1863, and most of the Federal expeditionary force, including the Eleventh Corps, returned to Chattanooga.[15]

———————

Illinois Staats-Zeitung
January 7, 1864
Camp near Brown[']s Ferry
December 19, 1863

The battles around Chattanooga were fought, the campaign ended, and we, the ever-present 11th Corps, returned on the 17th of this month to our peaceful old camp, after a time of horrible deprivation and of the greatest exertion, of which only the persons involved could have an idea. So on to it. We received marching orders at 2 o'clock in the afternoon on Nov. 22. The orders directed us to take only the barest necessities and only for approximately three days, after the end of which we would probably return to our camp. Because the weather was very pretty and warm, the orders were followed only too well. That evening we moved to our corps's designated position, in the familiar line of battle, forming the left center of the corps. The battle began on the 23rd, around 1 o'clock, and around three o'clock we received orders to advance. Then one-half hour later we were in the battle. It is not my intention to give you a report of the battles around Chattanooga, because it would be late, but I want to restrict it to give you some details of which you perhaps are not aware.

The 82nd Ill. had the honor to open the dance for our brigade (Hecker's). Two companies advanced as *"Skirmishers,"* and after several hours of lively fire were instrumental in pushing the enemy back to the other side of a *Creek* [named Citico].[16] You probably know this from different reports in which it was disclosed. The regiment lost 2 men from Company B in this *engagement: Private* Zander, wounded in the hand, *Private* Nicolay, dead. This was the total loss of the regiment

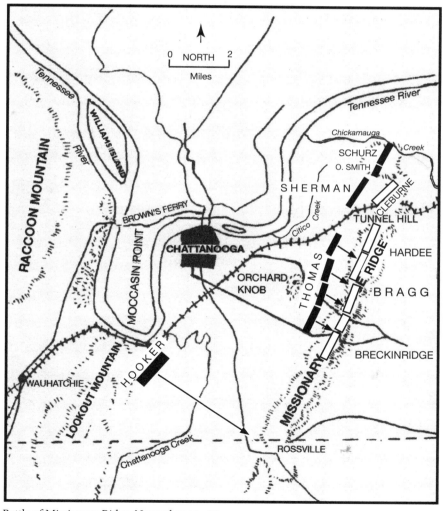

Battle of Missionary Ridge, November 25, 1863

during the battle. The 80th Illinois of our brigade, which relieved us (82nd) on the morning of the 24th, was less fortunate and lost 7 men, some lightly, some severely wounded. Among the latter was a lieutenant whom I fear will not live. This is all I know about casualties of our brigade.[17]

On the morning of Nov. 24 we had a lively *Skirmish* on our front but it was quiet the rest of the day and only single shots were fired. While we maintained the position we had won on the 23rd, Hooker went to work on Lookout [Mountain], which he, as you know, took with few casualties.[18]

On the morning of the 25th our line advanced up to the enemy *Rifle Pits* with insignificant resistance, then we received the order to hasten to reinforce Sherman. We arrived there toward 1 o'clock in the afternoon by marching in the double quick. I cannot help but impart to you the danger of this affair, in which the 27th and 73rd Pa. Reg. of the 2nd Division, Bus[c]hbeck's Brigade, took part on the morning of the 25th, and that took place under the following circumstances. When the connection between the 11th Corps and Sherman's corps was established, the above-mentioned (German) regiments were ordered, in conjunction with a division of Sherman's corps, to storm a mountain [Tunnel Hill] on which a Rebel fort stood and which covered their right flank. While Sherman's troops operated from one side, the veterans of the 11th Corps stormed it on the other side, under the leadership of a brave officer, Lieutenant Colonel Tafft [Taft] of the 143rd N.Y. Regt., who was temporarily commanding the 73rd Pa. Their bravery was in vain. Perhaps only 5[00]–600 men strong, they were repulsed by devastating flank fire from a far stronger enemy. Lt. Col. Tafft [Taft] was killed at the head of his command; the 73rd Pa. brought back about 90 out of 300 men. The 27th Pa. lost about 100 men. Most wounds of the 73rd were on the left side, those of the 27th on the right side; proof of how well the Rebels let their flank fire play.[19]

The 11th Corps, whose participation in the battle ended during the afternoon of the 25th, and from then on formed the reserve of the 15th [Corps], may have lost perhaps from 400–450 men in all. I must remark here that I indicated the losses of our brigade as 2 wounded of the 75th Pa. Regt. That is too low, our total losses were 11 men. On the evening of the 25th the [b]attle[s] of [around] Chattanooga ended. Bragg was in full retreat and we won a victory that will transform the rebellion with its impact, and through which it will bleed to death, if perhaps ever so slowly. Grant's skillful maneuvering of his troops, the demoralization of the enemy troops, and Bragg's incompetence, resulted in a victory accomplished with few battles and low casualties.[20]

At 4 a.m. on the 26th we ended our pursuit of the enemy and camped near Johnston's Station, perhaps 13 miles this side of it [three miles from Graysville], where we arrived late in the night. During the entire march we had the opportu-

nity to see traces of the Rebels' hurried retreat. Broken wagons, abandoned ammunition and provisions, etc., were everywhere. On Nov. 27 we marched above
Johnston's Station to Parker's Gap (also Taylors [Taylor's] Gap). [Illegible sentence.] Our brigade and one from the 2nd Division, both under command of
Colonel Smith, commander of the latter, had to depart after a short rest and pro-
ceed to Red Clay Station to destroy the R.R. and depot there, in order to prevent
the possibility of Longstreet rejoining Bragg. We arrived there toward evening
and immediately began the work of destruction, even though we were extremely
fatigued. We ripped up the rails for about 2 miles and set fire to the ties, the depot,
and several wagons. After this, we began the march back, which proceeded very
slowly. Meanwhile, it began to rain. Because we had to travel over a very steep
route it was very hard for Dilger's battery to advance.[21]

We reached Taylor's Gap around 11 p.m., dead tired because we had little rest
that day; we had marched about 28 miles in some terrible weather and over bad
roads. We rested on Nov. 28 to give the commissaries the opportunity to provide
us with provisions; however, I must confess that no one received any rest that day
because it was ice cold, rained very hard, and most of the men, because of the order
received on Nov. 23 (see above), were too poorly equipped to protect themselves
against the inclement weather, so no one even remotely thought about rest.[22]

Up until now we have experienced quite a lot. We have been short of rations,
made a tiring march, were soaked to the skin many times, have frozen like a dog,
etc., and many believed their troubles were at an end, because they presumed a
march back to the camp. However, they soon realized that they had been bitterly
deceived and found out that up to then they had just experienced the preliminaries.

The men received 12 rations for 3 days on the evening of the 28th and were
informed by a general order that they would still have to exercise patience for
a short time and endure the privations, stresses, and strains, until our brothers in Knoxville were free from all danger. They were being strongly pressed by
Longstreet. We broke camp the next morning to go to Burnside's relief under the
command of Sherman and in the following order of march: Sherman's corps on
the right, Granger in the center, and we, the 11th Corps, on the left.[23]

Toward evening our corps arrived in Cleveland, once a pretty place, which now
bears the traces of the destruction of the war. We camped close to the city in an
open field over which an ice-cold wind blew, and soon the temperature dropped
to North Pole–like. It was a horrendous night. I believe the cold allowed 5 minutes
sleep at most in spite of all our fatigue; at least that was the case with me.[24]

On November 30 we marched to Charleston on the double quick without rest,
reaching there about 2 o'clock in the afternoon. We encountered the enemy's cavalry for the first time in Charleston. They immediately crossed over the Hiawassee,

burned the R.R. bridge, and busied themselves on the other side of the river un-loading several railroad cars full of provisions; however, they were disturbed by several well-aimed shells from our side.[25]

Because of the destroyed bridge we had to remain in Charleston until the morning of Dec. 1, during which time the necessary repairs were made. We then crossed the Hiawassee (a rather large, important tributary of the Tennessee), where we took the provisions left behind by the Rebels on that side, consisting of *Meal, Corn Meal,* and some salt. Even though there was too little for us, it was favorably received because the rations previously provided to us, as you can easily understand, had been consumed long since. After the provisions were dis-tributed to the troops, we moved above Riceville to Athens, where we arrived in the evening and pitched camp approximately 2 miles beyond. Athens is a lovely, friendly little town and at the same time also a decidedly Rebel nest.[26]

On December 2 we marched over the *Hidway* [Highway?] leading to Sweet-water and to Philadelphia. We passed Philadelphia in the evening and marched about 2½ miles farther, then made camp late in the dark night. Our cavalry had small encounters with the enemy near Sweetwater and Philadelphia; several men were lost, if I do not have a false report.[27]

We decamped at 4 o'clock on the morning of the 3rd and reached Louden around daybreak. Earlier, this little city was a significant repository of provisions for the Rebels and was strongly defended by several forts. It appears to have recently been of significant value to Longstreet, in spite of the fact that the large railroad bridge over the Tennessee had been totally destroyed.[28]

Our sometimes forced marches of recent days gave the Rebels a disastrous surprise and left them barely time to destroy their munitions and provisions, as well as to plunge a railroad train of 3 locomotives and 43 cars into the Tennessee. A rather large part of the provisions still fell into our hands. This time besides meal, we received freshly baked biscuits, *Crackers,* pork, and hams. These provi-sions came to us at a very convenient time; we were all famished, because our entire nourishment up to that time consisted only of the little we had captured in Charleston. Moreover, we had taken several hundred prisoners, including a hos-pital full of sick patients, which gave them an opportunity to meet their brothers, whom our corps had picked up during the march from Chattanooga. This might raise the total number of them 15[?]—1,500. Still more cavalrymen remained in a fort on the opposite bank of the Tennessee. Dilger's battery sent over several greetings now and then, which meanwhile remained unanswered.[29]

On December 4 our brigade, including our regiment (82nd Ill.), was ordered to carry out a sham maneuver and reconnaissance. The brigade marched to the bank of the Tennessee and deployed in line of battle, while our regiment crossed the river in two old, rickety *"Flatboats."* We crossed over by company. Luckily, after two companies had arrived on the other bank, they advanced immediately toward the above-mentioned fort and, after several rifle shots, the entire garrison of about 20 cavalrymen fled. Meanwhile, the rest of the regiment crossed over and took possession of the fort. We found ammunition worth several thousand dollars and bagged a flag as well as six cannons, four of which were spiked. Our purpose was achieved and we returned the same way to London [Loudon]. The purpose of the sham maneuver was to make the Rebels believe that we would cross over at Loudon, while a bridge was being built for this purpose several miles above there. We camped by Loudon that night and I had the opportunity to sleep under a cover for the first time during this whole campaign, something I had always done earlier under the open sky without a tent. It was a pleasure.[30]

At 2:00 a.m. on December 5 we broke camp and crossed over the Tennessee about 9:00 a.m. on the above-mentioned bridge. This bridge was a splendid concoction about a ¼ mile long, consisting of wagons procured in the area and overlaid with boards so small that only two men could march on it side by side. Horses, wagons, etc., had to go through the water. The water was 3–4 feet deep here at its highest. This same day we reached the camp near Louisville [Tenn.], i.e., about 16 miles from Louisville.[31]

Our mission had ended, Longstreet was retreating to Virginia, and Burnside, thanking Sherman and his command for their prompt help, requested only Granger's corps for reinforcement to pursue the enemy. The other two corps were ordered back to Chattanooga. Our corps began its return march on Dec. 7. We passed the familiar wagon bridge about noon, and because the headquarters here had learned that a detachment of Wheeler's cavalry intended to destroy the bridge in Charleston, it was again our brigade that had the pleasure to double quick to that place.

We arrived in Charleston at 2 o'clock in the afternoon on the 9th. The cavalry had disappeared and the bridge had been destroyed. We crossed over in *Flatboats* and moved into a nice Rebel camp, where we remained several days and repaired the bridge. Shortly before reaching Charleston, we met Frank P. Blair and his entourage on the way to Washington.[32]

When the rest of our corps joined us we decamped and marched to Cleveland, followed by a significant number of Negroes consisting of men, women, and children, who had attached themselves to our corps in Athens and its environs. They had probably tired of their old masters. We pitched our camp in Cleveland about noon and rested until the next morning. Here we received for the first time, in a long, long time—Oh splendid! ! !—coffee, sugar, salt, and *Crackers* that had been sent to us from Chattanooga.

We marched again on the 16th. We arrived on the evening of the 17th at our old *Quarters,* and I can assure you it was time. The troops could not have held out much longer. We have suffered horribly. In a region devastated by two armies marching through it, where guerillas have resided for years, and the residents themselves have nothing to quiet their hunger, it is hard, very hard, to maintain an army for about three weeks, depending only on what can be foraged and seized from a very hostile enemy.[33]

We frequently made the day's strenuous march with empty wagons, and, although dead tired, could not sleep because of the cold. In the mornings, while preparing for the march, we did not once have a cup of hot coffee to warm our shivering bodies against the cold. A large number of the troops were totally worn out. Pants, jackets, shoes, all were ruined. We marched over 200 miles and a considerable number of the men were barefoot. I walked several days in totally torn up shoes and other officers of our regiment marched two days in their socks.

C. L. [probably 2nd Lt. Carl Lotz of Chicago.]

———

The 82nd Illinois and its division moved out of the Lookout Valley on January 25, 1864. The 82nd and its brigade relocated their camp to Whiteside, Tennessee; another brigade moved to the south side of the Tennessee River opposite Bridgeport, Alabama; and the third one camped at Shellmound.[34]

Meanwhile, General Hooker's official report of the Battle of Wauhatchie had been published in various newspapers and Colonel Hecker incorrectly believed that in one passage General Hooker had made an attack on his honor (regarding the brigades in Schurz's division not reaching General Geary's division at Wauhatchie before the battle ended). Hecker demanded a court of inquiry to clear his name. The court opened on January 29 and ended on February 15, with Hecker not being censured, "because the strictures contained in General Hooker's official report were not intended to apply to him or his command."[35] On February 17, 1864, Colonel Hecker received a leave of 20 days to go home to Illinois to attend to personal business. On March 13, the colonel submitted his resignation from the army stating his health was poor and he had important matters to take care of on his farm. Maj. Gen. George H. Thomas approved his request on March 17, 1864. General Howard opined that the real reason for the resignation was that he had not been promoted to brigadier general. Hecker's friend Gustav Struve attributed his departure to "injured dignity."[36]

Whiteside, Tennessee

*S*hortly after Colonel Hecker departed for Illinois on leave, 1st Lt. Rudolph Müller began writing the colonel to update him about what was happening in the regiment and to communicate details of battles and operations. The first four of his private letters appear below.

Born in Soest in the Rhineland Province of Prussia in 1835, Rudolph Müller immigrated to the United States at age seventeen and was working in a dry-goods store in Peoria, Illinois, when the war broke out. By enlisting on April 25, 1861, the five-foot, ten-inch, light-haired, blue-eyed, native German was among the early entrants into the Union army and mustered into the three-month 8th Illinois Volunteer Infantry Regiment at Springfield as a private. The predominately Anglo-American 8th Illinois mostly guarded railroad bridges spanning the Big Muddy River near Cairo, Illinois. When his enlistment ended on July 25, 1861, Müller returned to civilian life rather than joining the large majority of the 8th's members who enlisted in the new three-year 8th Illinois Regiment.[1]

The ambitious former private began recruiting a company of men for Hecker's new regiment early in August 1862, but fell short. After he and his contingent of forty-two recruits entered Camp Butler near Springfield, they combined with a slightly larger group of volunteers recruited by Robert Lender of Bloomington, a native of Pullendorf in Baden. This unit became Company E of the Second Hecker Regiment. Lender was elected captain of the new company and Müller became its first lieutenant. Lieutenant Müller was detached from his company on October 7, 1863, to serve as an aide-de-camp at the Third Brigade's headquarters and returned to the regiment after he was promoted to captain on March 12, 1864; on April 1, 1864, he became the commander of Company D. As far as is known, Rudolph took part in all the campaigns and battles of the 82nd, and he mustered out with the regiment on June 9, 1865. He received a brevet promotion to major retroactive to March 13, 1865.[2]

Rudolph Müller was likely not a Forty-eighter because he was only thirteen or fourteen years old during the German revolution; however, he was a Turner. He held a radical Republican viewpoint as evidenced by his letters. His friendship with Hecker and others in his regiment surely reinforced his strongly felt political views.[3]

———

Headquarters, 3rd Brig.[ade] 3rd Div.[ision], 11th Corps
Whiteside, Tenn.
February 23th, 1864

Dear Colonel Hecker,

It is very dull here since you have been gone. Apart from that everything is the same as when you left. Yesterday, a sensational dispatch came again from Corps. Cleborn's [Cleburne's] div.[ision] of the *Rebel Army are [is] reported at Lafayette, etc.* Frank took a *Cavalry* patrol over the mountains to Trenton. I rode with 5 men via Murphy['s] Hollow up to Trenton but could not learn anything new.[4]

McGroarty is here and wants to make a reconnaissance this afternoon. Howard came through yesterday. S[c]hurz is in Shellmound and is leaving for New York today. Grünhut's [Greenhut's] resignation was *approved* at Corps; he went there himself. Frank's Resg. [resignation] is back from Tyndale but sent in anew. [Hermann] Panse's leave was *approved* at the div.; therefore, he is not drinking any more water in order to work up a nice thirst when he arrives at the farm. Lt. Carl, Co. K, has also resigned, *disapproved* by Tyndale, as well as Frank's attempt, until the Veteran Regts. [Regiments] come back!! All Tyndale.[5]

The opinion of the *Court* is still not here.[6]

Warm greetings to your family. Regards.

McGroarty says he will try to use his influence to replace you.

You loyal friend, Rudolph Müller

Headquarters 3rd Brig. 3rd Div., 11th Corps,
Whitesid[e], Tenn.
February 24th, 1864

Colonel Hecker,

S[c]hurz and Robinson are away.[7] Eugene is the AAAG [acting assistant adjutant general]. Hector Tyndale is the absolute ruler in the div. and his *Scepter* for 25 days is certain. The men were under arms for 2 nights at Bridgeport and Shellmound, while we, after we convinced ourselves that the entire rumor was a *hoax,* slept peacefully. Hector is crazy, he sees 500,000 Rebels in every wooded hill. He was here today. Also, today, the poor fat Spraul had to go from Bridgeport up to Bus[c]hbeck in order to see if any patrols or *Scouts* had contacts.[8]

Rumors are circulating about where we will go. Nothing official. Greenhüt [Greenhut] brought news yesterday from the corps that even in Lafayette there was no sign of the enemy. Our *Scouts* have gone up to 6 miles past Trenton. Just now, 11:30 p.m., *Scouts,* who had been sent out to Frick's Gap about 20 miles back, reported no enemy there; however, a *Citizen,* who a *Scout* knew was reliable, and who was coming from Lebanon, had heard heavy firing there in the direction of Coffee Town at the mouth of Saute Creek (Tenn. River) about 10 miles above Ganter'sville [Guntersville], (reputedly Rody's Reb.[el] *Force*). No enemy is in Lebanon.[9]

McGroarty is very active. He would like to transfer from us to *the Cav.[alry]* Gottlob goes to Springfield tomorrow with 4 men (*to conduct recruits*).[10]

> Your trusted friend,
> Rudolph Müller

> Whitesid[e], Ten[n].
> *March* 10th, 1864

Dear Colonel:

McGroarty left today to go to Ohio with his regt.[regiment] Command of the brigade was transferred to Lt. Col. A. von Steinhausen. The 68th [New York] is occupying Ft. Heinzman on Sand Mtn., and has added about 62 recruits. Maj. Kummer is commanding the regt. Prince Salm[-]Salm was commissioned as colonel of the regt. but will not be mustered. He lives in New York.[11]

Kriszanowsky [Krzyzanowski], who entered New York decked out like an ox and was led through the streets crowned with a garland, is in Shellmound. I hear that on the 2nd of this month, the 75th Pa. was still in Philadelphia and is commanded by Mattsdorf [Matzdorff].[12]

This morning I fetched my little wooden box from Chattanooga containing excellent arrack. If you only were here again! Panse takes your place for the time being and drinks for you. However, I will reserve a bottle for you.

I saw Lt. Kaufmann from the 24th Regt., whose losses in the *Skirmish* near Tunnel Hill were only slight. Mihalotzy lies in Chattanooga severely wounded, shot through the right arm into the right breast. The bullet was not removed until 8 days later.[13]

I now begin to count the days until your return and hardly need to say how much we will all enjoy the day you return again. I send regards to your family and my best wishes for Arthur on his engagement.[14]

What do you have to say about publication of Gen. Order No. 9, Headquarters 3rd Brig. regarding Grünhut's [Greenhut's] resignation. Salomon must make use of everyone with *éclat*. Gr[eenhut] certainly has not done that himself.[15]

Those remaining from our staff are well. The *Provost's* nose glows more beautifully than ever and serves as the moon at our nightly *Picket* visitations. The men perform their duty well. We have put them to the test at each hour of the night.[16]

We have installed an embrasure in the entrenchments on the right; now the entrance to Murphy's Hollow can be completely covered. Enemy desertions are frequent, mostly *Cavalry*.

Yours,
Rudolph Müller
1st Lt. and A. A. A. G.

Colonel Hecker tendered a letter of resignation, dated March 16, 1864, while he was at home on sick leave, and it was accepted on March 21, 1864. General Howard noted with his endorsement that "Col. Hecker has been a good and energetic officer."[17] Rudolph Müller became aware of his colonel's resignation before he wrote the following letter, in which he reveals he is leaving his position as aide-de-camp at brigade headquarters. His departure from brigade headquarters is likely related to Col. James S. Robinson's appointment as brigade commander after the resignation of Colonel Hecker.[18] Even though he was promoted to the rank of captain on March 12, the leader of Company D is dejected and uncertain of his future. One reason for Rudolph's gloom is his extreme dislike for Lt. Col. Edward S. Salomon, whom he calls the "*Creole* from Jerusalem." Müller, as the letter reveals, is too proud to play up to a superior officer for a position, and much of his animosity toward his Jewish commander is based on Salomon's constant self-promotion with his superior officers and catering to certain officers under him.

Headquarters, 3rd Brig., 3rd Div., 11th Corps,
Whiteside, Tenn.
March 27th, 1864

Dear Colonel:

I am writing today for the last time from *Headquar.*, 3rd Br[ig]. The enclosed copy gives the details.[19] For the time being I am going back into the regt. and want to wait and see how the wind blows. Eugene wrote to me this morning that he put in a good word for me with Tyndale and advises me to pay my respects to him because he doesn't remember me exactly. However, I cannot do that—begging?

No. My sense of honor will not allow it, so he can find me if he needs me. Schurz is expected back; much could be said about that.

It is uninteresting and *gloomy* here since you departed, dear colonel; it is to all of us as if our lucky star had disappeared. I have no repose anywhere and have lost all desire. The same with Panse, who seeks to suppress his dolefulness through the familiar gallows humor. It is not otherwise.

I am in conflict with myself about my next move. I don't want to leave the regiment, don't want to give up and leave the game to the *Creole* from Jerusalem. Having to serve under him, whom I despise from the depth of my heart, is bitter. Then again, it appears that my duty is to remain with our flag, and to join in with the few brave officers so that they will remain free of the stain.

In the hope that you arrived home safe and sound and that I will hear from you soon. Regards to your family.

With affection and respect,

> Yours truly,
> Rudolph Müller, Capt.

Several important changes in the leadership and organization of the Union army occurred while the Second Hecker Regiment served at Whiteside, Tennessee. On March 2, 1864, Ulysses S. Grant was commissioned a lieutenant general and on March 17 was appointed commander of all United States' armies. This promotion prompted Grant to move east, where he could control the vast Army of the Potomac and work on his plan to quash the rebellion. Grant transferred command of the western armies to his protégé, Maj. Gen. William T. Sherman, who in turn selected Maj. Gen. James B. McPherson to head the Army of the Tennessee.[20]

Lieutenant General Grant believed that to win the war quickly the enemy's armies had to be destroyed, and on April 4 he ordered Sherman "to move against Johnston's army, to break it up and to get into the interior of the enemy's country as far as you can, inflicting all the damage you can against their resources." The general-in-chief left the planning of the campaign in the west up to Sherman. But Grant directed him to start his campaign at the same time the Army of the Potomac moved against Robert E. Lee's Army of Northern Virginia and to keep up the pressure so that Johnston could not send reinforcements to Lee. He would likewise keep hammering at Lee.[21]

On April 4, 1864, the unlucky Eleventh Corps and the Twelfth Corps passed into history in a reorganization that created a new Twentieth Corps. The new corps consisted of the former Twelfth Corps divisions of Brig. Gen. Alpheus S. Williams and Brig. Gen John W. Geary and a newly formed division commanded by Maj. Gen. Daniel Butterfield. The two former Eleventh Corps divisions were broken up and distributed among Williams's, Geary's, and Butterfield's divisions. A fourth division assigned to the Twentieth Corps served on post or garrison duty but never physically joined the others. Former Twelfth Corps generals commanded the First, Second, and Third divisions. Each division of the Twentieth Corps contained three brigades and approximately 8,000 officers and men present for duty.[22]

Maj. Gen. Oliver O. Howard became commander of a new Fourth Corps, while General Schurz was sent to head a camp of instruction for newly levied regiments near Nashville, Tennessee. The 82nd Illinois was assigned to the Third Brigade of the First Division of the new corps. Other regiments in the Third Brigade were the 101st Illinois Volunteer Infantry, 61st Ohio Veteran Volunteer Infantry, 82nd Ohio Veteran Volunteer Infantry, 45th New York Veteran Volunteer Infantry, and the 143rd New York Volunteer Infantry. Brig. Gen. Hector Tyndale and Brig. Gen. Alpheus S. Williams commanded the Third Brigade and the First Division, respectively.[23]

The 82nd Illinois remained at Whiteside, Tennessee, guarding the railroad throughout April of 1864 and waited for the start of a new campaign.

Nine

The Beginning of the Atlanta Campaign

By early May 1864, Maj. Gen. William T. Sherman had assembled most of his nearly 110,000-man grand army in and near Chattanooga and was waiting for Lieutenant General Grant's orders to move against Gen. Joseph E. Johnston's army. The Federal force comprised Maj. Gen. George Thomas's Army of the Cumberland consisting of the Fourth, Fourteenth, and Twentieth Corps—72,000 troops; Maj. Gen. James B. McPherson's Army of the Tennessee, consisting of the Fifteenth Corps and two divisions from each of the Sixteenth and Seventeenth Corps—24,000 troops; and Maj. Gen. John Schofield's small Army of the Ohio, consisting of the Twenty-third Corps—13,000 troops. Johnston's 54,000-man Confederate Army of Tennessee was massed at Dalton, Georgia, shielding the Confederacy's important railroad center, storehouses, and manufacturing facilities at Atlanta. Lt. Gens. William J. Hardee and John Bell Hood each commanded a corps. Johnston's army had 145 guns, just over half of Sherman's total. The numbers were clearly in the Federals' favor. Sherman's objectives required him to take the offensive. Joseph E. Johnston's strategy was to get his adversary to attack him in well-fortified positions, repel those attacks with great losses to the Federals, and then pursue the weakened Union army and crush or capture it. The result was the grueling Atlanta campaign that lasted over 100 days and cost both sides heavily.[1]

The warm spring weather, the burgeoning leaves, and blossoming flowers cheered the blue-clad soldiers as they began repositioning for the new offensive. Col. James S. Robinson now led the Third Brigade because Brig. Gen. Hector Tyndale had left the brigade on sick leave on May 2, 1864. The 82nd Illinois left Whiteside, Tennessee, on May 3 in the company of several other regiments of its brigade and arrived at Trickum P.O. on May 7, where the remainder of the First Division

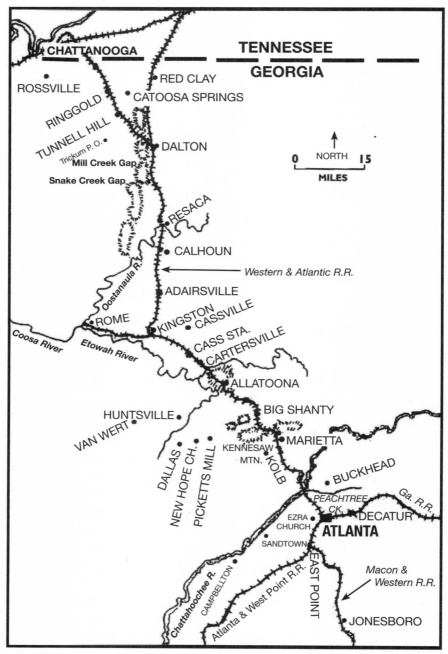

The Atlanta Campaign

was encamped. Fighting took place at Rocky Face Ridge beginning on May 8 but the 82nd Illinois and its brigade were not involved. During the night of May 10–11 the 82nd Illinois departed for Snake Creep Gap with its corps to reinforce the Army of the Tennessee. Sherman had sent McPherson through Snake Creek Gap hoping to get behind Johnston's army. Unfortunately for the Federals, the Confederates withdrew to Resaca before the Unionist force could slide in behind them.[2]

Capt. Rudolph Müller's first surviving letter of the Atlanta campaign informed Colonel Hecker of military movements and fighting, an interesting offer from Colonel McGroarty, and the return of Lt. Col. Edward S. Salomon after a long absence.

———

Camp at Snake Creek Gap, John's Mtn.[3]
May 11th, 1864

Dear Colonel,

Until today we have served only as a *Reserve* and have seen no enemy. There were sharp *Skirmishes* on the 2nd and 3rd. Bushbeck's brig. in Geary's div. lost about 300 men, 30–50 killed and the rest wounded on the afternoon and evening of the 9th [8th].[4] Butterfield stood before Buzzard Roost, where the 26th Wisc. skirmished with the enemy and Lt. Ju[e]nger received a flesh wound in the leg.[5] Geary was 5–6 miles (south of there) on the right with orders to reconnoiter; instead, he launched an unsuccessful attack on the very steep rocky heights (Rocky Face) with B.[uschbeck]'s brig., and lost many brave men. The *Ridge* is steep like *Look Out* [Lookout Mountain] and it is difficult to ascend even without baggage, knapsacks and weapons. I heard that Geary is under arrest because of the affair [not true]; however, little is said about it. I do not believe the rumor. Meanwhile we lie near Trickum's P.O., with our front facing east.

I last wrote to you from our camp near Taylor's Ridge on the 6th of this month [letter missing]. We finally moved at daybreak over Taylor's Ridge through Nic[k]ajack Gap. Butterfield moved right and parallel to us and went over the *Ridge* about 4 miles farther south. We halted for 3–4 hours in Dogwood Valley, 1½ miles from Trickum P.O., during which time a fight took place on Tunnel Hill. Our troops [were] on Tunnel Hill, the enemy on the next chain and continuous *Skirmishing* flared in the valleys in between.[6]

The 61st [Ohio] arrived on the 8th [7th?] with 240 men.[7] McGroarty told me yesterday that he wanted to take over command of the brig. and to have me as— imagine—*Topographical Engineer*. I told him, of course, that I would not be able to measure up to the position, because I am not an architect; however, he thought, *We will try it anyhow*. Should he really get the brig., I will go with him in any case. He would be more pleasant than Salomon, who arrived on the 9th *minus* recruits. The reception was very cool on all sides; I was as much amazed, as inwardly pleased. The *boy's* [*boys*] did not give him any *Hurrah*s, although it was suggested (rightly so!). The gentleman [Salomon] found the letter I wrote to you some time ago (regarding the responsibility), [he was] no doubt polite, but the politeness concealed his rudeness. His position in the regt. is no longer as rosy as before. He is generally seen through and he also knows everyone has found him out. Riese [Reese], earlier Adjutant of the 24th [Illinois], has enlisted as a *private* of the 82nd. What do you say to that? Surely Lt. Col. Salomon has a commission up his sleeve, and he stated that he would not hesitate to make Riese [Reese] a major if there was an opportunity.[8]

The 15th & 16th Corps are supposed to have destroyed the R. R. at Resacca [Resaca], and cut off the enemy's R. R. *Communication* with Atlanta. The *Gaps* are all occupied, and Johnston's army cannot fall back on Atlanta [only a rumor]. Shouldn't it be in the plans for Thomas, whose headquarters were at Tunnel Hill yesterday, to press the enemy toward South Carolina in order to make the capture of Atlanta easier for us? Scolfield [Schofield] and Howard on our left hinder him from going in the direction of Knoxville. It must be interesting for you to see the same movement conducted that you had suggested during the winter. I am eager to see whether a general attack on Dalton will occur or whether we will starve out the wretches in the Dalton basin. I believe the former. Our position, the 1st Div., is close to the western base of the *Ridge* at Johns Mtn. about 2 miles southeast or on the same elevation as Tilton. The regt. serves as support for Wütherich's [Wiedrich's] *Battery*.[9]

> With best regards to you,
> Rudolph Müller, Capt.

Lieutenant Colonel Salomon's cold reception mentioned above may have been caused by his long absence from his regiment and the fact that he did not bring any replacements with him. Salomon departed on a twenty-day leave on January 10, 1864 to visit Governor Yates regarding filling up the regiment with recruits. At the expiration of his leave he was able to get it extended, supposedly for recruiting purposes. While his men suffered through the cold winter in shelter tents, Salomon was at his warm home in Chicago.[10]

Captain Müller began his next letter on May 18, 1864, but did not finish it until May 21. The six-page handwritten letter gives an almost day-by-day account for the period. During this time Sherman's army closed up on the enemy's army fortified on Rocky Face Ridge; forced Johnston's army to retreat from Rocky Face Ridge and Dalton to strong fortifications around Resaca on the north bank of the Oostanaula River by threatening his line of communication to Atlanta; fought a

hard battle on May 14 and 15; followed the retreating Confederate army to Cassville, where the Rebels fortified their new position, and then abandoned it on the
night of May 19–20.[11]

Although the captain disliked Lieutenant Colonel Solomon personally, he reveals that he respected Salomon's leadership in battle and criticizes Major Rolshausen. Colonel Robinson receives sharp criticism and Müller alleges that Robinson's staff was drunk during the Battle of Resaca.

———————

Camp in the field, one mile south southeast of Calhoun
and 8–10 miles south of Coosawattic [Coosawattee] River, Georgia[12]
May 18th, 1864

Dear Colonel:

Received your letter of April 30. By now you will have received the latest news
of the results of the battles from Tunnel Hill to Resaca, where the last major
battle took place. The enemy was gradually pushed out of his strong position
and totally defeated. Too bad you could not take part in it. Johnston is retreating
rapidly and left his dead and many wounded on the field, even in field hospitals
some bodies lay on operating tables, one of whom still groaned, etc.[13]

The 82nd is healthy and in excellent spirits; it stands in high esteem as a result
of an opportune and really splendid *Charge* against an enemy brigade that was
just about to capture the 5th Indiana Battery; however, due to our unhesitating
attack and (without a command from the brig. commander) they retired immediately. We were fortunate to not lose a man. The enemy's bullets went too high,
more about this later.[14]

Salomon returned on the 9th of this month. It is considered fortunate for the
regt. that Maj. R.[olshausen] did not lead us in the battle. He is continually troubled by continuous diarrhea, so that even the drummer boys make fun of him.[15]

We heard yesterday that on the 16th and the day after, the 4th Corps, 14th,
15th & 16th [Corps], which follow on the heels of the enemy, hit the Reb[els] by
Calhoun, captured a large number of prisoners, and are supposed to have burned
an *Ammunition Train*.[16]

Last evening, May 20, [Müller did not change dateline of his letter started on
May18th] we encountered the enemy 2 miles in front of Cassville and a *skirmish*
occurred. The Reb[els] left their breastworks made of *Rails,* which they set on fire
before evacuating. One man accidentally discharged his rifle as we were crossing
over the entrenchments. Kaisberger bled to death.[17]

Yesterday, Sc[h]ofield's 23rd Corps formed the left flank; we connected with
his right wing; and the 4th, 14th and 15th [Corps] are on our right. Last evening

the Rebel force stood at Kingston; if the enemy moves toward Rome he runs into the trap set by Sherman. Hooker issued orders yesterday not to start a battle, probably only for the purpose of forcing the enemy toward Rome.[18]

Our current brig. commander is subject to much criticism. Robinson, who personally may be brave, has no more idea about management of a brigade than my [illegible word]. During the battle at Rasacca [Resaca] div. [illegible word] brig. staff was drunk.[19]

Now I want to briefly describe our entire march and the fighting. I wrote to you on May 6 from Taylor's Ridge. Carrying 7 days' rations, we began the march along the *Ridge* at approximately 7:00 a. m. and crossed over through Nic[k] ajac[k] Gap. Butterfield marched on our right to negotiate the *Ridge* 4-miles farther south. We rested for 3 hours in [D]ogwood [V]alley, 1 mile from Trickum P. O.; however, the *Cav.* skirmished in front. Toward 4:00 p. m. we pitched camp near the above-named P. O., and 5 miles in front of Buzzard Roost.

May 8 we tarried in our position waiting for the arrival of the 15th, 16th and 17th Corps; the skirmishes at Tunnel Hill & Buzzard Roost began.

May 10 at 1:00 a. m. we took up the march again; reached Snake Creek Gap about 10 o'clock at night. The gap lays 3 miles south of Tilton at the foot of John's Mtn. In a *skirmish* the day before, the 15th & 16th [Corps] had pushed the Reb[s] through the *gap*, which is 6 miles long. Col. Phillips of the 9th Ill. was wounded. McGroarty told me on the march to there that he would take over the brig. and wanted me on his staff as *Top.[ographical] Engineer*(?)[20]

I wrote this to you from Snake Creek Gap on the 11th, whether my letter arrived is still to say. The 15th Corps did not destroy the R. R. as I had informed you. They had indeed penetrated up to Resacca [Resaca], but after encountering a strong brig. withdrew to the exit of the *gap* and entrenched. Heavy fire was heard in the direction of Dalton.

May 12 on *Picket,* relieved about 8 o'clock. Around 3 p. m. we arrived in Sugar Valley about 4–5 miles from Resaca. An amusing incident occurred on this day. Hooker and his staff passed the whole column from *front to rear* and each regt. broke out with cheers when he was seen, but the 82nd did not cheer and marched on silently. The staff laughed; it was fun. The 14th Corps arrived; I saw the 24th (Illinois), Capt. Mauff commanding, but have seen nothing of it since then.[21]

May 13 we connected with the left of the 15th Corps. Osterhaus understood he would continue to maneuver and change position often in the battle. With the extremely irregular terrain there was little use for Art.[illery] and we could see little. There are many wounded. Howard's was [falsely] reported in Dalton. The enemy is still in *force* in our front and already half surrounded. Kilpatric[k] was wounded in the leg today. The onset of darkness ended the battle.[22]

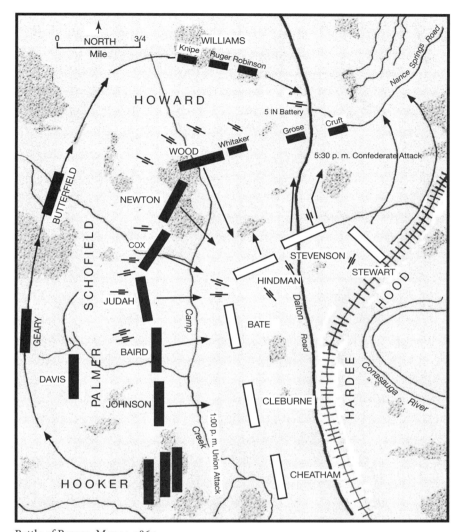

Battle of Resaca, May 14, 1864

May 14, 1864. Skirmishing began at daybreak and toward midday was conducted with great intensity. The Art.[illery] was needed only now and then. The news of victory from Va. was released to the troops today.[23]

Howard arrived from Dalton and immediately got into a hot fight. His troops drove the enemy out of 2 *rifle pits,* but he lost many men in a *defile* through which they had to pass. In the afternoon Howard was hard pressed, a terrible *fusil[l]-ade* raged on the whole line as we double quicked to Howard. [We] were ordered to the left, where the Reb[s] had almost reached and gone around. Over at that place we saw how a brig. retired in front of the thick raging Reb[s] (it was Groos's

[Grose's] brig., our Whiteside predecessor) and an entire 12-pounder battery was left standing. The Capt. had aimed his guns toward the left flank where the Reb[s] had penetrated, then almost instinctively we plunged down the hill, through a creek, and then tore into the miscreants with hurrahs, the [rest of the] brig. following us. At first, the major [Rolshausen] went back to deliver his existing cash of about $15 [?]to the Louis [?]. The Rebs were not expecting us there and ran back in a hurry. Sherman is supposed to have seen us and asked about us. After he was told who we were, he remarked *tell them, they are brave men.*[24]

On the 15th the battle expanded along the whole line. The 2 & 3 Div. moved out to flank the enemy; we joined the movement. Heavy fire was directed at the

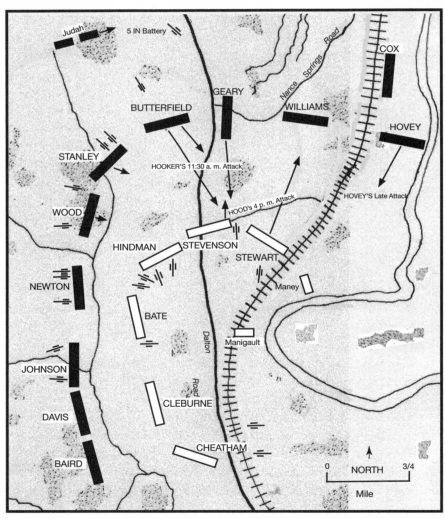

Battle of Resaca, May 15, 1864

enemy's *rifle pits* all day, and in the afternoon Butterfield assaulted and captured *rifle pits* and a *redoubt* with 4 guns. The 26th [Wisc.] was the first to plant its flag on the enemy works; three times our side was forced out of the *redoute* [redoubt] and in the end the enemy kept possession of it. The 26th lost about 40–50 wounded and only a few killed, among them a Lt.[25]

Around 2 o'clock we changed our position. We made a big turn to the right where our div. & brig. lay on the Plantation of J. G. Scales close to Green Station, and our main position was fiercely attacked (solely by Ga. regts.); their victory however was masterfully snatched away. Shells were thrown on them during the *movements,* their reserves came up with hurrahs, and the *Conflict* was hot. Our *boys* stood firmly behind breastworks built *of rails* while under fire from *Skirmishers* lying around in the woods; therefore they suffered few killed and wounded. The Rebs intended to hit our flank again and assumed we were not as strong there. The 27th Ind. captured a Rebel *flag.* Meanwhile, Scolfield [Schofield] closed up on our left—his left flank anchored at the Connasauga [Conasauga] Riv[er]. Our army now formed a large horseshoe with the enemy in the middle, so we awaited the renewal of the battle; however, on the 16th we received marching orders.[26]

During the night I was with my company on the battlefield serving as *Skirmishers.* The bright moon made a ghostly reflection on the pallid faces of numerous corpses lying around there; in addition, there were disturbing and veritably gruesome howls of pain from the wounded who believed they had been abandoned. A 1st Lt. from the 43rd Ga. was brought in about 10 o'clock. His regt. had intended to capture the *Battery.* He remarked, *"we thought sure we had that battery."* He marveled not a little that I was in the regt. that arrived there so suddenly and unexpectedly. I received a warning shot at this time. A spent bullet hit my left shoulder below the collarbone, ricocheted off my knapsack strap, but did not bruise my skin once. Too bad that it was not a little stronger.[27]

Perhaps in the following days the Reb[s] will make a stand in the Al[la]toona Mtns. on the other side of the Etowah Riv.[er]., which yesterday was vacated by the Rebels and was a very strong position.[28]

I believe the Reb[s] would decide to leave their splendid position at Cassville only in the circumstance that they were surrounded again. Yesterday evening Johnston & Hardee were there in *full force* and in person, and wanted us to attack, whereby many of our heads would have been smashed.

We stand north of Cassville. Scholfield [Schofield] is to the east. Howard waits about 1 mile away—West and S. W., and McPherson has already crossed the eminence in front of Kingston toward Atlanta. I don't know how it stands now. In any case Sherman knows exactly what he is doing. He gave Hooker orders not to make an attack; Howard is probably supposed to make a strong attack. On the 17th we crossed the Coosanatic [Coosawattee], then moved in a roundabout way over nice plantations and through forests until we arrived in front of Cassville on the 19th. We are still there today, the 21st, and are prepared for a 20-day march. I surmise that Johnston will abandon Atlanta and start for Va.; it would be a great march.

The expectation is that we must live off the country again. The Reb[s] even destroyed the interiors of houses, furniture, clothing, draperies, books, everything. As it was in Dalton, it also was in Cassville. Riese [Reese], earlier *Adjutant* of the 24th, is with Salomon who wants him as *Quar. Mr.* [quartermaster]; this I know through Riese [Reese] himself. Do you want to inform Panse, so that he will act accordingly and be doubly attentive?

Goodbye my dear colonel and remain in good spirits.

Yours truly,

Rudolph Müller

Subscribers to the *Illinois Staats-Zeitung* finally found some correspondence from a member of the 82nd Illinois among it pages. The Chicago news organ had not published any letters from the Second Hecker Regiment since January 7, 1864, probably because the regiment had not engaged in any significant combat or marches since that time.

Illinois Staats-Zeitung
May 31, 1864
On the battlefield, Resaca, Ga.,
16 May '64

We were in the battle three days: The first day we were in reserve; the second day we made a bayonet attack while under a most severe fire; and, on the third day we were subjected to dreadful artillery and infantry fire. The regiments to our right and left lost many men and it really is a wonder that we only had one man killed. Our regiment, under the splendid leadership of Lt. Col. Salomon, conducted itself so excellently that it was universally praised. The Rebels were beaten terribly.[29]

In camp by Cassville, Ga.,
20 May '64.

We finally have a rest day here by Cassville (Cassville lays somewhat east of Rome, nearly parallel to it; as is known, from there, Sherman's army advanced diagonally to Dallas. The *Staats-Zeitung* ed.). We had a small fight yesterday in which we lost one man killed. The enemy continues to retreat. In the great battle near Resaca the bullets whistled by our ears, so that it was a joy.[30]

I supplement the battle by Resaca for the time being as follows: On May 14 our division received orders to move to the left wing, because the enemy intended to flank us there. We had to march on the double quick and arrived just as our left wing, the brigade of Colonel Gross [Grose] of the 4th Corps, retreated in disorder. We were still in our position at the edge of the forest at the rather steep bank of a creek when Lieutenant Colonel Salomon noticed that the enemy in the forest opposite of us had come up to within nearly 30 paces of our battery, namely the Fifth Indiana Battery. Lieutenant Colonel Salomon recognized the danger and without waiting for an order from our irresolute brigade and division commanders, he commanded—forward *double quick*. With his saber in his hand he hastened us forward, and the entire regiment followed him with thundering hurrahs. The enemy was thrown into such confusion that they immediately took flight. We poured a terrible fire into them and through this clever feat of arms saved the battery and earned the honor of the day. We were universally complimented for our success, particularly by the generals. In our corps, and even in almost in the whole army, they talk about the charge of the 82nd under Salomon.

We have experienced terrible marches and still have to make them in the oppressive heat. We hope that the war will soon be over. This hope grips us everywhere here and with good grounds, because the Rebels are tired, and if Grant takes Richmond, there is no doubt that this story is over. We will ultimately defeat the Rebels.

[unsigned]

Readers of St. Louis's *Westliche Post* learned details of the Battle of Resaca on June 8, 1864.

> *Westliche Post*
> June 8, 1864
> Near Cassville, Ga.,
> May 19, 1864

We now stand eight miles north of Cassville and are seeking to drive the enemy toward Rome. On the 13th, 14th, and 15th we had a significant battle, which turned out in our favor, because the enemy retreated most swiftly, leaving his dead and wounded on the field.

Our regiment was not engaged on the first day, because our division was used as a mobile reserve and had to hurry here and there, where the need was the greatest. On the evening of the 14th we were sent on the double quick to the left wing. We arrived on a wooded ridge just as the brigade in front of us (Col. Gross's [Grose's] of the 4th Corps) that was supposed to support the 5th Indiana battery, was falling back in confusion. The Rebels had almost reached the battery.[31] At this moment our brigade, with our regiment in front, charged down the hill, fired a well-aimed volley into the Rebels and charged them with fixed bayonets. When the wretches saw this, they were gripped by a terrible panic and ran from there like the devil was behind them. They dared no more attacks on us. The captain of the battery thanked us with tears in his eyes because he had thought his battery was lost.

On the 15th we were again pushed here and there; however, our regiment did not suffer heavy casualties. On this day the Johnnies were severely cut up and moved back over the Ostanola [Oostanaula River].[32] The terrain was most unfavorable for artillery, because there were only a few open fields. For the most part this area consists of wooded ridges, where the undergrowth is so thick that you can hardly pass through it and cannot see 30 steps in front of you. It appears that Georgia consists of nothing but forests. There is no talk of nice plantations. Primarily, there are only cabins and these are mostly abandoned.

Incidentally, the people here are not lacking food as is continually said; poultry, sheep, and hogs are still plentiful, as is forage.

[unsigned]

———————

The bloodletting expected at Cassville was averted, in part, because Lt. Gen. John Bell Hood and Lt. Gen. Leonidas Polk convinced Joe Johnston that their lines could not hold. Johnston made another skillful retreat during the night, this time to the village of Allatoona, located in the Allatoona Pass, some five miles south of the Etowah River. The vital Western and Atlantic Railroad, Johnston's lifeline, ran through a deep cut here and continued southeast to Kennesaw Mountain, Marietta, and finally Atlanta. Sherman rested and resupplied his army at the Etowah River and on May 23 began crossing it. Instead of following the railroad to Allatoona, Sherman decided to pass around the Southern army using the few crude roads penetrating the rugged, densely wooded Georgia countryside.[33]

The following letter was written by Captain Müller to Colonel Hecker from the vicinity of Euharlee, located about eight miles south of Kingston and three miles south of the Etowah River.

———————

Near Euharfree [Euharlee], Ga. *on the March*
May 30, 1864

Dear Colonel,

We are again on the march toward the front, where bitter fighting has occurred near Dallas, Ga., since the 25th. Our entire brigade is escorting a large *Ord.[nance] Train* from Kingston, where we arrived from the front yesterday. We visited the 24th [Illinois]. My last letter to you from Cassville was dated May 21 [not found]. We left the little city on May 23 and crossed over the Etowah River on pontoons; these were a quite new type. The frame of each pontoon was made of wood and the sides were thick canvas (genuine Yankee). They are transported on wagons. Camped that night on the south bank while some miles to our left (east) a corps had a fight. I do not know which one. On the 24th we moved in the direction of Dallas.[34]

This morning as we were leaving Kingston, the 24th [Illinois] received ten barrels of beer. Imagine our anguish when we had to continue to march off without being able to refresh our thirsty throats from the heat and dust without one drink! We rested after we had crossed the Etowah again. Suddenly I saw 4 riders approaching over open fields and suspected Reb[el] *Cav.[alry]*; however, they were from the 24th. [Ill.], each with a canteen filled with the noble barley juice [beer]. What a surprise! And how we enjoyed this refreshing drink.

A few days ago I received your letter of the 10th of this month. As you have experienced, it is a pleasure to receive a letter in the field. Wish you commanded our brig., which is really excellent.

Our division's General Williams says: *The devil himself can't whip that Brigade,* and to Capt. Saalman[n], returning your greetings, he said: The 82nd is the best regt. in the brig. and in fact the best in my division, etc. That pleases you, doesn't it? Therefore, I wish that you led our brigade, although you have chosen the better part.[35]

Siegel [Sigel] has played out—that is what I saw as a headline for an article in the *Wheeling* [W. Va.] *Intelligencer.* Your observation, *the dutch have, etc.,* is only too true![36] Ahsmussen [Asmussen]? How does that strike you? An able soldier whose character is very dubious. Do not ever believe that he is your friend, at most he will be your friend as long as he can use you for his purposes. He must feel pressed like Joe [Hooker?], he does not play 1st fidle [fiddle] there.[37]

Krzyzanowski lives like a sultan in Bridgeport. Do not believe his command is so large. The Ala. *cav.* was mustered out in order to organize anew.[38]

Neussel, who performed very well before Resacca [Resaca], unfortunately suffered sunstroke on the 22nd [23rd?] and is probably in Chattanooga now.[39] Panse remains on Look Out [Lookout Mountain] in Summertown. Do you want to be so kind as to tell him that Salomon intends to displace him in order to put Riese [Reese] (earlier Adj. 24th) into his place. He must therefore be particularly good at *red tape*. Schurz is commanding the *Barracks* in Nashville, so far as I have heard. I saw Dilger on the left flank at Dallas on the 27th. I visited him while we lay in reserve. He fired at a Reb[el] *Battery* with his 12-pound Parrot [gun], a brave soldier. I was so fortunate to be able to offer a Commissary to him.[40]

        R. Müller

The preceding letter is surprising in that it does not mention that the 82nd Illinois fought in the Battle of New Hope Church on May 25; 11 men were killed and 59 wounded of the 245 engaged in the battle. The Twentieth Corps failed in its attempt to break through the hastily entrenched Rebel line, which was bolstered by sixteen deadly guns. Hooker's corps had 665 men killed, wounded, and missing; half of the casualties were in Williams's division.[41]

    Brig. Gen. Thomas J. Wood's Fourth Corps division suffered 1,500 casualties in their attempt to turn Johnston's right flank near Pickett's Mill on May 27. On May 28, the Fifteenth Corps soundly defeated attacks on its front. General Sherman then began to migrate his army back to the railroad in the vicinity of Acworth to alleviate its critical supply shortage. The *Illinois Staats-Zeitung* included the following letter excerpt about the aforementioned battle.[42]

        Illinois Staats-Zeitung
        June 9, 1864
        Kingston, Ga.
        May 29, 1864

    Our regiment just arrived here to get ammunition for the army. The 24th also lies here. On the 25th, 26th, and 27th we were in a terrible battle by the little town of Dallas. Our regiment fought heroically and has been much praised. We were not as lucky as at Resaca because we had to mourn the loss of 11 dead and 49 [59] wounded. Lieutenant Colonel Salomon's horse was hit by a piece of a bombshell and they plunged to the ground together. In the morning we depart again for the front. I can only send the casualty list in a few days.

        [unsigned]

Readers of the *Illinois Staats-Zeitung* of June 23, 1864, received details of the Second Hecker Regiment's role in the Battle of New Hope Church through another unsigned public letter dated June 7, 1864.

Illinois Staats-Zeitung
June 23, 1864
Field Camp by Lost Mountain, Ga.[43]
June 7, 1864

Our current campaign is a terribly difficult one and slow. I do not know why it is so slow. Our troops have fought excellently at every opportunity. The Rebels pull back, fighting for every inch of ground; however, I cannot understand the manner in which we pursue the enemy. As soon as the enemy evacuates a position, we follow and they come to a halt; we also halt and do not attack them, but fortify ourselves. This type of warfare is quite contrary to the soldiers' desires and we would much prefer if we attacked them, so that this exhausting campaign would end.

We left our camp at Huntsville, Ga., on May 25 and marched toward Dallas.[44] Two miles from that town we received the order to *about face* and hurry to help our 2nd Division because they had encountered the enemy on another road. Our regiment was last in the order of march on this day, and now marched back first because we *left in front* [about faced]. We crossed over Pumpkin Vine Creek 3 miles from the road that we marched up in the a.m., and a mile east of this stream we ran into the enemy, who had quickly thrown up light breastworks of wood and earth there. Our brigade formed a line of battle. The 82nd Ill. Regiment was on the left flank, next came the 101st Illinois, the 82nd Ohio and the 143rd N.Y. The 61st Ohio was advanced as skirmishers and the other 2 brigades of our division were 2nd and 3rd in the battle line. The signal to advance sounded and we moved forward. We soon overtook our skirmish line because they could not advance fast enough in the brush and were ordered back. Our line opened heavy fire on the enemy, which they answered in kind. The enemy had meanwhile brought a battery into position and regaled us with canister and grape[shot], i.e., not wine grapes. Nevertheless, our brigade advanced steadily and the Rebels fell back fighting. We received orders to halt, and the second line of battle advanced through our lines. Therefore, we had a half hour to catch our breath; however, the bullets, canister, and shells flew into our ranks. After half an hour, "*3rd Brigade forward*" was called and our line was sent to the front again. We advanced again and the battle began anew. We fought until all our 60 cartridges per man were fired.

The lieutenant colonel requested either relief or cartridges three times. Bayonets were fixed because our fire began to weaken from lack of ammunition. We feared the enemy would make use of this slackening and launch a bayonet attack. However, relief came and our brigade was ordered back. It had been a costly day. Our regiment entered the battle 250 [245] men strong and afterward between 60 and 70 dead and wounded from this group lay on the battlefield. The regiment

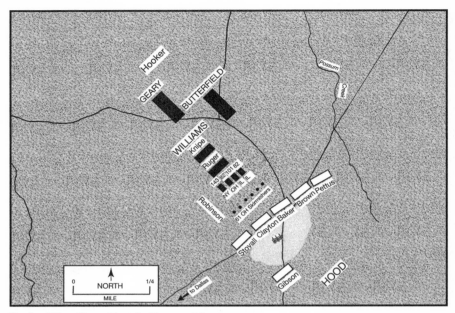

Battle of New Hope Church, May 25, 1864

had acquitted itself well and when we returned to the camp we heard many say: *"Hurrah for the 82d! Bully for the Illinois boys."*

On the 26th and 27th we lay in reserve; however, the sharpshooters' bullets flew over the heads of the front ranks and tore into ours. One hit the arm of Lt. Lotz and wounded Sgt. Major Bauer in the leg.[45] On the 28th, our brigade was ordered to Kingston with an ammunition train. We reached there on the 30th [29th]. We found the gallant 24th [Illinois] there. We met many old friends from Chicago and pleasantly chatted in the evening, and [illegible word] thought about the beer of the Garden City, which we really missed. We left for the front again on the 31st [30th], where we arrived on the evening of the 1st [31st].[46] We believed at the time of our departure for Kingston that we would next see our army directly before Atlanta. Unfortunately, we found it at the same place where we had left it. The next day Sherman's flanking maneuver began again, and until yesterday we have had only insignificant advanced post fights, with the results, *"nobody hurt."* Orders just arrived to make preparations for a 10-day march. I hope now it is said seriously:

"On to Atlanta."

Besides covering events since May 28, Müller's missive of June 1, 1864, criticized Colonel Robinson and his quest for a general's star.

Battlefield near Dallas, Ga.
June 1st, 1864
Camp 82nd Ill. Vols.[47]
9 o'clock in the morning

Dear Colonel,

Just yesterday I sent you, through a quartermaster, a long letter about our latest activities [letter dated May 30]. Whether you will receive it is very questionable. Last evening we reached the battlefield near Dallas again, finding everything in the same condition that we had left it on the 29th [28th] of last month. It has been a week since the battle and there have not been any noteworthy incidents with us. The losses on each side up until today might aggregate about 10,000, in our Corps 3,000.[48]

As usual, the densely forested terrain severely limits our visibility. Nonetheless, we know we are on a battlefield because of the continuous *skirmish* fire, a weak cannonade and the already numerous graves of the fallen soldiers. Now and then single bullets make their presence known by their well-known whistle. The enemy is supposed to have a very strong position on 70-foot-high cliffs, which position is impregnable. We must now wait on what will develop.

At present, we form a *Reserve;* but, as usual, we will be in the front again for the battle. This campaign is most stressful. We are constantly engaged with the enemy, eat bad food, have nothing to drink but bad water, not even a commissary, and are deprived of sleep. That means neither men of iron, as we are, nor the devil himself, can get anything.

Sherman has the absolute confidence of the army and is already engaged in a *flank movement.* Yesterday the pontoons' *Train,* which had joined us in Kingston, arrived. I do not know where they are going, maybe to the 17th Corps, which is in Rome on the march, in order to perhaps go over the Chattahootchee [Chattahoochee] down river.

Osterhaus distinguished himself again [on May 28] through his determination. The Reb[s] drove back a division [Harrow's] of the 15th Corps and captured 4 [3] guns with a night [mid-afternoon] attack. Osterhaus, seeing this, hastened to that div. with a brig., charged and [part of Harrow's division] recaptured the 3 cannon through a night [mid-afternoon] attack. [Several illegible words][49]

This afternoon at 1 o'clock, our div. immediately deployed on the extreme left of the army about 5–6 miles S.E. of our old position in the center. I do not know whether the whole corps will follow us here or if we will remain here.[50]

Eugene, Lotz, Gottlob and Grembelino Joe all are very happy that you think about them and return the greeting and express with me the wish that we had the old one back again as Com.[mander] of the brig.[51]

Robinson, as a soldier (apart from being a *Gentleman*), is not only a jackass but also an idiot; that is where the problem lies. Our *Charge* on the 14th of last month on Howard's left before Resacca [Resaca], which as is well known (and especially by the 82nd), was undertaken without commands, because each *Private* instinctively knew that the critical moment had arrived, has already been exploited for the benefit of Robinson, and thus he is pushing for his star.[52]

We read a description of the Battle of Resaca in the *Cincinnati Commercial* wherein Robinson's brig. is favorably mentioned. Eugene told me earlier that his adj. gen., Capt. Lee, sent the correspondence.[53] McGroarty has spoken badly about Robinson, who leaves all *Arrangements* to his staff, and if one complains will say: *That's not my business, I have nothing to do with that, go to Capt. so and so, etc.*

I close, hoping that you will write to me soon. You know how much we enjoy a letter in the field. Your good wishes to date have served as a talisman for us.

> Respectfully,
> Rudolph Müller, Capt.

Ten

Kolb's Farm to Atlanta

As General Sherman moved his three armies toward the Western and Atlantic Railroad in early June 1864, Joe Johnston moved his army in the same direction until the night of June 4, when he retreated southeast to protect the railroad. By June 19 Johnston had fallen back to Kennesaw Mountain and established a strongly entrenched arc-shaped line, with Hood's corps shielding Marietta to the northeast, Loring's corps (formerly Polk's) defending Kennesaw Mountain, and Hardee's corps stretching from the mountain to the road running from Lost Mountain to Marietta. Facing that line were McPherson's army on the Union's left, then Thomas's army, and finally Schofield's small army. The Twentieth Corps formed Thomas's right and Alpheus S. Williams's First Division manned the Twentieth Corps's right. Marietta lay four miles behind Kennesaw Mountain.[1]

Colonel Robinson's brigade of the First Division, including the 82nd Illinois, moved to its right on the morning of June 20 and encamped on Atkinson's plantation; its men built breastworks the next day. On June 22 the brigade advanced about one mile to the front, and, according to Colonel Robinson, "went into position on the left of General Knipe's brigade on the crest of a high wooded hill." Johnston sent Hood to his army's left and that evening Hood launched an attack against Brig. Gen. Joseph F. Knipe's brigade of Williams's division (to Robinson's immediate right). Although hard pressed, artillery and musketry from Knipe's brigade, assisted by Brig. Gen. Thomas H. Ruger's left, finally repulsed the strong attack. A column moving against Robinson's brigade was blasted head on by cannoneers from Winegar's battery and an enfilading fire from Geary's Second Division artillery. Another attack directed against Knipe's left flank was broken up by artillery and musketry, including that of the 61st Ohio of Robinson's brigade. This battle is known as the Battle of Kolb's Farm.[2]

The Battle of Kolb's Farm, his growing pride in the Twentieth Corps, and his negative feelings about several other officers are the topics of Rudolph Müller's June 24 letter to the colonel.

In the field 3 miles S.W. *of* Marietta, Ga.[3]
June 24th, 1864

Dear Colonel,

We had a hot, humid day today. The sun began shining again 3 days ago, after four weeks of rainy weather, and seems to want to make up for the missed time by scorching us. It is now 11 o'clock at night. The Reb[el] *Pickets* are firing at us unusually briskly, while ours answer in an equally unusual way, i.e., almost not at all. What is that supposed to mean? Do the Rebs intend to make a night attack or is it supposed to cover a retreat?

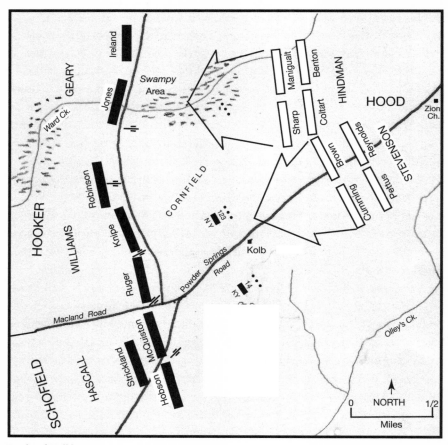

Battle of Kolb's Farm, June 22, 1864

We, that is our div., have a similar situation as at Gettysburg, where the open fields in front of us, approximately 1,500 yds deep, are completely controlled. Wüt-herich's batt[ery] [Winegar's battery] stands in our line behind good rifle pits. Batt. M stands to our right with the 2nd [1st] (Knipe's) Brig. in advance echelon formation, in an equally advantageous position, and where Hood's Reb[el] corps was repulsed yesterday with bloody heads. It was a joy for us to see our *shells* and *case shot* hit in the middle of their columns and how the wretches scattered like a flock of ducks after several salvos.[4]

We bypassed the left wing of the enemy, and in order to prevent our incursion into his rear, Hood's whole corps threw itself against our div. and primarily Knipe's brig., which held splendidly behind half-completed *Rifle pits*. Our div. was still alone with no connection on our right or left. It was a critical moment. Our Art. [illery] did its part and just when the enemy was at the point of turning our right, Schofield arrived and connected with our right. We still stood uncovered on the left of the div., and were only covered by the above-mentioned swamp; then our friend Geary finally arrived, and closed up on our left, still leaving a *Gap* of 1,000 yards, which today is still open and only covered by *Pickets* and the previously mentioned swamp.

The battle lasted several hours and moved toward the left after the Reb[s] at-tacked in our front and lost approximately 1,000 [1,500] men according to my (modest) estimate The Reb[s] removed their dead and wounded throughout the night and therefore our *Pickets* did not fire on them. I counted about 50 dead in-side our *Pickets*. Geary had a hot fight. One prisoner told us that on the morning of the battle, only one div. of their corps was present there, but after our arrival Hood's & Hardee's corps were deployed on their left wing, probably with the view to save the Dallas-Marietta Road, which now however is in our possession, so that the Rebels' retreat to the S.W. is blocked, and they only have the R. R. bridge as a crossing point.[5] Their right wing rests on Kennesaw Mtn., and therefore their entire line has to be parallel with the R. R., and it appears to me that Sher-man's Plan is to cross it.

Since Dallas we have made a large swing to the left, leaving Lost Mtn. to our right, pushing the Reb[s] out of one strong position after the other, partly through direct attacks, partly through maneuvering. The Reb[s] have a strong respect for us, they say: *If it were not for Hooker['s] Command we would whip the Yankees every time.* The corps has proven very competent with every affair and certainly has done more than any other in this campaign. Nevertheless, no one talks about this in any official reports. Hooker is personally brave, which I have observed several times, and even his enemies have to say this. It appears to me, however, that he plays a subordinate role with the other corps's chiefs.

Why was McPherson officially recognized by Sherman for Dallas [on May 28], where he lost 8–900 [379] men, a div. driven by the enemy, and what had been lost retaken by Osterhaus, while the 20th Corps on the 25th of the month [May] lost 3,000 [665] and drove the enemy off and all this was not mentioned at all? The prisoner mentioned above also remarked after he heard we were H.[ooker]'s men: *If we had known that, we would not have come out that way, we know them from Resaca.* These little incidents, very insignificant in themselves, nevertheless are very good and do not fail to boost the esprit de corps, so that finally, the star, which the Rebels so fear, must be attached to our crescent, which had not happened before now.[6]

Yesterday, there was a strong cannonade to our left that lasted for hours. I could not learn the particulars but the plentiful smoke from ignited powder and rifle fire let me conclude that there was a general engagement. Today, I heard that Osterhaus captured a Reb[el] *battery* at the foot of Kennesaw, although I do not know if it is true.[7]

The day before yesterday, Capt. Wheeler, Chief of Art.[illery] for the 2nd Div. was killed, shot through the heart. McGroarty had been ordered to support Knipe's left wing, but through his rashness, imprudently left his post, and against *Orders,* advanced the *Skir.[mish] Line* 300 yds with his regt. Major Becket[t] was killed on the spot by a shot into his face. There exists a general feeling of indignation toward him; he should be dismissed immediately because he, as usual, attacked. He displayed misdirected, inappropriate courage. Besides that he lost 7 men and had to return to his former position.[8]

My last letter to you was dated 12 miles N.W. of Marietta, June 8/9 [not found]. I want to convey to you our movements in sequence as best as I can. I have tried in vain to obtain special maps. They are promised to Salomon. I will copy them as soon as possible and send them to you.

Salomon leads the regiment very well, and yesterday Col. Robinson stated in the presence of Broughton (143rd N.Y.) it was the best of the brig., which it undisputedly is. The *Boys* stand like a wall. Salomon of course has learned that I said earlier that I would not serve under him. I had not let him know that up until now. I will tell him the plain truth and give him the reasons I feel like this. Apart from his moral courage, which is no greater than any soldier should and must have, he still vigorously promotes his own popularity.[9]

With every bullet flying by, Major R.[olshausen] plays the miserable role of a scaredy-cat. The fear of death is always written on his forehead and his back has become bent by his frequent *dodging.* He should let himself be sent home and not give his wife any grounds for anxiety. The rest are competent.

Your friends send their regards to you. Eugene is not entirely well today (tooth abscess).[10]

[unsigned]

––––––

Captain Müller was not alone in questioning why Sherman praised General McPherson and his command while the Twentieth Corps was ignored. After all, as historian Albert Castel states, Hooker's corps had "made every major Union attack, save Howard's ill-fated attack at Pickett's Mill; as a consequence it has suffered about 5,000 casualties, far more than any corps in Sherman's army." General Hooker and many other Cumberlanders resented Sherman's "flagrant favoritism for the Army of the Tennessee." Moreover, Hooker believed that he and his corps had also been the victims of Sherman's bad management of the campaign, a feeling that further increased his dislike of his army commander.[11]

Despite the army's chieftain's lack of praise for the Twentieth Corps, Colonel Hecker's personal war correspondent reveals that the merger of the Eleventh and Twelfth corps into the new Twentieth Corps had gone well and men of the former Eleventh Corps had now added the Twentieth Corps's star to their uniforms and were wearing it with pride. Some of the enemy called the Twentieth Corps "Hooker's Ironclads." The degree to which this newfound pride improved relations between individual German Americans and Anglo-Americans in the corps is uncertain.[12]

An unsigned letter published in the *Staats-Zeitung* in mid-July informed its readers in Chicago and elsewhere about the 82nd's role in the Battle of Kolb's Farm on June 22, 1864, and the Battle of Kennesaw Mountain, fought on June 27. Sherman made a serious blunder in ordering part of his army to attack the enemy's strongly fortified position on Kennesaw. Fortunately, the 82nd was not involved in the attack, which resulted in nearly three thousand Union casualties and a bitter defeat.[13]

––––––

Illinois Staats-Zeitung
July 15, 1864

By Marietta, Ga.
June 29, 1864

We have had a hard campaign and are still not finished with it. Fortunately, however, we have not made a major attack since the Battle of Dallas [New Hope

Church] on May 25. Despite this, since June 2, we have often been exposed to enemy musketry and cannon fire. We are in the first line in our present position. Our skirmishers are about 300 yards in front of us, and approximately 200 yards from the Rebels' skirmish line. We overlook the whole field to the right and the left and see and hear every cannon shot fired off along the entire line. On the 19th we lost 1 killed and 2 wounded in a brisk skirmish. On June 22 we arrived in our current position. Soon after our arrival the pickets on our right were driven in and the Rebels attacked in heavy columns with their usual yells. They threw themselves against the line of our First Brigade, which was busy constructing rifle pits. Our battery began playing on them with canister and grapeshot. The infantry opened a blistering fire at them, and the gray-clad troops were mowed down in heaps.

After half an hour of fighting, a heavy column appeared at our front; our artillery opened on them immediately, and we could see how the balls tore holes in their ranks. The Rebels scattered in all directions in great confusion and discovered that it is better not to attack the "*star corps*," as Joe Hooker's corps is called. The *Atlanta Appeal* reported that the Rebels lost 200 dead and 800 wounded in this affair. One can generally accept that their losses amounted to 1,500. Our division lost 150 [130] dead and wounded on this day. Since then our brigade has lost some men every day in skirmishes, but our regiment was lucky, because since then it has lost no men.[14]

On the 27th we received the order to prepare for a general attack. We expected a hard battle. Eight o'clock was the hour set for our army's advance. There was a large open field to our front. To advance over it would have cost us a large number of men, so we received the order to maintain our position and only our skirmish line was ordered forward with the line on their left. Geary's division stood to our left; left of it were the 4th and 14th Corps. The battle began shortly after eight o'clock.

We overlooked the entire battlefield from our position. It was a splendid view! Our left wing faced Ken[n]esaw Mountain, which we saw clearly from a distance of about 5 miles. The Rebels have 25 to 30 heavy guns on Ken[n]esaw Mountain. Our batteries began to toss a shower of shells toward the mountain and the enemy responded punctually, while our entire force advanced in three lines. It was an impressive view, with the stars and stripes fluttering in the air and the gleaming bayonets advancing steadily. Soon the whole line was engaged and for an hour we heard nothing but the sharp rattling of musket fire and the muted heavy thunder of cannon. The whole line was wrapped in a cloud and we saw nothing. The infantry fire ceased after an hour but an artillery duel continued for several hours along the whole line. One brigade of the 4th Corps lost all of its field officers. Our troops now have a good position 200 yards from the enemy works. I do not think another attack will be made. We will flank the enemy. Our brigade was ordered on an *Extra-Expedition*. You therefore should not expect a letter from me soon.

(As is known, the above-mentioned new flanking movement has been made by Sherman. The [*Staats-Zeitung*] Ed.)

After the bloody Battle of Kennesaw Mountain, Sherman began flanking Johnston's entrenched army again and by July 5 his Rebel army had retreated to fortifications along the north bank of the Chattahoochee River, just ten miles from Atlanta.[15]

In a long letter dated July 9, Rudolph Müller reported to Hecker events occurring between May 24 and July 9, 1864, though not in strict chronological order. The captain railed against corruption in the North and bemoaned what he believed was the lack of a good Republican presidential candidate for the upcoming election in November. Updates about certain officers in the 82nd, a change in the composition of Robinson's brigade, and praise for artillery Captain Dilger are also included.

Camp 82nd Ill. Vols. *in the field*
Near the Chattahootchie [Chattachoochee]
July 9, 1864

Dear Colonel,

Your valued letter dated the 19th of last month reached me on the 28th in our next to last position in front of Kennesaw. You should have received my letters dated June 8/9 [not found] and 25th [24th?] June. I am only able to reply to your last letter today because Sherman's order interrupting postal communications has now been lifted. Panse arrived on June 26 looking about 10 years younger, unfortunately with a crippled arm. He sends you greetings.[16]

Since the 5th of this month, we have had both wings resting at the river in a semi-circle. The enemy is on this same side of the river in a similar position, with the *Riv.[er]* at his back. He is strongly fortified and also has protection from forts on the south bank, and enjoys the peace and quiet, while the *Picket Line* maintains a lively fire here and there.

Yesterday, Howard, forming the left wing, removed a Reb[el] pontoon bridge to give the enemy the idea that it was being taken farther downstream. His infantry advanced under the concentrated fire of two enemy Parrot batteries and chased the crews to the devil. Our *Pickets* should already be over the river. The R. R. bridge within the range of our guns has not been destroyed.

Scolfield [Garrard not Schofield], on the right wing, crossed with a detachment of *Cavalry* and destroyed a [three] reb[el] *Govmt.* [*Government*] textile
factory [factories], where about 100 [400] girls were employed, and then he returned. These are mainly the events of the last few days.[17]

Our position is as follows: 4th Corps left of the 14th, 20th, 15th, 16th. The terrain
is very irregular, traversed by steep elevations and *Ridges* running parallel with the
river and intersected by numerous ravines. From several points in our position,
we can see the church steeples and houses (of Atlanta) lying at a distance of about
6 [8] miles as the crow flies; no trace however of the much discussed sandy plains
around Atlanta, just the same irregular terrain, thickly forested. A.[tlanta] lies at
the same altitude as our current position.

Visited Col. Maymann [Meumann] of 3rd Mo. yesterday where I heard that
a Reb[el] off[icer] who had deserted said: Johns[t]on has an order to fall back to
Macon (*lacks confirmation*), a stereotypical phrase one can use 100 times a day
with the many rumors. The 3rd, 12th, and 17th Mo. will go home in a month. Osterhaus wants to accompany them.[18]

Eugene, Panse, and Salomon have just gone over to the 15th Corps. The last
(Salomon) will take steps so you get the *Certificate* concerning *Ordnance.* He has
applied to the War Dept. for the eagle [colonel's rank] with the recommendation
of the brig., div., and corps [commanders]; thus the reason for his unusual activity
to cultivate popularity with our illustrious brigadier and the lion-headed Williams, about whom (especially the former) he otherwise, not unfairly, severely be-
rated, *tempora mutantur* [the times are changing]. The *Eagle* will probably come;
I have absolutely nothing against it. I fear only that he soon will not feel at home
on his cliff, and barely born will undertake a flight toward a [general's] star.[19]

We have here the comforting view of [Capt.] Bruhn gleaming like a new pearl
in our *field* & *staff.* Sgt. Sch[ö]n[e]wald (Co. K), who well deserves the disrespect
of every *Private* through his constant cowardice, will receive his commission as
2nd Lt. before long. Men like Bauer, Prell, Dörr [Doering], and others were overlooked. Regarding the above *Commission,* even Salomon wants nothing to do
with it because he is supposed to have procured it through connections behind
his back. What do you say about this?[20]

The 45th New York, which during the whole campaign never saw the enemy
and up to now was used as *Train* guards has departed for Nashville to provide
Provost service, which must make them feel ashamed. Their officers (i.e., only
individuals) said that they cannot let themselves appear before the eyes of the
82nd anymore. They are now ridiculed wherever they let themselves be seen. A
full Wisc. regt. should fill the hole created by the departure of the scaredy-cats,
hence an advantage for us.[21]

Your prediction about Augusta is quite correct and will probably come about, but that lies further in the future. Even after we have Atlanta, I would not think about that as long as Johnston's army also has not been destroyed. Although demoralized, behind their entrenchments they are a contemptuous enemy. Johnston does not dare an open field battle and I hope that Sherman will avoid ramming his head against these *Fortifications*. There is no fort, no entrenchment that we could not assault, but what useless sacrifices have we not already made! Our great, battle-eager army would be annihilated in the shortest time, while the Reb[s]. would fall back from one position to another without considerable losses. I had expressed doubt about Sherman earlier, but now know the slow advance is completely justified.

The campaign in Va. is beginning to become significantly doubtful. Grant is now operating on the same lines as McClellan did two years before. He is at Petersburg, which he recently thought to take through a coup (Kautz & Gillmore), but still is not able to take it with his whole army. If he considers the place so important, would he have not sent a larger force at the beginning that easily could have taken the city? Didn't he make a mistake? Then came the new incursions in Maryland & Penn., so is this right? This will probably make clear to the people in the northern metropoli the necessity of immediate conscription and elimination of the $300 clause. As long as a man can redeem himself for $300, it is clear that the government receives money but no soldiers.[22]

In the political *Chaos* it is difficult to find one's way and to find the man who can restore the country's sinking *Credit—Corruption* everywhere, above and below, *to live or not to live* is less the question than *to make the best of it*. One cannot go for Fr[é]mont, and can only go for Lincoln, the sleepy head, with reluctance. What is left? Should one wait on the revival of the decayed democracy? It would be best for one to cultivate his cabbage and beets far way from the disgusting body of the world in a remote corner of the primeval forest and to live only for oneself.[23]

Dilger has recently performed excellently with various opportunities, and any day now is expecting a *promotion* to chief of Art.[illery] of his div. Sherman and Thomas both watched him in the last *Actions*. His battery in the 14th Corps is not known as such, but notably as the *leather breeches battery* and *the captain with the leather breeches* is generally respected; as is well known, Dilger wears leather pants. During the last *charges* of the 14th and 4th Corps at the pos.[ition] at Kennesaw, he went to his Gen., asking why he had not sent Art.[illery] along? The Gen. answered him: No battery would venture into that musket fire. I will go, give me the order, and Dilger *Galloped* off, contributing not a little to warping of the enemy. [Dilger] [l]ost about 35 men, so he now has only enough men for 4 guns. Howard has already repeated the desire to have him again.[24]

On the 3rd of this month we left our position and marched through the Reb[el] [works] that were most hurriedly abandoned by the enemy as a result of several corps swinging to the right of our Army of the Cumberland. Scolfield's [Schofield's], along with the 15th & 16th Corps, had moved farther to the right during the two previous nights and arrived almost unnoticed in the rear of the Reb[s]. We followed hard on the heels of the enemy and on this and the following day took about 5,000 prisoners along our whole line, mostly deserters, who were all happy to be in our lines, and reported about the demoralization in their army. Johnston's army will only hold together through the sternest discipline.[25]

We rested on the 4th. The men received a ration of *Whisky* to celebrate the day, and toward evening we changed our Pos.[ition] again and were bombarded on the left wing. I heard that the enemy had been retreating for two days and he was cut off above the Powder [S]pring[s] road by McPherson.

The next morning we marched a long way until we reached our current position. The Reb[el] works we passed on the 5th were really like those at Kennesaw and would have been formidable to capture. There was an *Abatti* 250 paces deep, then 2 rows of *Pallisades* [*Palisades*] (pointed stakes densely anchored in the ground), then came the first line of bombproof breastworks with traverses of the same strength; 20 paces behind lay the 2nd line, then a third, and the 4th was just as strong as the first. We passed at least 2 *miles* of such works until we marched in another direction. Imagine the disturbing effect that the often-repeated abandonment of such a position must have on their troops.

Goodbye, dear colonel, with the request about [illegible word] your worthy family. I remain always with high esteem for you. Lotz, Lemberg [Lindbergh], Erickson, Gambelino, Gottlob, Lander [Lender], Capt. Saalman, Panse, Eugene [Weigel], the first wrote yesterday, all return your greetings.[26]

> Yours truly,
> Rudolph Müller,
> Capt.

The preceding letter is the first time we find Rudolph Müller discussing national politics or President Lincoln. He clearly airs his disgust with the wartime corruption in the North and expresses his lack of enthusiasm for Lincoln in the upcoming November 1864 presidential election. The reference to Lincoln as the "sleepy head" likely reveals a belief that Lincoln had not prosecuted the war aggressively enough. He also may have agreed with those Unionists who felt Lincoln had moved too slowly on the abolition of slavery and/or that Lincoln's plan for reconstruction was too lenient on the Rebels. Nevertheless, he would not support John C. Frémont, the candidate of the new Radical Democracy Party founded by

Radical Republicans opposed to Lincoln's re-nomination. This new party's planks included (1) a declaration that limitations on free speech, the press, and habeas corpus should only be applicable to areas under martial law; (2) the complete abolition of slavery; (3) reconstruction as the province of congress and not the president; (4) absolute equality of all men before the law; and (5) confiscation of the Rebels' lands and their distribution among soldiers and actual settlers. Party members comprised mostly radical Germans and non-German abolitionists. Friedrich Hecker did not support Frémont or the Radical Democracy Party because he believed they would reduce the political support for Lincoln and possibly result in a victory by George B. McClellan (the Democratic Party's candidate). Frémont would withdrew from the race in September 1864 and most Radical Republicans voted for Lincoln to prevent a Democrat from occupying the White House and thereby endangering the Union.[27]

In the preceding letter Müller again mentions that Salomon is militarily competent, but tempers this by saying his courage is no greater than should be expected of any soldier. He also repeats his belief that the lieutenant colonel's constant self-promotion is wrong. He points out that Salomon wanted nothing to do with Schönewald's promotion because it was obtained behind his back. By asking Hecker, "What do you say about this?" the captain emphasizes the irony of Salomon criticizing Schönewald's pressing for a promotion by using his contacts, when Salomon employs the same technique. This time Müller does not mention his commander's religion.

The following unsigned letter gave the *Staats-Zeitung* readers some information about the health of the 82nd Regiment, their location, and a personal evaluation of Gen. Joseph E. Johnston. When this letter was written its author did not know that General Johnston would be relieved of command just three days later for failure "to arrest the advance of the enemy to the vicinity of Atlanta, far into the interior of Georgia" or that there is "no confidence that you can repeat or repel him."[28] Aggressive corps commander John Bell Hood replaced General Johnston as army commander.

Illinois Staats-Zeitung
July 23, 1864
In the field at the Chattahoochie
[Chattachoochee], Ga.
July 14, 1864

Finally, after a 2½-month-long battle, we have received a short rest, which I can assure you we desperately need. This entire campaign has consisted of one continuous and more or less severe engagement with the enemy. Although this campaign cannot be compared to others that I have experienced in terms of strenuous marches, lack of provisions, unfavorable weather, and other things, the eternal commotion caused by the uninterrupted rattling of arms, the daily cannon thunder, and the continuous intense heat of the local climate, have all negatively impacted the health of even those who have the strongest natures. That is why the above-mentioned rest has become an indispensable necessity.

So far as I can learn, the present state of health of our army is satisfactory thanks to effective provisioning. Because we have never suffered from a lack of clothing and provisions (admittedly only consisting of *Crackers,* bacon, coffee, and sugar, as it is not to be expected otherwise), which have always been delivered in full rations, in spite of the destruction of our R. R. connection. Traces of scurvy frequently appeared at the beginning of the campaign, but were quickly eliminated by timely delivery of vinegar.[29]

As you see, up until now we have been quite successful in maintaining our physical health. In contrast, our mental well-being leaves much to be desired, because an illness that goes by the name of "camp *talk*" has afflicted most of our men and has almost degenerated into an epidemic. This sickness shows itself through an all too lively imagination and a strong desire for sensationalism. Such a sickness includes, e.g., the obsession to always want to be in possession of the latest news. There is talk about attacks in which the Rebels are assailed and their entrenchments captured, etc.; of flanking movements, which cut off Johnston from his line of retreat; of thousands of prisoners being taken, etc. Unfortunately, these events did not happen. I say unfortunately, because, remarkably, the results are always favorable for our cause. During the Battle of Resaca many afflicted with the above-mentioned illness had Johnston surrounded and calculated up to the minute when he would surrender with his army; later, they naturally condescended to wait a little longer for this grand moment. I hope God in his goodness will also soon free us from this evil.

Unfortunately, Johnston appears to have been a good acquisition to serve as the commander of the Rebel army, because he knew how to efficiently form an army of soldiers out of a demoralized, cowardly band under Bragg. He also understands that although numerically weaker than us in men and artillery, he can conduct a step by step fighting retreat without suffering considerable losses in any way, except for the land that falls into our hands through his retreats, although this is an irreplaceable loss for the Rebels. As if by magic, Johnston has constructed defenses in most of his positions that are almost impregnable and demonstrate the exceptional genius of well-educated engineers.

A few days ago, after a short stand on this side of the Chattahoochie [Chattachoochee], the Rebels withdrew to the other side, where they constructed a strongly fortified front again. The general view now is that Johnston is not sup-posed to have more than 45,000 men, while Sherman stands opposite him with perhaps 90,000.[30] Of our troops, the 23rd, 16th, 4th, and one division of the 15th Corps are on the other side of the *River*, while I believe that the 14th, 17th, and the rest of the 15th Corps, along with us, the 20th Corps, still remain on this side. We have occupied a heavily wooded chain of hills here, about 3 miles from the river, while our pickets stand at the bank of the Chattahoochie [Chattachoochee], and now and again peacefully bathe in its water with the Rebels. I am sorry that I can-not impart to you *en detail* our present battle line. It is generally unclear except in the highest circles.[31]

Earlier, I was of the opinion that Gen. Johnston would perhaps offer us a battle on the other side of the Chattahoochie [Chattachoochee] as the price for Atlanta; meanwhile, I have modified it and he will probably not do this. Rather, if pressed on his flanks, he will retreat to Macon. This view is generally accepted because Johnston is considered too weak to risk a decisive battle, and because Macon is the second most important strategic point. Atlanta, whose towers can be seen at individual points at a distance of perhaps 10 miles, might be in our hands within approximately two weeks.

Finally, permit me to remark that the 82nd Illinois Regiment is not composed purely of heroes, as one could have concluded based on the praise in an over-exu-berant correspondence in the *Ill. Staats-Zeitung* after the Battle of Resaca. Never-theless, the regiment has consistently done its duty during this campaign and has earned praise as one of the best regiments of the 1st Division of the 20th Corps.[32]

[Unsigned]

Captain Müller wrote a letter to Colonel Hecker on July 29, 1864, but, unfor-tunately, the missive did not reach the colonel or was lost after he received it. It is known that this missive contained information about the Battle of Peachtree Creek on July 20. The battle took place soon after the Twentieth Corps and New-ton's division of the Fourth Corps crossed Peachtree Creek, three miles north of Atlanta. Hood's attack focused mainly on the Twentieth Corps, and, in intense fighting, his Rebels suffered 4,800 casualties and a bloody repulse. Union losses were 1,700. The 82nd Illinois had one officer and nine men killed and 37 men wounded.[33] On July 22, Hood's army attacked McPherson's Army of the Ten-nessee east of Atlanta. Hood's soldiers fought hard but were defeated again. In this battle, known as the Battle of Atlanta, the Union suffered 3,722 casualties, including army commander Maj. Gen. James B. McPherson, who was killed. The Confederates incurred 3,300 to 3,800 casualties. Sherman appointed Maj. Gen. Oliver O. Howard, the Fourth Corps commander, to replace McPherson as head

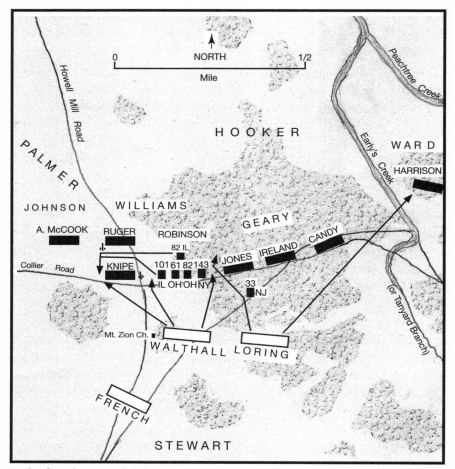

Battle of Peachtree Creek, July 20, 1864

of the Army of the Tennessee. Offended because he did not receive the army command, General Hooker, who was senior in rank to Howard, asked to be relieved of his command. General Williams temporarily commanded the Twentieth Corps (July 27–August 25), until Maj. Gen. Henry W. Slocum arrived from Vicksburg to assume command. Col. James S. Robinson asked to be relieved of his brigade command on July 24 due to severe illness and Col. Horace Broughton, 143rd New York, replaced him as commander.[34]

Sherman next swung the Army of the Tennessee behind both Schofield's and Thomas's armies to approach Atlanta from the west. While moving south on July 28, divisions led by Brig. Gen. John C. Brown and Maj. Gen. Henry D. Clayton of Stephen D. Lee's Corps and Maj. Gen. Edward C. Walthall's division of Maj. Gen. Samuel French's corps vigorously attacked Howard's new command near

Ezra Church. Again the Rebels were repulsed with heavy casualties but Sherman's army was blocked. Sherman then sent Schofield and his two divisions to the right of Howard's army on the west side of Atlanta to envelop Hood's left and destroy the railroad between East Point and Atlanta. After crossing Utoy Creek on August 6, Schofield attacked the Southerners but was defeated. At this point Sherman decided to lay siege to Atlanta and work to cut off its remaining railroad connections and thus its supplies. Meanwhile, the Twentieth Corps resumed its march toward Atlanta on July 22 and entrenched in view of houses and the enemy's entrenchments. Colonel Broughton reported that the right of the brigade's line "rested on Marietta Street a few hundred yards east of the Macon and Western Railroad, and almost one mile distant from the passenger depot in the city." The star corps would remain there until August 25.[35]

Captain Müller's lengthy mid-August letter mentions the boredom of a siege, comments about several current and resigned officers, as well as the military campaign and presidential politics.

···········

In the trenches before Atlanta
August 13th, 1864

Dear Colonel,

I received your valued letter of the 31st of last month on the 7th of this month, and if our letters offer you recreation, then it is doubly so the case with us. Eugene, Panse, and I read them to each other with great interest, thus many an hour is spent in pleasantly reminiscing. We occasionally ponder the future in order to briefly escape from the dreariness, the mind-deadening present, and quasi captivity. A siege like this is dreadful, boring to the point of insanity; in addition, our environment contains shallow people like those in our highly illustrious *Headquar*[*ters*], to which I will return later. I therefore praise the Knoxville campaign with all its discomforts, where we, at least in the evening by the camp fire, listened to your anecdotes and discussed the beauties of the country (remembering Mr. Maloon at Athens, East Tenn., and his neat kitchen, etc.).[36]

You will have my letter of the 29th of last month by now [not found]. It contains details about the battles that occurred, also Bechstein's death. Long before his death, Bechstein saw through our great mogul [Salomon], and hated him thoroughly, perhaps for self-serving reasons. In general, his death has caused little regret, but I pity him. For as long as I knew him, he was, for reasons related to miserliness, dishonest as an officer, often stingy in sordid ways, and even today owes many *Privates,* from whom he had borrowed *Cash.* He lived like a dog and denied himself many a thing; as you know, he let himself be disparaged by his own men and became openly despised. He had saved about $2,000 altogether and thought perhaps to re-enter life as a decent old fellow and had, so to say, secured his future when the fatal lead hit him. That is why I said that I pity him.[37] Lotz is listless, despair drives him to all corners and ends, nowhere peace.—He sends his cordial greetings to you.[38]

That Grünhut [Greenhut] sometimes feels the itch to return again may be so, and is also understandable because in private life, in society, he cannot move in circles and occupy positions like he did in the military. Salomon told me: Gr.[eenhut] is happy that he is at home. Frank, who loves business, had similar *spells,* and because I am in Jerusalem anyway, I want to mention the great mogul [Salomon] himself, who also has the colossal impudence to assure you of his unvarying love??? and loyalty ??? O! the trickster!—Yates, Hoffmann, Hirschbach, all of whom he imagines he has in his pocket will go out of office soon, then his grandeur will be at an end. You are not hostile to him in the field of politics in your uncommitted position, whichever turn things may take, but he could utilize *you,* your *name* in certain cases, for that reason, purely for that reason, to alter the unvarying? loyalty, sycophantic loyalty, that changes remarkably fast with otherwise better pastures. A true canine comedy.[39]

My dear colonel, I believe it is finally time that you disassociate yourself from anything with a trace of the *Creole* from Jerusalem [Salomon]. These people, as clever, smart, and as sly as they are, rejoice so little about the beauties of nature; one sees or hears little of them laughing heartily, just as little do they understand you, or recognize the traits of your character, and don't know to appreciate it. And should such people be allowed to boast at the beer table with letters from your hand? He must be an important man when he brings lengthy letters from the man who had shaken the crown of Germany. Will the neighbor and mother put their heads together?

Don't you believe that Gr.[eenhut], who formerly was the talebearer between your brig. *Headquar.[ters]* and reg., is now still the channel through which S.[alomon] thinks to get news? I have applied thick coloring, and with it allow me to express my fair-minded, candid opinion. It will appear strange to you that I judge Greenhut in such a way; however, S.[alomon] was always informed, and who else could it have been? He believes it must be forgotten because he only needs to draw advice from himself to know that he is well known by others and correctly judged. However, he is not truthful to himself, [so] he cannot be [truthful] to others. He has boasted so long about his fearsome bravery, his unsurpassable leadership of the regt. (*the old one was totally incapable of this*) until he now finally believes it himself, and does not fail to continuously show his own, elevated self to us and to *Outsiders.* They have prophesied Mihalotzy's destiny for him. They want him to take a giant step.[40]

Panse's comparison to a mosquito sets the stage. In order to complete the setting, take the flowers of the regt., Bruhn, Loeb, Kirchner, Stueven, as continuous besiegers of *Headquar.[ter]s,* who frequently bad mouth you with the brutish Major. It's almost as if after the lion's death the donkey comes around and kicks him. You can believe that I, Gottlob, Lotz, Eugene, Bal[c]k, Eri[c]kson, and Lemberg [Lindbergh] do not feel at home and content with these miserable, stupid boys, who, if just looked at, tremble. Every opportunity is seized to shun these nobles, if only for a day.[41]

Panse, Eugene, Lender, Boerner, and I visited Col. Maymann [Meumann] yesterday (3rd Mo.) lying 5 miles to our right and who will soon go home. The right wing, parallel with the R. R. and running 2–2½miles, swings around continuously with a large left wheel with daily fighting, while we remain in our old position appropriate for rest, and bombard the city day and night. The Reb[el] forts do not damage us at all, thus the wretches are unpretentious and silent. You will find a map of Atlanta showing our position enclosed. There is the usual understanding not to publicize it. With the next letter I will be able to send one to you showing our battlefield on the 20th. The corps stands in the following order: 4th, 20th, 16th, 17th, 15th, 14th, 23rd. In one of your earlier letters you expressed the desire to publicize a letter. I choose not to consent because I frequently refer to matters that are not suitable for this purpose, e.g., (today's letter).

As I hear through its com.[manding] off.[icer], the remainder of the 24th [Illinois] appears certain not to come to us because we were too often in the fire under Hooker. This did not originate with the men, because they wanted to join us. Osterhaus and Slocum, the latter for the 20th Corps, were expected yesterday evening.[42]

Deserters reported the fall of Mobile; one knows with certainty this could only have occurred by *reduction* of the forts that control the harbor.[43] Did you know that Capt. Newcomb is dead? He fell on the 21st of last month riding the picket line. He was wounded and died in Reb[el] hands. We found his grave during our advance on Atlanta. He was a brave officer. Schurz is supposed to go back to the East to attend a court of inquiry demanded by Siegel [Sigel]. According to a different tune, Schurz is supposed to obtain the Dept. of Miss. and Rosecranz [Rosecrans] active *Com.[mand]* in the field. That Kramer has accepted a position pleases me immensely. Laxforelle knew that Hooker passed through Louisville the next morning because of family circumstances, then back to New York. *La noblesse oblige* [*Noblesse oblige* is generally used to imply that with wealth, power, and prestige come responsibilities.][44]

The 75th [Pennsylvania] assists the 45th [New York] in Nashville, while the 68th [N.Y.] is supposed to be in Knoxville. Our siege appears to want to stretch into a long one. I believe however that before the middle of Sept. a significant battle will occur in the East as well as here. The Macon R. R. is again repaired; also, the *Raid* like all others was unsuccessful in that it cost many people. Stoneman is supposed to have been captured [on July 31]. No loss for us. He has never accomplished anything. [45]

With pleasure your kind invitation will be complied with, as soon as it is possible, only I fear we will obtain no peace. If only Eugene and I could get away together.

Debacles like Petersburgh [Petersburg] could become uncomfortable for the (Godlike) Abe [Lincoln]. I believe that his election is still very uncertain. Will he give McClellan command over Washington and the Potomac line? Would that not lend a hand to a coup by McClellan? The same could be achieved through a special army recruited for him with Seymour's help and the *Copperheads* of the other states. Wherefore I ask next, is Lincoln so cowardly not to have Vallandigham arrested? [46]

> With esteem
> Yours
> Rudolph Müller
> Capt.

In the preceding letter Müller displays his cynicism and tendency to criticize people who do not measure up to his high personal standards or who violate the rules of good military conduct. He describes Lieutenant Bechstein as greedy, stingy, and miserly; Lieutenant Colonel Salomon is viewed as an ambitious opportunist who uses exaggeration, politicians, other officers, and acquaintances for self-advancement; Major Rolshausen is brutish and cowardly; Lieutenant Loeb is stupid; former Captain Greenhut may have been an informant to Salomon; and Bruhn, Loeb, Kirchner, and Steveun [Stueven] all hang around the regimental headquarters and criticize Colonel Hecker with the major and are weaklings and miserable. stupid boys. Müller also wonders why his good friend Eugene Weigel is associating with Salomon. He identifies several officers who have negative opinions of many of the above-named men, indicating some discord within the 82nd's officer corps.

Müller's statement about being in Jerusalem implies that he was bothered by the sizable Jewish presence in the regiment. Prejudice against Jews was not uncommon in the United States; it also existed among some senior commanders in the army. It is difficult to determine the degree to which some of Müller's comments about Bechstein and several other Jewish officers were based on facts and/ or his own sense of propriety, and the degree to which such comments were due to anti-Jewish prejudices. His description of Bechstein's avarice, stinginess, and miserliness could have been factual and he would have described the lieutenant's behavior as such even if Bechstein had not been Jewish. However, his statements that, "These people . . . rejoice so little about the beauties of nature" and "one sees or hears little of them laughing heartily," indicate that he views Jews as racially inferior or at least distinguishably different from non-Jewish Germans.[47] This belief had to color his feelings about Jews. With respect to Captain Greenhut, Müller reveals an understanding of the social limitations of a Jew in America at this time.

Eleven

Atlanta Is Ours

he 82nd Illinois Regiment remained behind its works on the north side of the Chattahoochee River until August 25, 1864, enduring "the daily monotony of picket and artillery firing," while "sharpshooters kept doing their annoying work." On the 25th the regiment advanced to the Chattahoochee Bridge and built entrenchments for its entire brigade and then encamped. News arrived on September 2 that part of its division, including some regiments from its own brigade, had entered Atlanta, which had been abandoned by Gen. Braxton Bragg's army on the evening of September 1. Bragg vacated Atlanta after Sherman had wheeled six of his seven corps southwest and south of the city, cutting the Atlanta and West Point Railroad and the Macon and Western Railroad; an attack by Hardee's and Lee's corps failed at Jonesboro on August 31. Bragg concentrated his army at Lovejoy Station, seven miles south of Jonesboro. After the Secessionists defeated a Federal attack at Lovejoy Station, Sherman returned his army to the Atlanta area. Lieutenant Colonel Salomon reported that on September 4 "[w]e marched through the conquered city, with colors flying and bands playing, and occupied the works erected by our enemies." The 82nd Illinois and its brigade moved into the enemy works on the east side of the city, with its left covering the Buckhead road.

Lieutenant Colonel Salomon was placed in charge of the prison barracks and the 82nd guarded Rebel prisoners from September 12 until October 4. Salomon's command then worked on the defenses around Atlanta until October 15, when it engaged in extensive foraging expeditions. The 82nd Illinois would remain in Atlanta until November 15, when it and its corps joined in Maj. Gen. William T. Sherman's famous March to the Sea. The letters in this chapter were written during the regiment's stay in Atlanta.[1]

Group of Officers of the 82nd Illinois Infantry Regiment, Atlanta 1864. Seated in the center holding a sword and with a large hat on his knee is Lt. Col. Edward S. Salomon. To Salomon's right is Maj. Ferdinand Rolshausen. To Salomon's left is surgeon Charles E. Boerner. Standing on the far left in the second row is 1st Lt. Frank Kirchner. The soldier wearing the officer of the day sash is Capt. Eugene F. Weigel. To Weigel's right, with his hand on his hip, is Capt. Rudolph Müller. First Lt. Christian Erickson is on the far right of the photograph, 1st Lt. William Loeb is standing next to Erickson, and 1st Lt. Carl Lotz is standing fourth from the right. The other officers are unidentified. The above-named officers were identified by Eric Benjaminson and the editor of this book (courtesy of Chicago History Museum [ICHi-08203, photographer unknown]).

Müller reveals in the first letter that he is "emotionally sick" and would like to leave the army because cannot bear living in a "synagogue." Acting Adjutant Loeb and Major Rolshausen are mentioned again in unfavorable ways.

Atlanta, Ga.
September 15th, 1864

Dear Colonel:

Confirming receipt of your valued letter from the 14th of this month, I am finally giving you a sign of life from me again. Eugene [Weigel] has written to you about capturing Atlanta, so little remains for me to report about it. Enclosed is a map of the terrain showing Sherman's last movement toward Jonesboro, near where the battle took place from August 31 to September 1, 1864, the outcome of which you learned long ago. I have shown Sh[erman]'s march route in red. Hood arrived near J[onesboro] at the same time as our army and attacked immediately; however, he was repulsed with a bloody nose. An attack followed on the 1st, carried out mainly by the 14th and 17th Corps, which finally broke through the center of the Reb[s]. However, before the Reb[s] evacuated Atlanta they destroyed 4 R. R. trains, 4 [6 or 7] locomotives, and 84 [81] cars loaded with ammunition, weapons, etc., which turned the ruins of the Augusta Depot into a true Sodam [Sodom] and Gomor[r]a[h]. We saw fires and heard explosions during the night of the 1st to the 2nd while we lay at the Chattahotee [Chattahoochee] to protect communications.[2]

The enemy's main army is supposed to be at Griffin [Lovejoy Station] about 40 miles south of here, while ours has returned here in order to have a month's rest to reorganize. Then, as Sherman very naively announced in an order, *we will have a fine winter campaign,* one in which I meanwhile intend not to take part because I am strongly considering resigning. If I could only concoct a plausible lie I could use as a basis for resigning. You cannot imagine how things are here—I am actually emotionally sick. You should see what goes on here—just like a synagogue.[3]

Bal[c]k was wounded when he went to Ringgold to get *Regimental & Company* papers. He had the bad luck to be shot in the leg by bushwhackers while visiting the battlefield. The coffee buyer is from Fallmout[h] = the brave (?) Loeb, acting adjutant, whose cousins from Atlanta—Mr. Stern, Mr. Seligman, Mr. Bärman, etc., hang around High *Head*[q]*uar*[*ters*] every day, and since they are good, quite good Union people, even eat the Sabbath meal there, while the brutal major drivels about his misapplied rank and guzzles schnapps to give him formidable, fake courage. Now that is [illegible word].[4]

Neussel arrived here yesterday morning in a completely deranged condition (sunstroke and *Clemens* [seizures?]). Fortunately, Panse and I lugged him to a hospital, where he is receiving good treatment and is sedate. Since then he has become quite rational. We have made him aware that the Dr. Schroeder pursuing him, who must have mistreated him, was infamously cashiered and is in Canada, whereupon he [Neussel] then became considerably relieved and now wants to go home again.[5]

Osterhaus lies by East Point, the 23rd Corps in Decatur and the Army of the Cumb.[erland] is here. With cordial greetings to you and your family [illegible word] with great respect

Yours,

Rudolph Müller, Capt.

Captain Müller's next letter contains complaints about certain officers, including Lt. Col. Edward S. Salomon, Surg. Charles E. Boerner, Col. Horace Broughton, and Maj. Gen. Peter J. Osterhaus, but no mention of resigning his own commission. He also addresses presidential politics.

Atlanta, Georgia
September 27, 1864

Dear Colonel,

Your assumption that our Grand Inquisitor [Salomon] would share Mihalotzy's fate is beginning to become a reality because today he has come down from his high horse onto a mule through the enclosed petition [missing] of the *Officer Corps.* All the grandeur of his dizzying height suddenly came to nothing through this document—evidence of his powerlessness like there is no greater—and the nicest part of the affair is that it came from his closest friends, Heinzmann, Bruhn, Kirchner, etc. Eugene exposed it and it also became available to me; we have all signed it already. I followed the desire of the rest with pleasure. He put some of his favorites in a bad mood toward him by *non-approval* of resignations and disapproving *sick leaves,* and they have indeed not thought about the fact that they are giving him a slap in the face by this. That is what happens when you try to achieve popularity through any means. The document says very simply, we do not want you anymore; you, whom you alone consider as indispensable, because with a *consolidation* so many officers become *surplus.*[6]

Considering the numbers, 462 [men] in the *Aggegrate,* would yield 5 comp[anies]. and require 15 off.[icers]. Therefore, of the 13 [present officers] not a single one disappears, while 5 companies make a Lt. Col. unnecessary. What do you say to that? Insufficient leniency repays itself poorly. S.[alomon] was still so careless as to rip up the document in Lender's presence and threw it out of the window in a disdainful way.[7]

Col. Robinson returned yesterday as our brigade commander. Boughton had to relinquish his high place and return to his regiment (143rd N.Y.), which came hard to the arrogant man, who cursed! Duty bound, our tinny brass band began a serenade, providing quite good music for his diminished power, and Edw. S.[alomon], the major, and Dr. B.[oerner] came, the last more *Ass* than surgeon, also in order to booze (especially the last). Panse and I visited Lender and were sitting quite happily in his room when Dr. Boerner came in uninvited, and he really stepped into hot water. Panse, who naturally cannot get over his crooked right arm due to Dr. Boerner's incompetency, really let him have it. If that did not make Dr. Boerner feel like he was sitting on hot coals, I don't know what would have. This much is sure, Boerner has to have such a thick hide, so thick that not even a 12-pounder *solid shot* can penetrate it, which you, however, cannot assume with our major's significant [lack of] *Courage*.

Edward Salomon came somewhat late. The blame for this was the celebration of the so-called "long day" held at cousin Mrs. Löventhal's; but what harm was there in that, after all, it was cheap amusement for a ham, a bottle of wine, and some coffee, which the loyal Louis [Salomon?], as a young gallant of the lady cousin, balanced over dangerous footpaths while taking a stroll incognito during twilight. It is a bliss that the women and children at home do not see. I hardly believe that the earlier good discipline presently suffers through this amusement; even a private knows that "each animal wants his pleasure," and therefore views this with more complacency than earlier.[8]

Neussel has completely recovered and is back to his old self; he expects his release any day now. Also Schurz is really on the *Stump* for *Old* Abe.

Panse has probably written to you that you supposedly committed post office robbery. That borders on the laughable. Blair and Lincoln are probably behind it, perhaps because they remain neutral.[9]

Col. Robinson brought the news that the Ill. and Ind. troops will go home to vote, so they can pick up the *drafted men* for their regiments at the same time. The *disapprovals* of leaves for our *enlisted men* mean that they will not all go home, perhaps a larger % might be granted leaves later. So the whole affair appears improbable to me; it is, however, for us the single hope for a short leave.[10]

Sheridan's victories are pleasing. I hope that Grant will get down to work now. We need a decided victory on his part in order to crown our achievements up to now and to shake the rebellion to its foundation.[11]

There are no new actions to report from the army here. We are taking it easy with our guard duty, the army in the background. Logan, 15th Corps, and Howard and other generals are on leave and we do not expect a renewal of the campaign for about 6 weeks. Osterhaus will thus temporarily command the Dept. [of the] Tennessee. We (Panse, Eugene, and I) recently had the honor to visit him. I have become much disappointed in him because of his truly, conspicuously biased opinion expressed about the troops of the divs., corps [of the Army of the] Potomac, as well as [the] Cumberland; he stated that his Missourians are the only ones who actually strike and always sing. I would have liked to have laughed in his face when he described the Illinois men as completely worthless soldiers.[12]

> Farewell dear colonel,
> With best regards to you and your family, I remain, yours,
> Rudolph Müller, Captain

While the captain was penning the preceding letter Maj. Gen. Nathan Bedford Forrest's cavalry corps was busy attacking Sherman's line of communication with Nashville, and General Hood was preparing to send his Army of Tennessee north across the Chattahoochee River to sever Sherman's communication lines [the railroads] to force him out of Atlanta and into a battle.

On October 3, 1864, Müller began a missive that was not completed until October 20. In it he describes military operations and happenings with his regiment as far back as September 5, when Sherman issued his order expelling all the citizens of Atlanta who were not working for his armies. Important events occurring after September 5 include Maj. Gen. Nathan Bedford Forrest's cavalry capturing Athens, Alabama, and wrecking the railroad for various stretches from Chattanooga to Nashville; General Hood moving his 40,000-man army north of the Chattahoochee River to sever Sherman's line of communication between Atlanta and Chattanooga (the Western and Atlanta Railroad); Sherman sending six of his seven corps north to deal with Hood and Forrest; one of Hood's corps capturing Dalton, Georgia, on October 13; and Hood's army moving southwest to Gadsden, Alabama, where the army rested on October 20. In the following letter Müller also updates Colonel Hecker on Lieutenant Colonel Salomon's status and activities.[13]

―――――

Atlanta, Georgia
October 3rd, 1864

Dear Colonel,

I received your valued letter from Sept. 18 on October 1, and yet again the communication with you down here is intermittent. Our last newspaper was dated Sept. 21.

First, the bridges at Whiteside [Tenn.] and Bridgeport [Ala.] were supposed to be damaged and the 68th[?] and 58th[?] taken as prisoners; it turned out, however, that Forrest had destroyed the bridge over the Elk River [Sept. 29] and taken possession of Decart, Tenn. [Decatur, Ala.]. Troops continue to go to the rear. General Thomas himself has left for there. Last night, Oct. 3, the 4th Corps marched with artillery and train toward Marietta.[14]

During the 10-day armistice for an exchange of prisoners and moving the citizens Hood has caused a change of front, so that our left wing rests at Cambeton [Campbellton] where it entrenched itself to support Sandtown at the Chattahoochee. Part of the troops are supposed to march to Rome, perhaps in order to cut off Hardee's corps, which is thought to operate toward Huntsville [sent to command coasts of S.C., Ga., Fla.] (which rumor I do not believe). I cannot believe that Hood scattered his already weakened and demoralized army, and risks its complete destruction. His strength now is not at all sufficient to be able to induce Sherman to temporarily give up Atlanta. All that Hood could aim to achieve through such attempts would be more possible ways to refuse our immediate advance toward Macon and Mobile and even that might occur, as soon as we have accumulated enough supplies. As deserters reported, Georgia is nearly depleted of foodstuffs and no longer able to feed the army; the prov.[isions] now come from Mississippi. Atlanta will certainly become a more significant armed location and for the future will remain one of the most important military points. It becomes stronger through the erection of new forts, some even established in the city. The nicest buildings, structures, and villas must pay their last tribute out of strict necessity and be cleared away in order to construct our forts. Many persons would no longer recognize the places where they were born or lived. The 20th Corps appears to remain here as garrison for the present.[15]

Oct. 4th. Today the regt. was freed from night duty, guarding *Pris.[oners]*. We have pitched our camp by the brig. again, and expect to be moved again in a few days with the whole corps to another place in the city, in order to occupy more concentrated works. When the new works are finished, the very extensive Reb[el] works are supposed to be razed (reduced).

Hood has actually crossed over the Chattahoochee with ⅔ of his army, an act of desperation that will cost his army. The 20th Corps troops are the only ones south of the Chattahoochee, while Sherman's main body marched off to the rear. Yesterday, a battle is supposed to have occurred at Big Shanty, N.[orth] of Marietta, in which the dead on our side were reported to be 600. This suggests a total of 3,000 dead and wounded [casualties greatly exaggerated]. The Reb[s] were driven off and pursued.[16]

Could Lee perhaps have detached a part of his army in order to threaten us from the east or south? And Hood still needs to make his final movement—we have to wait and see. Yesterday we received good news from Va., appearing in a telegram from Stanton. Grant is supposed to have won a victory, taken 32 guns and is 4 miles from Richmond.[17]

Our noble commander, who still has not managed to get his eagle, departed with great pain from his nice headquarters. All remonstrance, all endeavors were fruitless because Ahsmuhsen [Asmussen], to whom he showed proof of an error in the prisoner rosters, was offended and insulted, and the result was, according to Edward S., that the 82nd was relieved of their present duty. Revenge is sweet.[18]

The provost marshall, a Col. Parkhurst (9th Michigan), made all imaginable efforts to keep us there because Edward S. had done an excellent job administering the post, and, firstly, saved him a lot of trouble by doing all kinds of work, which he actually did not have to do. Col. Parkhurst offered to give Robinson his own regiment, 100 muskets stronger than ours, but the latter (according to Edward S.) would not take two of his Michigan regiments for the 82nd Ill.—which always has an excellent standing.

But I mustn't forget the main joke. He gave Col. Parkhurst a present of a box of champagne, when not 5 minutes later the relieving order arrived, indeed annoying. We were highly amused by that; however, he cannot deny his nature, he had to be paid off. Be it Moses or Itzig, that's how that kind of business is done. Incidentally, it was not quite clear who had the ownership rights to the box, but it and 2 more were sent to Gen. Thomas C/O Lt. Col. Salomon—nobody knows by whom.[19]

After our consolidation projects were launched something had to be done, and what happened? A lightning rod was devised that was supposed to take our minds off of things and turn tempers in a less dangerous direction. A great artist came, Mr. Goldsticker, also one of our people, and he had to take pictures of us, a splendid

Group of Officers of the 82nd Illinois Infantry Regiment, Atlanta 1864. Seated on the far left is 1st Lt. Frank Kirchner; standing behind Kirchner, holding a pipe, is 1st Lt. Christian Erickson. Lt. Col. Edward S. Salomon is seated at the table touching a mug. 1st Lt. William Loeb is standing on the far right and Capt. Eugene F. Weigel is standing with his back to Loeb. The other officers are unidentified. The above-named officers were identified by Eric Benjaminson and the editor of this book (courtesy of the Chicago History Museum [ICHi-08204, photographer unknown]).

group. The lieutenant colonel is seated in the center like the sun, and around him are the great ones of the empire, like rays of light flowing from the sun. And if we had not just barely let our eyes tear up from the sun during the act of posing, the unacquainted could have assumed that we were also bedazzled by the radiance from his greatness. The counterpart to this constitutes a duplicate photograph, a boozing group. He occupied a table with an empty bottle and mug, with his well-known shrewd deceitful face the focal point, in the circle around him the minions of the court smoking and gambling; I am very sorry that Eugene has thrown himself away so far as to appear in the latter scene and generally wags too much around him, dines there, etc. Eugene cannot possibly respect and consider him to be honorable, and he does not. Why then a feigned friendship? Perhaps philosophy is in this smaller diplomatic game, *I can't see it.* The best figure in the first picture is the handsome *Quar Mr.* [quartermaster] with the now really slender waist and jaunty mustache. He appears as if he wanted to say: a true canine comedy, you should be so fit. I would send you copies, if both images were not fabrications.[20]

You would have been pleased today if you had seen our regiment, now again 170 muskets. The men are vigorous and it is really a delight to see them under arms, but it is torture that an ethically so worthless trio of *Field* and *Staff* reaps the fruit of the seeds planted with so much care. The stupid youth Loeb rides on horseback at the head of the regt. with drawn saber. It is a crying shame. The major with the mustached face lets his nebulous commands resound; if no bullets fly, it is very nice, and his mogul has, during this peaceful time, also been upstanding again, which is nicer, and the nicest is that he [at?] Whiteside no. 2, chased the demure Reb.[s] without success. I now think I have spent more pages than the whole blister is worth and end this theme.[21]

For the first time since Whiteside, Eugene and I revel under the Reb. *Fly* [tent] that you gave us, again in more splendid forest air, and I thought about forays from the farm, like hunting, fishing; unfortunately, warfare must remain the virtuous desire for now, and perhaps as before we have to be satisfied with half rations. The Chattahoochee R. R. bridge, as well as the wagon bridge above it have both washed away as a result of the recent heavy rains. Only one of the two wagon bridges still stands. Today, our animals still do not have any more fodder. Nice prospects.

Bal[c]k wrote recently that his self cure has worked well and the one opening of his wound is nearly healed; however, he says that he feels uneasy when he thinks of the synagogue, Jerusalem, and the reign of the high priests, and that he would have to carefully consider whether he wanted to wear the once discarded shackles again.

Oct. 6th—Much time has passed and if the postal connection is interrupted even longer, my letter will grow to be a true tapeworm. A lieutenant colonel [Salomon] with whom you are acquainted has lain very sick since the day before

yesterday with a Madam Löventhal, a pretty young wife, who lives in the city
and sometimes took strolls. Imagine our shock, when yesterday morning at daybreak, Mr. Löventhal came to our camp. He came in order to call our attention to
the condition of a suddenly and dangerously ill man, I meant to say officer. The
consequences of a strenuous campaign sometimes manifest themselves much
later; the symptoms may show up even after six weeks of rest. That might be the
case here, but bad people made remarks about punches and giving black eyes,
and rumor in the person of the major was the last straw. It was decided that such
a thing should remain a state secret, completely in confidence, because out here
news of a terrible defeat spreads like wildfire, so Eugene, Lender, and I set out to
inquire about the condition of the commander.[22]

Naturally, we were pleasantly surprised to find that our knight Edward came to
greet us not bathed in sweat, not in bed with feverish heat, but only with a black
eye and sundry marks from head to foot, and, incidentally, *in good spirits.* A quite
normal common *Quar. Mr.* [*quartermaster*], by no means our Panse, because he
can no longer be a blacksmith; no, one surnamed Erdmann from the 15th Mo.,
who had the audacity, first of all to insult the lady of the house (for whose honor
he naturally had to take up the cudgels) and still for good measure to play games
with our noble chief. Since the cat was out of the bag, much was said about the as-
sassin's vulgarity and according to his perspective each of us would have acted likewise, and even Gen. Thomas would vindicate him in this chivalrous action. Now, I
hope that at least our *Privates* will think with careful consideration about the affair,
because one hand washes the other.[23]

I still have not learned officially about our activities north of the Chatt.[ahoo-
chee]. One supposes that it is Hood's design to take possession of the 2 million
rations that we have piled up on Al[l]atoona Mtn. or also to press through East
Tenn[.] and Ky. to disrupt the theater of war there.

Thomas, who has traveled to Chattanooga, is supposed to operate from up
there, and according to the latest news has turned toward Dallas. The army has
taken 15 days of rations with it and for the 20th Corps, 100 days of them are on
hand, but not a granule for the mules and Art.[tillery] horses, which were collaps-
ing in great numbers.

Col. Maymann [Maumann] found himself in command of about 6[00]–700
men, nothing but the remainder of mustering out troops here.

October 20. Yesterday evening, returning from a 5-day *Forage Expedition,* I
heard that the mail would be dispatched in about 15 minutes. We brought back
692 wagons full of corn, some cattle, etc.; evidence that the South is still not
starved out. The *Expedition* went in a S.E. direction about 20 miles and 10 miles
south from Stone Mtn. It was strenuous, but interesting. According to a current

telegram, Hood has annihilated our occupying forces in Tilton and Dalton; Sherman is located in Snake Creek Gap. Otherwise, nothing new.[24]

   Yours truly,
   Your friend
   Rudolph Müller,
   Captain

  With his corps still posted in Atlanta and separated from the rest of Sherman's huge army, Captain Müller tells his friend Hecker about a lively celebration he and certain other officers held, much to Salomon's dismay. He also discusses the upcoming presidential election, the need for a decisive victory over the Confederacy, the demoralizing lack of support war on the home front, and agrees with the colonel's decision to personally support Lincoln but not to campaign for him.[25]

       Camp 82nd Ill. Vols.
       Atlanta, Ga.
       October 25, 1864

My dear Colonel,

  Barely back in action after the celebration of your silver wedding anniversary on the 23rd of this month, we continued the celebration last evening among our virgins with a bowl (*Camp kettle*) of *Punch*.[26] We recalled miseries and sorrows. We were happy and cheerful, and I hope that you have recovered from your rheumatic pain and spent the day in happy domestic circles. If premonition, sympathy, *etc.*, exist, then today your ears must still burn, because the manifold toasts given in your honor became so lusty that one man after another slipped under the table. Friend Gottlob fell first, then Lender. I had to try to tow them both home; and, Granbelino, when he at last attempted to guide himself home, got stranded on a sandbank, where he practiced swimming in 3 inches of water and got us wet, but finally reached his shanty. They tied on a big one and next morning had terrible hangovers when they had to do picket duty. Erickson and Lemberg [Lindbergh] also participated in the heavy drinking. Sadly, Lotz was absent on duty; however, our brave Captain Heinzmann became so enlightened that he finally played the role of a host with a white napkin for Eugene. Soon we all were so pleased; the thing could not have turned out better.

  The popularity-seeking blister [Salomon], which in any case will burst soon, listened with subdued rage, and how we amused ourselves while we celebrated your memory. About 9 o'clock when the *Bugler* was sent close to where Panse [illegible word] and blew taps, the Non Com *Quar*[*ter*]*master* staff, which celebrated the day with [illegible word] answered with the song *Hecker, Struve,* etc., melody *Schleswig-Holstein.* So it happened. The blister could not open his mouth. It has come so far that a Sgt. of Co. (C), could rail at the *Commander* G . . . rascal, *horse thief, Mule* seller, without anyone daring to say a word. *Don't like to create any bad feelings.* Shameful meekness!!! Pretty situation isn't it? I can report that you have justice, I also want no word more about the lost young fief[?]. Point made. Neus[s]el received his leave and is now on his way home. Panse has applied for a furlough and it has been *approved & recommended* at the regimental level. As for me, two officers are in line ahead of me but I hope that during the course of the winter I will be given the opportunity for a furlough.[27]

Rumors say that Sherman's army will occupy the railroad from Huntsville [Alabama]/Chattanooga to Atlanta and move into winter quarters. Hood stands about 40 miles west and southwest of Rome. Sherman is in Rome. The R. R. will be completely repaired in a few days and we will be provided with everything. Tomorrow we are in store for a 5-day foraging tour.

An off.[icial] dispatch from Grant to Sherman announced a new victory by Sheridan, who in spite of initially suffering setbacks beat the enemy and captured 50 guns.[28]

I am anxious about the election. The 61st Ohio had a majority of 8 for Lincoln out of a total of about 120 *votes.* Lincoln had better results in the 82nd Ohio. The numerous dispatches (*grape vine*) about our trip to Ill. to vote are *ausser Cours* [?].

I believe that the filling up of the regt. is something that stands in the distant future, and should we actually get recruits they would be a cheerful lot. What can be expected when patriotism has always been trampled on in the past, and which now is completely extinguished, and at most glimmers a little bit when news of a victory arrives? They are miserable shopkeepers, these citizens of the Republic, who are lacking almost all characteristics of genuine republicans, and after 3 years of bloody war still have not learned that peace can be achieved only through decisiveness and the rapid development of the North's entire strength.

Schurz is considered skillful on the *Stump.* In any case his political circle of activity detracts much from his soldierly honor, and he also will be tossed overboard as soon as Lincoln sits firmly in the saddle again, and like Siegel [Sigel], in the end, still will be given a court martial. Fremont [Frémont] is now finished and with him the St. Louis German radicalism, which, in spite of its Prussian loyalty, is being kicked aside by his American fellow believers. It is best for one to stand above the parties, that way one avoids being kicked and maligned. I believe that you are very smart to remain steadfast with your intentions; also, no one knows how it would harm you, and will try to in vain.[29]

I will try to get rid of my whims, have already begun and if first the various wines run down my thirsty throat, the last fresh liverwurst will be washed down by a new supply.

In the hope that we will celebrate your golden wedding anniversary with you, with kind regards,

>Yours, with esteem,
>Rudolph Müller, Capt.

Captain Müller wrote the following letter one week before he and his regiment marched off from Atlanta to participate in Sherman's famous "March to the Sea."

>*Camp at* Atlanta, Ga.
>November 8th, 1864
>12:00 a.m.

Dear Colonel,

This will be the last news you hear from me for months. The last mail leaves at 7 o'clock in the morning and then none until Mobile or Savannah. Atlanta will be vacated and we will go south and live off the land. The 14th, 15th, 17th, and 20th Corps comprises our *Force,* which is supposed to be led by Sherman himself. Thomas has organized a force in Nashville and if Hood crosses the Tenn. [River] he will tan his hide.[30]

I anticipate many stresses and strains and a few wild boars. Anyway, it will be an interesting hike. We will probably eat fresh oysters on this line. How I envy Panse, who has had a keen nose. Eugene is an aide to [General] Williams, who recently heard of some of your wit, which so pleased him that he expressed the desire to become acquainted with you, and opined that he would surely get along well with you, which I also believe. Williams is a really wild, tough guy and a good soldier. My command now extends to Co. A. & F. Bruhn has an ulcer on his leg and therefore cannot take part in the campaign. Just back from leave, Stueven suffers from the sins of his youth and was sent to the *Rear.* Lemberg [Lindbergh] takes the regt.'s money to Chicago. Few off.[icers] remain back.

Winkelried [Loeb] is the right hand, head and heart of our brave commander Friedensreich [Salomon]. The Great Mogul accompanied Mrs. Löventhal on a six-day trip to Nashville, and now can't reach his command despite his fearsome courage. For heaven's sake, how does the 20th Corps, how does Sherman start without him? So it will be done says Prof. Marx. What does Panse's appetite say to fresh liverwurst! O pain![31]

It was an all-important [election] day today, if *Old* Abe actually firmly sits in the saddle, I believe his *Shoulde[r], straps* sit darn loose.

Price has been dispensed with, but something does not seem quite right with Grant for it appears he only won 15 miles to the rear.[32]

Live well, with best regards, greetings to you, your family, and Panse.

Yours truly,
Rudolph Müller.

[P. S] Diefenbach no. 2 has again incorrectly set the arm of Franziscus, who broke it by a fall from his horse. Fortunately, the boy came into other hands at the right time.[33]

Twelve

The March to the Sea

ealizing that he could neither recapture Atlanta nor defeat Maj. Gen. William T. Sherman's Federal army, Gen. John Bell Hood moved his Army of Tennessee farther into Alabama on October 17, 1864, to prepare to invade Tennessee. Sherman sent the Fourth and Twenty-third Corps north to oppose this invasion, and on November 15, 1864, commenced his famous March to the Sea (Savannah campaign) from Atlanta. The victor at Atlanta planned to "make Georgia howl" by striking southeastward and destroying resources supporting the Southern war effort, including railroads, factories, and military stores. As historian David J. Eicher points out, the army chieftain, "defied military principles by operating deep within enemy territory and without lines of supply or communication." Once Sherman reached Savannah he could be resupplied by sea and then move north to cooperate with Maj. Gen. Ulysses S. Grant to capture Richmond, Virginia, and to eliminate Gen. Robert E. Lee's dangerous Army of Northern Virginia. Grant's Army of the Potomac had been stalled twenty miles south of Richmond in front of Petersburg's massive entrenchments since mid-June 1864.[1]

Sherman's force consisted of two wings that marched twenty to forty miles apart. The left wing consisted of the Fourteenth Corps and Twentieth Corps and was called the Army of Georgia. Maj. Gen. Henry W. Slocum commanded this army. Brig. Gen. Alpheus S. Williams headed the Twentieth Corps; Brig. Gen. Nathaniel J. Jackson led its First Division; and Col. James S. Robinson commanded the division's Third Brigade. Major Rolshausen commanded the 82nd Illinois in Lieutenant Colonel Salomon's absence.[2]

The right wing consisted of the Fifteenth Corps and Seventeenth Corps—the Army of the Tennessee. (One division of the Sixteenth Corps was transferred to the Fifteenth Corps and its other division joined the Twenty-third Corps for this

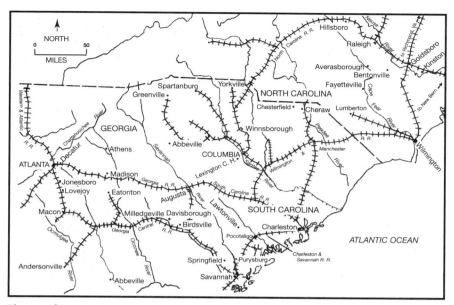

Theater of Operations August 1864 to May 1865

campaign.) Maj. Gen. Oliver O. Howard led the Army of the Tennessee. Only 3,000 Georgia militiamen and perhaps up to 10,000 troopers of Maj. Gen. Joseph Wheeler's cavalry command were available to oppose Sherman's overwhelming force of 55,000 infantrymen, 5,000 cavalry, 2,000 artillerymen, and 64 guns during the march to Savannah.[3]

The 82nd Illinois marched to Savannah with its corps by way of Decatur, Madison, Eatonton, Milledgeville (the capital of Georgia), Davisborough, Birdsville, and Springfield. They reached within four and a half miles of Savannah on December 11, and found flooded rice fields and 10,000 troops of Lt. Gen. William J. Hardee's command strongly entrenched and supported by artillery. During the march the German regiment participated in destroying stretches of railroad tracks and stations on the Georgia Central Railroad and the Charleston and Savannah Railroad. Their brigade did not engage in any significant fighting during its 350-mile journey. The 82nd Illinois and two other regiments of its brigade were withdrawn from the front lines late on December 11 and sent to protect the corps's trains from the rear. On December 19 Rudolph Müller penned a short letter to Colonel Hecker mainly advising that he was in trouble and describing the current military situation with respect to his corps.[4]

Under Arrest Camp 82nd Ill. Vols.
Cherokee Hill *near* Savanah[,] Ga.
December 19th, 1864

My dear Colonel,

Since about 3 days ago, I find myself sharing much of Panse's former fate in chains and bonds. I slapped that impertinent fellow Loeb in the presence of 4–5 officers and a *Forage party* that I commanded, because he accused me of a lie; the consequence of which is a now slumbering but revenge-seeking lion, and I minus my saber. I resigned immediately; however, I withdrew my resignation and resolved to await the judgment of a *Court Martial.* I doubt that Winke[l]ried [Loeb] has enough *Courage* to press charges, even though I and some other officers encouraged him to do so. I spoke to the president of the last *Court Martial,* who told me how he would handle such a charge and I at most could be reprimanded for the breach *of good order and discipline.*[5]

After a 24-day march we reached our current position in front of Sav's [Savannah's] works, which are protected by immense swamps, overgrown with impenetrable brushwood, and with felled trees blocking the only linking roads [causeways] for miles, barely permitting an encroachment. The enemy has batteries in position behind this blockade that much impedes our hacking through it. However, the seizure of Fort McAllister by the 2nd Div. of the 15th Corps on the 13th of this month and the capture of its occupants, consisting of about 80 cannoneers, and the *capture of* 23 guns, put them in connection with the fleet. The fleet, however, in spite of signaling, did not venture out after that until Sherman rowed out in a small boat to show the way (the harbor) was open [The navy knew the way was open]. We were very fortunate to capture a large quantity of *Rice;* the army lives on it for the moment (animals and men). We have beef in large quantities, no *pork* or *crackers.*[6]

Our lines stretch to the Savannah Riv.[er] where our corps rests, and over the Oguchee [Ogeechee River] by the fleet, and is at the nearest point about 3–3½ miles from the city. The enemy saves his *amm.[unition]* by not bombarding us day and night and is inflicting little damage, while we save our powder. There is a rumor that a combined artillery attack on the enemy works will occur today. We, my brig., therefore, located about 7 miles from Sv. [Savannah], were thrown to the *Rear,* because Monsieur Wheeler harassed our rear, but has since stopped. I will send a collection of my daily notes [not found] to you with the next steamer; for now, only this sign of life.[7]

Panse, the liverwurst devouring pig, is lazy; he does not write at all, what makes his waistline slim? And why does he send his *Su[r]g.[eon's] Certificate* from a *Civil[ian]* doctor not the certificate of the *justice of the peace?*[8]

I remain your *Swamp Angel*[9]
Rudolph Müller

Address [your letters] to: 20th Corps Left Wing Army of Georgia

---

Regarding the altercation with Loeb mentioned above, Lieutenant Loeb's court martial file reveals that on the morning of December 16, 1864, Major Rolshausen censured Captain Müller for "being too late" for a foraging expedition. Müller responded that he had not been given a time to appear. Lieutenant Loeb asserted that he had detailed him for 7:00 a.m. and the captain retorted that it was not so. Loeb then called Müller a liar and was struck by the latter. Loeb reacted back by throwing "a plate of victuals at him in the presence of a detail of enlisted men." Captain Heinzman separated them and Major Rolshausen, who described the fight as "rough and tumble," ordered both officers under arrest. The court martial hearing began on December 29, 1864, in Savannah, and adjourned on January 5, 1865. Loeb was found guilty of "conduct prejudicial to good order and military discipline," and was ordered dismissed from the service. The sentence was remitted, however, and he returned to duty with the regiment. The volatile captain was acquitted of all charges.[10]

On December 21, 1864, it was discovered that the Confederate troops had withdrawn from Savannah. Two days later the 82nd Illinois and its brigade entered Savannah, pitching their camps one mile above the city on McAlpin's Plantation on the right bank of the Savannah River.[11]

The following letter written by a German-born resident of Savannah describes the entry of Sherman's army into Savannah, conditions in the city, and his interactions with officers of the 82nd Illinois during their stay there. German American soldiers often sought out fellow Germans in places where they were posted. The letter also evidences fraternal bonds among Turners. Interestingly, Savannah's *Turnverein* was one of several in the South that withdrew from the *Turnerbund* in 1855 after the national organization announced it was against slavery and especially the spread of slavery into the free territories. The Savannah *Turnverein* denounced the organization's alliance with Northern abolitionists, asserting that its position regarding slavery was incompatible with Southern rights and interests and proved gross ignorance of Southern life. The Savannah group's withdrawal did not necessarily mean that the majority of Savannah's Turners were pro-slavery. This action may have been taken to forestall attacks on Savannah's Turners by Southerners who were already suspicious of the loyalty of Germans, and especially Turners. Savannah's *Turnverein* numbered forty members when it joined the *Turnerbund* in 1852.[12]

Illinois Staats-Zeitung
March 29, 1865
Savannah, Ga.
March 10, 1865

Dear friend Rapp,[13]

After Sherman's army occupied our city I obtained a copy of the *Illinois Staats-Zeitung* to read and saw in it that you are still alive and kicking. I have endured quite a lot since we last saw each other in Baltimore. The outbreak of the slaveholders' rebellion found me here in Savannah, and I was detained here quite against my will. I joined the local Turner society for the maintenance of the Turner principles. It's amazing that with the existence of *Klapperschlangen* [Rattle Snake]-Societies and *Conscription* we could still keep ourselves afoot. However, where there is a will there is a way, and where there is a Turner there is also strength and endurance.

When the hour of deliverance finally struck, the sound of Sherman's music was to us what the sound of Campbell's was for the British garrison at Kucknow's [Lucknow's] in East India.[14] Already weeks before we had expected this event with joyful anxiety and during the last days before the arrival of Sherman's army we used the highest houses as watchtowers both day and night, in order to be the first to greet the liberators. The local Turner Society and the German Fire Company were the first ones who raised the Federal flag and beat the troops of Gen. Geary to it.[15]

It was an impressive sight—to see these battle- and victory-accustomed heroes in dense incalculable columns, along with the sound of well-known marches. I will never forget it. Almost all the men appeared well, if somewhat in need of clothing, otherwise fresh and strong; quite different from the thin, narrow-shouldered, thin-armed Rebels. What also attracted our attention was the good behavior of the troops—no goose screams, and no jokes and no remarks about the onlookers as in the Rebel fashion. Everything indicated good discipline and only at the marketplace, where the Rebels began to plunder while retreating, and the Negroes and Irish wives plundered away, were the troops allowed to plunder with them. However, that stopped after a few days and the greatest security was established.[16]

Now the making of acquaintances began. I had the particular good luck to become acquainted with the officers of the 82nd Illinois (Hecker) Regiment through Capt. Heinzmann. Thanks to his lively Turner spirit, he inquired if a gymnastics society or Turner[s] were located here and he was referred to me. He called down to me from his horse, "*Gut Heil!*" and immediately confraternity was established.

We immediately went to the Turner Hall and in a very short time the officers of the above-mentioned regiment and the local Turners assembled. The soldiers were very surprised to find a Turner Society in this locality. We performed gymnastics, fenced, and drank, as long as time permitted, and it became immediately resolved to hold a Turner party to honor our guests. It soon took place and participation was good on the part of the Turners and the army, as well the local residents. There was the usual Turner festivity and sociability, and singing, gymnastics, and dancing.

We poor humans here felt as if we had awakened from the dead in the company of these energetic people and were very sorry that General Sherman issued marching orders so soon. Therefore, instead of another Turner gathering we had to hold a farewell party. Only Major Rolshausen, Capt. Heinzmann (now acting major), Quartermaster Panse, Capt. Müller, Lt. Lotz and Lt. Rieger[t], the *Doctor* of the regiment, and local Turners, were present at it. We had the luck to procure some good wine (which now is very difficult to find here) and we spent several good hours, which were tarnished for us only by thinking about the imminent departure of our dear friends.[17]

The stresses and strains that Sherman's army experienced since leaving here must have been terrible. The country between here and Charleston is very low, and the roads in this region are very bad and pass through miles-long swamps. Therefore, the army has had to build corduroy roads, etc., just to get through and not sink into the abyss. Unfortunately, a dam had also broken and the water of the rain-swollen Savannah River flowed incessantly into this lowland. The South Carolina side of the river appeared from here like a lake in which the woods looked like islands. The soldiers had to build their tents on poles and the water flowed through underneath them. So it also went for the new Hecker regiment, which, along with the 20th Corps, initially camped 25 miles beyond Savannah until the new campaign began. It is surprising under these circumstances that the soldier does not become ill humored; rather his mood elevates with difficulties and needs that he has to endure.

As an example of this gallows humor I want to tell of a small adventure of Capt. Heinzmann. He came back to Savannah from his camp with 3 other officers, a distance of about 27 miles. Their horses had to cover the last 12 miles of the trip partly by swimming. Everyplace in the region was under water; they had to use the bushes on the rice dams as guideposts. It continued to rain and they had to hand over their horses to a regiment located there to cross over the river in a small boat. After finishing their business they tried to return the same way. After going several miles, however, the horses they had picked up were tired from swimming for a long time, and were no longer able to bear up against the current. One of the horsemen was rescued from drowning by Heinzmann. They were forced to turn back and had to be happy to be on firm ground again. Several days later they took passage on a U.S. transport boat and later rejoined their command.

Postscript. We are not in such a trusting position with the troops still remaining here as we were with the new Hecker Regiment. Our acquaintance with the latter has spoiled us, i.e., we had developed too high expectations. Several other regiments compare unfavorably to them. They have no discipline, no *Subordination,* no morals: officer and *Private* swig out of a bottle and that leads them to become best friends; and the one rails at and curses the other. Then you come into the camp of the Hecker Regiment again. There it goes according to regulations and not otherwise. There the tents stand just so, the sentries march straight back and forth, the officer has this to do and the private that. You hear no private expressions, see no schnapps bottle circulating; there are no conflicts with superiors, but each does his duty, and what should not be done is made clear to them.

To such a model regiment belongs good material and also a Hecker was necessary to mold it. The Germans can be proud of these regiments and you can be particularly proud of yours from Illinois. It is a regiment of honorable men as far as I know it. My acquaintances among the officers especially gave me the opportunity to evaluate them. Such is the impression that they made, and as such it will long live on in the memories of the German population and the Turners. The picture of the officers adorns our assembly hall but we also remember them ourselves.

Now we have a part of the 19th Corps here as occupiers. They interact with residents quite differently than the 20th Corps. The latter treated us like a liberated people. These Nineteenth-ers, however, regard us as Rebels who have been brought to reason by Sherman. The population of Savannah does not deserve this treatment. We were denounced as Yankees in the Confederacy years ago. Generally, the state would return to the *Union* with the greatest pleasure, if it were only doable; unfortunately, however, the wrong people are still at the head in the South and the people themselves are not asked. If it had been left to the people, even of South Carolina, and a free election had been allowed, *Secession* would never have happened. Here is what happened. Each neighborhood had one or several rich planters who at the same time were judges, lawyers, etc., who determined in advance what was supposed to be the order of the day in an assembly, and woe to those who disagreed with them. The small planters, called *Cracker[s],* also knew very well that they were not able to object and therefore acquiesced uncomplainingly to the dicta of the large planters. There are generally no more patient people than the *Cracker[s].* [Cracker is a pejorative term for a poor white person, generally located in the rural south.] Some other people had rebelled against the Confederate economic system. They [the government] took all their money, cattle, grain, and their sons. They withdrew one thing after the other from the soldiers, sugar, soap, coffee, meat, meal, *Syrup,* payments, and everything, except some cornmeal and bacon and perhaps one shoddy uniform a year, and they did not grumble. Had they deprived them of everything and given them *in lieu thereof 30 lashes a day,* they would have been satisfied. We now hear much about secret assemblies in which these *Cracker* delegates vote to negotiate with the government about ways and means to return to the Union. Wish them luck. There will perhaps be better times here. Now it is really bad.

If my health permits it and I can arrange it accordingly, I will attend the session in Washington on the 3rd of April as a delegate from here. I am already elected for that purpose. I am already enjoying myself in advance and am also anticipating coming into the Turner group once again.

With brotherly greetings and a handshake.

F. K.[ürschner?][18]

––––––

The preceding letter contains several interesting passages. First, F. K. expressed joy about the liberation of the city by Union forces, indicating that he did not support the Confederacy. Second, he was happy that he had met fellow Germans of the 82nd Illinois and, perhaps even more, fellow Turners. Like so many other German Americans, the writer saw his native landsmen as superior in character and habits to Anglo-Americans. Third, he revealed that some of the Southerners in the area who had willingly endured ever increasing hardships for the Confederacy were now looking for ways to end the conflict and return to the Union. Finally, the writer revealed that Savannah had the reputation of being "Yankee" in sympathy. The composition of the city's 1860 population of 22,292 persons sheds light on this matter. There were 13,875 free whites, 7,712 slaves, and 705 free blacks. One-third of the free whites were foreign born, including over 3,000 Irish and nearly 800 Germans. Moreover, two-thirds of Savannah's 4,400 adult white males were of either foreign or Northern birth. With such a large percentage of its population being either enslaved or born outside of the South, Savannah was viewed in the Confederacy with a jaundiced eye.[19]

Thirteen

The Carolinas Campaign
to Fayetteville, North Carolina

With Savannah in hand, Sherman replenished his supplies by sea before launching an invasion of the Carolinas with 60,000 troops. "The plan of the campaign" as historian John G. Barrett explains, "called for feints on both Augusta and Charleston and a march directly on Columbia and thence to Goldsboro, North Carolina, by way of Fayetteville on the Cape Fear River. Goldsboro was chosen as the destination because that city was connected to the North Carolina coast by rail lines running from New Bern and from Wilmington. By this route Sherman could destroy the chief railroads of the Carolinas and devastate the heart of the two states."[1]

Like the trek to Savannah, Sherman's four corps proceeded in four columns, on separate roads where possible. The Fourteenth Corps and Twentieth Corps, under Major General Slocum, again formed the Left Wing, and the Fifteenth Corps and Seventeenth Corps comprised the Right Wing. As part of this new campaign the 82nd Illinois and most of its brigade (the Third under recently promoted Brig. Gen. James S. Robinson) broke camp on January 17, 1865, and crossed the Savannah River into South Carolina on pontoon bridges. The brigade reached Purysburg about noon on January 19 and had to remain there until January 28 due to exceedingly inclement weather. On January 28 the brigade headed north again, strengthened by the 31st Wisconsin, which had been detached on special duty.[2]

Pvt. Friedrich P. Kappelmann wrote to his parents two weeks after he departed from Savannah for South Carolina.

Camp near Sister's Landing, South Carolina
January 31, 1865

Dear Parents:

The New Year next year I will probably celebrate in Chicago. This will be a real relief because on the 26th of September, 1865, we shall be discharged from the U.S. service. Then we will be men again and not slaves and even less slave liberators.

This landscape is more fit for fish than for man. For everything is covered by moor and swamp, extremely unhealthy. Our wagons, which followed after us, had just arrived on an island opposite us when they were also attacked by the rainstorm. Many of the mules drowned and the drivers had to reach the shore in boats.

We are five miles from Sister Ferry and about forty miles from Savannah. Up to now every house was razed to the ground, particularly because all of them are quite empty. You can find whole little towns with not a living soul in them.

Many regards from your son
Frederich P. Kappelmann[3]

The Twentieth Corps, including Colonel Robinson's brigade, arrived near Fayetteville, North Carolina, on March 11, 1865, after an arduous trek of over 340 miles. During this march, which Confederate military leaders had dismissed as nearly impossible under winter conditions, the 82nd Illinois passed through Robertsville, Lawtonville, Buford's Bridge, Lexington (three miles west of Columbia), Winnsborough, Hanging Rock, Chesterfield, and Cheraw in South Carolina, before crossing the Lumber River at McFarland's Bridge. The Right Wing joined Slocum's wing at Fayetteville, traveling by way of Pocotaligo, Orangeburg, Columbia, and Cheraw.[4]

Captain Müller started a letter on January 31 at Robertsville, South Carolina, but after writing two paragraphs put it away and did not complete it until March 12, 1865, while resting at Fayetteville, North Carolina, located on high ground on the west bank of the Cape Fear River. Because Sherman's isolated bluecoats were living off the land as they advanced, without lines of communication to any Federal depot or base, Fayetteville offered the first opportunity for soldiers to send letters to the outside world. This became possible after Gen. Braxton Bragg, commander of the Confederacy's Department of North Carolina, ordered the abandonment of Wilmington, North Carolina, during the night of February 21 to 22, under threat of a 40,000-man Federal force led by Maj. Gen. John Schofield. Wilmington, located on the Cape Fear River (which empties into the Atlantic Ocean), was the last major port in Southern hands, and its loss was a strong blow to Robert E. Lee's army at Petersburg, Virginia. A Union gunboat arrived at Fayetteville by way of the Cape Fear River on March 12, 1865, establishing communication with Sherman's army.[5]

Sherman's march through South Carolina differed from his march from Atlanta to Savannah because the weather and terrain were more adverse in South Carolina and much more civilian property was destroyed. The severe storms that delayed Colonel Robinson's brigade at Purysburg were but a prelude to the rain between January 27 and March 10, which one soldier estimated occurred during half of this period. During one stretch of ten days, only one day passed without a steady drizzle or downpour. Roads in the low country were a nightmare to traverse and those in the uplands became mud pits. On the way from Purysburg to Fayetteville, the foot soldiers of the 82nd marched a total of thirty-two days on the forty-day journey and covered distances ranging from a few miles to up to twenty-two miles per day.[6]

A brief daily account of the 82nd Illinois's march through the "cradle of secession" prepared by Pvt. Max Schlund of Company B, mentioned, among other things, that on February 11, they "went across the South branch of the Edisto River, and marched through 2 miles of swamp. We walked knee high through water and swamp and reached our camp at 11 o'clock that night." They crossed the Catawba River on February 20, where "the water was very high and we were forced to push the wagons by hand." They helped move the wagons on February 26 because "the weather was so bad," waded through the Thompson River [Creek]" on March 3, "working way through a swamp territory" on March 4, and, after crossing the Great Pee Dee River on March 6, "helped army train (supply) 4 miles through a swamp region to the west side of the river, arrived at 2 a. m." Private Schlund mentioned a few contacts with Rebel cavalry during the march but no casualties.[7]

The soldiers of the Second Hecker Regiment also destroyed stretches of railroad track on February 8 and 10, were assigned to build a bridge over the Lumber River on March 8, and repaired roads and streets on March 10. Schlund's account omits mention of the seizure and destruction of military and civilian buildings, livestock, and foodstuffs by his army. Sherman's soldiers took special pains to wreak vengeance on both military and civilian property in the "mother of the secession," whose people, they believed, ignited the war. In South Carolina, four separate railroad lines were wrecked, including the Charleston and Savannah Railroad and the South Carolina Railroad, which connected Augusta, Georgia, to Charleston. Besides railroads, ordnance, factories, mills, and cotton, a tremendous number of homes and outbuildings and large quantities of stores and crops were destroyed. According to historian Joseph Glatthaar, "[i]n the countryside very little along the route of Sherman's march survived the destruction." On the

Twentieth Corps's route of march, portions or most of Hardeeville, Robertsville, Lawtonville, Blackville, and Lexington were put to the torch. Numerous homes in the countryside met similar fates.[8]

Columbia, the state's capital, was surrendered to General Howard's wing on February 17, and approximately one-third of its buildings were destroyed by fire while Federal troops were present. Columbia residents believed that General Sherman ordered the destruction, but a modern study by historian Marion Brunson Lucas disputes that and blames both sides in varying degrees. For example, Confederates set fire to bales of cotton in the streets to keep it from being captured, and drunken Union soldiers set some buildings on fire. A strong wind quickly spread the flames. The old State House and the interior of the new State House under construction were among things burned. Pillaging and plundering took place as well.[9]

The army had to live off the land and constantly seized huge supplies of food for its soldiers and forage for its animals; storehouses and the land were stripped bare. Some foragers (called "bummers") left enough food for the women and children to survive for a while, but not all did. Some women and children were left homeless and/or without provisions, in spite of pleading and crying.[10] Most blue-clad Unionists felt South Carolina and its people must suffer for starting and supporting this terrible war. Joseph T. Glatthaar found that a small number of the Federal soldiers, mostly new men, despised the forage system and the destruction. A Wisconsin soldier, Richard B. Satterlee, for example, informed his wife in a letter: "On the march we have live[d] pretty much off of the country; there is not enough left in the country to support the women and the children. This is a wicked, damnable, accursed war; if you could see and hear the poor women and innocent children crying and begging that they leave them a little meal or something to eat; yet the last morsel would be taken and they left to suffer."[11]

Resistance against Sherman's columns was light as they marched through South Carolina and the southern part of North Carolina, because the Confederate commanders were unable to mass their scattered brigades and divisions. It was February 22 before Joseph E. Johnston was appointed to take command of the Army of Tennessee and all the Confederate troops in South Carolina, Georgia, and Florida, and it was mid-March before Johnston concentrated approximately 20,000 troops in the vicinity of Smithfield, North Carolina, to attempt to drive back Sherman's army.[12]

Captain Müller briefly summarizes the march to Fayetteville in the following communication and reveals that in spite of his strong desire to prosecute the war against the Secessionists, he believes the army has been too hard on civilians and their property. Surprisingly, the captain makes no mention of Lieutenant Colonel Salomon, who returned to the regiment on February 2 from a long leave.[13]

On *Picket* by Robertsville, S.C.
January 31, 1865

Dear Colonel,

Since our arrival in Savannah and its capture I had hoped for a letter from you but to no avail. Panse has returned to the regt. [from his leave] safe and sound and about ten years younger. The fresh liverwurst, the good wine, and above all his ambience during the temporary stay on the farm have straightened wrinkles and rejuvenated him; in short, he is as cheerful as a little ear mite and revels in the memory of the past months.

On January 17 we left Sav.[annah] crossing to S.C., moving to Pewriesburgh [Purysburg] [L]anding where we were tormented for about 6 days by rain in the *Black Swamps.* It was a true frog and toad life, during which we camped in the water. The rain had so swollen the river that the 4-mile-wide *Rice plantations* were put completely underwater along the banks of the river.[14]

Near Fayetteville, North Carolina, March 12th 1865—

Continuing the letter started a long time ago, I announce to you that yesterday evening about 11, after an extremely exhausting march, we arrived here. The city is supposed to be pretty, lies about 2½ miles from the Cape Fear River, which is navigable all the time.

Today 2 gunboats arrived from Wilmington. We have established *Communication* to the sea. All corps will come together here in order to advance again after 1 day's rest, perhaps to Goldsboro. The Rebels, about 20,000 men under Hardee, according to information given by citizens, gave us trouble before our arrival.[15]

During the entire long march through South Carolina, the Rebels roved everywhere; their *Cav.* swarmed around us and individuals and foragers were taken prisoner. Columbia, S.C. lies in ashes; nearly all the plantations we passed and those lying 6–8 miles right and left of the line of our march shared the same fate. Our army has taken on the character of bandits and murdering arsonist bands through the forage system, which everyone [illegible word], and it is sad to have come so far that one must almost blush to say he belongs to Sherman's army and campaigned through S.C. The army has lived well, but is now worn down and especially suffers from lack of shoes and socks. Lee is supposed to have slipped away from Richmond with his army and possibly will march to the Mississippi; however, that is hard to believe. As soon as we have more time and leisure I will prepare a detailed account of our deeds and misdeeds. Today, only this as a sign of life.[16]

We had dreadful roads and as a result of the frequent rain, we encountered numerous swamps and rivers and puddles. We had many a hard day getting up to here; however, all obstacles have been overcome.

Panse, Lotz, Gottlob, etc. are well and send you warm greetings.

Yours truly,

Rudolph Müller, Capt.

Fourteen

The Final Battles

eneral Sherman reviewed his army on March 13 at Fayetteville and after this event the Twentieth Corps crossed the Cape Fear River on a pontoon bridge and halted four miles out toward Kyle's Landing. The march resumed on March 15 but was stalled by Brig. Gen. William B. Taliaferro's and Maj. Gen. Lafayette McLaws's divisions of Lt. Gen. William J. Hardee's corps and two divisions of Maj. Gen. Joseph Wheeler's cavalry that blocked the old Plank Road northeast of Fayetteville. This isolated the Twentieth Corps between the Cape Fear and Black rivers near Smithville (a few miles south of Averasboro). Kilpatrick's cavalry was unable to break through the enemy's blocking force and Col. William Hawley's brigade of Brig. Gen. Nathaniel Jackson's First Division was sent to reinforce the troopers. The next morning about 10:00 a.m. three batteries and Brig. Gen. William T. Ward's Twentieth Corps division arrived to help the hard-pressed Union troopers and Hawley, and drove the Confederates back to their second line of works. Jackson's First Division, including the 82nd Illinois, then came up on Ward's right, and Brig. Gen. John G. Mitchell's brigade of James D. Morgan's division, Fourteenth Corps, arrived on Ward's left. Kilpatrick's cavalry circled around to the right. Under severe pressure and wanting to avoid being flanked, Taliaferro withdrew his division back to a third line of fortifications. Despite heavy pressure from the Union forces up until early evening, the Confederate line held. After dark Hardee retreated to the area of Bentonville, having successfully stalled Sherman's progress while Joe Johnston assembled additional troops to oppose Sherman. Slocum's wing suffered 682 casualties and Hardee lost approximately 800 men.[1]

Colonel Salomon described the 82nd Illinois's actions on March 16 in his official report as follows:

We crossed the creek [Taylor's] and heard cannonading in our front. The road was very bad, leading through a swamp, and men and horses had to wade knee deep through the mud. About noon we came up to the Second Brigade of our division and the cavalry near the Black River. They were skirmishing with the enemy. You then ordered me to form my regiment in line of battle, my left connecting with the right of the Second Brigade, and to throw skirmishers to my front to relieve the skirmishers of the cavalry. These orders were immediately executed and when the line of the entire brigade was formed, we moved forward with the skirmish line in the front; the line of battle followed closely behind the skirmish line, and the enemy's fire being very heavy caused several casualties in my ranks before the regiment could fire. We advanced steadily, changing our lines and front several times, and drove the enemy toward a swamp. Firing was kept up on the picket line all night, and the next morning we found the works of the enemy evacuated. In this affair my regiment lost 1 private killed and 1 officer (Captain Heinzmann) and 9 enlisted men wounded. Captain Heinzmann was in charge of the skirmishers from my regiment, and I cannot omit to mention the gallant conduct of this officer.

Perhaps this battle changed Captain Müller's previous low opinion of Captain Heinzmann's courage.[2]

The first part of Rudolph Müller's next letter, dated April 2, 1865, refers briefly to the above-described Battle of Averasboro (also known as Averasborough, Taylor's Hole Creek, Smithville, Smiths Ferry, and Black River). The second part of the captain's letter focuses on his regiment and its brigade's role in the Battle of Bentonville on Sunday, March 19. On the next to last page of his letter the captain drew a map and indicated seven positions with numbers, which he referred to in his letter. Because Captain Müller omitted certain events occurring before his brigade reached the scene of the fighting, and some other events, it is useful to supplement his description of the battle, which lasted three days and cost the Unionists 1,527 casualties, and the Rebels 2,606.[3]

Slocum's and Howard's wings advanced toward Goldsboro on March 17 and 18, where Sherman planned to meet Maj. Gen. Alfred H. Terry's Provisional Corps (10,000 troops) and the bulk of Maj. Gen. John General Schofield's Twenty-third Corps (15,000 troops) by March 20. Terry was marching north from Wilmington and Schofield was moving west from New Bern. Unbeknownst to Sherman and his lieutenants, Joe Johnston had collected 21,000 troops in the vicinity of Smithfield (approximately twenty miles west of Goldsboro). Johnston's command consisted of the Army of Tennessee commanded by Lt. Gen. Alexander P. Stewart (eight divisions); Maj. Gen. Robert H. Hoke's division, plus artillery, all under

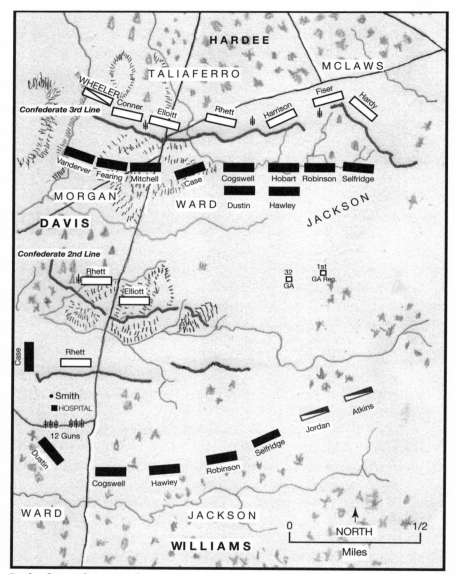

Battle of Averasboro, March 16, 1865

the command of Gen. Braxton Bragg; two divisions under Lt. Gen. William J. Hardee; and four cavalry divisions under Lt. Gen. Wade Hampton.[4]

Early on March 19 Johnston deployed his recently organized army in a some-what inverted fishhook-shaped formation to trap Slocum's force marching northeast on the Goldsboro Road. Taliaferro's division of Hardee's corps anchored the far right of Johnston's line; Stewarts's divisions continued the line to the left and then curved down to connect with Bragg's artillery and Hoke's division, which formed the lower shaft of the fishhook and blocked the Goldsboro Road. To General Slocum's disadvantage, the divisions of his two corps had become strung out and his distance from Howard's wing had increased. Johnston took advantage of this situation and attacked the head of Slocum's wing while it was isolated and lacked compactness. Although foragers from the Fourteenth Corps had encountered unusually stiff resistance from Confederate cavalry early on March 19, Sherman seriously doubted that Johnston would dare a major battle against his large army and he advised General Davis of this in the presence of Howard and Slocum.[5]

Brig. Gen. William P. Carlin's First Division of the Fourteenth Corps took to the road at 7:00 a.m. on March 19, and at approximately 10:00 a.m. his First Brigade, led by Bvt. Brig. Gen. Harrison C. Hobart, was surprised by musketry and artillery fire near the Willis Cole house. Hobart's soldiers quickly threw up some breastworks. At this time half his brigade was north of the road, facing north–northeast, and the other half was south of it, facing northeast. Carlin deployed Bvt. Brig. Gen. George P. Buell's Second Brigade to the left of Hobart and Lt. Col. David Miles's Third Brigade to Hobart's far right. This still left a dangerous gap between Hobart's left wing and his right wing. Around 11:00 a.m. Bvt. Maj. Gen. Jefferson C. Davis ordered Maj. Gen. James D. Morgan to insert two of his Second Division brigades to Carlin's right, facing Hoke's division. Morgan's third brigade later came up in support. General Carlin launched attacks on both sides of the road around noon and was repulsed with heavy casualties.[6]

Lt. Samuel D. Webb's 19th Indiana Battery arrived about 1:00 p.m. and joined Lt. Palmer Scovel's Illinois battery north of the Goldsboro Road. Scovell's four guns had been dueling with fourteen Confederate ones for several hours. One hour later, Col. William Hawley's First Brigade of Brig. Gen. Nathaniel J. Jackson's First Division, Twentieth Corps, arrived at the Reddick Morris farm and deployed about a mile behind Carlin. Brigadier General Robinson's Third Brigade (minus the 101st Illinois, which had been assigned to guard the Smithfield-Goldsboro crossroads) advanced a mile past Hawley's regiments and halted behind a small ravine. Robinson faced the gap in Carlin's line but was behind it and less than a quarter of a mile southwest of the Cole house. Soon the 82nd Illinois and 143rd New York were ordered back to support Hawley's brigade. Robinson was left with only three regiments and without connections to the brigades on his flanks. To worsen the situation, Carlin ignored the suggestion of Slocum's chief engineer to move back to connect with Robinson's line.[7]

At 2:45 p.m. all the Rebel divisions except Hoke's launched a strong attack against Carlin's positions, and his men, outgunned and outflanked, fled back to the Morris farm and were out of the fight for the rest of the day. After many of

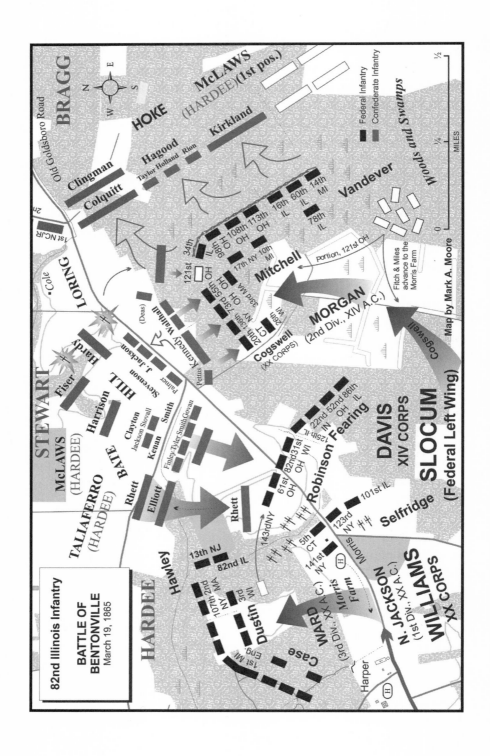

BATTLE OF
BENTONVILLE
March 19, 1865

82nd Illinois Infantry

Map by Mark A. Moore

Federal Infantry
Confederate Infantry

Woods and Swamps

MILES

0   ¼   ½

BRAGG

HOKE

McLAWS
(HARDEE)(1st pos.)

Old Goldsboro Road

Clingman

Colquitt

Hagood

Taylor Holland Rion

Kirkland

2nd

1st NCJR

Vandever

34th
IL

121st
OH

98th OH

108th
OH

113th
OH

16th
IL

60th
IL

14th
MI

78th
IL

55th
OH

73rd
OH

Mitchell

17th NY

10th
MI

33rd MA

20th CT

13th NY

35th
WI

Portion, 121st OH

MORGAN
(2nd Div., XIV A.C.)

Fitch & Miles
advance to the
Morris Farm

Cogswell
(XX CORPS)

Cogswell

•Cole

LORING

STEWART

Hardy

Fiser

McLAWS
(HARDEE)

Harrison

HILL

Stevenson

Palmer

J. Jackson

Kennedy Walthall

(Deas)

Pettus

Clayton

Jackson Stovall

BATE

Kenan

Smith

TALIAFERRO
(HARDEE)

Rhett

Finley Tyler Smith Govan

Elliott

Rhett

DAVIS
XIV CORPS

SLOCUM
(Federal Left Wing)

22nd
WI

52nd
OH

86th
IL

125th IL

Fearing

Robinson

61st
OH

82nd
OH

31st
WI

143rd NY

101st IL

123rd
NY

Selfridge

Hawley

13th NJ

82nd IL

5th
CT

141st
NY

Morris

Morris
Farm

H

WARD (XX A.C.)

N. JACKSON
(1st Div., XX A.C.)

WILLIAMS
XX CORPS

HARDEE

107th
NY

2nd
MA

3rd
WI

Dustin

1st MI
Eng.

Case

(3rd Div., XX A.C.)

Harper

H

Robinson's skirmishers were killed, wounded, or captured, and the troops on his left were driven back in disorder, the Ohioan withdrew his three regiments back to the Morris farm and constructed breastworks astride the Goldsboro Road. At 4:00 p.m., Hoke's division attacked Morgan's division and thanks to the timely arrival of Bvt. Brig. Gen. William Cogswell's Third Brigade of Maj. Gen. William T. Ward's Third Division, Twentieth Corps, Morgan's troops prevented a Confederate breakthrough. On Cogswell's front, fighting continued into the night.[8]

Meanwhile, Brig. Gen. Alpheus S. Williams had ordered Hawley's command (including the 82nd Illinois and 143rd New York) to move into a position about a quarter of a mile north of the Goldsboro Road in case the Rebels flanked Carlin. Hawley faced his regiments north. At 4:30 p.m., Brig. Gen. Stephen Elliott Jr.'s brigade and Col. Alfred M. Rhett's brigade, both of Brig. Gen. William B. Taliaferro's division, Hardee's corps, attacked Robinson's brigade at the Morris farm. The 143rd New York rejoined Robinson on his far left, while Hawley's 13th New Jersey and the 82nd Illinois crossed a ravine and deployed at a right angle to the rest of Hawley's brigade, facing Robinson's brigade. In fierce fighting, Robinson's four regiments fought the Rebels' charges head on, while the Jersey men and Lieutenant Colonel Salomon's Illinois regiment fired into the right flank of Elliott's and Rhett's brigades while they passed by them during their assaults on Robinson's line. All the while, an increasing number of Federal guns blasted the enemy's serried ranks with case shot, canister, and solid shot. Robinson's brigade withstood four separate charges before sundown. Then at sundown, Maj. Gen. William B. Bate's two divisions joined a final charge by Rhett's brigade and they, too, were repulsed, as was a later charge by part of McLaws division.[9]

Near Goldsboro, North Carolina

April 2nd, 1865

My dear Colonel,

I begin the day at sunup. I am answering your letter from Feb. 11 and can report that all your friends are well, with the exception of Heinzmann, who was shot on March 16 near Elk [Black] River [during the Battle of Averasboro]. He was shot like you were; the bullet not harming the bone, penetrating the outer part of the thigh and through the thick flesh of an unspeakable part beginning with A, causing a 12–14-inch-long wound. Besides him, 1st Sgt. Halverston [Halvorson] Co. (I) died as a result of a shot through his left breast. There was a man from Co. B killed and otherwise about 10 lightly wounded.[10]

In the March 19 battle by Be[n]tonville, about 7 miles from the Neuse Riv., our regt. was very fortunate, lost not one man and—according to quite precise communications via Edw. S.[alomon], the *great* man saved the rest of the army with his 172 men, in that we did not run pel[l-]mel[l] like a brig. of the 14th Corps, but at most did our duty and remained there. We were not [directly] attacked once and fired about 4 salvos into the flank of an attacking Reb[el] column, but we could see the Rebels in the dense undergrowth and about 800 yards *distance* [*distant*]. Was this not a heroic deed unlike any other? I tell you we almost bent under the burden of the fame and in spite of all this not one bird [eagle] flew by that landed on Salomon's shoulders. Winkelried [Loeb] delivers so much nonsense that in the near future we will solder a corona or halo for both heads together.

Should a shortage of laurel leaves occur in Ill., the 82nd is in a position to supply the entire state. The Lt. Col. is either very dumb or he displays a great brashness in that he considers us dumb enough to dare serve his naïve boasting to us. A single bow and one wraps the hero around his little finger, but *non est.* Will you not use your influence, so that the old phrase about the ungratefulness of the Republic also proves true for our genius? You would render a service to the world.

Apropos. My *Sentence* finally arrived. Am *Acquitted.*

Your prediction about the campaign up until now has been realized almost exactly. It was a considerable job, which we are happy to have behind us. An apt [enemy] leader commanding 25,000 men could have, if not indefinitely, delayed our train for several months if engaged at the right time inside South Carolina and, even if victorious, our army would have suffered dearly. As was the case, the Reb[s] did not have their *forces* together, thus were not in a condition to forcefully confront our encroachment.

Imagine how it would be with several thousand wounded without *Communication* and provisions—a fate that befell about 200 severely wounded Reb[s] (March 16); they were without provisions with the exception of a few head of cattle, and under care of a few paroled prisoners left behind and in a region (about 20 miles from Fayetteville) where no souls reside in a circle of about 4–5 miles and only pines and *swamp[s]* exist. It is terrible, but could not be different because we barely had *transportation* for our 3[00]–400 wounded, who, with the exception of the most severe cases were transported in army wagons. This transport over unearthly roads for 5 days was a hellish trip for our wounded and consequently many died. Major [John] Higgins 143 N.Y. was shot through the left leg. Capt. Schmidt and [1st] Lt. Klein from the 26th Wisc. were both killed [at Averasboro, N.C.] on March 16,the former shot in the chest, the latter through the head.[11]

I must describe to you in more detail the fight of the 19th to give you an opportunity to be aware of the skills of our *Gentlemen* generals. The details of the field campaign, however, I must save for my next letter. Only so much of it that we had to wade through *Swamps, Creeks, Rivers,* almost daily, often through water up to our stomachs. Had we not, according to good old custom, always preferred a good wine as well as a bad wine to the watery element, we would have become truly enchanted frogs, toads, or fish and could be used as underwater *Monitors* against the Frenchman [Emperor Napoleon III], who could, through a colossal daring deed, send over a fleet with an army. Can we not think that Napoleon would execute the blow? A landing in Mexico would be possible and further *Cooperation* with western [illegible word] situated Reb[el] troops could be disconcerting. As the affair now stands, I do not believe that those in Europe consider recognizing the South and even less of providing additional troops.[12]

I am strongly of the view that within the term of the enlistments of the r[e]gts., the rebellion will be concluded. If that is not the case then I fear a smaller gueril[l] a war will continue for years. They will work diligently in *Equipping* the troops. Everything points to an early continuation of the campaign toward Richmond. We expect perhaps a battle between here and there. The country should not [illegible word] to the defensive.

Now, to the fight by Bentonville that almost became a victory of the Reb[s], in that we lost about ½ mile of ground; however, we [Slocum's left wing] later repulsed 4 attacks by the enemy, one after the other, and in addition the next day the news arrived that the 15th Corps moved around the left of the Reb[s], and through this movement hospitals, prisoners, supplies, and a number caissons fell into our hands.

The 14th Corps marched in front of us and at 10:00 a.m. began skirmishing with the enemy, who had a battery in his picket lines. They pushed them back from hill to hill, so that we clearly heard the shooting always becoming more distant, during which time we constructed a *Cord du roi* [corduroy] *Road.*

Toward noon the cannonading became heavy. The 14th [Corps] had hit upon the Reb[el] *column.* We, the 1st and 3rd [d]iv.[isions], arrived; the 2nd [Division] escorted the train, and we were promptly deployed in the first line to the side of the *Road.* (No. 1)—the 143rd [N.Y.] and 82nd [Ill.] in the 2nd line. We [the 82nd Ill.] had barely arrived there when we were ordered to report to Col. Hawl[e]y, II Brig. (No. 2); this took place and we deployed in columns. Suddenly [musketry] rattled at position after position to our right. We immediately hastened through the ravine to the right on the double quick, arriving in the open fields. The brig. of the 14th Corps sailed off in full flight and was totally disbursed because after their *Reserve* was flanked on both wings they did not have connections on their right or left. Now the Reb[s] came through the gap between that brig. and mine (No. 1) on the exposed flank (left) and rear, while at the same time a column from the Reb[els'] position advanced over the open field. Naturally, our 3 regts.—the

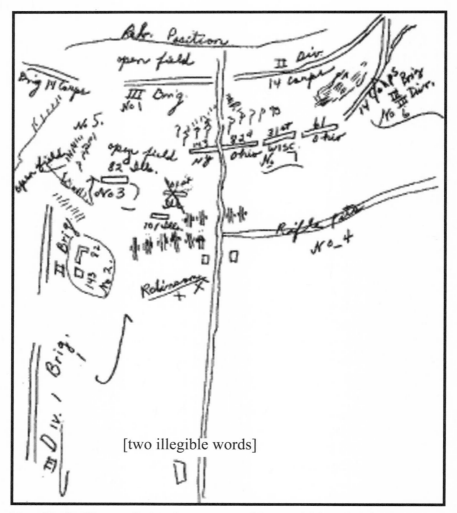

Map of Battle of Bentonville, March 19, 1865, traced from Rudolph Müller's hand-drawn map with English translations and enlarged

82nd Ohio, 61st Ohio, and 31st Wisc.—fell back. This is excusable, because neither general, nor colonel, nor capt., nor lt. knew our position. No one knew anything about this brig. of the 14th Corps. Just think about it! Gen. Jeff Davis left such gaps between each of his brigades; one was later plugged by the III Brig., III Div. [of our corps] (No. 6).

The other regiments of my brig. established themselves in position No. 7 again, because the 2nd Div[.] 14th Corps likewise made a backwards pivot of about 1 mile (toward No. 6). The 143rd N.Y. was deployed left of the road (No. 7); the 82nd Ill., meanwhile, hastened into position No. 3, awaiting the attack of the Rebs. Left of there on the open fields beyond some firs, an enemy column marched almost parallel with our front on No. 5 at the edge of a forest, from where a route led up to the 143[rd N.Y.], probably with a view to devastate our left flank there, to flank for the 2nd time. We opened a splendid fire on this column and immediately the artillery began to play toward No. 5. According to Edw. S., with his eagle's view of the open field in front of the 82nd Ill. and the interval between, we and the 143rd were so completely covered through our art.[illery] that the Reb[s] failed in spite of four attempts to break through. As well, they repeated the same on the entire line. Attacks came, soon right, soon left.

The 143rd N. Y.—Kudos to you! Stand tall. The 101st Ill. and our rgt. [regiment] are the core of the brig., [and] bear up together like a limpet. After the 143rd found that we covered the left flank, which we manifested through a few *Voll[e]y[s]*, the men of that rgt. said ["]Now we are all right.["] However, the 82nd Ohio and 31st Wisc., especially the former, are subject to strong criticism and have disgraced the brig. While the 14th Corps and III Brig., III Div. were strongly attacked, and still no shots fell on our brig., Maj. Crawl [Crall] cmdg. [commanding the] 82nd Ohio gave the order *to fall back*. Col. Watkins 143rd hurried there immediately and ordered the 82d [Ohio] back again, whereupon Maj. Crall answered: *There is danger for the boys out there. I can't get my men to go back.* What do you say about that? So we must honor a coward as a *superior* off.[icer].[13]

Incidentally, the 82nd Ohio is the regiment of Gen. Robinson, who distinguishes himself at every opportunity through incompetence and being drunk, including the whole of his staff. They are a jolly platoon.[14]

How often, dear colonel, we wish you were back. How often I hear this from off.[icers] of American regts.

Lotz, Ganlob [Gottlob?] Erickson, Lemberg [Lindbergh], Panse send their regards.

> Yours,
> Rudolph Müller

The battle of Bentonville did not end on March 19, but lasted until Joseph E. Johnston withdrew his army on the night of March 21. There was little fighting on March 20, but by late afternoon both of Sherman's armies were ready to challenge Johnston, who had contracted his lines to protect his flanks. On March 21, Maj. Gen. Joseph A. Mower of the First Division, Twentieth Corps, attempted to gain Johnston's rear with two brigades and cut off his line of retreat, but failed. Sharp skirmishing took place at other locations. Johnston withdrew that night, ending the battle. Sherman began moving his army to Goldsboro the next day to unite there with Terry's and Schofield's corps. Lieutenant Colonel Salomon reported that the 82nd Illinois reached Cox's Bridge on the Neuse River on the afternoon of March 23, after "crossing several nearly impassible swamps," and pitched camp three miles beyond the river. The regiment and its brigade arrived at Goldsboro, where they passed in review before General Sherman and encamped at 1:00 p.m. near the Weldon Railroad.[15]

Private Kappleman's last available letter dealt with the fact that not as much property was burned in North Carolina as in South Carolina, but that "nothing edible remained behind." His spirits were high and he believed the destruction wreaked by Sherman's army was a military necessity.

Camp in Goldsboro, North Carolina
March 26, 1865

Dear Parents:

We will not remain here long, for we are going forward again to Raleigh or to Richmond, for we have to help take that yet. But that doesn't matter, as long as it is *forward* to *victory!*—If the hardships are great, they will be borne willingly, if only we win, the end of the war is near, nearer then ever! The march from Savannah to here is 475 miles and the whole way there is not enough to eat to keep a regiment one week.

That is how it is everywhere we get to—everything edible is taken and no mercy; that is how it had to come, they would not have it otherwise.

Heartiest regards, Your son,
Friedrich P. Kappelmann[16]

On April 10, the regiment and its brigade broke camp and marched toward Raleigh, where it arrived on April 13, during which time the men learned that Gen. Robert E. Lee had surrendered his army in Virginia to General Grant. On April 16, it was reported that hostilities had been suspended and General Johnston was negotiating with Sherman. The happiness and good feeling of April 16 evaporated the next day and according to Lieutenant Colonel Salomon turned into "a feeling of hatred and revenge in the heart of every soldier," when the tragic news of President Lincoln's assassination arrived. On April 25, the Twentieth Corps, including Robinson's brigade, marched to Jones's Crossroads, expecting a fight. Robinson's brigade and its division returned to Raleigh on April 28 and learned that Johnston had formally surrendered his army on April 26.[17]

Sherman's army began its march to Washington, D.C. on April 30, passed through Richmond, Virginia, on May 11, and nine days later camped about two miles west of Alexandria. On May 24, Sherman's victorious army marched in review through Washington, D.C. and the 82nd Illinois and its division pitched camp three miles west of the Washington and Baltimore Railroad. It is from this camp that Captain Müller wrote the final letter in this volume.[18]

The disconsolate captain expressed no joy, in the following letter, that the war had ended, but instead criticized the generals who had ordered an unnecessary forced march to Washington, D.C., and provided some details of the arduous journey.[19] He also revealed that his relationship with Lieutenant Colonel Salomon had worsened and expressed the radical opinion that "the assassination of Lincoln on the whole will be regarded entirely as good fortune for the country."

Camp 82nd Rgt.
Near Washington, D.C.
May 27th, 1865

Dear Colonel,

By the time of our arrival in Illinois, the great review of both armies will already have been reported in the newspapers. We lie east of the Potomac, about 4 miles from Washington, and look forward to our mustering out, which will occur in a few weeks, or in any case within a month.

Eugene [Weigel] will return earlier than us; he has submitted his resignation. We still have much to do for the present with the mustering out of the men, etc., and as soon as our papers are finished, we will be sent to the state in order to muster out there and to be paid out. We will therefore soon be able to meet and greet you, and then will have much to tell you about the *Regime,* always led with amiable charitableness. The little emperor [Salomon] is beginning to become dreadful; imagine, today the *Creole* from Jerusalem summoned me, accusing me of making the men mutinous to undermine his reputation. From the outset the idea is too absurd to say anything about it.

I found that Kirchner, Hepp, et al., had slandered me behind my back, which means little, very little, and I entirely ignore it.[20] How should I deal with fellows who are guilty of such ignoble deeds and what is to be thought of a *Commander* who lends an ear to them, who is on familiar terms with those noble creatures who frequent houses of ill fame, while he neglects his family at home. I am sorry that Capt. Frey is so chummy with him, but this is evidence, which I appreciate and respect, that he possesses little knowledge of human nature.[21]

Our crossing from Raleigh, N.C., up to here was a true forced march. The troops were marched in a truly criminal way, without ever being allowed a midday rest. Our corps covered 190 miles from Raleigh to Richmond in 9 days. In the seven days before the 14th [May], about 20 men died, horrible casualties because of the lust for gambling by generals who sacrificed human life with impunity, just so that a star-studded master can say *I have beat them*.[22] The march led us over the classic fields in front of Spotsylvania, the Wilderness, and Chancellorsville. I visited the spot where we received our baptism of fire. At first glance it was barely recognizable again. Prolific bushes have shot up to a man's height where two years before only grass grew; the scene has changed. I came across several *Knapsacks* with our rgt.[']s, *No.* still there, while the graves of our fallen are no longer discernable, because rain has washed away the earth entirely and they are overgrown with grass again. Numerous Reb[el] graves on this small hill were better preserved. Boards with inscribed names identified their graves.[23]

We struck the Spotsylvania [battle]field where Hancock hit the left of the enemy, where a terrible massacre had to have occurred. Numerous skulls, hundreds of skeletons that never were buried, lie around here in several places where the dead had been covered with only a few shovels of earth. Due to rain one sees either a skull exposed or feet and legs sticking out. One place of about 50 paces in length was a slaughter *Rifle pit* on both sides, covered with perhaps 150 skeletons. Those of our men were on one side, the Rebs on the other side, and only separated by the breastworks, and it was only recognizable through remnants of clothing that a fight must have taken place. Nowhere before had I seen the impact of our cannon like at one place densely overgrown with high, thick fir trees, which had been cut off at a height of about 15 inches. By an inn near the *Courthouse* there was a piece of a rather thick tree that had stood in front of a Reb[el] battery and had became so shredded by our Minnie balls that it fell over; we saw the shot-up pieces.[24]

What a miserable end Jeff Davis had. Caught in a woman's clothes with spurs and boots, it is too beautiful. The Northern *Copperheads* should be condemned to have to mourn their former idol in the same costume for at least six months. Max[imilian] appears to make himself ready to travel, confiscates money, etc. The liberals [in Mexico], encouraged by our success, gain advantage after advantage, and at last are chasing Max to the devil without our help.[25]

S[c]hurz is in Washington.

In my opinion the assassination of Lincoln on the whole will be regarded entirely as good fortune for the country because, from all appearances, [Andrew] Johnson will take drastic actions with steadfast severity and clear out the traitors.[26]

Cordial greetings enclosed from Panse to you and your family, signed respectfully

> Yours
> Rudolph Müller

[P. S.] Recently he [Salomon?] told Gottlob that it felt to him as if he should put a bullet through his head, now that he had led the regiment gloriously and for so long—and now was being ridiculed by his own officers. However, it does not matter to him what people say. The eagle will come in spite of all the strain.

June 9/65—I just found the letter lying between my [?] that I believed you long ago possessed. The regt. mustered out today; we will leave for Chicago in 3 days, where the men should receive their pay and the final mustering out will take place. See you again soon.

Epilogue

*F*riedrich Hecker continued to engage in farming after his military career ended, became an active speaker in Republican circles, and wrote articles for German American newspapers. The talented orator wrote articles in favor of Ulysses S. Grant for the 1868 presidential election but did not go on the stump for him. Disappointed with Grant and his administration, *"der Alte"* joined the new Liberal Republican Party, whose aim was to prevent Grant's re-nomination and promote a reform platform for the Republican Party. Hecker opposed the patronage system, as well as the centralization of the national government and the concentration of power in the presidency that had emerged during the war. Nevertheless, Hecker later refused to support the Liberal Republican Party's unsuccessful nominee for president, newspaper editor Horace Greely—a temperance advocate. The colonel returned to the Republican Party's fold for the 1876 election and campaigned for Rutherford B. Hayes; he also supported former Union general James Garfield in 1880.[1]

In his speeches and articles for German American newspapers, Hecker opposed women's suffrage, railroad monopolies, socialism, and communism, while favoring finding new markets and building a canal in Panama. True to his earlier anti-Catholic views, he strongly supported German Chancellor Otto von Bismarck's *Kulturkampf* against the Catholic Church, which began in 1871. Bismarck's goal was to strengthen the secular state in the newly founded German Empire by reducing the political and social influence of the church. Hecker especially hated Jesuit clergy and the Papal doctrine of infallibility, and he believed that priests and the church had too much political influence over the laity. He also mistakenly warned of the potential danger of the growing number of Catholics in America.

The *Illinois Staats-Zeitung* disagreed with Hecker on this issue and stopped publishing his letters. The *Westliche Post* in St. Louis became his main outlet.[2]

Hecker, and most German Americans, expressed great pride and joy over the unification of Germany in 1871, after it defeated France in the Franco-Prussian War. One of the goals of the revolution of 1848 had finally been achieved and their native land was now a world power. Unfortunately, an emperor (Kaiser Wilhelm I) ruled Germany and true democracy and a true republican form of government were lacking. The old Forty-eighter embarked on a speaking tour of Germany in 1873 and sent dispatches back to the United States. In one speech on July 4, 1873, he identified himself exclusively as an American, praised America's liberty in contrast to the situations in Germany and many other lands, compared the modesty of American soldiers to the "German mania for medals," and noted Germany's press was not as free as America's. The German National Liberal Press detested him, while the democratic press praised him. Some German Americans were offended by his criticism of Germany.[3]

The man who had fought for liberty on two continents died from a lung infection at his farm in Summerfield, Illinois, on March 24, 1881. Colonel Hecker is buried in Summerfield Cemetery, St. Clair County, Illinois, under a standard U.S. Army vertical granite grave marker. Large monuments to the memory of Friedrich Hecker stand in Benton Park in St. Louis, Missouri, and in Washington Park in Cincinnati, Ohio.[4]

Rudolph Müller married Colonel Hecker's daughter, Malvina, a little over three months after his muster out and they took up residence in Peoria, where he worked as a wholesale dry goods merchant. Their wedding took place at the colonel's farm in Summerfield. The couple had three children; Hilda, born in 1869; Irma, born on September 23, 1871; and Albert, born on July 12, 1876. Hilda died before 1880. In 1880, Müller and his family were living in Chicago. There he had the following occupations: 1880, wholesale dry goods salesman; 1881, cigar maker; 1882, travel agent; 1883, unknown; and 1884, travel agent. By 1885 the family had relocated to Minneapolis, Minnesota, where Müller worked as a manager for the Val Blatz Milwaukee Bottling Company from 1885 to 1888. In 1889, he served as an agent for the aforementioned bottling company, and between 1890 and 1896 he worked variously as a manager, collector, and agent for the Val Blatz Brewing Company. In 1897, he became an agent for Anheuser-Busch Brewing Company, and in 1898 and 1899 he was an insurance agent. Müller had been a member of Minneapolis Lodge No. 41, Benevolent and Protective Order of the Elks, the Rawlins Post of the Grand Army of the Republic (G.A.R.), and the Military Order of the Loyal Legion of the United States.[5]

Müller died on October 12, 1899, from a self-inflicted gunshot wound incurred four days earlier at his home. He had been despondent over several years
of financial difficulties and had just suffered a painful injury in a fall. He was
cremated and his remains interred in the Elks Rest at Lakewood Cemetery in
Minneapolis. An article published in the *Minneapolis Tribune* on October 9, 1899
stated he "has always been known for his generosity and kindheartedness."[6]

Edward S. Salomon resumed his residence in Chicago after his muster out on
June 9, 1865. As Eric Benjaminson observed, he then "did just what Müller repeat-
edly accused him of, using his military record to advance his strong personal ambi-
tions." In 1866, the Republican war hero was elected to the lucrative office of clerk
of Cook County for a four-year term. President Ulysses S. Grant appointed him
governor of the Washington Territory in 1870. He resigned his governorship in
1872 after it was disclosed that he had loaned himself territorial funds for a specu-
lative land deal. Nevertheless, Salomon won official praise from the legislature for
his service. The ex-governor relocated to San Francisco in 1875 and resumed the
practice of law. In 1888, he was elected to the California legislature and served two
terms; in 1898, he was appointed assistant district attorney for San Francisco.[7]

Meanwhile, Salomon was active in the Grand Army of the Republic on the
Pacific Coast, and in 1887 was elected department commander of the G.A.R. He
was also a member of the Military Order of the Loyal Legion of the United States,
one of the organizers of the Army and Navy Republican League in San Francisco,
and for eight years functioned as the latter organization's commander-in-chief. A
large majority of the G.A.R. organization on the Pacific Coast supported him for
the commission of brigadier general in the campaign in the Philippines, but another candidate was selected. The ambitious soldier, lawyer, and politician died
on July 18, 1913, at the age of seventy-six, and is buried in Salem Memorial Park,
a Jewish cemetery in Colma, California.[8]

Eugene F. Weigel returned to St. Louis, Missouri, and was appointed chief clerk
of the secretary of state, a position he held until 1868. He next served as auditor
for the St. Louis Board of Water Commissioners in 1868 and 1869, and in 1870 was
elected Missouri's secretary of state as a Liberal Republican, in which capacity he
served for four years. Weigel then became the park commissioner of the City of
St. Louis from 1877 to 1887. In 1890, he was the United States supervisor for the
1890 census of St. Louis. He next joined the Department of the Interior and was
involved with the opening of the Oklahoma Territory to settlement; he also served
as a special land inspector. By 1895, he was working as a life insurance agent.[9]

The brevet major was active in the Grand Army of the Republic and served
as commander of the Frank P. Blair Post No. 1 in St. Louis for 1885. He also was
a member of the G.A.R.'s National Council of Administration in 1887 and served

as adjutant general at the national headquarters in Kansas City for 1888–1889. Finally, he was a member of the Military Order of the Loyal Legion of the United States. Weigel died of liver cancer on October 13, 1896, at the St. Louis home of his sister (Mrs. Atlanta E. Hecker). He was fifty-one years old. His remains were cremated at the Missouri Crematory in St. Louis and his ashes placed in the columbarium there.[10]

George E. Heinzmann remained in Chicago after his muster out and wed Fredericka S. Weidenbaum in or around 1866. A Reformed Lutheran minister married the couple and their marriage produced two sons and a daughter. In 1868, Heinzmann received a partial disability pension because of his shortened and weakened leg. Heinzmann sold worsted and wool goods until 1872 and then joined the city police force, where he advanced to lieutenant. In 1884 and 1885, he worked as an agent. His occupation for 1886 and 1887 is unknown, but from 1888 to 1895 he operated a saloon and imported spirits business. Finally, in 1896, he worked as a beer peddler. Heinzmann was admitted to the National Home for Disabled Volunteer Soldiers in Danville, Illinois, on December 15, 1899, and was discharged on April 23, 1903, at his own request. He died on January 21, 1907, at the Alexian Brothers Hospital in Chicago, from myocarditis and nephritis, at the age of sixty-six. He is buried in Chicago's Graceland Cemetery.[11]

Matthew Marx was discharged on October 7, 1863, and mustered into the army's Invalid Corps (later named the Veterans Reserve Corps). Captain Marx served as commander of Company I, 4th Regiment Veteran Volunteer Corps, then became acting assistant quartermaster, performing light office duty until he was discharged in April 1865. He practiced law in Chicago until 1879, when he married widow Eliza Moser in Topeka, Kansas. She already had three children. Marx and his family soon moved to San Francisco, but moved back East in 1881. The former captain lived in New York from July 1881 until he entered the Home for Disabled Soldiers in Hampton, Virginia, in April 1883. He was released from the soldiers' home in October 1883 and moved to Long Island, New York, where he lived until at least September 1890. On Feb 21, 1881, Marx was granted a monthly pension of $5.00 for a wound he claimed he received at the Battle of Gettysburg. The pension was increased to $10 per month effective May 30, 1883, but terminated in November 1885. Marx made several unsuccessful attempts to have the pension restored, the last papers being dated Sept. 23, 1890. His date and place of death are unknown.[12]

William Loeb was living in Chicago in 1866 but does not appear in the city directory again until 1870. Loeb worked as a real estate agent in partnership with his older brother Adolph (Adolph Loeb & Bros.) from 1870 to 1893; in 1894, he founded William Loeb & Company, bankers, real estate, and loans. William married Emma Mannheimer in Chicago in 1872; they had four daughters and three sons. Unfortunately, Emma, who was twelve years younger than Loeb, died in 1890 at the age of thirty-five. Loeb lived in a hotel after Emma's death. He died suddenly on March 3, 1904 at sixty-one while he was in Montevideo, Uruguay. His remains were returned to Chicago, where they were interred in Rosehill Cemetery on April 19, 1904.[13]

Carl Lotz made Chicago his home after the war, but traveled to Milwaukee, Wisconsin, in 1871 to marry Louise Lackner. Louise was born in Milwaukee to native-German parents. The couple produced three sons. Lotz worked as a coal merchant until 1883, when he became the editor and business manager for the *Neue Freie Presse* (New Free Press). Sometime late in 1884 or in 1885 Carl entered the real estate business and continued in that occupation until at least 1900. The lieutenant was long active in the Chicago *Turngemeinde* and served as its *Zweite Sprecher* (second presiding officer) in 1868 and as its *Sprecher* (presiding officer) in 1870, 1871, 1873, and 1876. He died on November 28, 1904 and his remains were cremated. Louise passed away two years before Carl.[14]

As disclosed in chapter 4, Capt. John Hillborg resigned from the 82nd Illinois Infantry on May 20, 1863. Eight months later, the native Swede enlisted in the 55th Illinois Volunteer Infantry Regiment as a private, probably motivated by a $400 bounty for enlistment. Hillborg was wounded in the shoulder and hand by a shell at the Battle of Kennesaw Mountain on June 27, 1864, for which he would receive a small monthly disability payment after the war. He was detached on September 15, 1864, to serve in the 1st Illinois Light Artillery, Battery H, in which he served until discharged on August 15, 1865, at Little Rock, Arkansas. His second wife Bernhardine (née Behrens), whom he married in St. Louis, Missouri, divorced him in April 1868, after she learned that he had a previous wife and daughter living in Sweden. Hillborg then brought his first wife Sophia and their daughter (also named Sophia) to the United States. In 1870 or 1871, the family moved from Chicago to Colmar, Iowa, where he operated a restaurant and saloon. He would continue to operate saloons in the various places he lived; sometimes he also farmed. In 1873, John took Sophia and their daughter back to Chicago, where the two women lived for the rest of their lives with his support. A second daughter born shortly after Sophia's relocation to Chicago was a life-long invalid. The next year John Hillborg traveled to Norway and brought his niece, Christiana M. Bugge, to the United States. Although he was still legally married to Sophia, he married Christiana on June 30, 1874, in New York. This marriage produced four daughters. The former captain and his new family lived in Colmar, Iowa, for several years then moved to near Albert Lea, Minnesota. After five or six years in Minnesota, the family moved to Grand Forks, North Dakota, where they lived for approximately five years. A final move was made to Forman, North Dakota, where Hillborg died on August 17, 1889, at the age of sixty-two. Christine received a small pension for herself and their children under sixteen until July 11, 1895, when the pension board determined she was not legally married to Hillborg because he was never divorced from Sophia.[15]

Frank Schönewald returned to Chicago after his muster out and reunited with his wife Angeline and their young son Orsemus. The couple later had a daughter they named Mary. Information about his postwar career is spotty, but he worked in various occupations; those known are: letter carrier 1869 and 1874; railroad employee, 1870; constable 1877–1880, 1882–1884; and clerk, 1869, 1876, 1881 and various years between 1885 and 1894. The former lieutenant died on March 20, 1895, at the age of fifty-six years, and is buried in the St. Boniface Catholic Cemetery in Chicago.[16]

Friedrich P. Kappelmann married Minnie Kliese in Chicago on March 10, 1867. Minnie was born in Wisconsin to German-born parents. The couple had seven children, including a set of twins. Two of their children died in infancy. Friedrich worked at his prewar occupation as a barber until his retirement. Active in veterans' organizations, Friedrich was a member of John A. Logan, G.A.R. Post No. 540, Evanston, Illinois, and served as its quartermaster for at least seven years, and officer of the guard for two years. The former ambulance corps member kept in touch with his comrades through the 82nd Illinois Veterans Club, and served as its financial secretary for some time. Minnie belonged to the Ladies Club of the 82nd Illinois Infantry and functioned as its treasurer. Finally, Friedrich won election to two terms as township supervisor for Evanston, Illinois. The sixty-eight-year-old veteran died at his home in Evanston on January 13, 1911. He is buried in Rosehill Cemetery in Chicago.[17]

Otto Balck and John Lebhertz left no postwar trails.

After 1865, most Forty-eighters tempered some of the radical idealism that drove them in the 1850s and worked to bring about changes in more practical ways.[18] They undoubtedly would be pleased that many of their "radical" ideas (prohibition of slavery, removal of the bible from public schools, anti-monopoly legislation, and wage and hour laws) are a part of modern America. However, Americans have rejected their ideals of socialism and communism, elimination of organized religions, and taxation of church property.

Turner societies flourished after the Civil War as returned soldiers resumed their active participation and new immigrants from Germany joined them. Physical education and cultural activities were central to the postwar *Turnvereine*. The formation of women's auxiliaries in the 1860s and the introduction of *Turnen* for women helped fuel membership growth. The boom that the Turner movement registered through the early 1890s ended, however, by the start of World War I. Annette R. Hofmann affirms that, "[t]he radical social revolutionary tendencies in the Turner movement had also declined and this was certainly due to the change in generations; most of the Forty-eighters and pioneers for social reform were dead."[19] World War II caused the American *Turnerbund* to change its name to American Turners. By 2011, it had fifty-four member organizations, with approximately 13,500 members.[20]

The 82nd Illinois and other German regiments succeeded in raising awareness of German participation and sacrifice in the Civil War well beyond the level that would have been achieved if their members had been scattered in Anglo-American–dominated units. In addition, as previously mentioned, these regiments were a means by which their members emphasized their ethnic identity, ethnic pride, and group solidarity, and they contributed to increased ethnic consciousness during the conflict. The same can be said for thousands of Germans serving in separate German companies in Anglo-American regiments, and there were certainly many Germans fighting for the Union who still considered themselves Germans first, and whose awareness of their ethnicity was enhanced by their wartime experiences.[21]

After the war most German Americans believed their right to a place in America had been bought and paid for in blood and exhibited little desire to abandon their *Deutschtum*. Their spokesmen emphasized the contributions they had and were making to their adoptive county, maintaining that German Americans could be good and productive citizens, while retaining their cultural Germanness.[22]

Although a fight against a common foe has been said to have fused soldiers together despite their ethnic and cultural differences, the letters in this book reveal little or no evidence that their German American authors experienced any such bonding with individual Anglo-American soldiers. Rather, the letters manifest ethnic solidarity and distinct cultural differences from Anglo-Americans, and no desire to surrender their German sensibilities.[23] Relatively few scholars have addressed this issue, and they are not unanimous in their views. Ella Lonn and William Burton, for example, claim that participation in the war accelerated or even completed the Americanization of prewar German immigrants. Their views have been widely accepted, although one cannot find substantive primary evidence supporting them.[24] Other scholars, including Stephen Engle, John Hawgood, and Christian Keller, argue that the war actually slowed or stalled their Americanization. Hawgood and Keller, in particular, strongly assert that American nativism manifested against Germans during the Know Nothing crisis, followed by nativist actions against Germans in the military during the Civil War, placed America's Germans on guard to protect their *Deutschtum,* and they remained on guard even after the crisis passed. Engle, Hawgood, Keller, and others contend that the conflict caused Germans to change their conceptions of their ethnic identity and of their place in American society, and after the war they constructed a national German American ethnic identity. This separate identity was based on cultural values, and, with help from post–Civil War immigration, lived on until it was finally shattered by the anti-German hysteria of World War I.[25] Recent works by Martin W. Öfele, Wolfgang Helbich, and Walter D. Kamphoefner also support the notion that Germans did not abandon their distinct ethnicity as a result of their participation in the Civil War.[26]

As stated in the introduction in this book, Stephen Engle credits Franz Sigel with successfully utilizing the link between community and battlefield to help unify the Union's Germans ethnically.[27] For evidence, Engle points to demonstrations in support of Sigel on the occasions of his two resignations (both because he thought he was being mistreated by nativist Anglo-American superiors) and his quests for more significant commands. Germans raised national outcries on behalf of their esteemed leader and, through demands by the German American press, mass meetings held in cities from Missouri to New York, and direct pressure on politicians (including President Lincoln), succeeded in having Sigel promoted to major general in 1862 and in having him assigned to several different higher commands even though he had not earned them by his performance on the battlefield. "Fighting on the home front was precisely the kind of solidarity that linked the Germans with the battlefront despite political differences," observes Engle. "In mobilizing demonstrations of support in Sigel's behalf," Engle concludes, "the German community gave evidence of moving in both directions (towards assimilation and towards constructing an ethnic identity) simultaneously—creating firmer ethnic solidarity, on the one hand, and acting effectively in the public sphere, on the other hand."[28] Substantial research is needed to prove or disprove the theories mentioned earlier.

German American identity in the United States was significantly boosted when Prussia and other German states achieved victory over France in the Franco-Prussian War (1870–1871), and German unity was achieved by the formation of what became known as the Second German Reich, headed by Kaiser Wilhelm I of Prussia. Most German Americans were elated that Germany was finally united and a respected European power. Even though long-hoped-for political reforms were not achieved, German American pride also received a tremendous boost.[29] One correspondent to the *Columbus Westbote* asserted that the German victory over France "had improved the status of German Americans by fifty percent."[30] Increased pride in their German roots and an inflow of immigrants from Germany helped maintain German American institutions and culture for decades. It was the 1890s before German American institutions began their long-term decline, because, as Russell A. Kazal explains, "[i]mmigration reached its peak and the children of immigrants turned away from the affiliations of their parents."[31] It took the anti-German hysteria ignited by the United States' declaration of war on

Germany in 1917 to shatter and then dissolve the hyphen in "German-American" that John Hawgood believed served "for so long at one and the same time as both a link and a bar between his Germanism and his Americanism, and as an obstacle to all his endeavors."[32]

Finally, the dearth of published information about the motives, opinions, and combat and other experiences of members of the largest ethnic group in the Union army is regrettable and deserves much more attention from historians and other scholars. The task will not be easy, however, because most of the necessary documents were written in German and few modern American historians can understand that language. In addition, these soldiers' writings are scarce because many archives in the United States concentrate on preserving documents written in English. Careful and painstaking mining for such documents in archives and in private hands will be necessary. Regardless, the fruits of such efforts would be immeasurable.

Notes

Introduction

1. Prior to 1990 the principal English-language sources of information about Germans in the Civil War were Ella Lonn, *Foreigners in the Confederacy* (Chapel Hill: University of North Carolina Press, 1940); Lonn, *Foreigners in the Union Army and Navy* (Baton Rouge: Louisiana State University Press, 1951); and William L. Burton, *Melting Pot Soldiers: The Union's Ethnic Regiments* (Ames: Iowa State University Press, 1988). Fordham University Press published a second edition in 1998. In 1999 a translated and edited edition of Wilhelm Kaufmann's *Deutschen im Amerikanischen Bürgerkrieg,* originally published in Munich in 1911, was published under the title *The Germans in the American Civil War: With a Biographical Directory* (Carlisle, Pa.: John Kallmann, 1999). Lonn, Burton, and Kaufmann must be used with caution because they are outdated, filiopietistic, tend to use ethnic stereotypes, or rely mainly on other secondary sources. As Christian B. Keller and David L. Valuska point out: "Both Lonn and Burton fail to treat Civil War-era Germans as that disunified, multifaceted conglomeration of people they were; they tend to view Germans largely as a bloc and play down the differences among them. This approach is . . . inaccurate." Lonn and Burton also maintain that the Civil War served to Americanize its German participants without providing supporting evidence. Burton also incorrectly concluded that there was little difference between the Germans in blue and their Anglo-American comrades and that German regiments lost their ethnic character as the war progressed. Despite their faults these studies do contain much useful information. Christian B. Keller and David L. Valuska, *Damn Dutch: Pennsylvania Germans at Gettysburg* (Mechanicsburg, Pa.: Stackpole Books, 2004), xiv, 205 n. 3. For further criticism of Kaufmann's and Lonn's books, see the introduction to Joseph R. Reinhart, ed. and trans., *Two Germans in the Civil War: The Diary of John Daeuble and the Letters of Gottfried Rentschler, 6th Kentucky Volunteer Infantry* (Knoxville: University of Tennessee Press), xx–xxii; Burton, *Melting Pot Soldiers,* 110. For further information on Germans and German-born soldiers in the Civil War era, nativism, ethnicity, and postwar memory, see Christian B. Keller, *Chancellorsville and the Germans: Nativism, Ethnicity and Civil War Memory* (New York: Fordham University Press, 2007); Wolfgang Helbich, "German-born Union Soldiers: Motivation, Ethnicity, and 'Americanization,'" in *German-American Immigration and Ethnicity in Comparative Perspective,* eds. Walter D. Kamphoefner and Wolfgang Helbich (Madison, Wis.: Max Kade Institute for German-American Studies, University of

Wisconsin–Madison, 2004), 296–325; Martin W. Öfele, *German-Speaking Officers in the U.S. Colored Troops, 1863–1867* (Gainesville: University of Florida Press, 2004), and *True Sons of the Republic: European Immigrants in the Union Army* (Westport, Conn.: Praeger, 2008). Histories of German regiments include Donald Allendorf, *Long Road to Liberty: The Odyssey of a German Regiment in the Yankee Army, The 15th Missouri Volunteer Infantry* (Kent, Ohio: Kent State University Press, 2006); James S. Pula, *The Sigel Regiment: The Twenty-sixth Wisconsin Volunteer Infantry, 1862–1865* (Campbell, Calif.: Savas Publishing Company, 1998); and Constantin Grebner, *"We Were the Ninth": A History of the Ninth Regiment Ohio Volunteer Infantry, April 17, 1861 to June 7, 1864*, trans. and ed. Frederic Trautmann (Kent, Ohio: Kent State University Press, 1987). Regarding German-born generals, see Stephen D. Engle, *Yankee Dutchman: The Life of Franz Sigel* (Fayetteville: University of Arkansas Press, 1993); Stephen D. Engle, "A Raised Consciousness: Franz Sigel and German Ethnic Identity in the Civil War," *Yearbook of German-American Studies* 34 (1999): 1–17; Earl J. Hess, "Sigel's Resignation: A Study in German Americans and the Civil War," *Civil War History* 26 (1980): 5–17; Mary Bobbitt Townsend, *Yankee Warhorse: A Biography of Maj. Gen. Peter J. Osterhaus* (Columbia: University of Missouri Press, 2010); Earl J. Hess, "Osterhaus in Missouri: A Study in German-American Loyalty," *Missouri Historical Review,* 78, no. 2 (Jan. 1984): 144–67; Lawrence G. Kautz, *August Valentine Kautz: Biography of a Civil War General* (Jackson, N.C.: McFarland & Co., 2008); and Hans L. Trefousse, *Carl Schurz: A Biography* (1982, reprint; New York: Fordham University Press, 1998). Recommended essays and journal articles also include Walter D. Kamphoefner, "German-Americans and Civil War Politics: A Reconsideration of the Ethnocultural Thesis" in *Civil War History* 37, no. 3 (1991): 232–46; Eric Benjaminson, "A Regiment of Immigrants: The 82nd Illinois Volunteer Infantry and the Letters of Captain Rudolph Müller," in the *Journal of the Illinois State Historical Society* 94, no. 2 (2001): 137–80; Marc Dluger, "The 82nd Illinois Volunteer Regiment—The Beginning" in *The Delano* 5, no. 2 (Spring/Summer 2003), 1–12; Mark H. Dunkelman, "Hardtack and Sauerkraut Stew: Ethnic Tensions in the 154th New York Volunteers, Eleventh Corps, during the Civil War," *Yearbook of German-American Studies* 36 (2001): 69–90; Christian B. Keller in "Flying Dutchmen and Drunken Irishmen: The Myths and Realities of Civil War Soldiers" in *Journal of Military History* 73 (2009): 117–245; Christian B. Keller, "'All We Ask is Justice': German-American Reactions to the Battle of Chancellorsville," *Yearbook of German-American Studies* 41 (2006): 1–26; Stephen D. Engle, "Yankee Dutchmen: Germans, the Union, and the Construction of Wartime Identity," in Susannah J. Ural, ed., *Civil War Citizens: Race, Ethnicity, and Identity in America's Bloodiest Conflict* (New York: New York University Press. 2010). For some primary sources, see note 7, below. See Lonn, Burton, and Öfele (*True Sons*), above and Dean. B. Mahin, *The Blessed Place of Freedom: Europeans in Civil War America* (Washington, D. C.: Brassey's, 2002) for information on German, Irish, and other nationalities in the military. For a detailed unpublished study of the 82nd Illinois Infantry, see Marc A. Dlugler, "A Regimental Community: The Men of the 82nd Illinois Infantry Before, During and After the American Civil War," Ph. D. diss., Loyola University Chicago, 2009.

2. Walter D. Kamphoefner and Wolfgang Helbich, eds. and Susan Carter Vogel, trans., *Germans in the Civil War: The Letters They Wrote Home* (Chapel Hill: University of North Carolina Press, 2006), xi. Estimates of the number of Germans in the Union army range from 176,187 to 216,000. The editor uses 200,000, a commonly accepted amount. These numbers exclude sons born in the United States to German parents. The terms German and German American in this work denote a person or persons born in any of the various nineteenth-century kingdoms, duchies, principalities, etc., in Central Europe collectively known as Germany, or their immediate offspring then living in the United States. The German-born population of the United States in 1860 was almost 1.3 million. Benjamin A. Gould, *Investigations in the Military and Anthropological Statistics of American Soldiers* (1969 reprint; New

York: Arno Press, 1979), 27; Kaufmann, *Germans in the American Civil War,* 70–74; Keller, *Chancellorsville and the Germans,* 169 n. 2; Mahin, *Blessed Place of Freedom,* 15, 21.

3. Kamphoefner and Helbich, eds. and Susan Carter Vogel, trans., *Germans in the Civil War,* 20; Mark M. Boatner III, *The Civil War Dictionary,* rev. ed. (New York: David McKay Company, Inc., 1987), 612; Keller, *Chancellorsville and the Germans,* 28.

4. Estimates of the percentage of native Germans in the Union army who served in ethnic German regiments range from 18 to 25 percent. William Kaufmann estimated that 36,000 native Germans served in German regiments. Christian B. Keller states that one in four fought in German regiments and Dean B. Mahin asserts that 20 to 25 percent did so. The editor of this work uses a conservative number of 40,000 Germans or 20 percent. Kaufmann, *Germans in the American Civil War,* 102; Keller, *Chancellorsville and the Germans,* 29; Mahin, *Blessed Place of Freedom,* 16. See Lonn, Burton, and Kaufmann for identified German regiments in the Union army. See Andrea Mehrländer, *The Germans of Charleston, Richmond and New Orleans during the Civil War Period, 1850–1870: A Study and Research Compendium* (Berlin, Germany: De Gruyter, 2011) regarding Germans in military units organized in certain cities in the Confederacy.

5. See Christian B. Keller, *Chancellorsville and the Germans,* for a description of the battle and a definitive study of its effect on the Union's Germans. The best books about the battle are Stephen W. Sears, *Chancellorsville* (Boston: Houghton-Mifflin Co., 1996) and Ernest B. Furgurson, *Chancellorsville, 1863: The Souls of the Brave* (New York: Knopf, 1992).

6. Approximately two-thirds of the 82nd Illinois's soldiers were native Germans. The proportion of Germans in the regiment was derived by the editor from microfilmed copies of the regiment's muster and descriptive rolls located at the Illinois State Archives, Springfield, Illinois (hereafter ISA). Illinois's German regiments were the 24th, 43rd, and 82nd Volunteer Infantry Regiments. Burton, *Melting Pot Soldiers,* 77; a compilation of the countries of birth of the 82nd Illinois's replacements prepared by the editor using copies of the muster and descriptive rolls at the ISA, refutes Burton's assertion that the ranks of the 82nd Illinois were "increasingly diluted by native born replacements," and it " . . . completed its Civil War service only a shadow of its original Germanic self." The regiment maintained its German majority throughout the war. Company C was the regiment's Jewish company. It affiliated with the Second Hecker Regiment in part because Hecker had had a liberal stance toward the Jews in Germany late in his political career there. A Jewish company was also organized in Syracuse, New York. It became Company A of the 149th New York Volunteer Infantry. Bertram Wallace Korn, *American Jewry and the Civil War* (1951 reprint; Marietta, Ga.: R. Bemis Publishing, Ltd., 1995), 97, 139. Robert N. Rosen argues, "Jews did not form distinctly Jewish companies because they fervently desired to be seen as citizens of their state and nation, not as a separate nationality. They had no desire to stand out as a group as they had been forced to do in Europe." Bertram W. Korn professes that many "Jewish men and officers in the Union and Confederate armies . . . thought they would avoid trouble by attempting to hide their background." Jews were as subject to anti-Jewish prejudices in the New World as they had been in the Old, and such prejudices escalated during the Civil War. Rosen, "Jewish Confederates," 167–68; Korn, *American Jewry and the Civil War,* 97, 139; <http://www.122ndnewyork.com/is.html> (accessed Oct. 28, 2011). For further reading about anti-Semitism during the Civil War, see Korn, *American Jewry and the Civil War,* and Gary L. Bunker and John Appel, "'Shoddy': Anti-Semitism and the Civil War," in Jonathan D. Sarna and Adam D. Mendelsohn, eds., *Jews and the Civil War: A Reader* (New York: New York University Press, 2010). Simon Wolf erroneously stated that "The 11th New York was more than half composed of men of Jewish faith," in his work *The American Jew as Patriot, Soldier and Citizen* (Boston: Gregg Press, 1972), 3. The editor's review of Wolf's listing of Jews in New York regiments on pages 236–301 did not disclose many more than a dozen Jews in the 11th New York Infantry. While the exact number

of Jews who wore blue or gray uniforms is unknown, scholars estimate that 6,000 to 7,000 Jews fought for the North and 1,200 to 2,000 battled for the South. A large majority of the 125,000 Jews living in the North and the 25,000 residing in the South were natives of German lands or of German ancestry. Robert N. Rosen, "The Jewish Confederates" in Ural, *Civil War Citizens*, 17, 167; Robert N. Rosen, *The Jewish Confederates* (Columbia: University of South Carolina Press, 2000), 162. Korn's *American Jewry and the Civil War* is the best history of Jews in the Civil War, but lacks coverage of the Jewish military experience. A reprint of Korn's 1951 edition published in 2001 contains a new preface and new material. Rosen's *The Jewish Confederates* chronicles both soldiers and civilians. Sabine Freitag and Steven W. Rowan, *Friedrich Hecker: Two Lives for Liberty* (St. Louis, Mo.: St. Louis Mercantile Library, 2006), 125–26, 129, 147 n. 12. Additional biographical information for Colonel Hecker is located in part II of the introduction to this work and in Chapter 2.

7. The letters in this book are among the rare collections of translated Civil War letters from soldiers fighting in a German regiment; further, only about a dozen different collections of letters by German-born soldiers are available in book form. Books comprising Civil War letters written by Germans that contain more than mundane information and that include information about issues such as motivation for enlisting, slavery, emancipation, ethnic prejudices, government policies, and changed opinions as the war progressed are: Joseph R. Reinhart, trans. and ed., *A German Hurrah! The Civil War Letters of Friedrich Bertsch and Wilhelm Stängel, 9th Ohio Infantry* (Kent, Ohio: Kent State University Press, 2010); Reinhart, trans. and ed., *August Willich's Gallant Dutchmen* (Kent, Ohio: Kent State University Press, 2006); Reinhart, trans. and ed., *Two Germans in the Civil War;* Robert Patrick Bender, ed., *Like Grass before the Scythe: The Life and Death of Sgt. William Remmel, 121st New York Infantry* (Tuscaloosa: University of Alabama Press, 2007); Walter D. Kamphoefner and Wolfgang Helbich, eds. and Susan Carter Vogel, trans., *Germans in the Civil War;* Frank L. Byrne and Jean Powers Soman, eds., *Your True Marcus: The Civil War Letters of a Jewish Colonel* (Kent, Ohio: Kent State University Press, 1985); Minetta Altgelt Goyne, trans. and ed., *Lone Star and Double Eagle: Civil War Letters of a German-Texas Family* (n.p.: Texas Christian University Press,1982); and William K. Winkler, ed, *Letters of Frederic C. Winkler 1862–1865* (n.p.: William K. Winkler, 1963). See also Earl J. Hess, ed., *A German in the Yankee Fatherland: The Civil War Letters of Henry A. Kircher* (Kent, Ohio: Kent State University Press, 1983) for an outstanding collection of letters authored by a soldier born in Illinois of German immigrant parents.

8. Available books about the home front include Reid Mitchell, *The Vacant Chair: The Northern Soldier Leaves Home* (New York: Oxford University Press, 1993); Phillip S. Paludan, *A People's Contest: The Union and the Civil War 1861–1865* (New York: Harper & Row, 1988); and Philip E. Webber, *Zoar in the Civil War* (Kent, Ohio: Kent State University Press, 2007). Zoar, Ohio, was a community founded in 1817 by German separatists seeking religious freedom. See also Engle, "A Raised Consciousness." Information about German Americans' activities on the home front in the Midwest appears in Lonn, chapter 18, but she attributes activities supporting the troops and their families to loyalty to the Union and ignores ethnic awareness and solidarity. Kamphoefner's and Helbich's *Germans in the Civil War* contains one or more letters written by each of twenty-two different civilians (in addition to letters from soldiers).

9. William Styple, ed., *Writing and Fighting the Civil War: Soldier Correspondence to the New York Sunday Mercury* (Kearny, N.J.: Belle Grove Pub. Co., 2000), 7.

10. Other major German American Republican newspapers included the *New Yorker Criminal-Zeitung, Philadelphia freie Presse,* Cincinnati *Volksblatt,* and the St. Louis, Missouri, *Westliche Post.* German American Democratic newspapers included the influential *New Yorker Staats-Zeitung* (edited by Forty-eighter Oswald Ottendorfer), the *Cincinnati Volksfreund, Die Chicago Union,* and the *Milwaukee Seebote.* John Charles Bodger Jr., "The

Immigrant Press and the Union Army," Ph. D. diss., Columbia University, 1951, 16, 20; Engle, "Yankee Dutchmen," 31–32; Bruce Levine, *The Spirit of 1848: German Immigrants, Labor Conflict, and the Coming of the Civil War* (Urbana: University of Illinois Press, 1992), 257–63; Christian B. Keller, "Germans in Civil War–Era Pennsylvania: Ethnic Identity and the Problems of Americanization," Pd.D. diss., Pennsylvania State University, 2001, 94–113, 143, 180, 316–24. See Bodger Jr., "The Immigrant Press and the Union Army," for a discussion of German American newspapers during the Civil War.

11. For a discussion of mid-nineteenth-century nativism, see John Higham, *Strangers in the Land: Patterns of American Nativism, 1860–1925* (New Brunswick, N.J.: Rutgers University Press, 2002), 3–11, and Tyler Anbinder, *Nativism and Slavery: The Northern Know Nothings and the Politics of the 1850s* (New York: Oxford University Press, 1992).

12. Franz Sigel was born in 1824 in Sinsheim, Grand Duchy of Baden, and educated at the military academy at Karlsruhe in Baden. Sigel came to the United States in 1852 and moved from New York City to St. Louis, Missouri, in 1857 to accept a professorship at the German Institute there. By 1861 the Forty-eighter was director of schools in St. Louis. The staunch Republican was commissioned a colonel of the 3rd Missouri Infantry Regiment on May 4, 1861, promoted to brigadier general on Aug. 7, 1861 (ranking from May 7, 1861), and elevated to major general on Mar. 22, 1862. Sigel resigned his commission on Dec. 31, 1861, because he was not promoted to command of the Federal Southwestern District of Missouri. He resigned again in March 1863 because he felt his Eleventh Corps (which was a little less than 50 percent German) was being neglected in terms of supplies, pay, promotions of Germans, and reinforcements, and he believed he was being demoted in a reorganization. Both times he blamed the nativism of his Anglo-American superiors for his perceived mistreatment, and German Americans and the German American press rallied to his support. After agreeing to return to the army he was given a small command in the District of Lehigh in Pennsylvania. He was appointed commander of the Department of West Virginia on March 10, 1864, after he and his German American supporters convinced the president to give him a more significant command. Defeated at the battle of New Market in Virginia on May 15, 1864, the inept general was sent to command the defenses of Harper's Ferry, West Virginia. On July 8, 1864, he was relieved of that command for ineffectual leadership and was without a command until he resigned from the army on May 14, 1865. He engaged in journalism in Baltimore then moved to New York, where he was active in publishing and politics. Sigel remained popular in the German American community after the war despite his unsuccessful military career. Engle, "A Raised Consciousness," 1–17; Engle, *Yankee Dutchman*, 2, 7; xvi–xvii, 55; For additional information about Franz Sigel, see Earl J. Hess, "Sigel's Resignation," *Civil War History* 26 (1980): 5–17. See Thomas Nipperdey, *Germany from Napoleon to Bismarck, 1800–1866*, trans. by Daniel Nolan (Princeton, N.J.: Princeton University Press, 1996), 527–98, for information about the German Revolution of 1848. Also see Veit Valentin, *1848: Chapters of German History*, trans. by Ethel Talbot Scheffauer (1940, reprint; Hamden, Conn.: Archon Books, 1965), and Wolfram Siemann, *The German Revolution of 1848–49*, trans. by Christiane Banerji (New York: St. Martin's Press, 1998).

13. Journalism attracted more Forty-eighters than any other profession or occupation, according to one professor. A. E. Zucker, ed., *The Forty-Eighters: Political Refugees of the German Revolution of 1848* (New York: Columbia University Press, 1950), 270; Wittke, *Refugees of Revolution*, 1; Burton, *Melting Pot Soldiers*, 110; The major generals were Franz Sigel, Carl Schurz, Peter J. Osterhaus, and August V. Kautz; the brigadier generals were Louis Blenker, Henry Bohlen, Frederick C. Salomon, Alexander von Schimmelfennig, Adolph Wilhelm August Frederick von Steinwehr, Max Weber, and August Willich. Compiled by the editor from Kaufmann, *The Germans in the American Civil War*, 260–328.

14. John B. Jentz, "The 48ers and the Politics of the German Labor Movement in Chicago during the Civil War Era: Community Formation and the Rise of a Labor Press," in Elliott

Shore, Ken Fones-Wolf, and James Danky, *German-American Radical Press* (Urbana: University of Illinois Press, 1992), 50–51, 7. Martin Öfele cautions, however, "One must be careful not to overemphasize their [Forty-eighters] impact on German-American identity building and their ability to shape ethnic public opinion in favor of Lincoln." Öfele, *German-Speaking Officers*, 7.

15. Wittke, *Refugees of Revolution*, 133–39, 122–33, 166–75; Engle, *Yankee Dutchman*, xv; Bonnie J. Krause, "German Americans in the St. Louis Region 1840–1860," *Missouri Historical Review* 83 (April 1989): 301.

16. Estimates of the number of Forty-eighters who came to the Unites States have ranged as high as 10,000 but the editor believes this number is too high. Many of these revolutionaries had taken refuge in other European countries before crossing the Atlantic, and many initially planned to return to Germany to resume the fight for liberty. LaVern J. Rippley, *The German-Americans* (New York: University Press of America, 1984), 51–53; Compiled by the editor from Levine, *Spirit of 1848*, table 1, p. 16; Engle, *Yankee Dutchman*, xv.

17. Ernest Bruncken, "German Political Refugees in the United States, 1815–1860," in *The German-American Forty-eighters, 1848–1998*, ed. Don Heinrich Tolzmann (Nashville, Ind.: NCAS Literatur, 1997), 32–33. Carl Wittke professes, "The arrogant air of superiority of some Germans, particularly editors of radical papers, toward the American 'way of life,'" was disturbing to many Americans. The Americans resented attacks on their "alleged low cultural and educational standards . . . eating and drinking habits, and the criticism of American art, architecture, literature, dirty cities . . . and the Americans absorption in business to the exclusion of all interest in intellectual and theoretical matters." Wittke, *The German-Language Press in America*, 132.

18. The demise of the American Party, which was strongest in the northeast, resulted from its internal failure to reach agreement on the issue of slavery; many of its followers in Northern states defected to the Republican Party. Similarly, the national Whig Party (anti-slavery, anti-Catholic, and pro-temperance) had fractured in 1854 over the issue of allowing the expansion of slavery into the western territories, and a large number of northern Whigs had joined the American Party. Engle, "Yankee Dutchmen," 28; McPherson, *Battle Cry of Freedom*, 141–42, 125–26; Robert P. Lockwood, *Anti-Catholicism in American Culture* (Huntington, Ind.: Our Sunday Visitor, 2000), 20–25; Mischa Honeck, *We are the Revolutionists: German-speaking Immigrants and American Abolitionists after 1848* (Athens: University of Georgia Press, 2011), 15–21.

19. Keller, *Chancellorsville and the Germans*, 10.

20. James M. Berquist, "The Forty-eighers and the Politics of the 1850s," in Hans L. Trefousse, ed., *Germany and America: Essays on Problems of International Relations and Immigration.* (New York: Brooklyn College Press, 1980), 114–15; James Stuart Olson, *The Ethnic Dimension in American History* (New York: St. Martin's Press, 1979), 99–100; Kathleen Neils Conzen, "German-Americans and the Invention of Ethnicity," in Frank Trommler and Joseph McVeigh, eds., *America and the Germans: An Assessment of a Three-Hundred Year History* (Philadelphia: University of Pennsylvania Press, 1985), 138–39; John A. Hawgood, *The Tragedy of German-America* (New York: Arno Press, 1970), 43, 271; Kamphoefner and Helbich, eds., *Germans in the Civil War*, 302; Keller, *Chancellorsville and the Germans*, 10.

21. Besides the Democratic Party's welcoming of German immigrants and opposition to strict Sunday and prohibition laws, Bruce Levine points out, "Northern Democrats attracted and retained this support by . . . verbally endorsing the cause of European freedom, . . . and in general presenting themselves as defenders of popular rights and welfare against 'monopolistic' designs ascribed to Whigs. Earlier support for homestead bills also drew German American support." Levine, *Spirit of 1848*, 151.

22. Andreas Dorpalen, "The German Element and the Issues of the Civil War," *Mississippi Valley Historical Review* 29 (June 1942): 70–71, 72–76; Frederick C. Luebke, "German Immigrants and American Politics: Problems of Leadership, Parties, and Issues," in Randall M. Miller, ed., *Germans in America: Retrospect and Prospect. Tricentennial Lectures Delivered at the German Society of Pennsylvania in 1983* (Philadelphia: German Society of Pennsylvania, 1984), 64–65; James M. Bergquist, "People and Politics in Transition: The Illinois Germans, 1850–1860," in Frederick C. Luebke, ed., *Ethnic Voters and the Election of Lincoln* (Lincoln: University of Nebraska Press, 1971), 224–26; German populations by location compiled by the editor from 1860 U.S. population census. See Freitag and Rowan, *Friedrich Hecker*, 153–216, for a discussion of the beginning of the Republican Party, the Kansas-Nebraska Bill and German American reactions. The *Dreissigers* ("the Grays") who came to the United States in the 1830s were more conservative than the Forty-eighters ("the Greens") and were slower to move to the Republican Party; some Grays remained Democrats, as did a small number of Forty-eighters. For a discussion of the differences, see Walter D. Kamphoefner, "*Dreissiger* and Forty-eighter: The Political Influence of Two Generations of Germans Exiles" in Hans L. Trefousse, ed., *Germany and America: Essays on Problems of International Relations and Immigration* (New York: Brooklyn College Press, 1980), 89–99. For information about how ethnoreligious identity impacted political identity, and how the Republican party's make up and development on the state level influenced German voters, see Kamphoefner, "German Americans and the Civil War Politics," 232–46.

23. Andreas Dorpalen, "The German Element and the Issues of the Civil War," 55; John A. Hawgood, *The Tragedy of German-America* (New York: Arno Press, 1970), 51–52; Augustus J. Prahl, "The Turners," in Zucker, ed., *The Forty- Eighters,* 100; Levine, *Spirit of 1858,* 154–55; Judith Conrad Wimmer notes that Catholics "were generally anti-abolitionists. . . . They spoke from a conservative, European background, believing that gradual emancipation would be of greater [b]enefit to both the nation and the slave." Judith Conrad Wimmer, "American Catholic Interpretations of the Civil War," Ph.D. diss., Drew University, 1979, 11. For additional information about German Roman Catholics and their church in the United States during the nineteenth century, see Coleman J. Berry, *The Catholic Church and German Americans* (Milwaukee, Wis.: Bruce, 1953).

24. Colonel Hecker mustered on Oct. 23, 1862. Unless otherwise stated: (1) the original muster in date for members of the 82nd Illinois was Sept. 26, 1862 (except for Company I for which the date was Oct. 29, 1862), and (2) the service information, residence, age, place of birth, and physical description for individual members of the 82nd Illinois were taken from the regiment's muster and descriptive rolls located at the ISA. Illinois. Hecker's letter to Gustav Struve appeared in German in *Die Gartenlaube,* Leipzig: Ernst Keil, 13, no. 4 (1865): 57–58. The translated letter is undated and appears in chapter 5 of this volume. Gustav Struve was born in 1805 in Munich, Bavaria, and studied law at Heidelberg and Göttingen. He agitated for a German Republic before 1848 and after the short-lived republic failed in 1849 he fled Germany and came to the United States in 1851. Struve served as a captain in the 8th New York Volunteer Infantry Regiment and resigned his commission after Prussian Prince Salm-Salm was appointed its colonel. The Forty-eighter returned to Germany in 1863 under a general amnesty and worked as an author. Zucker, ed., *The Forty- Eighters,* 273; Burton, *Melting Pot Soldiers,* 87–91; Freitag and Rowan, *Friedrich Hecker,* 104, 107–8. See Lonn, *Foreigners in the Union Army,* 291–93, for additional information on Prince Salm-Salm, a soldier of fortune.

25. Freitag and Rowan, *Friedrich Hecker,* 15, 129, 228–35. Hecker was elevated to command of the Third Brigade, Third Division of the Eleventh Corps. The new brigade consisted of the 80th Illinois, 82nd Illinois, 75th Pennsylvania, and 68th New York. Only the 80th Illinois was not a German regiment. Illinois and J. N. Reece, *Report of the Adjutant General of the State of*

Illinois (hereafter *RAGSI*), 9 vols. (Springfield, Ill.: Phillips Bros., 1900–1902), 5:121; *OR* vol. 31, 1:111–12, 206.

26. Rudolph Müller's original letters written in German are located in the Friedrich Hecker Papers, Western Historical Manuscript Collection, Thomas Jefferson Library, University of Missouri–St. Louis. Benjaminson, "Regiment of Immigrants," 137–80.

27. Benjaminson, "Regiment of Immigrants," 139.

28. Freitag and Rowan, *Friedrich Hecker*, 239, 237. An English translation of Eugene Weigel's letter previously appeared in Eric Benjaminson's "Regiment of Immigrants," 158–59. Information about Weigel, Salomon and Hillborg is located in the proximity of their letters.

29. *Illinois Staats-Zeitung*, Aug. 14, 1862, Aug. 15, 1862, Aug. 16, 1862, Aug. 19, 1862, Sept. 16, 1862, and March 29, 1865. The Jewish population of Chicago grew from 100 persons in 1850 to 1,500 persons in 1860; most were Germans. Edward Mazur, "Jewish Chicago: From Diversity to Community," in Melvin G. Holli and Peter d'Alroy Jones, eds., *The Ethnic Frontier: Essays in the History of Group Survival in Chicago and the Midwest* (Grand Rapids, Mich.: William B. Eerdmans Publishing Co., 1977), 265.

30. Freitag and Rowan, *Friedrich Hecker*, 160. Historian James M. McPherson asserts that Irish and German Catholics did not enlist in proportion to their percentage of the male population, while British and German Protestants did. Kamphoefner argues that it would be "far more accurate . . . to say that Republican immigrants were more eager recruits to the Union army than were Democrats; these categories overlapped with confession, but far from completely." James M. McPherson, *Ordeal by Fire: The Civil War and Reconstruction* (New York: Knopf, 1982), 358; Kamphoefner, "German-Americans and Civil War Politics," 243.

31. The aggregate number of enlistees mustered in to Oct. 29, 1863 (approximately 850) was compiled by the editor from *RAGSI*, 5:100–119.

32. In the nine companies in which Germans were in the majority, soldiers known to have been born outside Germany ranged from eleven in Company B and Company C to a high of thirty-seven in Company H. Besides Germans, Company H included twenty-three natives of Switzerland and small numbers of natives of Belgium, Bohemia, France, Holland, and one Missouri native. After its Swiss-born captain, Emil Frey, was captured at the Battle of Gettysburg, and its original first lieutenant was cashiered, Germans led this company. Colonel Hecker stayed with the Frey family after he fled to Switzerland in 1848. When Emil left his parents and came to America in 1860 he initially worked for Hecker as a farmhand. The Arlesheim, Switzerland, native joined the 24th Illinois Infantry in June 1861 as a private and was a first lieutenant when he resigned on June 17, 1862 and started recruiting a company for the Second Hecker Regiment. He mustered in as a captain on Sept. 26, 1862. After his capture at the Battle of Gettysburg, Frey was absent from the regiment for most of the remainder of the war. The governor nevertheless commissioned him as a major on June 8, 1865, but he was not mustered at that rank. He returned to Switzerland in August 1865, and became its president in 1894. The number of non-Germans was compiled by the editor from 82nd Illinois muster and descriptive rolls; Hedwig Rappolt, trans. and ed., *An American Apprenticeship: The Letters of Emil Frey 1860–1865* (New York: Peter Lang, 1986), 13–15; *RAGSI*, 2:317, 307, 5:113, 100.

33. Capt. Jacob Lasalle, 1st Lt. Mayer A. Frank, and 2nd Lt. Frederick Bechstein were the original officers for Company C. All three were Jews. Capt. Joseph B. Greenhut of Chicago was a twenty-year-old native of Teinitz, Austria. He mustered as a captain, Company K, on Oct. 23, 1862, and resigned on Feb. 24, 1864. Notably, he was the first Jew in Chicago to enlist in the Union army. He served as a private in Company A in the three-month 12th Illinois Infantry and mustered into the three-year 12th Illinois as a sergeant on Aug. 1, 1861. Greenhut was severely wounded in the right arm in the Battle of Fort Donelson in Tennessee in February 1862, and was discharged due to disability on Apr. 22, 1862. Meites, *History of the Jews of Chicago*, 91; muster and descriptive rolls, 12th Illinois Volunteer Infantry (three months

and three years), ISA, Springfield, Illinois; birthplaces of Jews in the regiment compiled by the editor from the muster and descriptive rolls, 82nd Illinois Volunteer Infantry, Adjutant General's Office Springfield, Illinois.

34. The 82nd Illinois was assigned to the First Brigade of the Third Division commanded by Brig. Gen. Alexander von Schimmelfennig and Maj. Gen. Carl Schurz, respectively. The First Brigade, Third Division, consisted of the following units: 82nd Illinois, 68th New York, 157th New York, 61st Ohio, 74th Pennsylvania, 1st Ohio Artillery, Battery I. *OR* vol. 27, 26–27. Alexander von Schimmelfennig served as an officer in the Prussian Army before siding with the revolutionists. In June 1849 he was wounded twice in the Battle of Rinnthal in the Palatinate, but escaped to Switzerland. This exile arrived in the United States in 1854. He was the colonel of the German 74th Pennsylvania Regiment before being promoted to brigadier general. After the Battle of Gettysburg he transferred to the Carolinas and commanded a brigade in the Tenth Corps. He died shortly after the war ended. Carl Schurz, a Forty-eighter, was born in 1829 near Cologne in the Rhineland Province of Prussia and came to America in 1852. Active in the Republican Party, he campaigned for Lincoln in 1860 and 1864. He resigned as Minister to Spain to enter the Union army as brigadier general on Apr. 15, 1862, despite his lack of prior military experience, and advanced to major general in 1863. After the Eleventh Corps became part of the new Twentieth Corps in April 1864, he was put in command of a Corps of Instruction at Nashville. He briefly returned to active service, where in the last months of the war he was with Sherman's army in North Carolina as chief of staff of Henry Slocum's Army of Georgia. He resigned from the army when the war ended. After the war Schurz engaged in journalism, and served as a senator from Missouri and Secretary of the Interior. *RAGSI*, 5:120; Keller, *Chancellorsville and the Germans*, 77, 33; Lonn, *Foreigners in the Union Army*, 196–97; Boatner, *Civil War Dictionary*, 727. See Hans. L. Trefousse, *Carl Schurz: A Biography* (Bronx, N.Y.: Fordham University Press, 1998) and Carl Schurz, Frederic Bancroft, and William Archibald Dunning, *The Reminiscences of Carl Schurz* (New York: The McClure Company, 1907).

35. Oliver O. Howard was a West Point graduate and career army officer. His right arm was amputated because of wounds received at the Battle of Fair Oaks in Virginia. He was promoted to major general in November 1862, and to command of the Eleventh Corps in April 1863. Howard was intelligent, brave, and dedicated but a poor tactician and lacked enterprise. The pious Methodist disliked alcohol and cursing and was poorly suited to command the Eleventh Corps. Albert Castel, *Decision in the West: The Atlanta Campaign of 1864* (Lawrence: University Press of Kansas, 1992), 98; John J. Hennessy, "We Shall Make Richmond Howl: The Army of the Potomac on the Eve of Chancellorsville," in Gary W. Gallagher, ed., *Chancellorsville: The Battle and Its Aftermath* (Chapel Hill: University of North Carolina Press, 1996), 23.

36. The 82nd Illinois and its corps fought only on May 2, 1863, although the Battle of Chancellorsville lasted from Apr. 30 to May 6, 1863. Recommended books about the Battle of Gettysburg are Stephen W. Sears, *Gettysburg* (Boston: Houghton Mifflin, 2003), Edwin B. Coddington, *The Gettysburg Campaign: A Study in Command* (New York: Simon & Schuster, 1997), and Harry W. Pfanz, *Gettysburg—The First Day* (Chapel Hill: University of North Carolina Press, 2001). For the battles around Chattanooga, see Peter Cozzens, *The Shipwreck of Their Hopes: The Battles for Chattanooga* (Urbana: University of Illinois Press, 1994) and Wiley Sword, *Mountains Touched with Fire: Chattanooga Besieged, 1863* (New York: St. Martin's Press, 1995); *OR* vol. 32, 3:258, 550.

37. Colonel Hecker said that his resignation was due to poor health and pressing personal matters on his farm. General Howard stated that an additional reason was that Hecker had been passed over several times for promotion. Gustav Struve believed that this was the overriding reason. The sensitive colonel was also upset because he believed General Hooker had attacked his honor in his official report about the Battle of Wauhatchie that was published in the *Cincinnati Commercial* and other newspapers in January 1864. Hecker demanded a court

of inquiry and was exonerated. Although Hooker was not referring to Hecker in his report, the latter refused to believe it. The battle had taken place the night of Oct. 28–29, 1863, near Chattanooga. Freitag and Rowan, *Friedrich Hecker*, 244–50.

38. William T. Sherman was a West Point graduate who succeeded Lt. Gen. Ulysses S. Grant as commander of the western armies in March 1864. His grand army aggregated 110,000 men during the Atlanta campaign and 60,000 troops during the subsequent campaigns. The Left Wing (Twentieth Corps and the Fourteenth Corps) became known as the Army of Georgia. General Joseph E. Johnston commended the Confederate Army of Tennessee during the initial phase of the Atlanta campaign, was replaced in July 1864 because of his failure to stop Sherman's army, and was reinstated as the army's commander in February 1865. McPherson, *Battle Cry of Freedom*, 808, 825. Some recommended books about the Atlanta campaign, March to the Sea, and Carolinas campaign are: Castel, *Decision in the West*; Noah Andre Trudeau, *Southern Storm: Sherman's March to the Sea* (New York: Harper, 2008); Joseph T. Glatthaar, *The March to the Sea and Beyond: Sherman's Troops in the Savannah and Carolinas Campaigns* (New York: New York University Press, 1985); John G. Barrett, *Sherman's March through the Carolinas* (Chapel Hill: University of North Carolina Press, 1996); and Mark L. Bradley. *Last Stand in the Carolinas: The Battle of Bentonville* (Campbell, Calif.: Savas Woodbury Publishers, 1996).

39. Aggregate dead compiled by the editor from 82nd Illinois muster and descriptive rolls and *RAGSI*, 5:100–119. A reception was held at the Turner Hall and Colonel Hecker, William Rapp of the *Illinois Staats-Zeitung*, and others, gave speeches. Lt. Col. Edward S. Salomon responded to the speeches on behalf of the regiment. *RAGSI*, 5:124.

40. Burton, *Melting Pot Soldiers*, 83; Helbich, "German-born Union Soldiers," 308; Keller, *Chancellorsville and the Germans*, 31.

41. Keller, *Chancellorsville and the Germans*, 26–28; Öfele, *True Sons of the Republic*, 69–70. George E. Heinzmann, Company B, was born in the Grand Duchy of Baden, and worked as a painter in Chicago before he enlisted. He was promoted from first lieutenant to captain on Mar. 12, 1863, and mustered out June 9, 1865. The muster and descriptive rolls show his village of birth as Walferhinen; the editor was unable to locate this village.

42. *Illinois Staats-Zeitung*, Aug. 6, 1862, Oct. 1, 1862; Rudolph Müller letter to Colonel Hecker, Mar. 27, 1864.

43. Helbich, "German-born Union Soldiers," 308–11; Keller, *Chancellorsville and the Germans*, 27–28.

44. Engle, "A Raised Consciousness," 11; Helbich, "German-born Union Soldiers," 306.

45. Keller, *Chancellorsville and the Germans*, 25; ages compiled by the editor from the 82nd Illinois muster and descriptive rolls, ISA. A study of the 12th Missouri Regiment (Union) yielded similar results as to ages. Earl J. Hess, "The 12th Missouri Infantry: A Socio-Military Profile of a Union Regiment," *Missouri Historical Review* 76, no. 1 (Oct. 1981): 61–62.

46. Occupations compiled by the editor from the 82nd Illinois muster and descriptive rolls. Bell Irwin Wiley, *The Life of Billy Yank: The Common Soldier of the Union* (Baton Rouge: Louisiana State University Press, 1952), 304. In sampling four Pennsylvania German regiments (the 27th, 73rd, 74th, and 98th), Keller found that "the majority of soldiers were day laborers, shoemakers, farmers, tailors, bakers and smiths, in descending order." *Chancellorsville and the Germans*, 25, 174–75 n. 3. The historian for the German 9th Ohio, organized at Cincinnati, reported that the regiment contained "about 400 common laborers before the war, the rest: lawyers, artists, merchants and craftsmen." The number of farmers is not given but it was probably fairly small and nowhere near half the regiment. Of the 781 soldiers in the German 12th Missouri who listed their occupations just less than 30 percent were farmers. Constantin Grebner, "*We Were the Ninth*": A History of the Ninth Regiment Ohio Volunteer

Infantry, April 17, 1861 to June 7, 1864, trans. and ed. Frederic Trautmann (Kent, Ohio: Kent State University Press, 1987), 199; Hess, "The 12th Missouri Infantry," 62.

47. Keller, *Chancellorsville and the Germans,* 25–26.

48. German was usually the language of both command and conversation in German regiments raised early in the war. Early on, information was entered into order and letter books in German script. By the time the 82nd Illinois mustered in during 1862, however, regimental records were being maintained in English. Evidence is lacking as to whether oral commands in Hecker's regiment were given in German. Robert Stoddard deserted right after the Battle of Gettysburg and claimed that after a few weeks in New York, he decided to return to the 82nd Illinois. On the way back, however, he began a drinking spree in Bridgeport, Connecticut, and joined the 5th Connecticut Infantry as a substitute, but never received the $300 bonus promised. He served ten months with the 5th Connecticut before being arrested. Capt. Joseph Gottlob of the 82nd Illinois and 1st Sgt. Fredrick H. Tanning of the 5th Connecticut testified in Stoddard's defense that he was a good and willing soldier based on their observations. Stoddard was found guilty of desertion and suffered the loss of $10 pay per month for ten months. Keller, *Chancellorsville and the Germans,* 31–32; Robert Stoddard Court Martial File, NN2447, NA.

49. *Illinois Staats-Zeitung,* Sept. 5, 1862; Keller, *Chancellorsville and the Germans,* 32–33. For a discussion about alcohol consumption in the Union army, see Thomas P. Lowry, *Irish and German Whiskey and Beer: Drinking Patterns in the Civil War* (Charleston, S.C.: CreativeSpace, 2011).

50. Helbich, "German-born Union Soldiers," 302–3. *Illinois Staats-Zeitung,* Dec. 19, 1864.

51. Annette R. Hofmann, "One Hundred Fifty Years of Loyalty: The Turner Movement in the United States," *Yearbook of German-American Studies* 34 (1999): 66.

52. *Illinois Staats-Zeitung,* Oct. 4, 1862.

53. Lonn, *Foreigners in the Union Army,* 309. So that their chaplain could be called Reverend, a *Freie Gemeinde* (Free Congregation) was formed, with a leader called a *Sprecher* (Speaker). Sermons were based on rationalism and not supernaturalism, revelation, dogmas, or creeds. After a protest by Jews, rabbis were allowed to serve as chaplains. Wittke, *Refugees of Revolution,* 122–43.

54. Reichhelm lost his job as a clerk and interpreter for the Surrogate Court in New York City because he dropped his support for Democrat Stephen A. Douglas and strongly supported Abraham Lincoln. Interestingly, Reichhelm's son had run away from home and joined Franz Sigel's 3rd Missouri Regiment (in which Hecker was then serving) because his father had forbidden him to join a New York regiment. During the organization of the 82nd, Hecker summoned the senior Reichhelm to become his new regiment's chaplain. *Schlegel's German-American Families in the United States,* 3 vols. (New York: The American Historical Society, 1916–1917), 164.

55. Friedrich August Braeutigam was a native of Grosspösna, Saxony. Friedrich August Braeutigam diary, Oct. 5, 1862, transcript, Gary Swick trans., Abraham Lincoln Presidential Library (hereafter ALPL), Springfield, Illinois.

56. Reinhart, *August Willich's Gallant Dutchmen,* x; Earl J. Hess, "The 12th Missouri Infantry," 62; Reinhart, *A German Hurrah!,* 6–7.

57. See Dunkelman, "Hardtack and Sauerkraut Stew," 69–90; Reinhart, *Two Germans in the Civil War,* 67; Burton, *Melting Pot Soldiers,* 202–3; Keller "Germans in Civil War–Era Pennsylvania," 143–53; Kevin, J. Weddle, "Ethnic Discrimination in Minnesota Volunteer Regiments during the Civil War," *Civil War History* 35 (1989): 239–59. Wolfgang Helbich does not favor using the "one-sided term 'nativism," but prefers "to speak of pluralistic ethnic competition—for power, for money, for recognition." Helbich, "German-born Union Soldiers," 308.

58. Keller, *Chancellorsville and the Germans*, 76–77. The *Illinois Staats-Zeitung* fought back against the slander by stating that "[t]he correspondent of the *N. Y. Times*, fueled by his nativistic perfidy and rage, seeks to create the impression that the German parts of the Corps performed especially bad [*sic*] and the American ones rather well." *Illinois Staats-Zeitung*, May 7, 1863. See Keller, *Chancellorsville and the Germans*, 114–17, 143–45. See note 59, below, for information about Maj. Gen. Joseph Hooker.

59. Keller, *Chancellorsville and the Germans*, 2–4; *Illinois Staats-Zeitung*, July 11, 1863; Keller, "Flying Dutchmen and Drunken Irishmen," 135–39. See also Christian B. Keller, "'All We Ask is Justice,'" 1–26. Maj. Gen. Joseph Hooker, a West Point graduate, became commander of the Army of the Potomac on Jan. 26, 1863, and was relieved of command after his army's defeat at Chancellorsville in Virginia. In September he was given command of the Eleventh and Twelfth Corps and moved to Chattanooga, Tennessee, with the two corps. Five months after the Confederate siege was broken, Hooker was given command of the new Twentieth Corps (consisting of the divisions of the Eleventh and Twelfth Corps at Chattanooga). He led the new corps until he asked to be relieved on July 28, 1864, because he was not given command of the Army of the Tennessee after its commander was killed during the Battle of Atlanta. He commanded several departments until he retired in 1868. Warner, *Generals in Blue*, 233–35.

60. Burton, *Melting Pot Soldiers*, 204–5.

61. Telegram from Capt. Ivar A. Weid to Governor Yates. Telegrams from a Frode Heergaard and Van H. Higgins, a lawyer, dated Sept. 13, 1862, were also sent to the governor. Mr. Heergaard stated he was writing on behalf of his fellow soldiers in Weid's company but he does not appear on the muster rolls. Frode Heegaard wrote in a letter to Yates, dated Sept. 13, 1862, "There have for many centuries existed a great national *Enmity* between the Scandinavian and German nations, which feeling of national hatred is daily exhibited in this country as much as it is in Europe." 82nd Illinois Infantry Correspondence File, ISA. Some non-Germans in German companies did receive last-minute promotions to officer rank. On June 8, 1865, the day before muster out, 1st Lt. Mons Lindbergh, a native of Sweden, was commissioned as a captain, Company E; Sgt. John U. Schimperil, a native of Switzerland, was commissioned as a 1st lieutenant, Company B; and 1st Sgt. John H. Porter, Company D, a native of York, Pennsylvania, and son of an Irish father, was commissioned as a 2nd lieutenant. U.S. population census for York, Pennsylvania, 1860. Capt. Ivar Alexander A. Weid, a twenty-five-year-old native of Odense, Denmark, resided in Chicago at his enlistment in the 82nd Illinois. Weid had previously joined the three-year 3rd Missouri Infantry on Sept. 21, 1861, and was discharged on June 2, 1862, because of a service-related rupture. He was a student at his enlistment in 1861 and a sergeant in Company D at discharge. The native Dane mustered into Hecker's second regiment on Aug. 30, 1862, and resigned on Jan. 17, 1863, due to impaired health. Ivar A. Weid pension file no. 661750, NA.

62. *Illinois Staats-Zeitung*, Sept. 1, 1862. In a study of letters written by thirty-six Germans in the military and twenty-three civilians of military age in the North, Wolfgang Helbich noted, "sixteen letter writers (including five civilians) explained that German officers "command better, German regiments fight better, German camps are cleaner, [and] German troops are healthier." Helbich also found about a dozen instances where Anglo-Americans were described "in the most unflattering terms—uncultured, hypocrites, money-crazed humbugs, swindlers, reckless wasters of human lives." Helbich, "German-born Union Soldiers." 299–300. Helbich and Kamphoefner, eds., *Germans in the Civil War*, 25. The letters of Henry Kircher, a second-generation German-American in the Union army, also express strong ethnic loyalty and pride. Kircher, *A German in the Yankee Fatherland*, 9, 13, 15, 28, 52, 62, 121.

63. Helbich, "German-born Union Soldiers," 301; Helbich and Kamphoefner, eds., *Germans in the Civil War*, 25. The letters were written to family and friends in Germany.

64. See note 62, above, regarding the letters in Helbich's study. Brig. Gen. Alpheus S. Williams, a Connecticut native, had served as a lieutenant colonel in a Michigan regiment in the War with Mexico. He served in the Twelfth Corps prior to its consolidation with the Eleventh Corps to form the Twentieth Corps. Williams commanded the First Division of the Twentieth Corps during the Atlanta campaign and the corps itself during the March to the Sea and Carolinas campaigns. See Alpheus S. Williams, *From the Cannon's Mouth: The Civil War Letters of General Alpheus S. Williams* (Detroit, Mich.: Wayne State University Press, 1959). Brig. Gen. Hector Tyndale began his military service on June 28, 1861, as a major in the 28th Pennsylvania Infantry. Promoted to brigadier general on Apr. 9, 1863, Tyndale was severely wounded at Antietam, given sick leave on May 2, 1864, and resigned on Aug. 26, 1864, because of poor health. Warner, *Generals in Blue,* 517. James S. Robinson, a printer and newspaper editor, joined the three-month 4th Ohio in April 1861. He later enlisted in the 82nd Ohio and became its major on Dec. 31, 1861, and its colonel on Apr. 9, 1862. Robinson achieved the rank of brigadier general on Jan. 12, 1865. He commanded the 1st Brigade, 3rd Division, Ninth Corps prior to commanding the 3rd Brigade, 1st Division, Twentieth Corps (Mar. 13, 1864–Apr. 16, 1864, and Sept. 27, 1864–June 7, 1865). He was seriously wounded at the Battle of Gettysburg. Warner, *Generals in Blue,* 406–7; Boatner, *Civil War Dictionary,* 704.

65. Rudolph Müller letters, Sept. 15, 1864, Mar. 27, 1864. Col. Stephen McGroarty, 61st Ohio Infantry.

66. Ibid., Mar. 27, 1864.

67. In 1864 some Republicans formed the Radical Democracy Party hoping to prevent Abraham Lincoln's re-election because they believed he had moved too slowly on the abolition of slavery and they opposed his plan to be lenient on the South during postwar Reconstruction. A large part of this party was comprised of radical Germans and some Anglo-American abolitionists, including some U.S. House and Senate members. John C. Frémont became the party's presidential candidate for 1864 but he dropped out of the race before the election and most Radicals voted for Lincoln to prevent a victory by a Democrat. Lincoln ran as the Union Party candidate, not the Republican candidate. It is not known if Rudolph Müller considered himself a Radical Republican or was a member of that party but his letters indicate his disdain for Lincoln's management of the war. See William Frank Zornow, *Lincoln and the Party Divided* (Norman: University of Oklahoma Press, 1954).

68. Rudolph Müller letters dated Oct. 25, 1864, and May 27, 1865.

69. Ibid., Apr. 2, 1865.

70. Rudolph Müller and Malvina Hecker married on Apr. 19, 1866, in St. Clair County, Illinois. Malvina Müller widow's pension file no. 499417, NA

1. Organization of the Regiment

1. *RAGSI,* 2:101–19.

2. McPherson, *Battle Cry of Freedom,* 491–94.

3. The companies would become Companies A, F, and G.

4. During 1862 the Chicago Board of Supervisors was disbursing bounties of $60 per volunteer and the Chicago Board of Trade offered bounties aggregating $200,000 to spur enlistments. Bessie Louise Pierce, *A History of Chicago,* 3 vols. (1937 reprint; Chicago: University of Chicago Press, 1975), 3:272.

5. C. Eugene Miller and Forrest F. Steinlage, *Der Turner Soldat: A German Soldier in the Civil War; Germany to Antietam* (Louisville, Ky.: Calmar Publications, 1988), 462–63; Wittke, *Refugees of Revolution,* 147; Burton, *Melting Pot Soldiers,* 3; Annette R. Hofmann, "The Turners' Loyalty for their New Home Country: Their Engagement in the American Civil War,"

The International Journal of the History of Sport 12 (1995), 153. For information on Turner militia and their arms, see Thomas B. Rentschler, *Rifles and Blades of the German-American Militia and the Civil War* (Hamilton, Ohio: Blue Hills Press, 2003).

6. Bruce Levine states that "Turners tended to be *Freisinnigen*—'religious liberals', rationalists, 'freethinkers' . . . who . . . harbored deep suspicion of organized churches and clerical hierarchies." They fostered social, political, and religious reforms, and viewed nativism, slavery, and prohibition laws as the most serious abuses of their time. Levine, *The Spirit of 1848*, 93–94.

7. Turners in the 82nd Illinois included Col. Friedrich Hecker, Maj. Ferdinand H. Rolshausen, Capt. George E. Heinzmann, Quartermaster Hermann Panse, Capt. Rudolph Müller, 1st Lt. Carl Lotz, 1st Lt. Joseph Rieger, Capt. Anton Bruhn, 1st Lt. Frank Kirchner, Sgt. Gustav Giese, 2nd Lt. Barthold Kruckenberg, Sgt. Charles Ohle, and Cpl. Peter Otto. *Illinois Staats-Zeitung,* Mar. 29, 1865; Frederick Bodo Bess, *Eine populäre Geschichte der Stadt Peoria* (Peoria, Ill: [s.n.], 1906), 539. *RAGSI,* 1:238–39.

8. Secretary of War, *Official Army Register of the Volunteer Force of the United States Army for the years 1861, '62, '63, '64, '65; Part 6: Indiana, Illinois* (Washington, D. C.: Government Printing Office, 1865), 341. Unless otherwise stated the source for all brevet promotions for officers of the 82nd Illinois is pages 341–42 of this publication. Rudolph A. Hofmeister, *The Germans of Chicago* (Champaign, Ill.: Stipes Publishing Co., 1976), 88–89.

9. After President Lincoln's call for 300,000 additional volunteers on July 2, 1862, failed to raise the requested volunteers, he called for the draft of 300,000 militia on Aug. 4, 1862, for nine months, and ordered that any state not meeting its assigned quota by Aug. 15, 1862, must have a special draft from its militia. Edward McPherson, *The Political History of the United States of America during the Great Rebellion, from November 6, 1860, to July 4, 1864* (Washington, D.C.: Philip & Solomons, 1864), 115.

10. Capt. Augustus Bruning, a native of Cloppenburg in the Grand Duchy of Oldenburg and a justice of the peace, was elected captain of Company B. He resigned on Mar. 12, 1863.

11. *Frisch, frei and frölich!* (Alert, free, happy) was another Turner slogan. In Germany the slogan was originally *Frisch, fromm, frei and frölich!* (Alert, devout, free, and happy). The writer dropped the word "devout" here.

12. This was probably Company A; however, it was mustered again on Sept. 26, 1862.

13. U.S. Mustering Officer Hill is unidentified except by the context. Hermann Panse of East St. Louis, Illinois, served as quartermaster of the 82nd Illinois until he mustered out in June 1865. He received a brevet promotion to captain in 1866. At enlistment he was forty years old, married, and a merchant. In 1860 he was secretary for the South St. Louis Insurance Company He was wounded on Aug. 10, 1861, during the Battle of Wilson's Creek, while serving in the three-month 3rd Missouri Regiment, Company K, and was discharged on Aug. 30, 1861.

14. Maj. John G. Fonda belonged to the 12th Illinois Cavalry and later became commander of the 118th Illinois Infantry. *RAGSI,* 1861–1866 (Springfield: Baker, Bailhache & Co, Printers, 1867), 8:121; John G. Fonda (118th Infantry): *RAGSI,* 1861–1866 (Springfield: Journal Company Printers & Binders, 1900), 6:292.

15. *Biographical Sketches of the Leading Men of Chicago* (Chicago: Wilson & St. Clair, 1868), 391; Benjaminson, "Regiment of Immigrants," 144–45.

16. Lorenz Brentano and Sheriff Anthony C. Hesing were the owners of the *Illinois Staats-Zeitung;* Brentano and Wilhelm Rapp were Forty-eighters and served as the newspaper's editors. Lieutenant Governor Francis A. Hoffmann was a native of Hereford in the Prussian Province of Westphalia. He arrived in the United States in 1839 and was ordained as a Lutheran minister in 1843. In 1851 he entered into politics and later worked in banking, journalism, and law. He was a founder of the Republican Party in Illinois and was elected

lieutenant governor in 1860. Jacob Lasalle of Chicago was a twenty-nine-year-old merchant and a native of Marburg in the Electorate of Hesse. He resigned on May 28, 1863. John Moses, *Illinois: Historical and Statistical, comprising the essential facts of its planting and growth as a province, county, territory, and state,* 2 vols. (Chicago: Fergus Printing, 1892), 2:636–37. The *Chicago Tribune* also reported on the war meetings on Aug. 14, 15, 16, and 19, 1862.

17. Concordia Hall was located on Dearborn Street near Monroe Street. The Jewish Concordia Club was formed early in 1862; Henry Greenebaum was the club's president. Irving Cutler, *The Jews of Chicago: From Shtetl to Suburb* (Urbana: University of Illinois Press, 1996), 20–21; Hyman L. Meites, *History of the Jews of Chicago* (Chicago: Jewish Historical Society of Illinois, 1924), 88.

18. M. M. Gerstley was a shirt manufacturer and president of his Jewish congregation *Anshe Ma'ariv.* The group's other officers were secretaries S. Flörsheim and Joseph Frank; and vice presidents B. Schönemann, Jacob Rosenberg, M. A. Meyer, Henry Greenebaum, S. Hyman, and I. S. Stettheimer. Max Gerstley is incorrectly listed as Mark Gerstley in the U.S. population census for 1860. I. J. Joseph Benjamin, *Three Years in America, 1859–1862* (Philadelphia, Pa.: The Jacob R. Schiff Library of Jewish Contributions to American Democracy: Jewish Publication Society of America, 1956), 274; *Illinois Staats-Zeitung,* Aug. 14, 1862. The Resolutions Committee consisted of Henry Greenebaum, M. Selz, Godfrey Snydacker, Samuel Cole, and Benjamin Schönemann. The resolutions can be found in Meites, *History of the Jews of Chicago,* 88–89, and also in the *Chicago Tribune,* Aug. 14, 1862.

19. Henry Greenebaum was a prominent Chicago banker, president of the German Emigrant Relief Society, first president of the Hebrew Relief Association, and a founder of the Sinai congregation. A native of Eppelsheim in Hesse, he also was elected as an alderman in Chicago in 1855. American Jewish Historical Society, *Publications of the American Jewish Historical Society* 11 (Baltimore, Md.: American Jewish Historical Society, 1903), 126–27.

20. Messrs. Schwarzenberg and Strauss are unidentified except by the context.

21. The mustering officer is unidentified except by the context.

22. Bryan Hall was located on Clark Street between Washington and Randolph Streets. Thomas B. Bryan built it. J. Seymour Currey, *Chicago: Its History and Its Builders; A Century of Marvelous Growth,* 5 vols. (Chicago: S. J. Clark Pub. Co., 1912), 3:248.

23. Unidentified except by the context.

24. The flag presenter was Mrs. Mary Leopold. Otto Steitz was a Chicago sign painter. Meites, *History of the Jews of Chicago,* 91. *Halpin and Bailey's Chicago City Directory, for the year 1862–63, containing, also, a classified business register and street and avenue directory; published annually after the removals of May first* (Chicago: Halpin & Bailey, 1862), 431.

25. Mr. Lombard is unidentified except by the context.

26. Korn, *American Jewry and the Civil War,* 118–19; *Chicago Tribune,* Aug. 14, 1862; Mazur, "Jewish Chicago: From Diversity to Community" in Holli and Jones, eds., *The Ethnic Frontier,* 265, 267–68. See also Meites, *History of the Jews of Chicago,* 83–100. Tobias Brinkmann, "The Dialects of Ethnic Identity: German Jews in Chicago, 1850–1870," in Helbich and Kamphoefner, *German-American Immigration and Ethnicity in Comparative Perspective,* 53–57.

2. Camp Butler

1. Burlington Station is unidentified except by the context.

2. The Tremont House was located at the southeast corner of Lake and Dearborn streets. *Chicago City Directory for 1860* (Chicago: D. B. Cooke and Company, 1860), 429.

3. First Lt. Mayer A. Frank, age twenty-one and a native of Nordstetter in the Kingdom of Württemberg, was promoted to captain on May 28, 1863, and resigned Feb. 29, 1864. He was single and a merchant.

4. The Union army was routed at the Battle of Bull Run (or Manassas) in Virginia on July 21, 1861. The Union army camped around Pittsburg Landing in Tennessee was not expecting an attack on Apr. 6, 1862, and had not prepared entrenchments. It was driven back to the vicinity of the landing, but on Apr. 7, with the help of reinforcements, the Union forces attacked and after hard fighting the Confederates withdrew to Corinth, Mississippi. This battle is also known as the Battle of Shiloh.

5. The arriving regiment was likely the 91st Illinois Infantry, whose colonel was Henry M. Day. *RAGSI,* 5:334.

6. The *Neuen Zeit* was published in St. Louis, Missouri.

7. The colonel was Henry M. Day.

8. In 1848 ethnic Germans living in the southern part of Schleswig and adjoining Holstein rebelled against Danish rule of the two duchies but were defeated. Prussia assisted the rebels. Geoffrey Wawro, *The Austro-Prussian War: Austria's War with Prussia and Italy in 1866* (Cambridge, England: Cambridge University Press, 1996), 41.

9. Col. Schnell is unidentified except by the context.

10. The Illinois adjutant general was Allen C. Fuller.

11. Friedrich Hecker initially fled to Switzerland. In the United States he promoted the formation of revolutionary societies to raise funds and enlist recruits for a second revolution. Hecker was residing in Belleville, Illinois, when he answered the call of the revolutionary People's Government of Baden to return to Germany in 1849, but only made it as far as Strasbourg, France, when he learned the latest uprisings had been put down. Hecker then returned to Belleville, the home of many Germans who had lived there since the 1830s. Wittke, *Refugees of Revolution,* 36–38.

12. Freitag and Rowan, *Friedrich Hecker,* 128, 168–69, 206–7.

13. Arthur Joseph Gabriel Hecker, born Nov. 6, 1842, was the oldest of four sons of Friedrich Hecker and Josefine Hecker, née Eisenhardt. One of the couple's daughters was stillborn, one died at about age two, and one, Malvina, lived until 1929. Arthur served his three-month enlistment in the 3rd Missouri Regiment, then mustered in the 24th Illinois, Company E, on July 8, 1861, and mustered out on Dec. 4, 1861. He was a sergeant. Organized at St. Louis, Missouri, on Apr. 22, 1861, for three-months service, the 3rd Missouri was involved in the capture of Camp Jackson at St. Louis on May 10, and later took part in the battles at Carthage and Wilson's Creek in Missouri. The regiment mustered out Sept. 4, 1861. A three-year 3rd Regiment was organized on Sept. 3, 1961. Freitag and Rowan, *Friedrich Hecker,* 220, 226, 227, 148 n. 21, 221–31; Arthur Hecker, 24th Illinois muster and descriptive rolls, ISA; Frederick H. Dyer, *A Compendium of the War of the Rebellion,* 3 vols. (Des Moines, Ia.: Dyer Publishing, 1908), 3:1323. For additional information about the 24th Illinois, see William Wagner, *History of the 24th Illinois Volunteer Infantry Regiment (Old Hecker Regiment)* (Chicago: s.n., 1911), and Ray W. Burhop, *The Twenty Fourth Illinois Infantry Regiment: The Story of a Civil War Regiment* (Tampa, Fla.: Burhop Associates, 2003). Dr. Wagner was the regiment's surgeon. The latter book is self-published with limited endnotes.

14. Caspar Butz, a native of Hagen, Westphalia, fled to the United States in 1849 to avoid capture by Prussian authorities. The Forty-eighter moved from Detroit to Chicago in 1854 where he was involved in the hardware business, writing, and politics. This German American powerbroker had close ties to the *Illinois Staats-Zeitung.* A Turner and anti-slavery man, Butz supported Lincoln in 1860 but became a radical Republican leading the movement of the Radical Democracy Party to nominate John C. Frémont for president in 1864. In a letter dated

May 27, 1862, Butz urged Governor Richard Yates, "to give Hecker a commission to raise a regiment. He will be able raise it in less time than any other Colonel." Butz included with his letter an article from the *Illinois Staats-Zeitung* urging Hecker's return to active service and stating Germans would rally around him to fight for the Union. Butz then asked, "Need I say anything else?" Richard Yates was originally from Warsaw in Gallatin County, Kentucky. He had previously served in the Illinois State Legislature and the United States Congress as a Whig. He lost his seat in Congress when he became a Republican but was elected governor of Illinois in 1860. He was elected to the United States Senate and served from March 1865 to March 1871. Zucker, ed., *The Forty-Eighters,* 283; Caspar Butz letter to Hon. Richard Yates, dated May 27, 1862, ISA; David Kenney and Robert E. Hartley, *An Uncertain Tradition: U.S. Senators from Illinois, 1818–2003* (Carbondale: Southern Illinois University Press, 2003), 56–58.

15. Capt. Anton Bruhn, thirty-four years old, a married barber from Chicago, mustered in as captain on Sept. 26, 1862, and mustered out on June 9, 1865. Bruhn was brevetted major after the war.

16. The maximum strength for an infantry regiment was 1,025 officers and enlisted men, consisting of the headquarters, and ten companies of 101 persons each. The minimum for a new regiment was 845 officers and men. Boatner, *Civil War Dictionary,* 612.

17. Lieutenant Bechstein was from Laufen in the Kingdom of Württemberg, a printer, and thirty-eight years old. He was promoted to 1st lieutenant on Mar. 1, 1863, Company I, and later transferred to Company F. He was killed on July 20, 1864, at the Battle of Peach Tree Creek in Georgia.

18. This was likely the artist Wilhelm Voegtlin, who was living in Milwaukee, Wisconsin, in 1860, and in New York in 1880. He was a native of Switzerland and twenty-seven years old in 1862. U.S. population census for 1860 and 1880.

19. First Lt. William Warner, Company D, was promoted to captain, Company I, on May 20, 1863, and was honorably discharged on Sept. 3, 1863. Second Lt. Frank Kirchner, Company D, was born in Heidelburg, Grand Duchy of Baden. A twenty-three-year-old cigar maker from Chicago, Kirchner was promoted to 1st lt., Company D, on May 21, 1863, and to captain, Company C, on Apr. 26, 1865. He mustered out on June 9, 1865. He received a brevet promotion to captain in 1866. Yates, Clark, and Southland are unidentified except by the context.

20. Meites, *History of the Jews of Chicago,* 92.

21. Mr. Burkhardt and the Jefferson House are unidentified except by the context.

22. Brig. Gen. John M. Schofield was in charge of the Missouri State Militia in 1862.

23. The Battle of Carthage took place in Missouri on July 5, 1861, and the Battle of Wilson's Creek on Aug. 10, 1861. Both battles were Confederate victories.

24. Major Rolshausen was from Hesse-Darmstadt and thirty-four years old at enlistment in the 82nd Illinois. He previously served as 2nd lt. in the Turner Union Cadets Militia Company (also known as Lt. Kewald's Independent Company of Illinois Infantry) and was captain of Company K, 24th Illinois Infantry Regiment from July 8, 1861, until he resigned on June 29, 1862. *RAGSI* 1:238, 2:319.

25. Chicago's German Workers Association (*Arbeitersverein*), a mutual benefit and social organization, was founded with the help of Forty-eighters during the economic crisis of 1857. *Arbeitersvereine* encompassed many crafts and occupations and many had singing groups. Hartmut Keil and John B. Jentz, eds., *German Workers in Chicago: A Documentary History of Working-class Culture from 1850 to World War I* (Urbana: University of Illinois Press. 1988), 34; Levine, *Spirit of 1848,* 113.

26. Joseph Frank was a merchant in Chicago. U.S. population census 1860.

27. Abraham Hart was a well-known furniture merchant and leader in the Jewish community. Esther L. Panitz, *Simon Wolf: Private Conscience and Public Image.* Sara F. Yoseloff

Memorial Publications in Judaism and Jewish Affairs (Cranbury, N.J.: Associated University Presses, Inc, 1987), 20.

28. These are two lines from the "Hecker Song" from 1848.

29. The 4th Polish Regiment of the Line fought for Napoleon I in the early 1800s. The incident referred to is unidentified except by the context.

30. The source of the other flag is unknown.

31. The Grand Duchy of Baden issued an amnesty on Aug. 7, 1862. Hecker qualified for amnesty but Gustav Struve did not. Freitag and Rowan, *Friedrich Hecker,* 253 n. 36.

32. Öfele, *True Sons of the Republic,* 128.

33. Pvt. Alexander Henschel belonged to Company C. He was a native of Berlin in Prussia, a barber in civilian life and twenty-three years old at his enlistment. He mustered out in June 1865.

34. Cpl. Constantin Drissen was discharged on Feb. 5, 1863, in Washington, D.C., due to disability from a wound.

35. Frank Schönewald mentions a temple in his letter, but the editor does not believe he was Jewish. He is buried in St. Boniface Catholic Cemetery in Chicago. Additional information about this soldier is included in the introduction to this volume. Record for Frank Schönewald, *Headstones Provided for Deceased Union Civil War Veterans, 1879–1903,* <http://search.ancestry.com/iexec?htx=View&r=an&dbid=1195&iid=MIUSA1879_113709-00535&fn=Frank&ln=Schoenewald&st=r&ssrc=&pid=100746> (accessed Apr. 4, 2013).

36. The *Evening Journal* is probably the *Illinois State Journal.*

37. Alexis B. Soyer was a celebrity chef who gained fame in London. Andrea Broomfield, *Food and Cooking in Victorian England: A History* (Westport, Conn.: Praeger Publishers, 2007), 27.

38. Julius Caesar was a Roman emperor and Horace and Virgil were classical Roman poets.

39. Col. Fritz Anneke, a Forty-eighter and former Prussian artillery officer, had served as Maj. Gen. John McClernand's chief of artillery, and later served as the colonel of the 34th Wisconsin Volunteer Infantry Regiment. *The War of the Rebellion: A Compilation of the Official Records of the Union and Confederate Armies,* 128 vols. (Washington, D.C.: Government Printing Office, 1880–1901), ser. 1, vol. 10, 1:757 (hereafter cited as *OR;* unless specified, all citations are to ser. 1). Burton, *Melting Pot Soldiers,* 109.

40. The writer is referring to Capt. Ivar A. Weid's company composed of Scandinavians.

41. Braeutigam, diary, Oct. 5, 1862, ALPL.

3. Off to the Seat of War

1. Braeutigam diary, Nov. 3–7, 1862, ALPL.

2. Ibid., Nov. 8–18, 1862; *Illinois Staats-Zeitung,* Dec. 11, 1862.

3. George W. Fuchs was Company K's 1st lieutenant. The Ottawa, Illinois, resident was a native of Schweinheim, Kingdom of Prussia. A locksmith and married, he resigned on May 17, 1863.

4. The man shot, a Mr. Vines, is unidentified except by the context. *Illinois Staats-Zeitung,* Dec. 8, 1862

5. Capt. William Neussel of St. Louis, a twenty-eight-year-old married bookkeeper and Hesse native was the officer of the day. The captain was discharged for disability on October 4, 1864, but due to a clerical error is listed in the *RAGSI* 5:111 as dishonorably dismissed from the service on Oct. 4, 1864. Evidence in his Civil War pension file indicates he was an excellent and well-respected officer before he was disabled by sunstroke, causing almost chronic severe mental problems until his death on Dec. 25, 1894. Margaretha Neussel widow pension file no. 456311, NA.

6. The Battle of Second Bull Run (also called Second Manassas) took place on Aug. 29–30, 1862. Following Maj. Gen. John Pope's orders, General Sigel's First Army Corps attacked Maj. Gen. Thomas J. "Stonewall" Jackson's corps on Aug. 29, 1862, and was falsely told by General Pope that Maj. Gen. Irvin McDowell's corps was on the way to help him. McDowell had not received the pertinent orders. Sigel's corps fought well on Aug. 29 and 30 but was defeated because Maj. Gen. James Longstreet's corps reinforced Stonewall Jackson late on Aug. 29. Maj. Gen. Philip Kearny purposely delayed following General Pope's orders to move his division up to Sigel's corps on Aug. 28 and then refused Sigel's request to attack his right flank on Aug. 29. Kearney's hatred for the German general was the reason. Kearny was killed in the Battle of Chantilly on Sept. 1, 1862, and, therefore, was not held accountable for his reprehensible inaction. Maj. Gen. James Longstreet commanded the First Corps (Right Wing) of Gen. Robert E. Lee's Army of Northern Virginia. Maj. Gen. Thomas J. Jackson led the Second Corps (Left wing) of the Army of Northern Virginia. Maj. Gen. John Pope transferred from the Army of the Mississippi to assume command of the Union's new Army of Virginia in June 1862, and was replaced by Maj. Gen. George McClellan after his defeat. General McCllelan had purposely delayed moving his troops to the battlefield to reinforce John Pope's army. Engle, *Yankee Dutchman,* 143; John J. Hennessy, *Return to Bull Run: The Campaign and Battle of Second Manassas* (New York: Simon & Schuster, 1993), 194–95, 220–22, 468; *OR* vol. 12, 2: 546, 548.

7. New Baltimore is twenty miles southwest of Fairfax, Virginia.

8. See note 24 to the introduction regarding Prince Salm-Salm. The prince's wife's first name was Agnes. The writer is referring to Lt. Col. Carl B. Hedterich of the 8th New York Infantry. *OR* vol. 12, 2:285.

9. The 107th Ohio was composed mostly of Germans from Cleveland and its county. It mustered in Sept. 9, 1862.

10. Carl Lotz is listed in the regimental records as Carl Lotz, C. Lotz, and Earl Lotz. His residence at muster in is listed as St. Louis, Missouri, but at the dates of his promotions is listed as Chicago, Illinois. The muster rolls incorrectly indicate his place of birth as Hollenzollern, Prussia.

11. The editor believes Camp Seward was at or near Ball's Crossroads (now the intersection of N. Glebe Road and Wilson Boulevard) in Arlington, Virginia.

12. The Battle of Port Royal took place in South Carolina on Nov. 7, 1861. The Union captured Port Royal Sound.

13. Aranjuez is a town south of Madrid in Spain. It is at the confluence of the Tagus and Jarama rivers and was once a royal summer residence with elaborate gardens.

14. Lieutenant B. was probably Frederick Bechstein, 2nd lieutenant, Company C.

15. "O you dear Augustin ("*O, du lieber Augustin*") is an old Viennese folk song composed by Marx Augustin. It concerns Augustin being dumped into a pit containing the dead bodies of plague victims. <http://www.tutorgigpedia.com/ed/Oh_du_lieber_Augustin#Text_of_the_song > (accessed Apr 4, 2013).

16. Camp Banks may have been named after Maj. Gen. Nathaniel P. Banks, who had commanded the defenses of Washington, D.C. until October 27, 1862, when he left that position to become commander of the Department of the Gulf.

17. Mr. Sch. is unidentified except by the context.

18. Desertions compiled by the editor from 82nd Illinois muster and descriptive rolls; D. L. Costa and M. E. Kahn, *Heroes and Cowards: The Social Face of War* (Princeton, N.J.: Princeton University Press, 2008), 99–109. For additional information about desertion during the Civil War, see Ella Lonn, *Desertion during the Civil War* (New York: The Century Company, 1928). Aquia Creek is a tributary of the Potomac River.

19. Engle, *Yankee Dutchman,* 30; Keller and Valuska, *Damn Dutch,* 91.

20. See note 32 to the introduction regarding Capt. Emil Frey.

21. Pvt. Johann Wittmer stood six feet, six inches tall. Pvts. Wittmer, Justus Wildhaber, Wilhelm Wildhaber, Johann Geisbühler, Jacob Bircher, Johann Kissting, Rudolph Müller, and Cpl. Franz Tseharner, were all natives of Switzerland.

22. Dumfries, Virginia, is approximately thirteen miles north of Stafford, Virginia.

4. A New Year Begins

1. *RAGSI*, 5:120.

2. McPherson, *Battle Cry of Freedom*, 560–61; *Illinois State Register*, January 7, 1863, in Henry Steele Commager, ed., *Documents of American History*, 6th ed. (New York: Appleton-Century-Crofts, 1958), 421–22.

3. Yates Family Papers, ALPL.

4. 82nd Illinois muster and descriptive rolls, ISA.

5. Peter Hanson was a twenty-one-year-old native of Christiana, Norway. The Chicago resident resigned on December 10, 1862. Christian Erickson was a twenty-three-year-old native of Bergen, Norway. He is also listed as Christian Ericson in some muster and descriptive rolls. Erickson mustered in as a 2nd lieutenant on December 19, 1862, and was mustered in as a 1st lieutenant and transferred to Company F on March 12, 1864. He mustered out June 9, 1865, and later received a brevet promotion to captain

6. 82nd Illinois Infantry correspondence file, ISA.

7. Ibid.

8. Captain Hillborg's resignation was accepted on May 20, 1863. John Hillborg, Compiled Service Records, Record Group 94, NA; 55th Illinois muster and descriptive rolls, ISA.

9. Braeutigam diary, transcript, trans. unknown, Jan. 20, Mar. 20, Feb. 6, Apr. 5, and Apr. 10, 1863.

10. Keller, *Chancellorsville and the Germans*, 46–47; Engle, "A Raised Consciousness," 5.

11. Jeffrey D. Wert, *Lincoln's Sword: The Army of the Potomac* (New York: Simon & Schuster, 2005), 221; Pula, *The Sigel Regiment*, 103.

12. Wert, *Lincoln's Sword*, 225–26.

5. The Battle of Chancellorsville

1. *OR* vol. 25, 1:197; Charles P. Roland, *An American Iliad: The Story of the Civil War*, 123; McPherson, *Battle Cry of Freedom*, 639; Keller, *Chancellorsville and the Germans*, 49.

2. David J. Eicher, *The Longest Night: A Military History of the Civil War* (New York: Simon & Schuster, 2001), 477–78.

3. Sears, *Chancellorsville*, 202–13; Wert, *Sword of Lincoln*, 160, 238–39; Keller, *Chancellorsville and the Germans*, 51–53; Furgurson, *Chancellorsville 1863*, 105, 159. Lt. Gen. Thomas J. "Stonewall" Jackson headed the Second Corps, Army of Northern Virginia, and was army commander Robert E. Lee's best general. Brig. Gen. Francis C. Barlow's brigade (von Steinwehr's division), containing approximately 1,500 troops, had been detached and was not with its division at the time of the attack. Oliver O. Howard, "The Eleventh Corps at Chancellorsville," in Robert Underwood Johnson and Clarence Clough Buel, *Battles and Leaders of the Civil War* (1887 reprint; Secaucus, N.J.: Castle, n. d.), 3:192, 193.

4. Keller, *Chancellorsville and the Germans*, 54–55; Sears, *Chancellorsville*, 247–48, 264–70.

5. Keller, *Chancellorsville and the Germans*, 56–62.

6. *OR* vol. 25, 1:653–654.

7. Ibid., 1:654–57, 662; Keller, *Chancellorsville and the Germans*, 64–66.

8. Keller, *Chancellorsville and the Germans*, 63–64.

9. Ibid., 64–72.

10. The 82nd Illinois reported 29 killed, 88 wounded, and 38 missing. None of the missing died in Confederate prison camps. *OR* vol. 25, 1:182–83.

11. Ibid., 1:558–61, Sears, *Chancellorsville*, 426–29, 440, 442.

12. Sears, *Chancellorsville*, 431.

13. General Schurz's report also erroneously stated Hecker was shot while carrying the flag. *OR* vol. 25, 1:656. *Belleviller Zeitung*, May 21, 1863; *Illinois Staats-Zeitung*, May 13, 1863; *Die Gartenlaube* 13, no. 4 (1865): 57–58.

14. Two Rebel pieces were withdrawn from beyond Devens's left before a regiment of General Schimmelfennig's brigade arrived there. This regiment suffered some casualties in a skirmish on the way to find the guns. *OR* vol. 25, 1:650.

15. The reconnaissance went as far as Carpenter's farm, which lay along the Brook Road, roughly three-fourths of a mile due south of Devens's brigade of Schurz's division. *OR* vol. 25, 1:663.

16. Second Lt. Ferdinand Babst of Chicago mustered in as a lieutenant on Apr. 23, 1863; he died on Aug. 2, 1863. First Lt. Erich Hoppe was wounded but lived. He was promoted to Captain of Company F on May 29, 1863, and transferred to the Veteran Reserve Corps on Aug. 3, 1863. Second Lt. Lorenz Spönnemann of Lebanon, Illinois, was a native of Homburg, Prussia. Second Lt. Conrad Schonder was a native of Gosbach, Kingdom of Württemberg, and resident of Belleville, Illinois.

17. This is Mayer A. Frank.

18. Frederick A. Dammann mustered in as 2nd Lieutenant, Company E, on Apr. 27, 1863. He was previously the commissary sergeant, resided in Lincoln, Illinois, and resigned on Jan. 18, 1864. Capt. Frederick L. Weber of St. Louis, Missouri, aged thirty, was discharged on May 28, 1863.

19. Surgeon George Schloetzer mustered in on Sept. 26, 1862, and was discharged on Jan. 1, 1864. He was a native of Bavaria who resided in Chicago, Illinois; 1870 U.S. population census.

20. Friedrich P. Kappelmann to "Dear Parents," May 10, 1863, Jan. 18, 1863, transcript, unknown trans., in Civil War Times Misc. Collection, U.S. Military History Institute, Carlisle, Pennsylvania (hereafter USAMHI).

21. Colonel Hecker stayed at the Philadelphia home of his sister Charlotte and her husband Dr. Heinrich Tiedemann. Tiedemann was a Forty-eighter. Freitag and Rowan, *Friedrich Hecker*, 243. The excerpt appeared in *Die Gartenlaube* 13, no. 4 (1865): 57–58. See note 24 to the introduction regarding Gustav Struve.

22. Union soldiers occasionally claimed that enemy soldiers were given a concoction of whiskey and gunpowder to make them brave. These accounts are highly suspect. James M. McPherson, *For Cause And Comrades: Why Men Fought in the Civil War* (New York: Oxford University Press, 1997), 53.

23. Capt. Francis A. Dessauer, 45th New York Infantry Regiment, died from his wound. Von Seille is unidentified except by the context. *OR* vol. 25, 1:680.

24. See note 17 in chapter 2 regarding Lieutenant Bechstein.

25. Lt. Col. Lorenz Cantador, 27th Pennsylvania Volunteer Infantry Regiment. *OR* vol. 12, 2:285.

26. Maj. Gen. Henry W. Slocum, a New Yorker and West Point graduate, was commander of the Twelfth Corps. He was originally colonel of the 27th New York Infantry, and later held brigade and divisional commands. Warner, *Generals in Blue*, 451–52.

27. See note 23, above.

28. Lt. Col. Edward S. Salomon and Adjutant Eugene Weigel.

29. First Assistant Surgeon Emil Brendel mustered in on Oct. 23, 1862, and resigned on May 21, 1863. Surgeon George Schloetzer was honorably discharged on Jan. 12, 1864.

30. Pvt. Anton Bihl died of wounds and Joseph Schellkopf was killed in action. The editor was unable to identify the other two men whom Müller mentions were dead. The orderly, Pvt. Charles Zaisser, a native of Blaublasen, Württemberg, was killed on May 5, 1863.

31. The 26th Wisconsin mustered in at Milwaukee on Sept. 17, 1862. It was called the Sigel Regiment after Maj. Gen. Franz Sigel. The 157th New York mustered in on Sept. 19, 1862, at Hamilton, New York. It was not a German regiment. Dyer, *Compendium*, 3:1684, 1464.

32. *New York Times*, May 5, 1863; *New York Herald*, May 5, 1863; Keller, *Chancellorsville and the Germans*, 97–105. Some editors, mostly Democrats, blamed the Lincoln administration for the defeat, not the individual German soldiers. They erroneously claimed Lincoln had let Franz Sigel go and left the Germans to be led by Carl Schurz, who lacked formal military training and who was only promoted to general because he had campaigned for Lincoln. "Why the Germans Ran," *Cleveland Plain Dealer*, May 8, 1863; Keller, *Chancellorsville and the Germans*, 89–90. The exact percentage of Germans in the Eleventh Corps is uncertain. On May 21, 1863, General Howard sent a *List of German Troops in the Eleventh Army Corps* to General Hooker. Out of twenty-six regiments in his command Howard listed eleven "exclusively German" regiments and four regiments of "mixed nationalities." The aggregate of officers and men "present" for the "exclusively German" regiments totaled 4,206; the "present and absent" numbered 5,777. Further, the aggregate of officers and men "present" for the fifteen listed regiments totaled 6,136; the "present and absent" numbered 8,345. As Bigelow indicates, however, Howard's list "does not indicate how the count was taken nor what was understood or meant by 'German Troops.'" The corps's aggregate troops "present" on April 30, 1863, and May 10, 1863, were 15,412 and 12,826, respectively. The aggregate troops "present and absent" for the entire Eleventh Corps on April 30, 1863, and May 10, 1863, were 19,180 and 17,411, respectively. Totals compiled by the editor from *OR* vol. 25, 1:660–61, 2:320, 464; John Bigelow, *The Campaign of Chancellorsville: A Strategic and Tactical Study* (New Haven, Conn.: Yale University Press, 1910), 479.

33. Keller, *Chancellorsville*, 88–89.

34. Ibid., 91.

35. Ibid.

36. Ibid., 105.

37. Ibid., 122.

6. The Battle of Gettysburg

1. Scott Hartwig, "The Campaign and Battle of Gettysburg," in Christian B. Keller and David L. Valuska, eds., *Damn Dutch*, 74–75.

2. *OR* vol. 27, 1:60–61.

3. Bradley M. Gottfried, *The Maps of Gettysburg: An Atlas of the Gettysburg Campaign, June 3—July 13, 1863* (New York: Savas Beatie, 2007), 9; Harry W. Pfanz, *Gettysburg: The First Day*. Civil War America (Chapel Hill: University of North Carolina Press, 2001), 21–22. Richard S. Ewell commanded the Army of Northern Virginia's Second Corps and Alexander Powell Hill led its Third Corps.

4. Ibid., 53; Wert, *The Sword of Lincoln*, 274; *OR* vol. 27, 1:114–15, 702, 734.

5. R.'s letter, dated July 5, 1863, in *Illinois Staats-Zeitung*, July 11, 1963; Scott Hartwig, "The 11th Army Corps on July 1, 1863: The Unlucky 11th," *Gettysburg Magazine* 2 (Jan.1990): 135; *OR* vol. 27, 1:727. Emmitsburg, Md., lay approximately twelve miles southwest of Gettysburg.

6. Hartwig, "The 11th Army Corps," 38–40 and 40 n. 28.

7. Ibid., 38–40 and 40 n. 28. For further information about Dilger's battery, see Kenneth M. Kepf, "Dilger's Battery at Gettysburg," *Gettysburg Magazine* 4 (1991): 49–63.

8. Hartwig, "The Campaign and Battle of Gettysburg," 91; Hartwig, "The 11th Army Corps," 39–40; James S. Pula, "Fighting for Time: Carl Schurz on the First Day at Gettysburg," *Gettysburg Magazine* 35 (July 2006): 30–31.

9. *OR* vol. 27, 1:727–28.

10. Hartwig, "Campaign and Battle of Gettysburg," 88–92.

11. Stephen W. Sears, *Gettysburg* (Boston: Houghton Mifflin, 2003), 216–17, 221–22. For a brief description of the retreat through Gettysburg by Capt. Joseph B. Greenhut, Company K, see John L. Beveridge, David B. Vaughan, and Joseph B. Greenhut, *Illinois Monuments at Gettysburg* (n. p.: H. W. Rokker, State Printer, 1892). See also Edward S. Salomon, *"Gettysburg," by Past Commander Edward S. Salomon . . . Read Before the California Commandery of the Military Order of the Loyal Legion of the United States, at a Banquet at San Francisco, California, January Seventeenth, Nineteen Hundred and Twelve* (San Francisco: Shannon-Conmy Print. Co, 1913), 395–411.

12. Hartwig, "Campaign and Battle of Gettysburg," 91–93.

13. Ibid., 94; Hartwig, "The 11th Army Corps," 49.

14. Gottfried, *Maps of Gettysburg*, 142–43, 216–17.

15. Beveridge, et. al., *Illinois Monuments at Gettysburg*, 34.

16. Hartwig, "Campaign and Battle of Gettysburg," 97–103; Sears, *Gettysburg*, 282–83, 326; Harry W. Pfanz, *Gettysburg—Culp's Hill and Cemetery Hill* (Chapel Hill: University of North Carolina Press, 1993), 213–14; *OR* vol. 27, 1:731.

17. *OR* vol. 27, 2: 470–71; 1:730–31, 722, 751–52; Hartwig, "Campaign and Battle of Gettysburg," 103.

18. *OR* vol. 27, 1:237–38; Hartwig, "Campaign and Battle of Gettysburg," 105; Sears, *Gettysburg*, 361–71.

19. Hartwig, "Campaign and Battle of Gettysburg," 105–9; *OR* vol. 27, 2:320; Sears, *Gettysburg*, 419.

20. Sears, *Gettysburg*, 496, 498; *OR* vol. 27, 1:183; Hartwig, "The 11th Army Corps," 33–34; John W. Busey and David G. Martin, *Regimental Strengths at Gettysburg* (Baltimore, Md.: Gateway Press, 1982), 85. The number of missing who died in Confederate prison camps compiled by the editor from the 82nd Illinois muster and descriptive rolls.

21. Hugo Schröder, Company H, born at Kaiserwalden in Prussia, was promoted from sergeant to 2nd lieutenant on Apr. 22, 1863, and was honorably discharged on May 15, 1865. He was married and a miner at enlistment. Eugene Hepp was promoted from sergeant, Company A, to 2nd lieutenant of the same company on Feb. 14, 1863, and to 1st. lieutenant, Company B, on Apr. 29, 1865. He mustered out June 9, 1865.

22. *Illinois Staats-Zeitung*, July 20, 1863. This may be a reference to the advance of the 45th and 157th New York. It is known the 45th advanced to the McLean barn, where they captured a number of Col. Edward A. O'Neal's men who had taken shelter there. The 157th advanced to near the barn, but to the east and north of it, before they changed front to attack Doles, and captured a number of Maj. Eugene Blackford's 5th Alabama skirmishers in this advance. Hartwig, "The 11th Army Corps," 39.

23. *OR* vol. 27, 1:734.

24. Wright's Grove was located at the corner of North Clark and Diversey streets in Chicago, Illinois, and was a popular picnic place and beer garden for Germans. It was the site of Camp Fry, an assembly and mustering site for troops during the Civil War. Cliff Terry, *Chicago Off the Beaten Path*. Off the beaten path series (Guilford, Conn.: Globe Pequot Press, 2005), 59.

25. The writer is referring to Adj. Eugene Weigel.

26. First Sgt. Barthold Kruckenberg, Company D, a butcher from Chicago, was born in Hamburg, Germany. He was promoted to 2nd lieutenant on May 20, 1863, and discharged on Nov. 13, 1864. His name appears as Krukenburg and Krugenberg in the 82nd Illinois muster and descriptive rolls.

27. Dr. Brown is unidentified except by the context.

28. Ernst Fuhrmeister from Chicago mustered in as a first sergeant. He was mortally wounded on July 1, 1863. The former clerk was born in Magdeburg, Prussia. Pvt. Friedrich Calmback, a tailor, was born in the Kingdom of Württemberg. John Boher is actually Pvt. John Bolken. He was born in Havel, Oldenburg, and mustered out as a corporal on June 9, 1865; Sgt. Gustav Giese was wounded at Peachtree Creek in Georgia on July 20, 1863, and mustered out with his regiment in 1865. An upholsterer at enlistment, Gustav was a native of Prussia. Cpl. Emil Giese was discharged for disability on Mar. 14, 1864. A fresco painter in civilian life, he was born in Prussia. Finally, Heinrich Meins does not appear on the regimental rolls. Captain Marx may be referring to A. H. Mignell (also listed as J. H. Mignett), a musician in Company D, who transferred to the Veteran Reserve Corps on Feb. 15, 1864. Mignett was a Prussian-born musician. All five soldiers were from Chicago.

29. The writer is referring to Capt. George E. Heinzmann, Company B.

30. Margaret S. Creighton, *The Colors of Courage: Gettysburg's Hidden History: Immigrants, Women, and African-Americans in the Civil War's Defining Battle* (New York: Basic Books, 2005), 171–72.

31. Dr. George Schloetzer was the regiment's original surgeon. He was discharged on Jan. 12, 1864. The doctor, a native of Germany, practiced medicine in Chicago before he enlisted.

32. Pvt. John Ackermann, a native of St. Gallen, Switzerland, was the only member of Company K killed during the three-day battle. He was a sailor before he enlisted. The muster and descriptive rolls incorrectly list his date of death as July 3, 1864, ISA. Ackerman was killed by a shell that cut off more than half of his head, according to Capt. Joseph B. Greenhut. Beverage, et. al., *Illinois Monuments at Gettysburg*, 35.

33. Confederates taken prisoner July 1–July 5 totaled 12,227. *OR* vol. 27, 2:346.

34. Union losses in the march north, the battles at Gettysburg and Winchester, and the pursuit after July 3 aggregated 30,100 men. Union casualties at Gettysburg totaled almost 23,000 men. Sears, *Gettysburg*, 496.

35. Mathias Greenwalt is also listed as Mathias Greenwaldt in the regimental records. Originally a corporal, he was promoted to commissary sergeant at an unknown date and mustered out on June 9, 1865 as a quartermaster sergeant; Cpl. Henry O. Briegel is listed as missing on July 1, 1863, with no further information. Briegel, a native of Wierbuntz, Germany, had worked as a clerk in Milwaukee prior to enlistment; Anton Karsten [Carstons] mustered out on June 9, 1865.

36. Lieutenant Colonel Salomon did not command the 153rd Pennsylvania for long because the regiment mustered out of service on July 24, 1863.

37. Eugene F. Weigel, Compiled Service Records, 3rd Regiment United States Reserve Corps; 4th Missouri Infantry Regiment; Record Group 94, NA; MOLLUS, circular no. 154, May 1, 1897, at the Missouri History Museum, St. Louis, Missouri.

38. In 1860 Eugene Weigel was living in St. Louis, Missouri, with his parents, Dr. Phillip and Theresa Weigel, and six siblings ranging in age from nine months to twenty-two years old. U.S. population census for 1860.

39. Dr. Charles E. Boerner of East St. Louis, Ill., joined the 82nd Illinois in the field on July 8, 1863, and mustered in as first assistant surgeon on July 29, 1863. He was forty-one years old. Boerner was promoted to surgeon on Mar. 12, 1864, and mustered out on June 9,

1865. He had previously served in the 3rd United States Reserve Corps, Missouri, and the 4th Missouri Infantry. Boerner was court martialed and dismissed from the 4th Missouri for misapplication of stores and provisions drawn for the hospital of the 4th Missouri Infantry and misapplication of money constituting the hospital fund. Charles E. Boerner, Compiled Service Records, 3rd United States Reserve Corps, Missouri, and 4th Missouri Infantry, Record Group 94, NA. In the last two regiments he was listed as Dr. Edmund Boerner. The Civil War pension index card for Charles E. Boerner indicates he served in the 82nd Illinois and 3rd United States Reserve Corps, Missouri.

40. Lou is likely Eugene's older sister, Louisa Weigel.

41. *OR* vol. 27, 1:733–34. Engle, *Yankee Dutchmen,* 194–95.

7. After Gettysburg to Chattanooga

1. Christian B. Keller, "Pennsylvania's German-Americans, a Popular Myth, and the Importance of Perception," in Christian B. Keller and David L. Valuska, eds., *Damn Dutch,* 157–61.

2. Ibid., 139–40, 148–49.

3. Pula, *The Sigel Regiment,* 163–75.

4. Creighton, *Colors of Courage,* 171–72.

5. Compiled by the editor from *OR* vol. 29, 1:8; *OR* vol. 27, 1:164; 3:802–3; Keller, "Pennsylvania's German-Americans," 155–56.

6. See Peter Cozzens, *This Terrible Sound: The Battle of Chickamauga* (Urbana: University of Illinois Press, 1992), and Glenn Tucker, *Chickamauga: Bloody Battle in the West* (Dayton, Ohio: Morningside, 1976) for descriptions of the battle.

7. *OR* vol. 30, 1:37, 39–40; 31, 1:817; 2:568–69; McPherson, *Battle Cry of Freedom,* 675. General Grant commanded both the Army of the Tennessee and the Department of the Tennessee. The four western divisions brought to Chattanooga were the First, Second, and Fourth divisions of the Fifteenth Corps and the Second Division of the Seventeenth Corps. On Oct. 16, General Grant was named commander of the Military Division of the Mississippi, comprising the departments of the Ohio, the Cumberland, and the Mississippi. Grant had previously achieved important victories at forts Donelson and Henry in Tennessee and Vicksburg in Mississippi. "Opposing Forces in the Chattanooga Campaign," in *Battles and Leaders of the Civil War,* 3:729; *OR* vol. 30, 4:404.

8. *OR* vol. 31, 1:801, 817. Maj. Gen. William T. Sherman was commander of the Fifteenth Corps.

9. A Union-loyal Virginian born in 1818, George H. Thomas was a West Pointer and a Mexican War veteran. He was appointed brigadier general on Aug. 17, 1861, and on Dec. 2, 1861, was appointed commander of the Army of the Ohio's First Division. Thomas rose to major general on Apr. 25, 1862, and was later dubbed the "Rock of Chickamauga" for his courageous leadership at the Battle of Chickamauga in September 1863. He became commander of the vast Army of the Cumberland on Oct. 20, 1863. Warner, *Generals in Blue,* 500–501; *OR,* vol. 30, 4:404. See Gerald J. Prokopowicz, *All for the Regiment: the Army of the Ohio, 1861–1862* (Chapel Hill: University of North Carolina Press, 2001) for a history of the Army of the Ohio.

10. McPherson, *Battle Cry of Freedom,* 675; *OR* vol. 30, 4:41.

11. *RAGSI,* 5:121; *OR* vol. 31, 1:111–12, 206.

12. General Geary, a veteran of the War with Mexico, had organized the 28th Pennsylvania Infantry Regiment and became its first colonel. He assumed command of the Twelfth Corp's Second Division on Oct. 15, 1862. Boatner, *Civil War Dictionary,* 327–28; *OR* vol. 31, 1:84–85, *OR* vol. 31, 1:32; See Peter Cozzens, *The Shipwreck of Their Hopes: The Battles for Chattanooga* (Urbana: University of Illinois Press, 1994).

13. *OR* vol. 31, 1:32.

14. *OR* vol. 31, 2:359–60, 381–84.

15. Major General Burnside at one time had been commander of the Army of the Potomac. Now serving in the West, his command, consisting of the Ninth Corps and Twenty-third Corps, occupied Knoxville, Tenn., and was expecting to be attacked by Lt. Gen. James Longstreet's Confederate corps. Longstreet's corps had been sent to reinforce the Army of Tennessee in September 1863, fought in the Battle of Chickamauga, and was sent from Missionary Ridge in late November 1863 to reclaim Knoxville, Tennessee. *OR* vol. 31, 1: 267.

16. Citico Creek, located east of Chattanooga, arced southwest and flowed into the Tennessee River.

17. Pvt. August Zander was born in Lütz, possibly in Rhenish Bavaria, and mustered out on May 18, 1865. Pvt. Gotthelf Nicolai was a native of Gotha in the Duchy of Saxe-Coburg-Gotha. Coincidentally, both privates were from Chicago, married, and painters before enlistment. The lieutenant of the 80th Illinois Infantry mentioned is unidentified except by the context. *OR* vol. 31, 2:83.

18. A force of almost three divisions led by Maj. Gen. Joseph Hooker cleared Lookout Mountain of three Confederate brigades on Nov. 24, 1863. Federal losses did not exceed 500 men. McPherson, *Battle Cry of Freedom,* 677–78.

19. Lt. Col. Joseph B. Taft was killed in the battle. *OR* vol. 31, 2:89, 349–50.

20. The Eleventh Corps lost 350 men in the battles around Chattanooga, mostly from the Second Division. *OR* vol. 31, 2:98.

21. *OR* vol. 31, 2:385, 374–75.

22. Ibid., 2:382

23. Maj. Gen. Gordon Granger was the commander of the Fourth Corps, Army of the Cumberland. *OR* vol. 31, 2:4.

24. *OR* vol. 31, 2:382.

25. Ibid., 2:382.

26. Ibid.

27. Ibid.

28. *OR* vol. 31, 2:383.

29. Ibid.

30. Ibid.

31. Ibid.

32. Frank P. Blair Jr. was a member of a powerful American family and influential Republican. While a member of the U.S. House of Representatives from Missouri, Blair was appointed as a brigadier general in August 1862 and major general in November 1862. General Sherman selected Blair to lead the Fifteenth Corps after his own promotion to head of the Army of the Tennessee in October 1863. The general returned to Congress early in 1864 to defend Lincoln's reconstruction plans and aid in his reelection effort. He returned to the army and took command of the Seventeenth Corps on May 5, 1864. Warner, *Generals in Blue,* 36; *OR* vol. 38, 4:33.

33. *OR* vol. 31, 2:383.

34. *OR* vol. 32, 2:197. Whiteside, Tennessee, is located about sixteen miles west of Chattanooga near the state line with Georgia.

35. Freitag and Rowan, *Friedrich Hecker,* 248–49; *OR* vol. 31, 2:137ff and 210.

36. Friedrich Hecker, Compiled Service Records, Record Group 94, NA; Freitag and Rowan, *Friedrich Hecker,* 249; Gustave Struve, "Hecker in America," *Die Gartenlaube* 13, no. 4 (1865): 59.

8. Whiteside, Tennessee

1. Benjaminson, "Regiment of Immigrants," 139–40; "The End Has Come," *Minneapolis Tribune*, Oct. 13, 1899.

2. Benjaminson, "Regiment of Immigrants," 139–40, 141; Robert Lender served as a 1st Sgt. in the 24th Illinois until he was mustered out on Dec. 1, 1861, by special order of General Buell. Twenty-fourth Illinois muster and descriptive rolls, ISA. He was a native of Pullendorf, Baden, was married, and resigned on May 16, 1865. Rudolph Müller also temporarily commanded Company A and Company F in November and December 1864. Rudolph Müller, Compiled Service Records, Record Group 94, NA.

3. Frederick Bodo Bess, *Eine populäre Geschichte der Stadt Peoria* (Peoria, Ill.: n. p., 1906), 539.

4. Patrick R. Cleburne commanded a division in Lt. Gen. William J. Hardee's corps in the Confederate Army of Tennessee, commanded by Gen. Joseph E. Johnston, who replaced Braxton Bragg after his defeat in the battles around Chattanooga. Lafayette, Ga. lay thirty miles south of Chattanooga. *OR* vol. 32, 3:867.

5. Stephen J. McGroarty was a native of Ireland, and Tyndale was the son of Irish immigrants. McGroarty was seriously wounded at the Battle of Peachtree Creek on July 20, 1864, and his left arm was amputated. He was brevetted as brigadier general on May 26, 1865. Tyndale was colonel of the 28th Pennsylvania Infantry prior to being elevated to brigadier general on Apr. 9, 1863. He previously commanded the First Brigade, Third Division, Eleventh Corps. Mayer A. Frank of Company C had his resignation approved on Feb. 29, 1964, due to a disability. He had incurred a rupture or hernia on July 1, 1863, at the Battle of Gettysburg when his horse was shot and he was thrown onto a pile of rails. He worsened this old wound at Missionary Ridge when he was thrown against the pommel of his saddle. He was serving as an aide-de-camp in both battles. Mayer A. Frank pension file no. 175764, NA; Stephen J. McGroarty, 61st Ohio, Compiled Service Records, Record Group 94, NA; Warner; *Generals in Blue*, 516–17. See Benjaminson, "A Regiment of Immigrants," page 161, regarding an article in the *Illinois Staats-Zeitung* of Mar. 15, 1864, about Captain Frank's resignation. Second Lt. Leander Carl was promoted from 1st Sgt. to 2nd lieutenant on May 17, 1863, and resigned on Mar. 16, 1864. He was married and a piano maker from St. Louis, Mo. Trenton, Ga., is located approximately ten miles south of Whiteside, Tenn.

6. Lieutenant Müller is referring to the court of inquiry about the actions of Colonel Hecker during the Battle of Wauhatchie.

7. Major General Schurz left to go on leave. The writer is referring to Col. James S. Robinson of the 82nd Ohio Infantry. Kramer is unidentified except by the context. The army tried to retain veteran soldiers whose three-year terms would expire in 1864 by offering a $400 bounty and a thirty-day furlough. Approximately 136,000 of the eligible soldiers accepted this offer; more than 100,000 did not veteranize. *OR*, series III, vol. 5, 635–36; McPherson, *Battle Cry of Freedom*, 719–20.

8. Spraul is unidentified except by the context. Buschbeck's is the camp of Col. Adolphus Buschbeck, commander of the First Brigade, Second Division, Eleventh Corps. Cozzens, *This Terrible Sound*, 401.

9. The writer is referring to locations in Alabama. Frick's Gap lay south–southeast of Whiteside, Tennessee; Lebanon lay approximately ninety-five miles southwest of Whiteside; and Guntersville lay seventy-five miles southwest of Whiteside and east of Lebanon.

10. At his enlistment, 1st Lt. Joseph Gottlob, a native of Prussia, resided in Alton, Ill., was a merchant, and was twenty-two years old. On Mar. 12, 1864, Gottlob was promoted to captain and transferred from Company G to I; on June 22, 1867, he was brevetted as a major. Joseph Gottlob, Compiled Service Records, Record Group 94, NA.

11. Lt. Col. Albert von Steinhausen served in the 68th New York (known as the "Cameron Rifles" and "2nd German Rifles"); Major Kummer's given name was Arnold. See note 24 to the introduction regarding Prince Salm-Salm. *OR* vol. 31, 1:805; *The Union Army: A History of Military Affairs in the Loyal States, 1861–65—Records of the Regiments in the Union Army—Cyclopedia of Battles—Memoirs of Commanders and Soldiers*, 8 vols. (Madison, Wis: Federal Pub. Co., 1908.), 2:100.

12. Lieutenant Müller humorously described Col. Wladimar Krzyzanowski's return to New York on leave. The 75th Pennsylvania had veteranized on Jan. 2, 1864, and was on furlough. Lt. Col. Alvin von Matzdorff mustered out with the regiment on Sept. 1, 1865. Samuel P. Bates, *History of Pennsylvania Volunteers 1861–1865* (Harrisburg, Pa: [s.n.], 1869), 921–22.

13. The writer is referring to 1st Lt. Moritz Kaufmann of Company H. Kaufmann mustered out on Aug. 6, 1864. Mihalotzy is Col. Géza Mihalotzy of the 24th Illinois, who later died from his wound. The 24th Illinois was part of a large reconnaissance in force from Rossville toward Dalton, Georgia, from Feb. 22 to Feb. 27, 1864. *RAGSI*, 2:316; *OR* vol. 31, 1:451–53.

14. Rudolph Müller is referring to Colonel Hecker's son Arthur.

15. General Order No. 9, issued by Colonel McGroarty, temporarily commanding the brigade, stated that Rudolph Müller was replacing Capt. Joseph B. Greenhut as the brigade's assistant adjutant general due to the latter's resignation from the army. McGroarty stated that "[t]he colonel commanding feels it both a duty and a pleasure to bear testimony to his diligence, zeal and fidelity in his performance of his duty in the office, as well as in the field, and he regrets to see so excellent and brave an officer as Captain Greenhut leave his command." McGroarty added, "Matters of important character only could induce Captain Greenhut to leave the army." Quoted in Wolf, *The American Jew as Patriot, Soldier and Citizen*, 144.

16. The identity of the provost is unknown.

17. Friedrich Hecker, Compiled Service Records, Record Group 94, NA.

18. Boatner, *Civil War Dictionary*, 704.

19. The editor found no attachment or copy with this letter.

20. McPherson, *Battle Cry of Freedom*, 718, 744.

21. *OR* vol. 32, 3:246.

22. *OR* vol. 32, 3:258, 550. Maj. Gen. Daniel Butterfield commanded the Third Division, Twentieth Corps. Prior to the reorganization he was Maj. Gen. Joseph Hooker's chief of staff.

23. Carl Schurz, Frederic Bancroft, and William N. Dunning, *Reminiscences*, vol. 3, *1863–1869* (London: John Murray, 1909), 95; *OR* vol. 38, 2:85; *OR* vol. 32, 3:555.

9. The Beginning of the Atlanta Campaign

1. *OR* vol. 38, 1:115, 120, 52; 2:745; 3:676–77; *OR* vol. 32, 3:246; Thomas Lawrence Connelly, *Autumn of Glory: The Army of Tennessee, 1862–1865* (Baton Rouge: Louisiana State University Press, 1971), 294. Lt. Gen. William J. Hardee, a Georgian, had declined command of the Army of Tennessee after Gen. Braxton Bragg resigned in December 1864. Albert Castel, *Decision in the West: The Atlanta Campaign of 1864* (Lawrence: University Press of Kansas, 1992), 28–29.

2. Pula, *Sigel Regiment*, 228; *OR* vol. 38, 2:85; *OR* vol. 38, 1:59; Castel, *Decision in the West*, 129–30. Resaca is located approximately fifteen miles south of Dalton, Georgia.

3. Snake Creek Gap ran through Rocky Face Ridge approximately eleven miles south of Mill Creek Gap (also called Buzzards Roost Gap). The Western and Atlantic Railroad ran through the latter gap to Dalton and its terminus at Atlanta.

4. General Geary was ordered to try to force his way through Dug Gap while the Fourth Corps and Twenty-third Corps held the enemy's attention at Mill Creek Gap and its vicinity.

Dug Gap lay about three and one-half miles south of Mill Creek Gap. Col. Charles Candy's First Brigade and Col. Adolphus Buschbeck's Second Brigade of Brig. Gen. John W. Geary's Second Division, Twentieth Corps, were repulsed at Dug Gap on May 8, 1864. Aggregate casualties for both brigades were 357. *OR* vol. 38, 2:114–17.

5. First Lt. Sigmund Juenger, Company A, 26th Wisconsin, was discharged for disability on July 30, 1864. *OR* vol. 38, 1:99; Pula, *Sigel Regiment,* 361.

6. Taylor's Ridge begins northeast of Ringgold, Georgia, and extends southwest to below Ringgold. Nickajack Gap runs east–west through Taylor's Ridge and leads east to Trickum P.O. Tunnel Hill lies on the Western and Atlantic Railroad about midway between Ringgold and Dalton, Georgia, and is northeast of Trickum P.O. Dogwood Valley begins east of Taylor's Ridge.

7. The 61st Ohio was returning from its veterans' furlough.

8. This is Charles M. Reese, who was discharged on Aug. 22, 1861 as first sergeant, Company I, 24th Illinois, to become its adjutant but before mustering at that rank became a major in the 15th Wisconsin infantry. He resigned his commission on June 8, 1862. A native of Denmark, Reese mustered into the 82nd Illinois, Company B, on Dec. 14, 1863, as a private. He mustered out July 3, 1865. *RAGSI,* 2:318; Wisconsin. Adjutant General, *Roster of Wisconsin Volunteers, War of the Rebellion, 1861–1865,* 2 vols. (Madison, Wis.: Democrat Printing Company, 1886), 804.

9. This is Capt. Michael Wiedrich's 1st New York Light Artillery, Battery I.

10. Edward S. Salomon, Compiled Service Records, Records Group 94, NA.

11. See Philip L. Secrist, *The Battle of Resaca: Atlanta Campaign, 1864* (Macon, Ga: Mercer University Press, 1998), for additional information about the Battle of Resaca.

12. Calhoun is located approximately eight miles due south of Resaca. The Twentieth Corps camped east of Resaca, at the bank of the Coosawattee River on May 16, 1864, after crossing the north–south running Conasauga River. The next morning the corps crossed the east–west flowing Coosawattee River, which joins the Conasauga about four miles southeast of Resaca to form the Oostanaula River. The brigade arrived six miles east of Adairsville after dark on May 18. *OR* vol. 32, 2:87.

13. General Johnston retreated because he feared that Sherman's troops would gain his rear after a crossing was made at Lays Ferry on the Oostanaula River. His troops were not driven from their fortifications, but withdrew. Castel, *Decision in the West,* 173, 178–79, 181; *OR* vol. 38, 1:64. See also Secrist, *The Battle of Resaca.*

14. At Resaca, the arrival of five brigades from Gen. Leonidas Polk's corps strengthened Johnston's army, which was deployed in a strong fishhook-shaped line west and north of the town. Around 4:00 p.m. on May 14, after General Johnston learned that the left flank of Maj. Gen. David S. Stanley's Fourth Corps division on the far left of Sherman's line was "in the air," he ordered Hood to attack Stanley's flank. Hood sent Stevenson's and Stewart's divisions, which drove Stanley's troops back in confusion, while also turning his left flank. Fortunately for Stanley, Peter Simonson's 5th Indiana Battery, whose infantry support had fled, was able to hold its position on the far left using double-canister until Col. James S. Robinson's brigade arrived and repulsed this dangerous attack. The remainder of Williams's division and its corps followed the Third Brigade and extended Sherman's left. Albert E. Castel, *Decision in the West,* 164–66.

15. Rudolph Müller used the German word *Eilgang* here rather than *Durchfall. Eilgang* can mean either rapid motion or diarrhea.

16. Skirmishing took place on May 16, 1864 on the direct road from Resaca to Calhoun and there was some fighting at Adairsville, seven miles south of Calhoun, as elements of Sherman's army approached the town. The editor found no evidence that an ammunition train was burned. *OR* vol. 38, 1:293. Castel, *Decision in the West,* 190–94.

17. Pvt. William Kaisberger of Company D, a native of Hesse, was killed in action on May 2, 1863 at the Battle of Chancellorsville. The editor could not find a death in the 82nd Illinois on May 20, 1864.

18. Kingston lay on the Western and Atlantic Railroad, approximately eight miles west of Cassville; Rome, Georgia, lay about fourteen miles west of Kingston.

19. The editor found no evidence to support Müller's allegations.

20. Müller is referring to Major Jesse J. Phillips of the 9th Illinois Infantry. His wound was not fatal and he returned to service. *RAGSI,* 1: 288, 432, 463.

21. August Mauff was captain of Company E. He was a native of Saxony and mustered out on Aug. 6, 1864. *RAGSI,* 2:310.

22. Osterhaus is Maj. Gen. Peter J. Osterhaus, a native German commanding the First Division of the Fifteenth Corps. See Mary Bobbitt Townsend, *Yankee Warhorse: A Biography of Major General Peter Osterhaus* (Columbia: University of Missouri Press, 2010). Brig. Gen. Hugh Judson Kilpatrick, commander of the Third Division of Sherman's cavalry corps, was shot in the left thigh while reconnoitering. Castel, *Decision in the West,* 151–52; *OR* vol. 38, 1:102.

23. The reports of Grant's victories are greatly exaggerated. Grant was stopped by Robert E. Lee in bloody combat in the Wilderness in Virginia, but rather than retreat continued his campaign. Castel, *Decision in the West,* 185–86.

24. Müller is describing the battle at Resaca on May 14, 1864. See note 13 and 14 to this chapter. Col. Willam Grose, a Hoosier, led the Third Brigade, First Division, Fourth Corps. The captain mentioned was Peter Simonson. *OR* vol. 38, 1:90. A letter written on May 19, 1864, and published in the *Westliche Post* (St. Louis, Mo.) on June 8, 1864, indicated the regiment was located eight miles north of Cassville on May 19. Regarding the saving of Captain Simonson's battery, the soldier wrote: "Our brigade, our regiment in front, charged down the hill, fired a well-aimed salvo into the Rebels and charged them with fixed bayonets. When the wretches saw this they were gripped by a terrible panic and ran from there like the devil was behind them." Soldier Louis is unidentified.

25. The four guns captured and briefly held were from Capt. Max Van Den Corput's "Cherokee Battery." First Lt. Christian Phillip of Company F, 26th Wisconsin, was killed on May 15. Total losses for the 26th for May 14 and 15 were seven killed and forty-three wounded. Castel, *Decision in the West* 174–75; Pula, *Sigel Regiment,* 239.

26. John G. Scales, a South Carolina native, lived in Coosawattee, Gordon County, Georgia, U.S. population census, 1860; *OR* 38, 2:29.

27. The enemy lieutenant is unidentified except by the context. The 43rd Georgia belonged to Brig. Gen. Marcellus Stovall's brigade, Stewart's division, Hood's corps.

28. The Etowah River was about nine miles south of Cassville.

29. The soldier lost in battle is unidentified except by the context.

30. Colonel Salomon reported one member of the 82nd Illinois killed in a skirmish with Southern cavalry near Cassville. The editor was unable to determine the identity of the soldier allegedly killed. *OR* vol. 38, 2:97.

31. Lieutenant Colonel Salomon stated in his official report that he ordered his regiment to charge the Rebels attacking Simonson's battery "although the brigade was not in line yet." Ibid.

32. Union soldiers sometimes called Confederate soldiers Johnny Reb or Johnnies.

33. Castel, *Decision in the West,* 205–6; William T. Sherman, *War is Hell: Personal Narrative of His March through Georgia,* ed. Miles Lane (Savannah, Ga.: Beehive Press, 1974), 35, 37; William R. Scaife, *Campaign for Atlanta* (Atlanta, Ga.: W. R. Scaife, 1985), 49: *OR* vol. 38, 4:271–72.

34. The Battle of New Hope Church took place on May 25 several miles east of Dallas, Georgia. Dallas lay about sixteen miles southwest of Allatoona. Troops of the Twentieth Corps were unsuccessful in dislodging A. P. Stewart's fortified division and suffered approximately 665 casualties, including eleven killed and fifty-nine wounded from the 82nd Illinois. Johnston had learned of Sherman's maneuver and sent his three corps to stop him. Thomas Van Horne, *History of the Army of the Cumberland,* 2 vols. (1875 reprint; Wilmington, N.C.: Broadfoot,

1992), 2:75–77; Castel, *Decision in the West*, 226; *OR* 38, vol. 2:97–98. See Russell W. Blount Jr., *The Battle of New Hope Church* (Gretna, La.: Pelican, 2010), for more about the battle.

35. Capt. Saalmann is Charles Saalmann of the 75th Pennsylvania, Company C. <http://soda.pop.psu.edu/cgi-bin/broker?e2=saalmann&_PROGRAM=pubprogs.cw3c.sas&_SERVICE=sodapop> (accessed Oct. 29, 2011).

36. Maj. Gen. Franz Sigel, who headed the Department of West Virginia, took his command into the Shenandoah Valley and was badly defeated at New Market, Virginia, on May 15, 1864.

37. Col. Charles. W. Asmussen, was Maj. Gen. Joseph Hooker's assistant inspector general. *OR* vol. 38, 1:855.

38. The 1st Alabama Cavalry, United States Volunteers, was the only Union cavalry regiment from that seceded state. It served with the headquarters of the Fourteenth Corps during the Atlanta campaign. Nine of its original companies enlisted for one year. When the one-year men were discharged, new companies of three-year men were organized. Margaret M. Storey, *Loyalty and Loss: Alabama's Unionists in the Civil War and Reconstruction* (Baton Rouge: Louisiana State University Press, 2004), 103. See Glenda McWhirter Todd, *First Alabama Cavalry, U.S.A.: Homage to Patriotism* (Bowie, Md: Heritage Books, 1999).

39. See note 5 to chapter 3 regarding William Neussel.

40. See note 8, above, regarding Charles M. Reese.

41. *OR* vol. 38, 2:97–98; Castel, *Decision in the West*, 223–26.

42. *OR* vol. 38, 1:377–79; 4:331.

43. Lost Mountain stands about five miles east of Dallas, Georgia, and due south of Acworth.

44. Dallas, Georgia, lay approximately nine miles south of Huntsville, Georgia.

45. George Bauer was promoted from private, Company B, to sergeant major on June 22, 1863, and to first lieutenant, Company K, on Apr. 26, 1865. A prewar clerk from Chicago, Ill., Bauer was married, a barber in civilian life, and a native of Celle in the Kingdom of Hanover. He mustered out on June 9, 1865. Lt. Lotz is 1st lieutenant Carl Lotz, Company G.

46. *OR* vol. 38, 2:98.

47. Robinson's brigade camped in the vicinity of New Hope Church on June 1. *OR* vol. 38, 2:88.

48. The *Official Records* (*OR*) show that aggregate casualties for the Army of the Cumberland and its Twentieth Corps during the month of May 1864 were 8,774 and 3,917 officers and enlisted men, respectively. In his memoirs, General Sherman admitted to a total of 9,299 casualties in his grand army for May 1864 but shows casualties for the Army of the Cumberland and its Twentieth Corps of only 6,856 and 3,568, respectively. *OR* vol. 38, 1:145; William T. Sherman, *Personal Memoirs of Gen. W. T. Sherman*, 2 vols. (New York: Appleton, 1891), 2:47.

49. The three Federal guns captured were in front of Brig. Gen. William Harrow's Fourth Division, not Osterhaus's, and the Rebel brigade was driven back soon after it penetrated into a gap between two brigades on Harrow's right. Osterhaus did lead a brigade from his division to assist in repelling the enemy assault but it did not recapture the guns. Osterhaus did return with the brigade just in time to participate in a sound and bloody repulse of an attack on his fortified division by two enemy brigades. This is called the Battle of Dallas. Castel, *Decision in the West*, 244–46. *OR* vol. 38, 3:131.

50. On June 1 the Fifteenth Corps moved east into the Twentieth Corps' position, and the Twentieth Corps swung northeast about six miles toward Acworth and rested at the rear of its army's left, near Pickett's Mill. Castel, *Decision in the West*, 255.

51. Eugene is Adj. Eugene Weigel. Lotz is 1st Lt. Carl Lotz. Gottlob is likely Capt. Joseph Gottlob, a native of Germany and an Alton, Illinois, resident, who was promoted from first lieutenant, Company G, to captain, Company I, on Mar. 12, 1864. Gottlob mustered out on June 9, 1865. He was single and a prewar merchant. Grembelino Joe is unidentified except by the context.

52. Col. James S. Robinson was named a brigadier general on Jan. 12, 1865, and brevetted as a major general on March 13, 1865. Mark M., Boatner, III, *Civil War Dictionary*, rev. ed. (New York: David McKay, 1988), 704.

53. Capt. Lee is probably Alfred E. Lee of the 82nd Ohio.

10. From Acworth to Atlanta

1. Van Horne, *Army of the Cumberland*, 2:86, 88; Castel, *Decision in the West*, 259, 283, 285.

2. Brig. Gen. Joseph F. Knipe headed the First Brigade of Alpheus S. Williams's division, and Brig. Gen. Thomas H. Ruger led its Second Brigade. Van Horne, *Army of the Cumberland*, 2:91–92. *OR* vol. 38, 2:89–90.

3. Marietta, Georgia, lay on the Western and Atlantic Railroad, approximately twenty miles northwest of Atlanta.

4. Lt. Charles E. Winegar's Battery I and Capt. John D. Woodbury's Battery M both belonged to the First New York Light Artillery and Alpheus Williams's division. *OR* 38.1:98.

5. Federal casualties aggregated 250, at most. The 82nd Illinois suffered one killed and three wounded on June 22, 1864. Castel, *Decision in the West*, 295; *OR* vol. 38, 1:99, 98.

6. Castel, *Decision in the West*, 246.

7. General Osterhaus pushed his skirmishers to within two hundred yards of the top of Kennesaw Mountain but withdrew under orders of Fifteeenth Corps commander John Logan after encountering a heavy enemy line from Hardee's corps. No mention is made in Osterhaus's report of capturing any guns. Maj. Gen. Peter J. Osterhaus, a native German, commanded the First Division of the Fifteenth Corps. Maj. Gen. John A. Logan succeeded Maj. Gen. William T. Sherman as commander of the Fifteenth Corps in November 1863. *OR* vol. 38, 3:98, 103; 31, 2:584.

8. An enemy sharpshooter killed Capt. William Wheeler, Second Division chief of artillery and commander of the 13th New York Independent Battery, Twentieth Corps, on June 22, 1864, while he was directing a section in battle. *OR* vol. 38, 2:181. Müller mistakenly criticizes Colonel McGroarty. The colonel was ordered to take his regiment to assist Knipe's brigade in the battle on June 22, 1864. Major Beckett is David C. Beckett, 61st Ohio. *OR* vol. 38, 2:109.

9. Müller is referring to Col. Horace Broughton.

10. Eugene is Eugene F. Weigel, who mustered in as captain of Company F on May 12, 1864. Company F had been without a captain since August 1863, when Capt. Erich Hoppe was discharged and transferred to the Veteran Reserve Corps.

11. Confederate losses at the Battle of Kennesaw Mountain aggregated about 700. Castel, *Decision in the West*, 290–91.

12. Ibid., 291.

13. Ibid., 319–21; *OR* vol. 38, 1:69.

14. General Williams reported that total casualties for his division on June 22, 1864, were 130 killed, wounded, and missing. Lieutenant Colonel Salomon reported losing two men on the skirmish line. Salomon's casualties must have consisted only of wounded because the muster rolls show no one killed on that day. Castel, *Decision in the West*, 295; *OR* 38, 2:32, 99.

15. The Chattahoochee River begins in far northeastern Georgia and flows in a southwesterly direction, then turns due south and forms the bottom half of the Georgia–Alabama state line.

16. Quartermaster Panse's arm was crippled at the Battle of Wilson's Creek in Missouri in 1861 and not while on leave.

17. The young women were initially sent north to a prison in Louisville, Kentucky, then freed and disbursed to work in northern states, never to return to Roswell. Castel, *Decision in the West*, 336.

18. Col. Theodor Meumann, who had served in Prussia, succeeded Franz Sigel as colonel of the 3rd Missouri on November 1861. Kaufmann, *Germans in the American Civil War*, 310–11. General Osterhaus formerly commanded the brigade containing the three Missouri regiments identified and whose soldiers' enlistments would soon expire.

19. Müller likely referred to Alpheus Williams as lion-headed because of his long, curly hair; his wild and wooly beard; and his thick moustache, which extended well beyond the sides of his beard.

20. Anton Bruhn was the original captain of Company A. Why he is referred to as being part of the field and staff is unknown. Sgt. Frank Schönewald was commissioned as a second lieutenant on Mar. 16, 1864, but not mustered in at that rank. Bauer was probably Sgt.-Maj. George Bauer of Chicago, who became first lieutenant, Company K, on Apr. 11, 1865. Andreas Prell was the commissary sergeant. He later became acting first lieutenant of Company D, but mustered out on June 9, 1865, with the rank of quartermaster sergeant. Prell was born in the Kingdom of Bavaria. Sgt. Fritz Doering of Company K, a married laborer, was German-born, and mustered out on June 9, 1865. All these men hailed from Chicago.

21. The editor could not discover what the 45th New York did to cause them to be held out of the fighting during the Atlanta campaign or why Müller looked down on them. The 45th New York was transferred to the Fourth Division, Twentieth Corps. The 31st Wisconsin joined the Third Brigade, First Division, on July 21, 1864. It previously was part of the Fourth Division, Twentieth Corps, and added more than 700 troops to the brigade. *OR* vol. 38, 2:91.

22. After seven weeks of campaigning, in which his Eastern army had suffered 65,000 casualties, General Grant resorted to a siege of Petersburg, Virginia (located about twenty-five miles south of Richmond). The siege lasted nine months. Grant sent forces north into the Shenandoah Valley in early June, and Confederate partisans under Mosby and a corps under Jubal Early moved to deal with these Federals. The Federals under David Hunter and Phil Sheridan accomplished little. Müller criticizes the Union's policy of allowing a conscripted soldier to buy his way out of serving by paying $300 to the government. On July 10, 1864, Maj. Gen. Benjamin F. Butler, commander of the Army of the James, sent an infantry force under Brig. Gen. Quincy A. Gilmore and a cavalry force under Brig. Gen. August V. Kautz to try to capture Petersburg, Va., and destroy the railroad and the bridges over the Appomattox River. Militia defended Petersburg. After observing the works in his front Gilmore believed they were too strong to take and withdrew. Kautz's troopers carried the works on the south side of the city but Home Guards and artillery forced him to abandon the mission. McPherson, *Battle Cry of Freedom*, 737–79; Lawrence G. Kautz, *August Valentine Kautz, USA: Biography of a Civil War General* (Jefferson, N.C.: McFarland & Co., 2008), 127–29.

23. Frémont was nominated as the presidential candidate of the new anti-Lincoln Radical Democracy Party in Cleveland, Ohio, on May 31, 1864. Levine, *Spirit of 1848*, 261, See also note 27, below.

24. Dilger's losses for early July 1864 appear to be exaggerated. His battery's losses for the entire Atlanta campaign were one officer and four enlisted men killed and one officer and nineteen enlisted men wounded. *OR* vol. 38, 1:826.

25. The number of prisoners captured (5,000) for one day is greatly exaggerated. Sherman's army reported taking 7,480 prisoners during the four months ending Aug. 31, 1864, and receiving 2,438 deserters. *OR* vol. 38, 1:85.

26. Mons O. Lindbergh mustered into Company A as a sergeant, was promoted to first lieutenant, Company E, on Mar. 12, 1864, and commissioned a captain on June 8, 1865, but was not mustered in at that rank. Mons was a native of Gårdlösa in Skåne, the southernmost province of Sweden, and enlisted in Chicago. He is listed in the muster rolls as M. O. Linberg and Moses Lindbergh. Interestingly, the Swede was born Mons Olssen and added Lindbergh to his name while attending college. Mons served one year in the British army beginning

in 1855 (partly in Turkey during the Crimean War). He served five years in the Royal South Scanlan Infantry Regiment in Sweden before coming to the United States in 1862. Erickson is 1st Lt. Christian Erickson, Company F. Lender is Capt Robert Lender, Company E. Grace Lee Nute, "The Lindbergh Colony," *Minnesota History* 20, no. 3 (Sept. 1939): 244.

27. Frémont was nominated in Cleveland, Ohio, on May 31, 1864. He withdrew as a candidate on Sept. 22, 1864, after Lincoln promised to remove Postmaster-General Montgomery Blair from his cabinet. Frémont also opposed the confiscation and redistribution of Rebel property and stated that a united Republican Party was superior because the Democrats would accept a Union with slavery. He also announced that the Lincoln administration had been a failure. Ruhl J. Bartlett, *John C. Fremont and the Republican Party* (New York: Da Capo Press, 1970), 102–3, 130–31; William Frank Zornow, *Lincoln and the Party Divided* (Norman: University of Oklahoma Press, 1954), 85–86; Freitag and Rowan, *Friedrich Hecker*, 257–58.

28. Quoted in Castel, *Decision in the West*, 361.

29. Scurvy is a disease caused by a lack of vitamin C and characterized by spongy gums, loosening of the teeth, and a bleeding under the skin.

30. Russell S. Bonds, *War Like the Thunderbolt: The Battle and Burning of Atlanta* (Yardley, Pa.: Westholme, 2009), 47.

31. At this time many soldiers on both sides agreed not to fire upon one another without warning and fraternized.

32. The letter referred to appeared in the May 31, 1864, *Illinois Staats-Zeitung*.

33. *OR* vol. 38, 1:131, 2:100.

34. *OR* vol. 38, 2:92; 3:28–29; 5:273; Gary L. Ecelbarger, *The Day Dixie Died: The Battle of Atlanta* (New York: Thomas Dunne Books/St. Martin's Press, 2010), 271 n. 12, 217. See Ecelbarger, *The Day Dixie Died,* for a study of the Battle of Atlanta.

35. *OR* vol. 38, 1:78–79; 2:100, 93; 3:872.

36. Mr. Maloon is unidentified except by the context.

37. See note 17 to chapter 2 regarding Bechstein.

38. Lotz is 1st Lt. Carl Lotz, Company G.

39. Greenhut is former captain Joseph B. Greenhut. Frank is former captain Mayer A. Frank. Müller used the German name *Reinecke* (Reynard the Fox), an anthropomorphic red fox and trickster figure in fable. Yates is Illinois governor Richard Yates; Hoffmann is Illinois lieutenant governor Francis A. Hoffmann; Hirschbach is unidentified, but probably was a politician or other influential person.

40. Mihalotzy is Col. Géza Mihalotzy of the 24th Illinois, who died after being wounded at Buzzards Roost Gap in Georgia.

41. Bruhn is Capt. Anton Bruhn, Company A; Loeb is 1st Lt. William Loeb, Company C; Kirchner is 1st Lt. Frank Kirchner, Company D; Stueven is 2nd Lt. Charles E. Stueven, Company A, who was promoted to first lieutenant on Feb. 14, 1863, and commissioned as a captain, Company K, on an unknown date (but not mustered in as a captain). He was a barber in Chicago, unmarried, and twenty-two years old at enlistment. Gottlob is Capt. Joseph Gottlob, Company I; Lotz is 1st Lt. Carl Lotz, Company G. Eugene is Capt. Eugene Weigel, Company F. Erickson is 1st Lt. Christian Erickson, Company F. Mons O. Lindbergh, an original sergeant of Company A, was promoted to first lieutenant, Company E, on Mar. 12, 1864, and commissioned as a captain on June 8, 1865, but was not mustered in at that rank. He mustered out June 9, 1865. Lender is Capt. Robert Lender of Company E; Boerner is Dr. Charles E. Boerner, the regimental surgeon.

42. First Lt. Frederick Zengle was the commander of the 24th Illinois, Company A, which at this time consisted of men who had not completed their three-year enlistments when the rest of the regiment mustered out in July and August 1864. *RAGSI*, 2: 327. Maj. Gen. Peter J. Osterhaus and Maj. Gen. Henry W. Slocum.

43. The Union navy won the Battle of Mobile Bay on Aug. 5, 1865, shutting the port of Mobile, but the city was not captured until Apr. 12, 1865. McPherson, *Battle Cry of Freedom*, 761; *OR* vol. 49, 1:145–46.

44. Capt. Edward H. Newcomb, 61st Ohio Veteran Volunteer Regt., aide-de-camp, was mortally wounded on July 21, 1864. *OR*, vol. 38, 2:35; Schurz was Maj. Gen. Carl Schurz; Maj. Gen. Franz Siegel asked for a formal inquiry after he was relieved of command of the Reserve Division, Dept. of West Virginia. No inquiry took place. Engle, *Yankee Dutchman*, 207–8; Maj. Gen. William S. Rosecrans remained in command of the Dept. of the Missouri until December 1864. Boatner, *Civil War Dictionary*, 708; Kramer and Laxforelle are unidentified except by the context.

45. The 68th Regiment is unidentified except by the context. Stoneman is Maj. Gen. George Stoneman, commander of the Cavalry Corps, who was captured on July 31, 1864, near Macon, Georgia, with 700 of his troopers. *OR* vol. 38, 2:914; Boatner, *Civil War Dictionary*, 802.

46. Maj. Gen. George B. McClellan, former commander of the Army of the Potomac, was seeking the Democratic Party's nomination for president. He became the Democratic nominee at the convention convened on Aug. 29, 1864, in Chicago. Perhaps Rudolph Müller believed President Lincoln might offer McClellan command of the Union army to eliminate him as a political opponent. Horatio Seymour was a Democrat, the governor of New York, and an opponent of Lincoln. He opposed the 1863 military draft law and was considered as a presidential candidate in 1864. Copperheads were Democrats who opposed the war and favored a negotiated settlement. Clement L. Vallandigham was a leading Copperhead, who served as a state legislator, and a U.S. Congressman, who ran for governor of Ohio in 1863. On May 25, 1863, Vallandigham was exiled to the Confederacy and then moved to Canada. He returned to the United States in 1864 in violation of the 1863 order exiling him. He was not arrested and was active in the Democratic Party for the remainder of the war. *New York Times*, Sept. 1, 1864; *Ohio Archaeological and Historical Publications* 23 (Columbus: Ohio Historical Society, 1914), 261, 263–64. See Stephen W. Sears, *George B. McClellan: The Young Napoleon* (New York: Ticknor & Fields, 1988), for a biography of McClellan. See Jennifer L. Weber, *Copperheads: The Rise and Fall of Lincoln's Opponents in the North* (Oxford: Oxford University Press, 2006), and Frank L. Klement and Steven K. Rogstad, *Lincoln's Critics: The Copperheads of the North* (Shippensburg, Pa.: White Mane, 1999), for information about the anti-war Copperhead movement.

47. Paul Lawrence Rose states that the famous German composer Wilhelm Richard Wagner was an anti-Semite and that Wagner took "the Jews as the alien enemy of the 'organic' German culture." According to Rose, Wagner saw, "the threat of the Jews to German art as residing in Jewish foreignness, in Jewish money-mindedness and egoism, a materialism sublimated in the characteristics of Jewish art itself, which is incapable of the organic, the natural, the truly beautiful." Rudolph Müller's comments are along this line. Paul Lawrence Rose, *Wagner: Race and Revolution* (New Haven: Yale University Press, 1992), 42–43.

11. At the Gates of Atlanta

1. *OR* vol. 38, 2:95–96,100–101; Richard M. McMurry, *Atlanta 1864: Last Chance for the Confederacy* (Lincoln: University of Nebraska Press, 2000), 169–76.

2. General Slocum reported on Sept. 3, 1864, that the enemy "destroyed 7 locomotives and 81 cars, loaded with ammunition, small-arms and stores." On Sept. 19 he revised the number of locomotives destroyed to six. During an attack on Sept. 1, 1864, several Unionist regiments broke through Hardee's line at Jonesboro and captured most of the defenders at that point; however, the Rebels were able to check the attack and darkness ended the fighting. *OR* vol. 38, 2:20, 21; McMurry, *Atlanta 1864*, 174–75.

3. *OR* vol. 38, 3:765.

4. Balck is 1st Lt. Otto Balck of Company C. He likely was a Jew. He originally mustered into Company A. Mr. Stern, Mr. Seligman, and Mr. Baerman are unidentified except by the context.

5. Capt. William Neussel, Company G, resigned because of disability on Oct. 4, 1864. Dr. Schroeder is unidentified except by the context.

6. The editor is uncertain as to what fate of Col. Géza Mihalotzy of the 24th Illinois Rudolph Müller is referring. Capt. George E. Heinzmann, Capt. Anton Bruhn, and 1st Lt. Frank Kirchner were referred to in this letter only by surname.

7. Because the number of men in regiments had decreased so significantly due to deaths, disabilities, desertions, and other reasons, many regiments had excess officers for the remaining enlisted men. Consolidation was proposed to bring the strength closer to one thousand men and eliminate excess officers. Five companies required only a major, but not a colonel or lieutenant colonel.

8. The identity of Mrs. Löventhal is unknown except by the context. Whether she is a cousin by blood or the writer refers to her as such because she was Jewish or for some other reason is unknown.

9. The reason the colonel was referred to as a post office robber is unknown but it was in jest. Blair is Maj. Gen. Frank P. Blair Jr. commander of the Seventeenth Corps. The matter in which Blair and Lincoln remained neutral is unknown. S. M. Bowman and Richard Biddle Irwin, *Sherman and His Campaigns: A Military Biography* (New York: C. B. Richardson, 1865), 262.

10. Nineteen states allowed soldiers to vote in the field. Three important states that did not allow absentee balloting were Illinois, Indiana, and New Jersey. Some soldiers were transported to their home states to vote but not members of the 82nd Illinois. McPherson, *Battle Cry of Freedom*, 804.

11. Maj. Gen. Philip H. Sheridan defeated Confederate forces near Winchester, Virginia, on Sept. 19, 1864, and at Fisher's Hill on Sept. 21–22, 1864. Grant was stalled in front of Petersburg, Virginia. Castel, *Decision in the West*, 547.

12. Perhaps General Osterhaus was needling Müller and his Illinois comrades. After immigrating to the United States in November 1849, Osterhaus and his family settled in Belleville, Illinois, and by 1852 moved to nearby Lebanon. The family moved to St. Louis, Missouri, in 1860. Townsend, *Yankee Warhorse*, 16–19.

13. George S. Bradley, *The Star Corps or, Notes of an Army Chaplain, During Sherman's Famous "March to the Sea"* (Milwaukee: Jermain & Brightman, printers, 1865), 166. Castel, *Decision in the West*, 552–53; *OR* vol. 39, 1:807.

14. John Allan Wyeth, *Life of Lieutenant-General Nathan Bedford Forrest* (New York: Harper & Bros., 1908), 498.

15. Macon lay approximately ninety miles south–southeast of Atlanta and Rome lay roughly seventy miles northwest of Atlanta. Sherman initially decided to turn Atlanta into a fortress and hold it; he later decided to destroy its militarily useful facilities and materials, cut its railroad connections, and abandon the city. Castel, *Decision in the West*, 549.

16. On Oct. 3, 1864, Confederate forces seized Big Shanty and Moon Station and on Oct. 4 Acworth fell to Rebel troops. Up to 600 Unionist soldiers were taken prisoner at these places. On May 5, Confederate troops were repulsed at Allatoona, with a loss of about 1,000 men. *OR* vol. 39, 2:812, 552; Castel, *Decision in the West*, 552.

17. Müller is likely referring to an attack against Fort Harrison on the James River on Sept. 29, 1864, and fighting near Poplar Springs Church, southwest of Petersburg, from Sept. 30 to Oct. 2, 1864. The Federals gained ground in both cases. Eicher, *The Longest Night*, 740–41.

18. Lt. Col. Charles W. Asmussen was the assistant adjutant general of the Twentieth Corps. *OR* vol. 44, 626.

19. Col. John G. Parkhurst was the provost marshal general of the Army of the Cumberland. Rudolph Müller may have been referring to Moses, the biblical leader of the Jews, and Daniel Itzig, a Berlin banker appointed by Frederick the Great as Chief Elder of all Jewish congregations in Prussia. *OR* ser. 2, vol. 7, 908; Nahida Remy, *Nahida Remy's the Jewish Woman,* trans. Louise Mannheimer (New York: Bloch, 1916), 192; Robinson was Col. James S. Robinson.

20. Mr. Goldsticker is unidentified except by the context. Eugene is Capt. Eugene Weigel of Company F, formerly the regiment's adjutant. *OR* vol. 32, 1:453. Müller is giving Colonel Hecker a description of the two group photographs that have survived and appear in this book.

21. The trio of field and staff referred to were Lieutenant Colonel Salomon, Major Rolshausen, and Acting Adjutant Loeb.

22. Mr. Löventhal is unidentified except by the context.

23. Second Lt. Adolphus Erdmann was quartermaster of the 15th Missouri Infantry. Allendorf, *Long Road to Liberty,* 211.

24. The regiment also went on a foraging expedition commanded by Col. James S. Robinson on Oct. 16, 17, 18, and 19. The Union garrison of approximately 800 soldiers at Dalton, Georgia, and a smaller number of troops at Tilton, Georgia, surrendered on Oct. 13, 1864; the number of casualties was not high. *OR* vol. 44, 260; 39, 1:732, 717, 720.

25. Freitag and Rowan, *Two Lives for Liberty,* 257–58.

26. Friedrich Hecker married Marie Josefine Eisenhardt, the daughter of a prosperous Mannheim merchant, in October 1839. Ibid., 50.

27. The "Hecker Song" was sung in connection with the 1848 Revolution and contained the refrain "Hecker, Struve, Blenker, Zitz, and Blum, slay the German princes!" http://www.marxists .org/archive/marx/works/1885/letters/85_05_15.htm. (accessed June 25, 2013).

28. Sheridan defeated Jubal Early's Confederate army at the Battle of Cedar Creek on Oct. 19, 1864, ending Early's army as an effective fighting force. Eicher, *The Longest Night,* 749–53.

29. Freitag and Rowan, *Two Lives for Liberty,* 257–58. Many Germans believed that they were being used by the Lincoln administration and were or would be ignored after their immediate usefulness waned. On the other hand, Germans used their political influence to obtain favors and concessions from the Lincoln administration, including generalships for Germans.

30. Apparently, the captain knew there would be a long campaign but was not sure of the objective. Mobile lay approximately 350 miles southwest of Atlanta; Savannah lay about 250 miles southeast of Atlanta.

31. The reason Müller refers to Salomon as Friedensreich (peaceful realm or abundant peace) is unknown. The lieutenant colonel went to Nashville, Tennessee, on leave to sign papers in connection with a personal financial matter. Professor Marx is unidentified except by the context. Arnold von Winkelried, a legendary Swiss hero, sacrificed his life at the Battle of Sempach (July 9, 1836) by rushing at the Austrians, grabbing as many as of the enemy spears as he could with his hands and burying them in his body, thus opening the way into the enemy's ranks for his comrades, who defeated the Austrians. Charles Morris, "Sempach and Arnold Winkelried," in *Historical Tales* (in German) (Philadelphia: Lippincott. 1908), 5:189, 192–93.

32. Maj. Gen. Sterling Price began a raid into Missouri from Arkansas on Sept. 19, 1864, with a Rebel force of 12,000 men and 14 guns. Price retreated from Missouri late in October and when he arrived at Confederate lines in Laynesport, Arkansas, his command had dwindled to 6,000 men. The editor does not know the basis for Captain Müller's comment about General Grant. Boatner, *Civil War Dictionary,* 669–71.

33. The only Diefenbach in the 82nd Illinois was Cpl. John Diefenbach of Company E, a native of Hartrung in the Duchy of Nassau. He was a single farmer from Peoria and mustered out with the regiment. Diefenbach no. 2 might have been a substitute name for one of the regiment's medical personnel. Pvt. James Franziskus, an 18-year-old-farmer at enlistment, was a native of Glasburg, France, and was from Chicago, Ill. He mustered out on June 9, 1865.

12. The March to the Sea

1. Trudeau, *Southern Storm*, 41–42; Larry J. Daniels, *Days of Glory*, 420; Eicher, *The Longest Night*, 761–62, 765–66.

2. *OR* vol. 44, 7, 853.

3. Maj. Gen. Joseph Wheeler claimed he never had more than 3,500 soldiers in his own force. Boatner claims that there were 13,000 troops (including 3,000 Georgia militiamen) around Lovejoy Station, Georgia, to oppose Sherman. *OR* vol. 44, 7, 16, 411; Boatner, *Civil War Dictionary*, 509.

4. *OR* vol. 44, 259–61, 599, 654, 959.

5. In a court martial proceeding held on Mar. 24, 1863, Quartermaster Hermann Panse was found not guilty of being drunk while on duty on Feb. 5, 1863, and not guilty of refusing to transport the shelter tents of Company K's officers and the baggage of the officers of Company A. Panse allegedly had the tents and baggage thrown out of the wagons for the march between Hartwood Church to Potomac Creek in Virginia. Rudolph Müller testified that when he saw Panse on the march he was not drunk. Herman Panse Court Martial File, LL274, folder 1, Records Group 153, NA. Müller referred to Loeb as a revenge-seeking lion because *Loeb* can mean "lion" in German.

6. The total garrison at Fort McCallister was nearly 200 men of whom 16 were killed and 28 wounded; the remainder was captured. Federal losses were 24 killed and 110 wounded. The earthwork fortifications were built in 1861 at Genesis Point near the mouth of the Ogeechee River to protect the southern flank of Savannah. Trudeau, *Southern Storm*, 417–18, 427, 439.

7. *OR* vol. 44, 261, 410–11. Maj. Gen. Joseph Wheeler's cavalry corps of the Army of Tennessee was left in Georgia to resist Sherman after Major General Hood took the rest of the Army of Tennessee north to Tennessee.

8. Quartermaster Panse departed on leave on October 30, 1864. He submitted a medical certificate signed by a doctor on November 23, 1864, stating that he had fallen from a horse and fractured his ulna and dislocated his radius, and would not be fit for duty or to travel for twenty days. Below the doctor's signature was a statement signed by a justice of the peace, "Sworn to and Subscribed before me this 27th day of November 1864." Hermann Panse Compiled Service Records, Record Group 94, NA.

9. Swamp Angel was also the name given to a 200-pound (8-inch) rifled gun used by Union troops to shell Charleston, South Carolina, on Aug. 22–23, 1863. Boatner, *Civil War Dictionary*, 822.

10. William Loeb Court Martial File, MM1759, Records Group 153, NA.

11. *OR* vol. 44, 259–61.

12. *Jahrbücher der Deutsch-Amerikanischen Turnerei, Band.* I, *Heft* 1, Nov. 1890: 269, 21; *Heft* 4, July 1891: 174; for a discussion of foreign and Northern immigrants in the South and its larger cities, see Dennis C. Rousey, "Friends and Foes of Slavery: Foreigners and Northerners in the Old South," *Journal of Social History* 35, no. 2 (Winter, 2001): 373–396. Walter J. Fraser, *Savannah in the Old South* (Athens: University of Georgia Press, 2003), 254–55.

13. William Rapp was editor of the *Illinois Staats-Zeitung*.

14. Lt. Gen. Sir Colin Campbell was appointed to command in India after the outbreak of the Indian Mutiny of 1857. He led the relief of Lucknow in November of 1857 and by 1858 had crushed the rebellion. Archibald Forbes, *Colin Campbell, Lord Clyde* (London: Macmillan, 1895), 132–33.

15. The Savannah *Turnverein* was one of several southern *Turnvereine* that withdrew from the national organization (the *Turnerbund*) when the latter formally fostered gradual emancipation in 1855. Dennis Rousey states, "The Savannah Turnverein protested the influence of 'Northern Abolitionists' on the national convention, accused it of 'gross ignorance of South-

ern life,' and condemned its support of the emancipation proposal for being 'in direct conflict with Southern rights.'" This does not necessarily mean that the majority of Savannah's Turners were against gradual emancipation, but the protest may have been made to forestall attacks on Savannah's Turners by Southerners who were already suspicious of the loyalty of Germans and especially Turners. Rousey, "Friends and Foes of Slavery," 381.

16. Noah Andre Trudeau mentions this plundering incident in his book; see Trudeau, *Southern Storm: Sherman's March to the Sea* (repr. ed. 2009; New York: Harper Perennial, 2008), 492.

17. First Lt. Joseph Riegert, Company H, was a native of Oberkirch in Baden. The married machinist from Chicago was promoted from 2nd lieutenant, Company H, to 1st lieutenant on Apr. 22, 1863, and transferred to Company B. The day before his muster out on June 9, 1865, he was commissioned as captain, Company H, but not mustered in at that rank. He mustered in at twenty-six. The regiment's doctor was Charles E. Boerner.

18. The editor believes that the author of the letter might be an F. Kürschner, whom Pvt. Friedrich P. Kappelmann mentioned was a Turner who helped him obtain a letter from his parents while he was in Savannah. Friedrich P. Kappelmann to "Dear Parents," Jan. 31, 1865, transcript, unknown trans., USAMHI.

19. Walter J. Fraser, *Savannah in the Old South* (Athens: University of Georgia Press, 2003), 254–55; Mehrländer, *The Germans of Charleston, Richmond and New Orleans*, 397.

13. The Carolinas Campaign to Fayetteville, North Carolina

1. Goldsboro, North Carolina, lay approximately sixty miles northeast of Fayetteville. The Atlantic and North Carolina Railroad connected New Bern to Goldsboro; the Wilmington and Weldon Railroad ran from the port of Wilmington to Petersburg, Virginia. John G. Barrett, *Sherman's March through the Carolinas* (Chapel Hill: University of North Carolina Press, 1996), 39. United States, *The Official Atlas of the Civil War* (New York: T. Yoseloff, 1958), plates 137, 138.

2. *OR* vol. 47, 1:1718, 659, 668–69.

3. Friedrich P. Kappelmann letter to "Dear Parents," Jan. 31, 1865, transcript, unknown trans., USMHI.

4. Ibid., 668–70, Joseph T. Glatthaar, *The March to the Sea and Beyond: Sherman's Troops in the Savannah and Carolinas Campaigns.* The American Social Experience 1 (New York: New York University Press, 1985), 141; Eicher, *The Longest Night*, 799–800. For the burning of Columbia, South Carolina, see Marion Brunson Lucas, *Sherman and the Burning of Columbia* (College Station: Texas A & M University Press, 1976).

5. Eicher, *The Longest Night*, 799–800.

6. Glatthaar, *March to the Sea and Beyond*, 100, 108–110; *OR* vol. 47, 1:668–70; Mark A. Moore, *Moore's Historical Guide to the Battle of Bentonville* (Campbell, Calif.: Savas Pub., 1997), 26.

7. Max Schlund Diary, Feb. 11, 20, 26, 1865, and Mar. 3, 4, 6, 1865, transcript, unknown trans., Newberry Library, Chicago, Ill.

8. *OR* vol. 47, 1:669–70; Barrett, *Sherman's March through the Carolinas*, 88–89; Glatthaar, *March to the Sea and Beyond*, 137, 142–42, 148; Max Schlund Diary, February 8 to March 10, 1865.

9. McPherson, *Battle Cry of Freedom*, 828. See Lucas, *Sherman and the Burning of Columbia*.

10. Glatthaar, *March to the Sea and Beyond*, 124–25, 141.

11. Quoted in Glatthaar, *March to the Sea and Beyond*, 133, 242 n. 25. See also *OR* vol. 47, 1:487 for Brig. Gen. James D. Morgan's condemnation of foragers in his command who "are a disgrace to the name of soldier and the country." Morgan was commander of the Second Division, Fourteenth Corps.

12. *OR* vol. 47, 1:659; 2:1247; Barrett, *Sherman's March,* 112.

13. *OR* vol. 47, 1:659.

14. Ibid., 1:668.

15. Major General Hardee was not able to concentrate all the troops under his command against Sherman and it was not until Joseph E. Johnston was able to collect 20,000 troops near Smithfield, North Carolina, that Sherman's troops were seriously challenged. Moore, *Moore's Historical Guide,* 3.

16. See note 11 to this chapter.

14. The Final Battles

1. Brig. Gen. William T. Ward commanded the Third Division of the Twentieth Corps. Col. William Hawley led the Second Brigade of the First Division of the Twentieth Corps. Brig. Gen. John G. Mitchell headed the Second Brigade of Brig. Gen. James D. Morgan's Second Division of the Fourteenth Corps. *OR* vol. 47, 1:585, 65, 64, 63; Barrett, *Sherman's March,* 150–55.

2. *OR* vol. 47, 1:670–71.

3. Ibid., 1:76, 1060.

4. The Provisional Corps was made up of detachments of the Twenty-fourth and Twenty-fifth Corps. Sherman ordered Schofield and Terry to repair the railroads while advancing to Goldsboro. General Johnston's infantry and artillery effectives totaled 18,000 as follows: Stewart, 4,000; Bragg 6,500; Hardee, 7,500. Hampton had 4,200 cavalrymen. Bradley, *Last Stand in the Carolinas,* 111; Barrett, *Sherman's March,* 39 n. 57, 149, 160; *OR* vol. 47, 1:1058.

5. Moore, *Moore's Historical Guide,* 26, 23.

6. Bradley, *Last Stand in the Carolinas,* 153–54, 157, 174, 176; Moore, *Moore's Historical Guide,* 23.

7. Lt. Palmer F. Scovel led the 1st Illinois Light Artillery, Battery C. The 101st Illinois was later relieved from guarding the Smithfield-Goldsboro crossroads in order to join Col. James L. Selfridge's brigade (First Brigade, First Division, Twentieth Corps), which was located in reserve about 300 yards behind Robinson's brigade but was not engaged in any fighting. Bradley, *Last Stand in the Carolinas,* 194–95, 168, 173–79, 194, 168, 273, 200; *OR* vol. 47, 1:612.

8. Stephens's battery (1st Ohio Light, Battery C) dropped trail to the left and rear of Robinson's brigade, and Rich's battery (2nd Illinois Light, Battery M) set up south of the Goldsboro Road behind Robinson. Winegar's battery (1st New York Light, Battery I), Newkirk's battery (1st New York Light, Battery I), and Scovel's battery joined Stephens's battery north of the road behind and to the left of Robinson. One gun of Webb's battery joined Rich's battery; the remainder was captured earlier and Captain Webb was killed. Bradley, *Last Stand in the Carolinas,,* 200, 203, 266–67; *OR,* vol. 47, 1:666, 52, 55; Moore, *Moore's Historical Guide,* 33, 34, 42.

9. Col. William Butler was commanding Rhett's brigade because Col. Alfred M. Rhett had been captured near Averasboro on Mar. 15, 1865. *OR* vol. 47, 1:1084, 1060; Bradley, *Last Stand in the Carolinas,* 200–201, 280, 289, 293, 282–95. Barrett, *Sherman's March,* 149, 160; Glatthaar, *March to the Sea and Beyond,* 169.

10. Sgt. Ole K. Halvorson died from his wound on March 19, 1865. A native of Tinn, Norway, and a farmer, the sergeant was living in Leland, Illinois, when he enlisted. Pvt. Anton Schneider of Chicago, a native of Weisenheim, Prussia, was killed on Mar. 16, 1865. The editor is uncertain whether he was from Weisenheim am Sand or Weisenheim am Berg. The two villages are about five miles apart.

11. Maj. John Higgins of the 143rd New York Infantry was shot through the left leg. Capt. Charles Schmidt and 1st Lt. Friedrich Rudolph Klein belonged to Company B and Company C, respectively, of the 26th Wisconsin Infantry. *OR* vol. 47, 1:665, 66.

12. French troops invaded Mexico in 1862 because Mexico refused to pay its foreign debts. In 1863, supported by Mexican conservatives and French troops, French Emperor Napoleon III installed a Hapsburg prince, Maximilian I, as emperor of Mexico. Ousted president Benito Juárez and his republican forces continued fighting against the French troops and the Mexican monarchists. The French fleet landed soldiers, who captured Guaymas on Mar. 29, 1865. This is likely the blow to which Rudolph Müller was referring. The republicans defeated the imperial forces at Tacámbaro in Michoácan. Napoleon III removed the French forces from Mexico in February 1867. The French did not intervene on behalf of the Confederacy. Charles Morris, *The Story of Mexico: A Land of Conquest and Revolution, Giving a Comprehensive History of This Romantic and Beautiful Land from the Days of Montezuma and the Empire of the Aztecs to the Present Time, Including a Graphic Description of the Mexican Country*. (s.l.: L. T. Myers, 1914), 205, 206–7; Hubert Howe Bancroft, *History of North Mexican States and Texas* (San Francisco: History Company, 1889), 696–97.

13. Lt. Col. Hezekiah Watkins commanded the 143rd New York. He coerced the retreating troops of Maj. James S. Crall's regiment back into the line. *OR* vol. 47, 1:53. Moore, *Moore's Historical Guide*, 41.

14. The editor found no evidence that Colonel Robinson or his staff were drunk during this battle.

15. *OR* vol. 47, 1:27–28, 672. The vital Wilmington and Weldon Railroad ran north–south from Petersburg, Virginia, to Wilmington, North Carolina.

16. Friedrich P. Kappelmann letter to "Dear Parents," Mar. 26, 1865, transcript, unknown trans., USAMHI.

17. *OR* vol. 47, 1:125, 131, 673.

18. Ibid., 1:668, 673.

19. Captain Müller is referring to the corps commanders driving their men to march twenty-five to thirty miles per day in high heat and high humidity on the stretch to Richmond because they had bet on whose corps would arrive first. Dozens of men died from heat prostration. Glatthaar, *March to the Sea and Beyond*, 179.

20. Müller refers to Capt. Frank Kirchner of Company C and 1st Lt. Eugene Hepp of Company H.

21. This was Capt. Emil Frey, Company H.

22. See note 19 to this chapter.

23. The Battle of the Wilderness was fought May 5–7, 1864, and the Battle of Spotsylvania took place May 8–24, 1864. Both battles were part of Lt. Gen. Ulysses S. Grant's Overland campaign in Virginia and produced huge casualties. The Battle of Chancellorsville in Virginia occurred Apr. 30–May 6, 1863.

24. Maj. Gen. William Scott Hancock led the Union's Second Corps.

25. When captured by Union cavalry Jefferson Davis was wearing his wife's "raglan" (a light waterproof overcoat without sleeves) and a shawl over his head. Davis claimed he accidentally put on his wife's raglan that was similar to his, and she had put the shawl over his head to protect him from the weather. From this the rumor spread that he was trying to escape disguised as a woman. William C. Davis, *Jefferson Davis: The Man and His Hour* (New York: HarperCollins, 1991), 636–37.

26. Andrew Johnson, a Union-loyal Tennessean, was vice president at the time of Lincoln's assassination.

Epilogue

1. Freitag and Rowan, *Friedrich Hecker,* 268–69, 273, 338.

2. Ibid., 378, 377–78.

3. Ibid., 336.

4. Ibid., 437, 441, 453, 457.

5. Rudolph Müller, pension file no. 954848, NA; 1870 and 1880 U.S. census, Chicago, Illinois; *Chicago City Directory,* 1881, p. 863; 1882, p. 881; 1883 (unknown); 1884, p. 994; *Minneapolis City Directory,* 1885, p. 542; 1886, p. 557; 1887, p. 701; 1888, p. 976; 1889, p. 916; 1890, p. 901; 1891, p. 892; 1892, p. 870; 1893, p. 1038; 1894, p. 682; 1895, p. 732; 1896, p. 787; 1897, p. 858; 1898, p. 838; 1899, p. 920. In 1870 Alexander Hecker, brother of Malvina Hecker Müller, age sixteen, was living with Rudolph and Malvina.

6. *Minneapolis Tribune,* Oct. 9, 13, and 14, 1899.

7. Oscar T. Shuck, *History of the Bench and Bar of California* (Los Angeles, Calif.: Commercial Printing House, 1901), 987–88; Benjaminson, "A Regiment of Immigrants," 177; Edmond S. Meany, *Governors of Washington, Territorial and State* (Seattle: University of Washington, 1915), 43–44; Edward S. Salomon, pension file no. 397004, NA.

8. Edward S. Salomon, pension file no. 397004, NA; Military Order of the Loyal Legion of the United States (MOLLUS), *Register of the Loyal Legion of the United States Compiled from the Registers and Circulars of the Various Commanderies* (Boston: n. p., 1906), 199; "Death Comes to General Salomon," *San Francisco Chronicle,* July 19, 1913.

9. Eugene Weigel's death certificate incorrectly states he died at the home of his niece Atlanta E. Hecker. Atlanta was Eugene's younger sister and the widow of Alexander Hecker (son of Col. Friedrich Hecker). St. Louis, Missouri, Department of Health, Certificate of Death, No. 8359, Oct. 23, 1896; Missouri Commandery of MOLLUS, Circular No. 154, May 1, 1897, at Missouri History Museum, St. Louis, Missouri.

10. Missouri Commandery of MOLLUS, Circular No. 154, May 1, 1897, at Missouri History Museum, St. Louis, Missouri.

11. George E. Heinzmann, pension file no. 93730, NA; occupations compiled by the editor from Chicago city directories for the years 1872–1906, <http://www.fold3.com/browse.php#5|h25JYODs2> (accessed Apr. 5, 2013); U.S. census for 1900, shows Heinzmann residing in Danville, Illinois, but incorrectly shows his birthplace as Virginia; *Chicago Tribune,* Jan. 23, 1907.

12. Matthew Marx, pension file no. 183253, NA, 1880 U.S. census.

13. Occupations compiled by the editor from Chicago, Illinois, city directories for 1866–1903; U.S. population census for 1870, 1880, and 1900. Chicago, Illinois; <http://search.ancestry.com/cgi-bin/sse.dll?rank=1&new=1&MSAV=0&msT=1&gss=angs-c&gsfn=william&gsln=loeb&msydy=1872&msypn__ftp=cook+county+illinois&uidh=iz2&pcat=34&h=72979&recoff=6+7&db=FSCookILMarriage&indiv=1> (accessed Apr. 5, 2013). Death and burial information provided by Fran Luebke.

14. Milwaukee County Register of Deeds—Registration of Marriages, 1871, vol. 5, p. 72 (certified copy); U.S. population census, 1880 and 1900: *Chicago City Directory,* for each of the years 1865 through 1901; Theodor Janssen, *Geschichte der Chicago Turn-Gemeinde: Aus mündlichen Ueberlieferungen und Vereins-Dokumenten zuusammengestellt* (Chicago, Ill.: [M. Stern], 1897), 91; *Chicago Daily Tribune,* Nov. 29, 1904, Feb 11, 1902.

15. John Hillborg, Compiled Service Records, Record Group 94, NA: 82nd Illinois Infantry and 55th Illinois Infantry; John Hillborg pension file no. 130070, NA.

16. Occupations for Frank Schönewald compiled by the editor from Chicago, Illinois, city directories for 1866–1895; Card Records of Headstones Provided for Deceased Union Civil War Veterans, ca. 1879–ca. 1903 Microfilm Publication M1845 (22 rolls) roll 18, NA.

17. Document titled "To All Whom It May Concern" found at <http://trees.ancestry.com/tree /25091940/person/12567628201/media/2?pgnum=1&pg=0&pgpl=pid|pgNum> (accessed Apr. 5, 2013); *Chicago Tribune*, Jan. 14, 1911.

18. Wittke, *Refugees of Revolution*, 367, 27.

19. Hofmann, "Turners' Loyalty," 72–73, 28.

20. Phone call to American Turners National Headquarters in Louisville, Kentucky, June 23, 2011.

21. Engle, "Raised Consciousness," 10. Pvt. Gottfried Rentschler exhibited enhanced ethnic consciousness in a letter published in the *Louisville Anzeiger* on Mar. 15, 1864: "The German soldier is generally far more faithful, conscientious, and zealous than the native-born American. This is part of the German nature, which is our reason to be proud of our nation. One more thing: The German soldier is obedient and loyal to duty without regard to reward or punishment. The American considers only reward or—the *Guard-House*. This is caused by the national education on either side, in the broadest sense of the word." This outburst of ethnic pride followed the private's disclosure about a statement a nativist officer made to him: "Germans had no business to bear arms and become soldiers, because they value the country so little just like the Negro." In the same letter he also declared, "The German is a 'Dutch soldier' and as a 'Dutchman' he is, if not despised, disrespected, and not regarded or treated as an equal." Then he warned, "The conclusion that the mixing of Germans and Americans in the Army may be beneficial to both parties . . . is in error." Reinhart, *Two Germans in the Civil War*, 67–68.

22. Conzen, "German-Americans and the Invention of Ethnicity," 140; Hawgood, *The Tragedy of German-America*, 279.

23. Engle, "Raised Consciousness," 1.

24. Lonn, *Foreigners in the Union Army and Navy*, 659–60; Burton, *Melting Pot Soldiers*, 227–28, 233; Keller, "Germans in Civil War–Era Pennsylvania," 2, 2 n. 2; Engle, "Raised Consciousness," 1.

25. Engle, "Raised Consciousness," 1–2; Keller, "Germans in Civil War–Era Pennsylvania," 1–2, 2 n. 2, 221, 233–34; Valuska and Keller, *Damn Dutch*, 192–98; Hawgood, *The Tragedy of German-America*, 253–54, 267–98, 234. See also James S. Olson, *The Ethnic Dimension in American History* (New York: St. Martin's Press, 1979), 93–108.

26. Öfele, *German-Speaking Officers*, 230; Helbich, *German-born Union Soldiers*, 321. For a recent analysis of existing literature on Germans in the Civil War and a discussion of such issues as their military effectiveness, allegiance, and assimilation, see Christian B. Keller, "New Perspectives in Civil War Ethnic History and Their Implications for Twenty-First-Century Scholarship," in Andrew L. Slap and Michael Thomas Smith, eds., *This Distracted and Anarchical People: New Answers for Old Questions about the Civil War–Era North* (New York: Fordham University Press, 2013).

27. See note 12 to the introduction for information about Franz Sigel.

28. Engle, "Raised Consciousness," 1–17.

29. Tolzmann, *German-American Experience* (Amherst, N.Y.: Humanity Books, 2000), 219–23.

30. Quoted in Wittke, *Refugees of Revolution*, 359.

31. Russell A. Kazal, *Becoming Old Stock: The Paradox of German-American Identity* (Princeton, N.J.: Princeton University Press, 2004), 8.

32. Hawgood, *Tragedy of German-America*, 253–54, 287–303. In a recent work, Russell A. Kazal argues that even before the United States entered World War I, "institutional German America—which encompassed everything from secular gymnastic and singing societies to German Lutheran congregations and German Catholic national parishes—was unraveling." Kazal notes, "Guido Andre Dobbert, James Berquist and other scholars have portrayed

German ethnic institutions as suffering a long-term decline beginning in the 1890s." Kazal, *Becoming Old Stock*, 4. See also Guido Andre Dobbert, *The Disintegration of an Immigrant Community: The Cincinnati Germans, 1870–1920* (New York: Arno Press, 1980), and Erik Kirschbaum, *The Eradication of German Culture in the United States, 1917–1918* (Stuttgart: H.-D. Heinz, 1986).

Bibliographic Essay

Yankee Dutchmen under Fire is based on letters written by soldiers of the 82nd Illinois Volunteer Infantry Regiment. In addition, many books, articles, essays, and public documents have been used in preparing this book.

Vol. 5 of *Illinois and J. N. Reece, Report of the Adjutant General of the State of Illinois,* 9 vols. (Springfield, Ill.: Phillips Bros., 1900–1902), provides brief but important data about the military service of the officers and enlisted men of the 82nd Illinois Volunteer Infantry Regiment. More detailed service information for individual soldiers is available in their compiled service records, Records Group 94, at the National Archives in Washington, D.C., and in the regiment's muster and descriptive rolls in the Illinois State Archives, Springfield, Illinois. Pension files in the National Archives can yield valuable postwar information about certain individuals, where extant.

Undeniably, the greatest source about the Civil War is the *War of Rebellion: A Compilation of the Records of the Union and Confederate Armies,* 128 vols. (Washington, D.C.: Government Printing Office, 1880–1901), containing campaign and battle reports and dispatches from officers on both sides. These volumes are often referred to as the *Official Records,* or the ORs.

Modern histories of German regiments include Donald Allendorf, *Long Road to Liberty: The Odyssey of a German Regiment in the Yankee Army, The 15th Missouri Volunteer Infantry* (Kent, Ohio: Kent State University Press, 2006), and James S. Pula, *The Sigel Regiment: The Twenty-sixth Wisconsin Volunteer Infantry, 1862–1865* (Campbell, Calif.: Savas Publishing Company), 1998.

Among the most helpful specific campaign and battle accounts are Ernest B. Furgurson, *Chancellorsville: The Souls of the Brave* (New York: Alfred A. Knopf, 1993), and Steven W. Sears, *Chancellorsville* (New York: Houghton Mifflin Company, 1996); Stephen W. Sears, *Gettysburg* (Boston: Houghton Mifflin, 2003); Edwin B. Coddington, *The Gettysburg Campaign: A Study in Command* (New York: Simon & Schuster, 1997); and Harry W. Pfanz, *Gettysburg—The First Day* (Chapel Hill: University of North Carolina Press, 2001). For the battles around Chattanooga, see Peter Cozzens, *The Shipwreck of Their Hopes: The Battles for Chattanooga* (Urbana: University of Illinois Press, 1994), and Wiley Sword, *Mountains Touched with Fire: Chattanooga Besieged, 1863* (New York: St. Martin's Press, 1995). For Sherman's Atlanta Campaign and subsequent campaigns and battles, see Albert Castel, *Decision in the West: The Atlanta Campaign of 1864* (Lawrence: University Press of Kansas, 1992); Noah Andre Trudeau, *Southern Storm: Sherman's March to the Sea* (New York: Harper,

2008); Joseph T. Glatthaar, *The March to the Sea and Beyond: Sherman's Troops in the Savannah and Carolinas Campaigns* (New York: New York University Press, 1985); John G. Barrett, *Sherman's March through the Carolinas* (Chapel Hill: University of North Carolina Press, 1996); and Mark L. Bradley, *Last Stand in the Carolinas: The Battle of Bentonville* (Campbell, Calif.: Savas Woodbury Publishers, 1996).

The best histories of the Army of the Potomac are Bruce Catton's trilogy: *Mr. Lincoln's Army* (New York: Doubleday, 1951); *Glory Road* (Garden City, N.Y.: Doubleday, 1952); and *A Stillness at Appomattox* (Garden City, N.Y.: Doubleday, 1953); and Jeffry D. Wert, *Lincoln's Sword: The Army of the Potomac* (New York: Simon & Schuster, 2005).

The best histories of the Army of the Cumberland are Thomas Van Horne, *History of the Army of the Cumberland: Its Organization, Campaigns, and Battles,* 2 vols. (1875, reprint, with an introduction by Peter Cozzens; Wilmington, N.C.: Broadfoot Publishing, 1992), and Larry J. Daniel's more recent *Days of Glory: The Army of the Cumberland, 1861–1865* (Baton Rouge: Louisiana State University Press, 2004).

Information about general officers is presented in Ezra Warner's *Generals in Blue: Lives of the Union Commanders* (1964, reprint; Baton Rouge: Louisiana State University Press, 1992), and Ezra J. Warner, *Generals in Gray: Lives of the Confederate Commanders* (Baton Rouge: Louisiana State University Press, 1959). Mark M. Boatner III, *The Civil War Dictionary,* rev. ed. (New York: David McKay, 1988), also contains brief information on generals of both sides. Stephen D. Engle's *Yankee Dutchman: The Life of Franz* Sigel (Fayetteville: University of Arkansas Press, 1993), is worthwhile reading not only because it is an insightful biography of a military leader highly exalted by his fellow German Americans but also because it reveals the vast cultural dimensions of the war.

Notable works that cover the entire war are James B. McPherson, *Battle Cry of Freedom: The Civil War Era* (New York: Ballantine Books, 1989), and David J. Eicher, *The Longest Night: A Military History of the Civil War* (New York: Simon & Schuster, 2001). Charles P. Roland's *An American Iliad: The Story of the Civil War,* 2nd ed. (New York: McGraw-Hill, 2001), is the best concise narrative of the Civil War.

Useful works on the German Revolution of 1848 are Veit Valentin, *1848 Chapters of German History,* trans. by Ethel Talbot Scheffauer (1940, reprint; Hamden, Conn.: Archon Books, 1965), and Wolfram Siemann, *The German Revolution of 1848–49,* trans. by Christiane Banerji (New York: St. Martin's Press, 1998). Leading studies concerning Forty-eighters and Turners include Carl Wittke, *Refugees of Revolution: The German Forty-Eighters in America* (Philadelphia: University of Pennsylvania Press, 1952); A. E. Zucker, ed. *The Forty-Eighters: Political Refugees of the German Revolution of 1848* (New York: Columbia University Press, 1950); Don Heinrich Tolzman, ed. *The German-American Forty-Eighters 1848–1998* (Indianapolis: Max Kade German-American Center, Indiana University-Purdue University at Indianapolis and Indiana Germanic Heritage Society, 1997).

Historical information about the German American press is found in Karl J. Arndt and Mary E. Olson, *German-American Newspapers and Periodicals 1732–1955* (Heidelberg, Ger.: Quelle & Meyer, 1961), and Carl Frederick Wittke, *The German-Language Press in America* (Lexington: University of Kentucky Press, 1957). John Charles Bodger Jr., "The Immigrant Press and the Union Army," Ph. D. diss., Columbia University, 1951, is a unique work containing much translated commentary from the German-language press.

Secondary sources examining German soldiers in the Civil War are small in number but growing. The most useful are Ella Lonn, *Foreigners in the Confederacy* (Chapel Hill, University of North Carolina Press, 1940); Ella Lonn, *Foreigners in the Union Army and Navy* (Baton Rouge: Louisiana State University Press, 1951); William L. Burton, *Melting Pot Soldiers: The Union's Ethnic Regiments,* 2nd ed. (New York: Fordham University Press, 1998); and Wilhelm Kaufmann, *The Germans in the American Civil War,* trans. Steven Rowan, ed.

by Don Heinrich Tolzmann with Werner D. Mueller and Robert E. Ward (1911, reprint; Carlisle, Pa.: John Kallmann, Publishers, 1999). Ella Lonn's two books contain much valuable information but they also perpetuate old ethnic stereotypes, are filiopietistic, and lack critical analysis. Burton's study also contains much valuable information about German regiments and their leaders, but, like Lonn, he fails to point out that Germans were a diverse lot and both profess that the war served to "Americanize" Germans without providing supporting evidence. Kaufmann's narrative, like Lonn's, is dated, contains quite a few factual errors, and reflects the bias of its German-born author.

Bruce Levine, *The Spirit of 1848: German Immigrants, Labor Conflict, and the Coming of the Civil War* (Urbana: University of Illinois Press, 1992), sheds light on some significant areas such as German immigrant arrivals, living and economic conditions, political attitudes, and the labor movement. Helpful studies of the diverse German American political attitudes for the period include Frederick C. Luebke, "German Immigrants and American Politics: Problems of Leadership, Parties and Issues," in Randall M. Miller, ed., *Germans in America: Retrospect and Prospect, Tricentennial Lectures Delivered at the German Society of Pennsylvania in 1983* (Philadelphia: The German Society of Pennsylvania, 1984); and Walter D. Kamphoefner, "German-Americans and Civil War Politics: A Reconsideration of the Ethnocultural Thesis," *Civil War History* 37, no. 3 (September 1991): 232–46.

Among the works questioning the theory that the Civil War rapidly accelerated "Americanization" of German immigrants are John A. Hawgood, *The Tragedy of German-America* (New York: Arno Press, 1970), and Kathleen Neils Conzen, "German-Americans and the Invention of Ethnicity," in Frank Trommler and Joseph McVeigh, eds., *America and the Germans: An Assessment of a Three-Hundred-Year History* (Philadelphia: University of Pennsylvania Press, 1985). More recent works include Stephen D. Engle, "A Raised Consciousness: Franz Sigel and German Ethnic Identity in the Civil War," *Yearbook of German-American Studies* 34 (1999): 1–13, and Christian B. Keller and David L. Valuska, *Damn Dutch: Pennsylvania Germans at Gettysburg* (Mechanicsburg, Pa.: Stackpole Books, 2004). Christian B. Keller's excellent *Chancellorsville and the Germans: Nativism, Ethnicity, and Civil War Memory* (New York: Fordham University Press, 2007) also quashes the myth that cowardly behavior on the part of German American regiments caused the Union's defeat at the Battle of Chancellorsville and engages the issues of nativism, ethnic identity, and the postwar effects on German Americans of their Civil War experiences. Interested persons should also refer to Wolfgang Helbich, "German-Born Union Soldiers: Motivation, Ethnicity and 'Americanization,'" in *German-American Immigration and Ethnicity in Comparative Perspective*, Wolfgang Helbich and Walter D. Kamphoefner, eds. (Madison, Wis.: Max Kade Institute for German-American Studies, University of Wisconsin–Madison, 2004). Also see Martin W. Öfele, *German-Speaking Officers in the U.S. Colored Troops, 1863–1867* (Gainesville: University of Florida Press, 2004).

A little over a handful of the books containing letters and diaries of German American soldiers comment on issues such as motivation for enlisting, slavery and emancipation, ethnic prejudices, government policies, and changed opinions as the war progressed. Recommended works include Walter D. Kamphoefner and Wolfgang Helbich, eds., and Susan Carter Vogel, trans., *Germans in the Civil War: The Letters They Wrote Home* (Chapel Hill: University of North Carolina Press, 2006); Joseph R. Reinhart, *A German Hurrah!: The Civil War Letters of Friedrich Bertsch and Wilhelm Stängel, 9th Ohio Infantry* (Kent, Ohio: Kent State University Press, 2010); Joseph R. Reinhart, *August Willich's Gallant Dutchmen: Civil War Letters of the Thirty-second Indiana Infantry* (Kent, Ohio: Kent State University Press, 2006); Joseph R. Reinhart, *Two Germans in the Civil War: The Diary of John Daeuble and the Letters of Gottfried Rentschler, 6th Kentucky Volunteer Infantry* (Knoxville: University of Tennessee Press, 2004); William K. Winkler, ed., *Letters of Frederic C. Winkler, 1862–1865* (n.p.: William K. Winkler, 1963). See Frank L. Byrne and Jean Powers Soman, eds., *Your True Marcus: The Civil War Letters of a Jewish Colonel* (Kent, Ohio: Kent State University Press, 1985); Minetta Altgelt Goyne, trans. and ed., *Lone Star and Double Eagle: Civil War Letters of a German-Texas Family* (n.p.: Texas Christian University Press, 1982); and Earl J. Hess Jr., ed., *A German in the Yankee Fatherland: The Civil War Letters of Henry A. Kircher* (Kent, Ohio: Kent State University Press, 1983), for an outstanding collection of letters authored by a soldier born in Illinois of German immigrant parents.

Most of the above-mentioned resources are available through libraries and/or bookstores. For other sources used in editing this work, please refer to the endnotes.

Index